Congress and Policy Making in the 21st C

Congress is frequently said to be "broken," "dysfunctional," and "weak," but how does the contemporary Congress really work? Does Congress have the capacity to solve major policy problems? Can it check an aggrandizing executive, oversee a powerful Federal Reserve, and represent the American people? Can Congress cope with vast changes in the American political economy, including rising income inequality? *Congress and Policy Making in the 21st Century* takes a fresh look at the performance of Congress in the domestic arena, focusing on issues such as immigration, health care, and the repeal of "Don't Ask, Don't Tell." With original contributions from leading scholars, this important volume examines how Congress tackles – and fails to tackle – key policy challenges in an era of growing social diversity and ideological polarization. Rich in analysis and illuminating detail, the book reveals the full complexity of the institution at work.

JEFFERY A. JENKINS is Professor of Politics at the University of Virginia and Editor-in-Chief of *The Journal of Politics*. He has published more than thirty-five articles in peer-reviewed journals, such as the *American Journal of Political Science*, *The Journal of Politics*, *Legislative Studies Quarterly*, and *Studies in American Political Development*. He is also the author (with Charles Stewart III) of *Fighting for the Speakership: The House and the Rise of Party Government* (2013) and the editor (with Sidney M. Milkis) of *The Politics of Major Policy Reform in Postwar America* (Cambridge University Press, 2014) and (with Eric M. Patashnik) *Living Legislation: Durability, Change, and the Politics of American Lawmaking* (2012).

ERIC M. PATASHNIK is Professor of Public Policy and Politics and Director of the Center for Health Policy in the Frank Batten School of Leadership and Public Policy at the University of Virginia. He is also Nonresident Senior Fellow at the Brookings Institution and an elected fellow of the National Academy of Public Administration. Patashnik is the author of several books including *Putting Trust in the U.S. Budget: Federal Trust Funds and the Politics of Commitment* (Cambridge University Press, 2000) and *Reforms at Risk: What Happens After Major Policy Changes Are Enacted* (2008), which won the Louis Brownlow Book Award for outstanding contribution to the literature on public administration.

Congress and Policy Making in the 21st Century

Edited by

JEFFERY A. JENKINS
University of Virginia

ERIC M. PATASHNIK
University of Virginia

CAMBRIDGE
UNIVERSITY PRESS

CAMBRIDGE
UNIVERSITY PRESS

32 Avenue of the Americas, New York, NY 10013-2473, USA

Cambridge University Press is part of the University of Cambridge.

It furthers the University's mission by disseminating knowledge in the pursuit of education, learning, and research at the highest international levels of excellence.

www.cambridge.org
Information on this title: www.cambridge.org/9781107565555

© Cambridge University Press 2016

First published 2016

Printed in the United States of America

A catalog record for this publication is available from the British Library.

Library of Congress Cataloging in Publication Data

Congress and policy making in the 21st century / edited by Jeffery A. Jenkins, Eric M. Patashnik.
    pages   cm
Includes bibliographical references and index.
ISBN 978-1-107-12638-1 (Hardback) – ISBN 978-1-107-56555-5 (Paperback)
    1. United States. Congress.   2. Decision making–Political aspects–United States.   3. Legislation–Political aspects–United States.   4. Policy sciences.   5. United States–Politics and government.   I. Jenkins, Jeffery A.   II. Patashnik, Eric M.
JK1021.C5526 2016
320.60973–dc23   2015030288

ISBN 978-1-107-12638-1 Hardback
ISBN 978-1-107-56555-5 Paperback

Contents

Figures

Tables

Contributors

R. Douglas Arnold, Princeton University
Sarah Binder, George Washington University and Brookings Institution
Nicholas Carnes, Duke University
Alexander Hertel-Fernandez, Harvard University
Jeffery A. Jenkins, University of Virginia
Nolan McCarty, Princeton University
Jonathan Oberlander, University of North Carolina at Chapel Hill
Bruce I. Oppenheimer, Vanderbilt University
Eric M. Patashnik, University of Virginia
Barbara Sinclair, University of California, Los Angeles
Theda Skocpol, Harvard University
Mark Spindel, Potomac River Capital, LLC
Daniel J. Tichenor, University of Oregon
Rick Valelly, Swarthmore College
Craig Volden, University of Virginia
Alan E. Wiseman, Vanderbilt University

Acknowledgments

This volume is being published during one of the most fluid, unpredictable, and tumultuous periods in the history of the American Congress. Government shutdowns, eleventh-hour deals to raise the national debt ceiling and avoid economic calamity, the rise of the House Freedom Caucus and the fracturing of the Republican conference, the surprising resignation of House Speaker John Boehner (R-OH), and the emergence of "strange bedfellow" coalitions on a number of issues – these are just some of the remarkable developments of the past several years.

It is too soon to know how these developments will shake out, but it is already clear that political science needs to catch up with events on the ground. Toward that end, we invited some of the nation's most insightful scholars of Congress and public policy to gather at the University of Virginia on June 3–4, 2013, to address fundamental questions about the consequences of partisan polarization, the evolving activities of individual lawmakers as entrepreneurial shapers of public action, and the role of Congress as a problem-solving institution across critical domestic arenas such as immigration, healthcare, and transportation. From these essays came the chapters in this volume.

The authors do not reach a consensus on either the causes or the consequences of congressional performance. However, using a variety of research approaches, tools, and data sources, they identify empirical patterns and theoretical puzzles that scholars will be wrestling with for years to come.

We are grateful to the Miller Center of Public Affairs and the Frank Batten School of Leadership and Public Policy at the University of Virginia for supporting this project. We would also like to thank Governor Gerald Baliles, former Director of the Miller Center, and Sidney Milkis, the White

Burkett Professor of Politics, for their sponsorship and encouragement. They saw a conference on Congress and policy making in the 21st Century as a novel and important undertaking. We also wish to express our appreciation to the anonymous reviewers for Cambridge University Press, whose comments and suggestions improved the volume significantly.

The Evolving Textbook Congress

Polarization and Policy Making on Capitol Hill in the 21st Century

Jeffery A. Jenkins and Eric M. Patashnik

In 2009, the U.S. Congress, led by House Democrats, sought to tackle the issue of climate change and pass major energy legislation. The American Clean Energy and Security Act (ACES), sponsored by Rep. Henry Waxman (D-CA) and Sen. Edward Markey (D-CA), proposed a "cap and trade" system to limit the amount of greenhouse gases that companies could emit nationally. "Emission permits" would be bought and sold in a marketplace, and the cap would be reduced over time to curb carbon dioxide gases. The ambitious bill generated significant controversy. Environmental groups lobbied for the measure while the petroleum and natural gas industries and conservative advocacy groups sought to block its passage. The bill passed in the House by a slim 219–212 vote, with just 8 Republicans in support. But, the following year, ACES died in the Senate, when Majority Leader Harry Reid (D-NV) acknowledged that he did not have the sixty votes necessary to overcome a Republican-led filibuster.

Since 2010, President Obama has been urging the Congress to pass climate change legislation. But little has been accomplished congressionally, with meaningful policy change made more difficult since the Republicans regained majority control of the House in 2011. In his 2013 State of the Union address, Obama announced that he was prepared to move forward without legislative action. "If Congress won't act soon to protect future generations, I will," he said (Restuccia and Dixon 2013). Working through the Environmental Protection Agency (EPA), Obama in 2014 established a new regulation that would cut carbon emissions produced by coal-burning power plants by 30 percent from 2005 levels by 2030. Congressional Republicans were immediately up in arms about the executive "overreach" and warned of significant job losses in the coal industry. Obama made no apologies for seizing the initiative, however, and castigated Congress for failing to tackle climate change. And, in June 2014, the Supreme Court largely upheld the EPA's authority to regulate greenhouse gases, though the decision also left open the possibility of future judicial review of rules imposing limits on power plant emissions.

On combating carbon pollution, then, national policy making in the 21st Century is being led primarily by the president with significant input from the judiciary. Individual lawmakers have certainly taken positions and made public statements, but Congress is not a central institutional player in climate-change-mitigation policy making.

* * *

Executive-led policy making on core national issues is not the way James Madison intended the U.S. political system to work. When the framers established the Constitutional system in 1787, they cast Congress in the starring role. Article I established Congress as the premier site of political representation and lawmaking in the national government. And Congress lived up to its star billing for some time. Policy making in the 19th century was predominantly a legislative branch affair. The president typically played the part of patronage dispenser and occasional veto player, and the federal bureaucracy remained modest in scale and scope (Kernell and Jacobson 2006). The federal courts determined the meaning of the law, arbitrated jurisdictional disputes between the states and the national government, and served as a surrogate for a more fully developed administrative apparatus (Skowronek 1982). Nonetheless, the courts' role in governance was essentially procedural and reactive. Party politics was the driver of substantive debates, and Congress remained the key institutional forum where sectional and economic interests and clashing ideas about the future of the republic vied for influence (Cooper 2009).

As the 20th century dawned, the American state expanded, new regulatory agencies emerged, and Congress struggled to maintain its institutional prominence. During the Progressive and New Deal eras, the president became far more active in domestic affairs, and the size of the executive branch mushroomed. To be sure, the outpouring of social legislation during the Great Society was a joint production of the White House and Congress (Zelizer 1999), but Richard Nixon's effort to preempt congressional authority in areas such as impoundments and war powers forced Congress to reassert its basic constitutional prerogatives (Sundquist 1981; Schickler 2001). By the 1960s, the federal judiciary had also emerged as a formidable rival and partner to the political branches through its willingness to take a "hard look" at bureaucratic discretion, interpret statutes, and articulate rights claims (Kagan 2001).

The present era finds Congress on the political defensive, both on Pennsylvania Avenue and in elite discourse. A policy-driven president, more willing to steer government unilaterally (Howell 2003), and a vast if overloaded bureaucracy, politicized to engineer the president's preferred outcomes (Lewis 2008), have transformed the executive branch into a formidable policy-making force under Republican and Democratic presidents alike. The federal judiciary continues its activist bent, in a liberal direction on social issues such as same-sex marriage and a more conservative direction on economic policy, federalism, and voting rights issues. Congress, by comparison, often seems feckless and feeble in the face of national challenges. Heightened levels of partisan polarization, in tandem with close levels of party competition that bring control of Congress within reach of both parties in every election, seem to have made it harder for lawmakers to reach timely agreements on the issues of the day (Binder 2003; Sinclair 2006; Lee 2013). Public confidence in the institution is at a postwar low: in a recent Gallup survey, only 7 percent of the public said they approved of Congress's job performance (Riffkin 2014). Lawmakers have also been sharply critical of the institution. As Sen. Joe Manchin (D-WV) stated about Congress's inability to keep the government funded without threatening a default on the national debt, "Something has gone terribly wrong when the biggest threat to our American economy is the American Congress" (see Steinhauer 2012).

To be sure, distress about Congress's ineffectiveness is nothing new. Reformers have criticized Congress's lack of productivity and limited problem solving capacity since the 1940s (Adler and Wilkerson 2012; see Polsby 1990). But some experts insist that the current legislative dysfunction is different from the past, in degree if not in kind, and that Congress has become "the broken branch" (Mann and Ornstein 2006). Even when Congress manages to act, its performance is often disappointing. As Sarah Binder argues, "Half-measures, second bests, and just-in-time legislating are the new norm, as electoral, partisan and institutional barriers limit Congress's capacity for more than lowest common denominator deals" (Binder 2014, 18).

Yet other scholars argue that the American political system has self-correcting properties, and that many of the alleged problems in legislative performance will prove to be limited and short-term (Mayhew 2009; Sinclair 2009; Shepsle 2009). Both sides of the debate tend to offer general assessments of the institution's overall capacity, with relatively little analysis of Congress's ability to perform specific problem-solving tasks such as developing policy options and confronting trade-offs.[1]

The goal of this volume is to offer a more nuanced assessment of Congress's performance in the contemporary American state. We seek to understand and evaluate how well Congress fulfills its roles as lawmaker and representative body across key domestic policy areas, including health, energy, and fiscal policy. In doing so, we recognize that the behavior of the institution and its members is mediated by contextual forces, including polarization and economic inequality, the growing complexity of activist government, declining public trust in government, fiscal pressures, and a vast increase in the number and variety of interest groups. How have these broad changes in the social and economic environment shaped the internal operation of Congress? How has Congress in turn used its governing capacities to address problems and remake the economy and the society? Any effort to answer these questions must recognize that Congress's performance cannot be understood in a vacuum, but only within the separation of powers system of which it is a part (Mayhew 2009). The crucial issue is not only how many bills Congress passes, but also how it governs in cooperation and competition with other political actors and institutions.

Because Congress is the foundation of the American state, the study of Congress has long been at the center of American political science. Some of the most important works on American politics emerged within the legislative politics subfield during the 1970s, 1980s, and 1990s. This is an opportune moment to take a fresh look at some of these arguments. In an era of gridlock and polarization, do the classic scholarly models and approaches – including David R. Mayhew's "electoral connection," Richard Fenno's "congressmen in committees," and Keith Krehbiel's "pivotal politics" – still provide purchase on congressional behavior? That is, do the typical ways of approaching the study of the postwar Congress still apply today? Or do procedural developments, such as the decline in "regular order" in the law-making process and the near requirement of sixty votes in the Senate on most policy issues, suggest that attention should shift away from individual members and committees to parties and the "unorthodox" mechanisms that party leaders use outside regular order, including party task forces, complex floor procedures, and the budget reconciliation process (Sinclair 2011; 2014)?

This volume is also concerned with analyzing the effects of growing partisan polarization in Congress. There is a scholarly consensus that Congress has polarized over the last three decades (Sinclair 2006; Poole and Rosenthal 2007); the two parties have become increasingly ideologically homogenous (Democrats liberal, Republicans conservative) as well as distinct from one another. The effect of increased polarization on Congress's ability to perform its constitutional functions and representational duties is much more of an open question, however (Nivola and Brady 2008). We explore the consequences of polarization throughout the volume, and do so by policy area.

A final goal of the volume is bring into dialogue two separate research communities: traditional Congress scholars and public policy scholars. Both sets of scholars often focus on law making, but they seldom speak to one another. The rising prominence of deductive theory and large-N roll call analyses has led to the marginalization of policy substance within congressional studies (Lapinski 2013). The focus has been on how institutions, rules, and procedures are formed and influence the behavior of members and party caucuses. At the same time, policy scholars have tended to focus on presidents, bureaucracies, and the media as the key sites of agenda setting, decision making, and implementation. We believe that congressional and public policy scholars can learn a great deal through closer intellectual engagement, and we hope this volume takes a significant step toward encouraging productive exchange.

THE ESSAYS

A volume of this kind, with a topic as broad as "Congress and policy making in the 21st century," could be assembled in a multitude of ways. The four headings under which we have grouped the essays – "Congressional Policy Making in a Polarized Age," "Congress and Society," "Congress and Economic Policy," and "Congress and Domestic Policy Dilemmas" – do not exhaust the connections to be drawn among them, but this organization highlights some central themes. We describe these themes in the following, in the context of summarizing the content of the various chapters.

In Part I, "Congressional Policy Making in a Polarized Age," we begin with two essays that explore the broader setting in which the major actors of Congress – members, committees, and parties – seek to advance their legislative objectives. These essays draw attention to the factors that increase the probability of policy gridlock, as well as the factors that open the window to major legislative accomplishment. Significant in the chapters included in Part I is the insistence that it is possible to generalize about the politics of policy making on Capitol Hill. While no two bills are alike, there are nonetheless systematic patterns in how Congress makes policy that reflects the procedural rules of the game, the evolving partisan and ideological context in which each chamber operates, and the nature of proposed policy changes themselves.

A central theme that emerges from this volume is that congressional parties are far stronger and more prominent today than they were in the 1970s when classic books by scholars such as David R. Mayhew and Richard Fenno were published. Nonetheless, some of the authors argue that individual lawmakers remain an important unit of analysis for understanding congressional behavior. Members vary greatly in their law-making activities. Some law makers leave a major imprint on the legislative process while others are far more passive participants.

In Chapter 2, Craig Volden and Alan E. Wiseman focus on the role of skillful "policy entrepreneurs" in bringing about legislative action. These are members who – because of ideological commitment or simply the desire for power or impact – invest their (scarce) time and energy in sponsoring bills and moving them forward in areas where the electoral rewards for doing are often lacking. Drawing on James Q. Wilson's classic policy typology, Volden and Wiseman argue that any legislative proposal can be classified in terms of those who benefit and those who are harmed by the proposal. If the citizens who support a proposal are broadly distributed across society but the opponents are concentrated – as is the case with respect to the thorniest issues before Congress in the early 21st century, such as mitigating climate change – the potential for legislative gridlock is high. The opponents of the policy proposal will place tremendous pressure on Congress not to act, while the supporters (each of whom has a low per capita stake in the outcome, and therefore lacks a strong incentive to engage in political action) are unlikely to be effective advocates. Policy change can be secured under such difficult policy circumstances only if policy entrepreneurs advocate for the proposal on behalf of its dispersed supporters. Volden and Wiseman carefully review law-making activities – including bill sponsorship, committee action, and floor passage – across nineteen issue areas from the 93rd to the 107th Congress (1973–2002) and find that policy gridlock is indeed much greater in entrepreneurial domains compared with those where entrepreneurial politics is less prevalent, with only 2 to 3 percent of sponsored bills becoming law in entrepreneurial areas compared with 6 percent in less entrepreneurial areas. However, there are members who are willing to take on the difficult challenge of pushing legislation forward even in such difficult circumstances. Highly skilled entrepreneurs such as Henry Waxman (D-CA) and Philip M. Crane (R-IL) have been able to use their innate abilities, political knowledge, and institutional positions to overcome the hurdles to action in areas such as health and foreign trade.

If Volden and Wiseman show that policy making in Congress in the 21st century cannot be characterized properly without attending to the nature of the policy challenges Congress faces and the effectiveness of individual lawmakers as policy entrepreneurs, Barbara Sinclair emphasizes in Chapter 3 that congressional performance also cannot be understood without accounting for the impact of partisan polarization. The best-known model attempting to explain policy gridlock and policy change holds that increasing polarization inhibits legislative productivity: As the two parties become more internally ideologically homogeneous, and more distant from each other, it becomes harder for leaders to build a winning coalition for a policy change that is preferred by all its members to the status quo. Sinclair argues that while this model has yielded useful insights, its explanation of the policy consequences of polarization is incomplete, because it only captures the direct effect of polarization. What also needs to be recognized, she argues, is that polarization facilitates stronger party leadership and greater internal rewards for team behavior, especially in the House of Representatives. She argues that the net impact of polarization on legislative productivity depends on whether partisan control of the branches and chambers is unified or divided, and illustrates her claim by examining policy making in the 111th (2009–10) and 112th (2011–12) Congresses.

Having begun with a section that looks at the role of general factors such as member entrepreneurship and polarization in both encouraging and impeding congressional productivity across issue areas, we move to sections that explore in more fine-grained detail how the contemporary Congress responds to specific political challenges and policy problems. Congress does not exist in a vacuum. As a representative body, one of the Congress's most important roles is to mediate between government and the conflicting sets of preferences and demands emanating from the activists, policy elites, interest groups, and ordinary citizens who comprise America's ever-changing society. An open question is whether congressional responses will map onto, reinforce, alter, or ignore the cleavages found in society. Over the past fifty years, American society has changed in fundamental ways. The civil rights and women's movements of the 1960s and 1970s opened mainstream American life to new groups, revised norms about the meaning of equality, and both reinvigorated and tested the nation's commitment to fair play (Patterson 1997). As these vast changes in the membership of the American social community were occurring, American families were also being buffeted by powerful economic and demographic forces, including globalization, technological change, and shifts in family patterns (Levy 1999). These forces have combined with shifts in the political landscape, such as the decline of unionization, to generate rising income inequality in the United States (Hacker and Pierson 2011). While the period of the 1940s through the 1970s was characterized by the "Great Compression," in which the distribution of income between rich and poor became more equal than it had been previously, the period since the 1980s has witnessed the emergence of what some refer to as a "New Gilded Age," marked by a growing gap between the middle class and the rich (Bartels 2010). How has the contemporary Congress responded to demands from previously stigmatized social groups to further liberalize access to American civic life? And how has Congress responded to rising income inequality? In Part II of the book, Rick Valelly and Nicholas Carnes take up these questions by looking at the interplay between Congress and society.

In Chapter 4, Valelly recounts the fascinating saga of the repeal during the lame-duck session of the 111th Congress (just before the Republicans regained control of the House) of "Don't Ask, Don't Tell," the statutory ban on gay men and women serving openly in America's armed forces. The case merits close attention from scholars of Congress and public policy not only because it ended an era of official federal discrimination against an identity-based minority, but also because it illustrates the importance of individual members' parliamentary skills in making Congress work (a point quite consistent with Volden and Wiseman's emphasis on entrepreneurship). Drawing on John Kingdon's classic model of the policy-making process (Kingdon 2002), Valelly describes how recognition of the DADT's flaws connected temporally with favorable electoral results and changes in the menu of policy solutions to make repeal possible in 2010–11. But while a window of opportunity opened, there was no guarantee that repeal would be accomplished before the window closed. The legislative tale Valelly tells is complicated, with many unexpected twists and turns, but one key to success was the strategic partnership between Congress and the Pentagon. Rather than ordering an end to discrimination in the armed forces, members of Congress set in motion a "self-repeal" by the military that Congress then certified. This strategic collaboration between Congress and the Pentagon ensured that repeal would gain support in Congress not only from social liberals committed to gay rights, but also from conservatives who were unwilling to second guess a decision by respected military leaders.

If Congress has demonstrated a capacity to promote social equality in civic life, Nicholas Carnes's Chapter 5 highlights the reluctance of the legislative branch to push back against the forces generating rising inequality in the economy. Using legislative report card data on high-stakes legislation related to economic inequality, Carnes examines the determinants of congressional support for twenty-four bills and amendments during the 2011–12 congressional session with important implications for economic inequality, such as a bill to repeal the estate tax, increases in the minimum wage, and a bill to enact the so-called Buffet Rule. He finds that the two parties are separated by an enormous gulf: Democrats are much more supportive of steps to reduce economic inequality than Republicans. There are also important intraparty differences that stem from divergent opinions across districts. Members who represented constituents who care less about inequality or who were more conservative were more likely to support politics that would increase inequality. In addition, Democrats are more likely to support inequality-increasing policies when they represent less heavily unionized districts. Carnes's findings about the responsiveness of legislative voting on inequality to both constituent opinion and union penetration underscore the importance of looking at Congress as an institution embedded within society. As he writes, "Our legislative branch itself isn't the problem – it's the *inputs* into the legislative process that make it difficult for Congress to deal with inequality."

Part III of the book examines how Congress shapes national economic policy in three important areas – taxation, budgeting and appropriations, and monetary policy. These areas are each distinctive in some ways, but all three provide tests of Congress's capacity to overcome partisan and ideological divisions to fund government, promote good economic outcomes for the country, and maintain an institutional balance of power with the executive.

Article 1, Section 8, of the Constitution gives the Congress the power to tax, but *how* Congress chooses to exercise that power has become one of the flashpoints of modern American politics (Campbell 2011). A key puzzle is why majority parties in Congress are able to achieve their tax policy goals sometimes, but not at other times, even when their goals enjoy political support and are backed by economic logic. Alexander Hertel-Fernandez and Theda Skocpol take up this puzzle in Chapter 6 by examining why Democrats have had such a hard time raising revenues or reconfiguring the politics of taxation to reflect their preferences despite favorable political and economic conditions. The authors contrast Democrats' efforts in 2009–10 to allow tax cuts for upper-income earners to expire – which would have helped to combat rising income inequality – with Republicans' major tax-cutting drive during the first term of the George W. Bush administration. The comparison between the Democrats' handling of tax policy at the start of the Obama administration and the Republicans' tax policy during the early Bush years might seem asymmetric since it is inherently easier, all else being equal, to cut taxes than to raise them. Hertel-Fernandez and Skocpol forcefully argue, however, that repeal of the Bush tax cuts for top incomes was politically advantageous for Democrats at a time when the vast majority of ordinary Americans were struggling economically, and that mainstream economic analysis indicated that a full extension of the Bush tax cuts was a much less effective stimulus measure than alternatives, such as extending unemployment insurance. To explain the divergent capacities of the two parties on tax politics, Hertel-Fernandez and Skocpol highlight four factors: the timing of tax initiatives in relation to economic trends; management of the majority party's congressional caucus; agenda setting by party leadership; and mobilization of outside interests. In sum, their analysis suggests that both state and society need to be foregrounded to fully explain congressional behavior.

Congress currently struggles not only to raise taxes, but also to pass the appropriations and budget bills to provide for federal spending. Indeed, as Nolan McCarty observes in Chapter 7, the House and Senate have been increasingly unable to pass or reconcile budget resolutions. Moreover, Congress is often unable to pass appropriations bills on time. As a result of the collapse of "regular order" in the congressional budget process, Congress has been forced to rely on continuing resolutions and omnibus bills to keep the government's fiscal machinery running, circumventing the traditional annual appropriations process. On the basis of statistical models of appropriations delays, McCarty argues that split chamber control, divided government, and heightened partisan polarization are associated with impaired congressional procedural performance on fiscal policy. Pundits bemoan the collapse of regular order, viewing it as a sign of a dysfunctional Congress. The empirical question remains, however, whether poor procedural performance has any clear impact on fiscal policy outcomes or the broader U.S. economy. McCarty finds that there is no clear relationship between the tardy passage of appropriation bills and either spending or deficit levels, seemingly ruling out first-order effects on major fiscal aggregates. At the same time, McCarty does uncover some modest evidence that poor procedural performance increases policy uncertainty, although the causal mechanism remains unclear.

Legislative debates over taxes and spending often receive a great deal of media attention because they are public and because they frequently highlight congressional dysfunction. The irony is that the Federal Reserve Board's monetary policy decisions – which are made behind closed doors – arguably have a much larger influence on economic growth, inflation, and employment. Congress created the Fed, and in theory Congress could abolish it. An important subject for inquiry is how much influence Congress has over the Fed's decision making – and how that influence is used. Supervising the Fed poses a dilemma for Congress. On the one hand, Congress wants to hold the Fed accountable for its policy decisions, particularly during periods of high unemployment. On the other hand, Congress recognizes that central banks need to be able to make decisions without excessive political interference in order to develop the institutional autonomy and policy credibility necessary to keep the inflation rate

stable and low. In sum, there is a trade off between independence and democratic accountability. Why and when does Congress seek to revise the degree of
independence it affords the Fed?

In Chapter 8, Sarah Binder and Mark Spindel track congressional attention
to the Fed in the postwar era. They find that lawmakers' prescriptions for the
Fed are largely driven by changes in economic conditions. When the economy is
doing well, lawmakers propose stronger powers for the Fed; when the economy
falters, lawmakers look for ways to reduce the Fed's independence. While
congressional attention to the Fed is sporadic and ad hoc, the authors' results
suggest that Congress is not powerless to bring democratic values to bear on the
contours of monetary policy.

The final section of the book examines how Congress responds to three of
the most difficult domestic policy dilemmas: controlling health care costs,
reforming the immigration system, and increasing energy efficiency. Each
dilemma presents members with a different mix of constituency pressures,
partisan divisions, ideological cleavages, and interest group alignments. In each
case, we see members struggling to find a path forward that allows Congress to
address the underlying policy dilemma without jeopardizing members' individual reelection chances. Finding such a path is never easy for an institution with
535 members, and sometimes impossible.

In Chapter 9, Jonathan Oberlander examines the role of Congress in health
care cost control, past, present, and future. Health experts agree that a great
deal – perhaps as much as one-third – of U.S. medical spending is wasteful and
does not improve health outcomes (Health Affairs 2012). While waste could be
trimmed without harming patients, there are many reasons to expect that
Congress will not be able to control the level or growth of health care spending.
A dollar spent on medical care is a dollar of income to hospitals, drug companies, and doctors, all of whom are represented by powerful lobbies who
seek to protect their members' concentrated interests in health care debates.
Moreover, millions of citizens work in the health care sector, and there is a
deep-seated fear among many Americans that health care cost controls will
reduce the access to and quality of medical care enjoyed by insured Americans.
The challenges of controlling health care costs are amplified by Congress's
fragmented committee structure, myopia, and partisanship. As Oberlander
writes, "There seemingly could not be a worse match between the magnitude
of a policy problem and the depths of institutional incapacity." Yet, Oberlander
argues, Congress's record in health care cost containment is, if hardly perfect,
better than commonly believed. Under pressure to reduce the federal budget
deficit, Congress has repeatedly enacted measures – often attached to omnibus
legislation – to constrain Medicare spending. Congress has done so mainly by
reducing payments to providers, not by directly cutting Medicare benefits. To
make up for the lost Medicare revenues, providers have shifted at least some of
their costs onto the states and private insurers. In sum, Congress has done far
more than many assume – but much less than is needed to solve the health care

cost problem. As Oberlander concludes, "It remains to be seen whether Congress can overcome its parochial budgetary perspective and embrace the politically more challenging task of implementing system-wide cost controls."

Health care debates pit the concentrated interests of medical industry groups who seek to protect their incomes against the diffuse interests of taxpayers, businesses, and workers who have a less tangible stake in cost control. As Daniel J. Tichenor argues in Chapter 10, the divisions that emerge in debates over illegal immigration and the future of undocumented workers are, in contrast, much more complex and fluid. Not only do constituency groups disagree over immigration reform proposals, there is not even a consensus on the problem definition. Tichenor argues that four traditions clash in national debates over immigration: cosmopolitism, economic protectionism, probusiness expansionism, and cultural protectionism. These distinctive ideological fissures make the formation of "strange bedfellow" coalitions and difficult compromises necessary for congressional action on major immigration reform – and elusive. Rather than supplanting the four immigration policy traditions, the mistrust created by heightened partisan polarization has created additional barriers for immigration reformers to overcome in seeking to fashion a "grand bargain." Tichenor concludes that comprehensive immigration reform may not be feasible until changes in national demography (including the growing number of Latino voters) make their influence felt across a larger share of congressional districts, reinforcing the need for scholars to examine the interplay between congressional actions and social forces.

While there is no consensus among lawmakers on whether the U.S. should tighten or loosen legal restrictions on immigration, there is a strong congressional agreement that the country should be less dependent on foreign sources of energy. As Bruce I. Oppenheimer shows in Chapter 11, however, this energy policy consensus has not eliminated legislative conflicts over the potential solutions. The dilemma is that many energy policy proposals require the public to bear short-term costs – such as higher energy costs or increased taxes – to reap long-term benefits. Because of the well-documented myopia and negativity bias of voters, supporting such policies exposes members to electoral risk. Accordingly, Congress has only passed significant energy legislation over the past half century when exogenous events – such as rising energy prices and uncertainties about the supply of gas and heating oil in the aftermath of oil embargoes – have made the political costs of adopting policy changes lower than the political costs of maintaining the status quo. Even then, the parliamentary skill of congressional leaders in packaging the legislation to minimize the traceability of costs was essential to winning the support of rank-and-file members. In recent years, heightened polarization and the fraying of bipartisanship on committees has made it even harder to resolve energy policy issues within Congress, increasing the incentive for the president to adjust energy policies (such as corporate average fuel economy standards on motor vehicles) through unilateral action. The result has been a clear decline in congressional influence over energy policy, even as American national government maintains some capacity to advance national objectives in this arena.

In Chapter 12, distinguished political scientist R. Douglas Arnold provides his reflections on the essays contained in the book. He begins by posing two fundamental questions: What makes for a productive Congress? And why are some congresses more successful in achieving legislators' policy goals than others? Raising concerns about the conventional ways these questions have been addressed in the literature, Arnold argues, first, that bill production is not a reliable and unbiased measure of legislative achievement because conservatives are less inclined to government action than are liberals; and second, that fidelity to poll results also does not provide a firm foundation for political scientists to evaluate legislative accomplishments both because of the shallowness of public opinion (poll results are highly sensitive to question wording) and because lawmakers seek to respond to the intensity of citizens' opinions. Finally, Arnold draws on the findings of the chapters to discuss whether policy making has changed over the past decade as the parties became increasingly polarized. Contrary to claims of a completely broken Congress, Arnold points out that recent congresses have been productive in passing important stimulus, financial services, tax, and health care legislation (a fact that should not be obscured by the increasing resort to omnibus law making). While Arnold states that policy making under unified control is more likely to be dominated by the majority party today than in earlier eras – with the minority party more likely to be disgruntled with the results – he emphasizes that bipartisan coalitions are still a primary vehicle for making policy in Washington, even if building such coalitions is increasingly difficult.

THE EVOLVING "TEXTBOOK CONGRESS"

Taken together, the picture that emerges from Arnold's wrap-up and the individual chapters is of a 21st century Congress that is highly polarized and frequently deadlocked, with a record of mishandling many issues, even as it retains a capacity to contribute to the resolution of major policy challenges through the political entrepreneurship and skill of its members; the ambition and team behavior of its party coalitions; and a periodic willingness to defer to, or enter into strategic collaborations with, other institutional actors. How does this complex portrait compare to views of Congress from previous eras?

In "The Changing Textbook Congress," Kenneth A. Shepsle (1989) evaluated Congress as a law-making body in the late 1980s, relative to his generation's common understanding of how Congress operated and governed. Shepsle argued that the "textbook" view of Congress that was being taught to students in introductory American government courses was outdated; that textbook view was based on the politics of the 1940s and 1950s, when a "conservative coalition" of Southern Democrats and Republicans dominated Congress and the committee system was the prime repository of power.

The textbook Congress of the early postwar era reflected an equilibrium among jurisdictional, geographical, and partisan forces. By the 1960s, however, the overall mood in the country had tilted to the left, a geographic realignment and voting-rights revolution were underway, and the committee-based system was increasingly under stress. Pressure for change ramped up in the 1970s, and internal reforms (especially in the House) shifted power away from committees and toward both individual members (through the expansion of subcommittees) and parties (though increased deference to party leaders).

At the time Shepsle was writing, the decentralizing and centralizing tendencies of the reforms seemed in conflict, and a new "equilibrium" wasn't obvious. The postreform Congress featured many power centers and was characterized by a high level of fluidity and uncertainty. By the early 1990s, however, political scientists studying Congress (Rohde 1991; Cox and McCubbins 1993) had determined that the centralizing tendencies had won out; that is, that a new governing equilibrium based on parties, rather than subcommittees, had emerged.[2] In effect, the days when the two parties were to varying degrees "big tents" – with the Democratic caucus including scores of Southern conservatives and the Republican caucus counting among its members a large faction of northern liberals – were long past. In their place were two rival teams, a liberal Democratic Party and a conservative Republican Party, committed to fundamentally different principles and representing distinct constituencies. And that became the storyline over the next quarter century. Indeed, the "textbook Congress" taught to today's millennial generation revolves around the notion that strong parties dominate Congress and polarization is at an all-time high.

The authors of this volume, taken together, provide a more nuanced view of this textbook Congress, and suggest perhaps that we are in the beginning stages of a new era of congressional policy making. Clearly, strong parties and polarization are still in evidence. But governing, by all accounts, has become more difficult under conditions of *both* unified and divided government. A sixty-vote threshold on most policy matters has emerged in the Senate, brinkmanship tactics have become the norm in both chambers, and the institution as a whole seems to be constantly on the verge of one self-created crisis or another.

And yet, Congress has not ground to a halt because of "dysfunction." Legislative productivity is still relatively high on matters of importance. As David R. Mayhew has shown in his list of "important enactments" through 2014, the increasingly polarized and divisive atmosphere in Congress has not led to a significant decline in landmark law making. In sum, despite its various problems (many of which are self-inflicted), Congress remains a consequential policy maker in a number of areas (which is not necessarily to pass judgment on either the quality or the adequacy of its actions relative to the problems the nation faces).[3]

That said, the partisan environment in Congress seems a bit different than it did in the recent past. Intraparty stress has increased significantly since the

George W. Bush era, as intraparty homogeneity is being tested by the difficulty of reconciling conflicting promises to different groups of constituents and party supporters. The prime example is the Tea Party element within the Republican Party. In the House, this conservative group has repeatedly bucked the leadership and forced a new kind of bipartisanship to emerge to keep the institution afloat. On a variety of issues, for example, Speaker John Boehner (R-OH) found he had no choice but to rely on the minority Democrats to provide the key votes to enact important policies, such as the revision and extension of the Bush-era tax cuts, Hurricane Sandy Relief, the Violence Against Women Act, and the raising of the debt ceiling. These moves were rational strategic compromises during a period of divided government, but they incensed conservative House Republicans who favored an even more adversarial and aggressive posture toward the Obama Administration. Exhausted from fights within his party and criticism of his actions by the House Freedom Caucus (a Tea-Party-inspired group of forty Republican hard-liners), Boehner in late 2015 announced he would relinquish his gavel and resign from Congress. Majority Leader Mitch McConnell (R-KY) faced a more fluid and open lawmaking environment in the Senate, but he too was compelled to work with Democrats on issues such as measures to repair the formula for reimbursing Medicare physicians (the "doc fix") and to combat human trafficking. These efforts exposed him to attacks from his right flank, led by Ted Cruz (R-TX) and others. As a result, McConnell sometimes gave in to their demands and scheduled votes on conservative priorities (like defunding Planned Parenthood), rather than risk the Tea Party's wrath.

Thus, just as the party-based textbook model supplanted the committee-based textbook model in the late 20th century, a new model of congressional policy making seems to be emerging in the 21st century – more due to necessity than to design. As of this writing, what the final shape of this new model will be is unclear. Parties are still important during this institutional transition, without question. But the strong, internal cohesion that was central to the party-based model seems to be fraying, especially when a party like the Republicans is in the majority and faces the difficult task of balancing its ideological aspirations with the demands of governing and funding a vast policy state. Odd bipartisan coalitions have been forming – sometimes with the majority party being "rolled" – to pass important laws (often at the eleventh hour), while legislative entrepreneurship of individual members continues to be a driving force in policy origination and development. And finally, external actors in the American separation of powers system – the president and the bureaucracy – are increasingly vying with Congress for policy making control, and taking advantage of Congress's inability to act quickly and decisively on various issues.

What does this all add up to? Our sense, based on the essays contained in this book and other recent scholarship, suggests that any understanding of the evolving textbook Congress should take into account the following trends and developments:

- The evolving textbook Congress operates in an era characterized not only by significant partisan polarization but also by unusual *partisan parity*, in which nearly every election can potentially shift majority control (Lee 2009). The high level of electoral competitiveness between the two parties raises the stakes in all policy debates and discourages bipartisan cooperation on the crafting of legislation even when ideological disagreement is not deeply rooted – unless a crisis (such as the prospect of national default) absolutely compels it.
- The institution today faces an increasingly *unilateral presidency*, more willing than during the postwar era to address domestic (not just foreign policy) challenges without substantial legislative buy-in or support. The era when the president's main governing power was the "power to persuade" is long past.
- Because of the vast expansion of the federal government over the past fifty years, the evolving textbook Congress confronts what Suzanne Mettler (2014) calls a "policyscape" – a landscape in which policies created in the past have themselves become institutions that shape the legislative agenda, such as the need to pay for rising Medicare costs. The statutes passed by previous congresses have spawned constituencies, created hard-to-reverse organizational adaptations, and shaped public expectations about government's role. The policies have also created problems and unintended consequences that demand current legislators' attention, such as the ongoing financial problems of the Highway Trust Fund stemming from changes in driving patterns, increased fuel economy, and the failure to index the gas tax to inflation. In sum, established policies now form the institutional terrain on which American politics plays out (Pierson 2014). The upkeep, maintenance, and repair of existing policies today constitutes a central task for legislators. This task is particularly difficult for the GOP given its aim to fundamentally scale back the size and scope of the American state despite the inertia and upward spending pressure from preexisting policy commitments, but it also creates challenges for Democrats given their struggles with taxation and policy reform.
- Finally, the evolving textbook Congress confronts an American community whose membership and identity are changing as a result of shifting and often contested norms on issues such as same-sex marriage and immigration as well as vast changes in the material circumstances of Americans due to globalization, technological change, and rising inequality.

The common theme of this list is that the functioning of the 21st century Congress cannot be understood by examining only the procedural rules and internal organization of the House and the Senate. The key to understanding the evolving textbook Congress will be to analyze how legislators, both individually and as factions and party units, represent and help to constitute the membership of a changing American society, as well as how legislators manage and respond to the pressures emanating from the policy environment.

Congress scholars will need to look beyond Capitol Hill to understand why Congress behaves the way it does; public policy scholars will need to gain a better appreciation for how legislative incentives mediate the politics of problem solving. The total number and kinds of laws that Congress passes will still be worthy of investigation, but so will many other dimensions of legislative output and performance, such as how Congress's decisions *and* nondecisions shape economic growth, the distribution of income, and national security. At the same time, the evolving textbook Congress presents an opportunity to revisit traditional questions about the tension between governance and responsiveness, about conflict and cooperation between the branches, about distributive justice versus efficiency, and about state–society relations (see Fiorina 2011).

This is an exciting research agenda for scholars of Congress and public policy in the 21st century.

Notes

1. For a study of this topic, see Patashnik and Peck (forthcoming).
2. On the transition from the committee-based textbook model to the party-based textbook model, see Sinclair 2014.
3. Consistent with a point raised by Arnold in his chapter in this volume, Mayhew notes that the common tendency to focus on the total number of bills enacted – a trend that has been sloping downhill since World War II – gives a misleading portrait of congressional productivity. For example, Mayhew observes, "Harry Truman's Congress of 1949–50, during which in reality that president's program did not do very well, is reported to have chalked up over 2,000 enactments; Obama's first Congress, which featured the jam-packed $787B stimulus, the Dodd-Frank financial services reform, and Obamacare, chalked up just 385 enactments. What's going on in these summary numbers? Has the U.S. government grown dramatically less active? Not likely. A moment's thought will stir in you a well-grounded suspicion that Congress has drifted over the decades into stuffing its production into big, thick, capacious, sometimes 'omnibus' bills as distinguished from individual smaller free-standing ones." See Mayhew's commentary posted at: http://campuspress.yale.edu/davidmayhew/files/2015/05/dataset-DWG-laws-2013-14.pdf. For Mayhew's list of significant legislation, see http://campuspress.yale.edu/davidmayhew/datasets-divided-we-govern/.

References

Adler, E. Scott, and John D. Wilkerson. 2012. *Congress and the Politics of Problem Solving*. Cambridge: Cambridge University Press.

Bartels, Larry. 2010. *Unequal Democracy: The Political Economy of the New Gilded Age*. Princeton, NJ: Princeton University Press.

Binder, Sarah A. 2003. *Stalemate: Causes and Consequences of Legislative Gridlock*. Washington, DC: Brookings Institution Press.

     2014. "Polarized We Govern?" Center for Effective Public Management at Brookings, May. www.brookings.edu/~/media/research/files/papers/2014/05/27%

20polarized%20we%20govern%20binder/brookingscepm_polarized_figreplaced textrevtablerev.pdf.

Campbell, Andrea L. 2011. "Paying America's Way: The Fraught Politics of Taxes, Investments, and Budgetary Responsibility." In Theda Skocpol and Larry Jacobs, eds., *Reaching for a New Deal: Ambitious Governance, Economic Meltdown, and Polarized Politics in Obama's First Two Years.* New York: Russell Sage.

Cooper, Joseph. 2009. "From Congressional to Presidential Preeminence: Power and Politics in the Late Nineteenth Century and Today." In Lawrence C. Dodd and Bruce I. Oppenheimer, eds., *Congress Reconsidered,* 9th ed. Washington, DC: Congressional Quarterly Press.

Cox, Gary W., and Mathew D. McCubbins. 1993. *Legislative Leviathan: Party Government in the House.* Berkeley: University of California Press.

Fiorina, Morris P. 2011. "Reflections on the Study of Congress." In Eric Schickler and Frances E. Lee, eds., *Oxford Handbook of the American Congress.* New York: Oxford, pp. 861–74.

Hacker, Jacob S., and Paul Pierson. 2011. *Winner-Take-All Politics.* New York: Simon & Schuster.

Health Affairs. 2012. "Health Policy Brief: Reducing Waste in Health Care." December 13.

Howell, William G. 2003. *Power without Persuasion: The Politics of Direct Presidential Action.* Princeton, NJ: Princeton University Press.

Kagan, Robert A. 2001. *Adversarial Legalism: The American Way of Law.* Cambridge, MA: Harvard University Press.

Kernell, Samuel, and Gary C. Jacobson. 2006. *The Logic of American Politics,* 3rd ed. Washington, DC: Congressional Quarterly Press.

Kingdon, John. 2002. *Agendas, Alternatives, and Public Policies,* 2nd ed. New York: Longman.

Lapinski, John S. 2013. *The Substance of Representation: Congress, American Political Development, and Lawmaking.* Princeton, NJ: Princeton University Press.

Lee, Frances E. 2009. *Beyond Ideology: Politics, Principles, and Partisanship in the U.S. Senate.* Chicago: University of Chicago Press.

2013. "Presidents and Party Teams: Debt Limits and Executive Oversight, 2001–2013." *Presidential Studies Quarterly* 43 (4): 775–91.

Levy, Frank. 1999. *The New Dollars and Dreams.* New York: Russell Sage.

Lewis, David E. 2008. *The Politics of Presidential Appointments: Political Control and Bureaucratic Performance.* Princeton, NJ: Princeton University Press.

Mann, Thomas E., and Norman J. Ornstein. 2006. *The Broken Branch: How Congress Is Failing American and How to Get It Back on Track.* Oxford: Oxford University Press.

Mayhew, David R. 2009. "Is Congress the 'Broken Branch'?" *Boston University Law Review* 89 (2): 357–70.

Mettler, Suzanne. 2014. "The Politics of the Policyscape: The Challenges of Contemporary Governance for Policy Maintenance." August 21, 2014. http://ssrn.com/abstract=2484837 or http://dx.doi.org/10.2139/ssrn.2484837.

Nivola, Pietro S., and David W. Brady. 2008. *Red and Blue Nation? vol. 2: Consequences and Correction of America's Polarized Politics.* Washington, DC: Brookings Institution Press.

Patashnik, Eric, and Justin Peck. Forthcoming. "Can Congress Do Policy Analysis? The Politics of Problem Solving on Capitol Hill." In Alan Gerber and Eric Schickler, eds., *Governing in a Polarized Age: Elections, Parties, and Political Representation in America*. Cambridge: Cambridge University Press.

Patterson, James. 1997. *Grand Expectations*. New York: Oxford University Press.

Pierson, Paul. 2014. "Conclusion: Madison Upside Down." In Jeffery A. Jenkins and Sidney M. Milkis, eds., *The Politics of Major Policy Reform in Postwar America*. New York: Cambridge University Press, pp. 282–302.

Polsby, Nelson W. 1990. "Congress-Bashing for Beginners." *The Public Interest* 100: 15–23.

Poole, Keith T., and Howard Rosenthal. 2007. *Ideology and Congress*. New Brunswick: Transaction Publishers.

Restuccia, Andrew, and Darius Dixon. 2013. "Obama to Congress in State of the Union: Act on Climate or I Will." *Politico*, February 12, 2013. www.politico.com/story/2013/02/obama-to-congress-act-on-climate-or-i-will-87555.html

Riffkin, Rebecca. 2014. "Public Faith in Congress Falls Again, Hits Historic Low." *Gallup Politics*. June 19. www.gallup.com/poll/171710/public-faith-congress-falls-again-hits-historic-low.aspx.

Rohde, David W. 1991. *Parties and Leaders in the Postreform House*. Chicago, IL: University of Chicago Press.

Schickler, Eric. 2001. *Disjointed Pluralism: Institutional Innovation and the Development of the U.S. Congress*. Princeton, NJ: Princeton University Press.

Shepsle, Kenneth A. 1989. "The Changing Textbook Congress." In John Chubb and Paul Peterson, eds., *Can the Government Govern?* Washington, DC: Brookings.

  2009. "Dysfunctional Congress?" *Boston University Law Review* 89 (2): 371–86.

Sinclair, Barbara. 2006. *Party Wars: Polarization and the Politics of National Policy Making*. Norman: University of Oklahoma Press.

  2009. "Question: What's Wrong with Congress? Answer: It's a Democratic Legislature." *Boston University Law Review* 89 (2): 387–98.

  2011. *Unorthodox Lawmaking: New Legislative Processes in the U.S. Congress*. Washington, DC: Congressional Quarterly Press.

  2014. "Is Congress Now the Broken Branch?" *Utah Law Review* 2014 (4): 703–24.

Sundquist, James L. 1981. *The Decline and Resurgence of Congress*. Washington, DC: Brookings Institution Press.

Skowronek, Stephen. 1982. *Building a New American State: The Expansion of National Administrative Capacities, 1877–1920*. Cambridge: Cambridge University Press.

Steinhauer, Jennifer. 2012. "A Showdown Long Foreseen." *New York Times*, December 30, 2012. www.nytimes.com/2012/12/31/us/politics/fiscal-crisis-impasse-long-in-the-making.html.

Zelizer, Julian E. 1999. *Taxing America: Wilbur D. Mills, Congress, and the State, 1945–1975*. Cambridge: Cambridge University Press.

PART I

CONGRESSIONAL POLICY MAKING
IN A POLARIZED AGE

2

Entrepreneurial Politics, Policy Gridlock, and Legislative Effectiveness

Craig Volden and Alan E. Wiseman*

A common and compelling narrative about policy making in the U.S. Congress in the 21st century revolves around party polarization and gridlock. According to such a narrative, the vast ideological divide between Democrats and Republicans leaves insufficient common ground on which to forge the coalitions that are necessary to properly govern America's complex republic. Especially absent a sizable unified government, wherein the president's party also controls the House and a filibuster-proof Senate majority, the natural result is gridlock.

In this chapter, we argue that such a narrative, while useful, has a variety of limits, all of which point toward the need to focus not merely on party and ideology but also on the law-making effectiveness of individual policy entrepreneurs in Congress. First, it is important to recognize that not all policy making in Congress is driven by partisan politics. Notably, as we discuss in the following, interest group politics, client politics, and entrepreneurial politics are all common and important, often with the potential to cut across partisan divides. Second, the overarching story of polarization-induced stalemate misses the fact that policy gridlock varies substantially over time and across different issue areas, in ways that partisan polarization cannot adequately explain. Third, this variance in rates of gridlock is closely linked to the extent to which issues are dominated by the incidence of entrepreneurial politics at specific points in time. (As we define in the following, entrepreneurial politics involve issues for which there is concentrated opposition to policy change, yet widely distributed supporters for such change.) Highly effective lawmakers are needed to act as entrepreneurs in

* The authors thank Claire Abernathy, James Austrow, Tracy Burdett, Matt Hitt, Jeff Jenkins, Chris Kypriotis, Lauren Mattioli, Eric Patashnik, Brian Pokosh, and Dana Wittmer for valuable research assistance, and conference participants at the University of Virginia, and the University of Michigan for helpful feedback on earlier drafts of this work.

overcoming gridlock on such issues. And many of the same skills that they use to advance policy change in the presence of entrepreneurial politics are also valuable in overcoming the gridlock of partisan politics.

Throughout this chapter, we develop this argument through both qualitative case studies and large-N quantitative analyses. Taken together, the evidence we advance points toward a greater need for scholars and practitioners alike to focus not just on the ideological positions of members of Congress, but perhaps even more so on which lawmakers in Congress have the ability and inclination to "get things done."

We begin with an illustrative example from one of the most pressing policy problems facing the United States in the early 21st century – soaring health care costs. These costs can be traced, among other causes, to many of the behaviors that Americans engage in on a daily basis. For instance, on countless occasions in an average day, Americans make a choice to smoke or not, to eat healthy foods or not, and to exercise or not. We would often prefer a silver bullet solution to the hard work necessary to live healthy lifestyles.

In this context, a *Washington Post* article in the summer of 1989 presented more bad news. It began by noting that "for people eager to watch their weight without giving up cheesecake, Sara Lee Light Classics must seem like a gift from the gods."[1] With only "200 Calories Per Serving," Sara Lee "light" cheesecake promised a wonderful alternative to more conventional cheesecake offerings. Closer inspection revealed, however, that the only substantive difference between the "light" and regular Sara Lee cheesecakes was the prescribed serving size. That is, ounce-for-ounce, "light" cheesecakes were no healthier than regular Sara Lee cheesecakes. Such unclear and potentially misleading labeling was yet another example of the state of the industry that led Marion Nestle, the chairwoman of the Department of Home Economics and Nutrition at New York University, to claim that "labels are worse than useless, they are dangerous . . . it's not an exaggeration to say that [misinformation] is killing people."

In light of a growing list of such misleading labels, consumer health advocates had been pushing for more transparent (and truthfully informative) labeling practices and standards for years. Yet they had failed to experience any success when pressing their cases directly with companies or indirectly through lawmakers on Capitol Hill. Such failures should not have been surprising to even the most casual observer of American politics. After all, the status quo of opaque labeling practices clearly favored a concentrated, wealthy, and well-organized collection of interests that consisted of food producers, marketers, and other links in the American food economy rent-chain. Any change to current policy that required them to alter their lucrative marketing and labeling practices would likely lead to significant costs and lower profits.

On the other side, the most obvious beneficiaries from truth-in-labeling regulations were a relatively diverse and poorly organized public, who would benefit (on the margin) from having access to clearer and more accurate information, with which they could make better-educated decisions about their diet and food consumption habits. While such issues are of obvious importance to public health advocates, they are not the kinds of political matters that generally compel members of the public to turn out in the streets (figuratively speaking) demanding policy change. In light of the stark differences between the concentrated benefits that flowed to a narrow set of interests under the status quo and the dispersed benefits that would flow to a diverse coalition of interests under a policy change, it seemed likely that "light," yet not-so-light, cheesecakes were here to stay.

But that was all about to change. A little over a year after the aforementioned story was published in the *Washington Post*, President Bush signed into law "one of the most substantial revisions of law governing the regulation of food ... in the nation's history."[2] The Nutrition Labeling and Education Act of 1990 had been sponsored in the U.S. House by Representative Henry Waxman (D-CA). It was Waxman who served as the policy entrepreneur on this issue, advocating, pushing, begging, threatening, and bargaining, to ensure that his proposal ultimately found its way into law. How was Representative Waxman so successful at bringing about such a momentous change in health policy? And what might be extracted from the experiences of Waxman and other entrepreneurs in Congress to inform us more broadly about the determinants of health policy change, as well as changes in other policy areas, more generally considered?

As one considers the policy-making activities and abilities of the U.S. Congress in the 21st century, a number of features stand out. First, some problems seem more intractable than others. As the scholars writing in this volume discuss, health care spending, tax policy, and immigration reform all present thorny problems that Congress has difficulty addressing. Other issues, such as fuel economy standards and financial crises, have been tackled partially by Congress and partially by other institutions including executive agencies and the Federal Reserve. In still other policy areas, Congress surprises observers with its ability to act quickly, such as in its repeal of the "Don't Ask, Don't Tell" policy for gays in the military. What is it about some policy areas that lead to greater policy change than others?

Second, given the complex legislative organization of Congress, the strategic choices of policy entrepreneurs are crucial in bringing about significant change. For example, in the 2010 maneuverings over health care reform, most observers felt that reform efforts had reached their end with the election of Republican Scott Brown to fill the Senate seat from Massachusetts when Ted Kennedy passed away.[3] This party switch limited supporters to only fifty-nine of the sixty votes that would be needed to overcome a filibuster of modified legislation to resolve House–Senate differences. However, House leaders developed a plan to pass the identical bill that had previously succeeded in the Senate and to throw all of their amendments into a separate bill, passed just minutes later. Who are the entrepreneurs who rise to such policy-making challenges?

Third, the strategic decisions of policy entrepreneurs are most crucial on the exact issues that are the most intractable. Put simply, issues that have broad support in Congress can pass, and can even pass by wide margins, without too much in the way of political wrangling. Even with Congress as polarized as it has been in recent years, and even with divided government across chambers or across branches, agreements are struck to bring about hundreds of new laws in each two-year period between congressional elections. Most of these new laws address substantive issues, rather than just commemorative matters, although successes have received much less publicity than recent high-profile failures. In contrast, on the more heavily gridlocked issues, the law-making effectiveness of individual members of Congress becomes critical. Someone must construct policy proposals that address major problems before the country. Someone must modify those proposals to make them viable to members obsessed with reelection. And someone must then shepherd such bills through subcommittees and committees, across the floors of the House and Senate, and into law. Such a "someone" is typically a lawmaker, a member such as Henry Waxman, who uses his policy expertise, his institutional position, and his ability to build support within or across party lines to bring about a policy change.[4] How can we identify the effective lawmakers in Congress and their role in helping to overcome policy gridlock?

In this chapter, we answer these questions and paint a picture of policy making in Congress in the 21st century that returns to some of the lessons learned in the 20th century. Specifically, we revisit an idea developed by James Q. Wilson, who argued that the politics of policy making is often determined by the nature of the proposed policy change itself. In particular, we emphasize *entrepreneurial politics*, wherein the policy change being advocated benefits a broad but disorganized set of individual and collective interests, but with costs to be paid by a single or small group of concentrated and well-organized interests. Given the ability of the organized interests to stop policy change, entrepreneurial politics is often the politics of policy gridlock, with little change likely without the efforts of an effective policy entrepreneur.

We argue that policy areas facing entrepreneurial politics can be identified by focusing on the entrepreneurs themselves. In particular, we demonstrate that in any major issue area that Congress confronts, at any given point in time, it is possible to identify whether policy-making advances are spread out broadly across the members of Congress or are limited to a single or small set of policy entrepreneurs. In contrast to the difficult cases of entrepreneurial politics, instances of client politics feature numerous policy advocates, all willing to act on behalf of the organized (and often well-funded) clients in support of a policy change over the disorganized and widely dispersed policy opponents. We identify effective lawmakers in order to label as *entrepreneurial politics* those issue areas wherein a single legislator accounts for a large fraction of the law-making activities.

Having identified issue areas featuring entrepreneurial politics, and relying on the theoretical claim that entrepreneurial politics are more likely to feature policy gridlock, we next identify the rates of gridlock across issue areas over time. Specifically, across the same policy domains in which we identify policy entrepreneurs, we measure the percentage of lawmakers' proposals that actually become law. If the theory is correct, the same policy areas featuring entrepreneurial politics will have the highest levels of policy gridlock.

Consistent with expectations, in focusing on the U.S. House, we find policy gridlock to be much greater in the issue areas facing entrepreneurial politics than in those where entrepreneurial politics is less prevalent. For example, in the 107th Congress (2001–02), more than 6 percent of low entrepreneurial bills became law, while less than 2 percent of bills in highly entrepreneurial issue areas succeeded. Moreover, upon tracking the extent to which the more highly entrepreneurial policy issues are also the most gridlocked across Congresses, we find strong evidence that such a relationship has grown in its intensity over time.

Having engaged in such aggregate analysis, we conclude with a return to the specific law-making strategies of two policy entrepreneurs themselves. We highlight how Henry Waxman and Philip M. Crane (R-IL) used their innate abilities, their cultivated skill sets, and their institutional positions to overcome entrepreneurial politics in the areas of health and of foreign trade. In sum, building on analysis from the 20th century, we argue that policy making in Congress in the 21st century cannot be characterized properly without first classifying the nature of the politics involved and without then focusing on the effectiveness of individual lawmakers as policy entrepreneurs.

Taken as a whole, our argument contrasts significantly with recent portrayals of policy making in Congress as completely mired in gridlock due to partisan polarization. As Sinclair eloquently describes in Chapter 3 of this volume, partisan polarization can likely have both a direct and an indirect effect on the likelihood of policy change.[5] The most obvious direct impact of party polarization is that, as the parties become more distinct from each other (and ideologically homogeneous), the prospect for cross-party coalitions is diminished, and the nature of plausible winning coalitions within the majority party changes, as well. Hence, gridlock might become increasingly pervasive, as an increase in partisan polarization would often correspond to an expansion of the distance between various pivotal actors in both chambers whose acquiescence would need to be secured in order to move bills further in the legislative process (i.e., Brady and Volden 2006; Krehbiel 1998). Likewise, one would expect that the prospects for coalition building via side payments by party leaders (e.g., Snyder 1991; Wiseman 2004) would become increasingly difficult, as members of the minority party will essentially become too expensive to be won over with favors and other forms of political currency.[6]

A more subtle consequence of political polarization, however, is its indirect impact on the nature of law making. Sinclair and others argue that as the parties become more internally homogeneous, rank-and-file party members become more comfortable delegating various parliamentary tools to their leaders. Such delegation to party leaders will have consequences for both the kinds of policies that will come up for consideration on the floor (i.e., Cox and McCubbins 2005) and the tools that leaders possess to induce members to toe the party line (e.g., Rohde 1991).

While Sinclair's arguments are consistent with spatial models and other dominant perspectives on the consequences of polarization in Congress, we offer three main points of departure from such a view in this chapter. First, as alluded to earlier, we build on Wilson's (1980) work to suggest that many proposed policy changes are better understood based on entrepreneurial polit-ics or client politics than solely through the lens of partisan politics. Second, we establish that some policy areas are much more gridlocked than others, and account for such differences based on whether the nature of the surrounding policy choices tends to be entrepreneurial or not. And, third, rather than focusing on parties as collective entities, we turn our gaze to individual members of Congress. Some of those members are particularly adept at using their expertise, coalition-building skills, and institutional positions to become highly effective lawmakers. Such entrepreneurs play a major role in determining whether gridlock will be overcome in Congress and therefore in determining which public policies will govern the nation.

ENTREPRENEURIAL POLITICS

Political scientists seek broad generalizations that allow for a coherent under-standing of the underlying politics of policy making, without treating each new policy proposal as unique. If unique, then little can be said based on past experience to inform scholars and practitioners about what they should expect in the upcoming policy-making process. In contrast, if the current case is in some ways similar to early instances of a comparable political phenomenon, then prior experiences can be brought to bear in forming expectations about current or future behaviors.

Such a quest for generalizations has been engaged by political scientists across the generations, with some insights being more useful than others. Among the sets of generalizations that has stood the test of time is a classifi-cation system advanced by James Q. Wilson in a variety of his writings. Perhaps best articulated in Wilson (1980), he classifies any given policy change in terms of those who benefit from and those who are harmed by the proposal.[7] For each side, he identifies whether the interests are widely distributed (and thus unlikely to generate much direct political action) or highly concentrated (and thus likely to be politically impactful). Such classifi-cations are captured concisely in what has come to be known as the Wilson matrix, replicated in Figure 2.1.[8]

Benefits from Policy Change

	Concentrated	Widely Distributed
Concentrated	*Interest Group Politics*	*Entrepreneurial Politics*
Widely Distributed	*Client Politics*	*Majoritarian Politics*

Costs of Policy Change

FIGURE 2.1: The Wilson Matrix

Note: Based on Wilson (1980), this matrix illustrates the nature of politics associated with policy proposals, depending on whether those who benefit from the proposal or those paying the costs are concentrated (and thus likely to be politically active) or widely distributed (and thus likely to be politically inactive).

If those receiving the benefits and those paying the costs from a policy proposal are both highly concentrated (and thus likely to be well organized), the result is interest group politics. For example, high-profile disputes between business and labor fall in this category. Interest group politics is the subject of countless scholarly works (e.g., Denzau and Munger 1986; Hansen 1991; Leech 2011; Truman 1951; Wright 2003). These works flesh out the details of Wilson's claim that the result of interest group politics tends to be a policy choice in favor of the side that is stronger in generating effective political pressure.

In contrast to interest group politics, majoritarian politics tends to take place when neither side is particularly concentrated. Widely distributed across society, each side places little pressure on policy makers, neither through lobbying nor through other modes of advocating their positions. This is not to say that politicians are inactive in this area, however. Political parties, seeking issues that will mobilize their bases or looking to capture the support of broad segments of society, will take up the various sides of such majoritarian issues. An example of majoritarian politics may be a broad set of budget and tax priorities, which influence most Americans, but only at an insufficient level to generate interest group pressure. The strength of the parties acting through legislative institutions will then determine the policy outcome. In this area, the vast and growing literature on parties in Congress offers numerous insights into policy making (e.g., Aldrich and Rohde 2000; Cox and McCubbins 2005; Gailmard and Jenkins 2007; Krehbiel 1993; Krehbiel, Meirowitz, and Wiseman 2015; Lebo, McGlynn, and Koger 2007; McCarty, Poole, and Rosenthal 2001; Minozzi and Volden 2013; Snyder and Groseclose 2000).

Entrepreneurial politics takes place when the supporters of a policy change are broadly distributed but the opponents are concentrated. For example, new restrictions on business practices designed to aid consumers or to help the environment may be opposed by organized business interests, without concentrated support from the policy's beneficiaries. In such instances, policy change is unlikely because the organized opponents have many venues in which to stop policy change, such as relying on blocking mechanisms in committees or subcommittees, erecting procedural obstacles, or counting on the inherent complexities in bicameral negotiations and supermajority requirements (such as cloture votes to end a filibuster in the Senate or veto override votes in both houses). Policy change in entrepreneurial politics can only be secured on the intensive action of policy entrepreneurs, who advocate for the new proposal on behalf of its broadly distributed supporters. Entrepreneurs may arise based on their own personal convictions about the issue at hand or for some larger political purpose, such as to set the stage for an attempt at gaining a higher office. Nevertheless, the nature of the opposition they face means that, even where entrepreneurs arise, they often face insurmountable odds.

Finally, the converse of entrepreneurial politics is client politics. Here, the supporters of a policy change are concentrated and well organized, while the opponents are widely dispersed. Examples include targeted tax breaks, crop subsidies, or some types of public works projects. In contrast to entrepreneurial politics, policy change is quite easily achieved under client politics. Supporters of the policy change seek out policy makers to advocate on their behalf and secure their aid through electoral assistance or other support.

While the politics of these four types of policy change may each play out quite differently, one broad but important relationship emerges from Wilson's matrix. Specifically, in terms of policy gridlock, we take from Wilson's work the following hypothesis.

Entrepreneurial Politics and Policy Gridlock Hypothesis: *Policy gridlock is more likely in policy areas and during times featuring entrepreneurial politics than under other types of politics.*

Few scholars would disagree that the nature of entrepreneurial politics undermines policy change. Indeed, examples abound of gridlock in such policy areas prior to the rise of an effective entrepreneur. Baumgartner and Jones (2009) and Kingdon (2011), for example, point to several cases of the crucial role that political entrepreneurs played in overcoming gridlock in policy areas such as environmental policy, auto safety, and health policy.[9]

Our hypothesis extends beyond such individual examples, however. In our view, if one looks at the types of policy problems prevalent in specific issue areas at particular points in time, the likely nature of the politics becomes clear on a broader scale. For instance, the massive deficits and mounting debts accumulated over the past decade mean that current budget and macroeconomic policy making is likely to be characterized by entrepreneurial politics.

Proposals to tackle the fiscal imbalance may offer broad benefits, but those whose programs need to be reined in or whose tax loopholes must be eliminated will be organized in their resistance. Likewise, the benefits of reductions in auto emissions are broadly distributed while the costs are borne largely by the auto industry. Indeed, numerous environmental policy proposals currently feature entrepreneurial politics.

In this view, if we can characterize major issue areas as best represented by entrepreneurial politics or by other political arrangements, we can then rely on the hypothesis to formulate a clear expectation about the likelihood of policy change in some areas compared to others. Our task is therefore quite clear. We need to develop a method to capture whether each issue area in each Congress is best characterized as facing entrepreneurial politics or as facing other, likely less gridlocked, political circumstances. We confront this task in the next section.

IDENTIFYING POLICY ENTREPRENEURS
AND ENTREPRENEURIAL POLITICS

In "Breaking Gridlock: The Determinants of Health Policy Change in Congress," we (Volden and Wiseman 2011) developed an Interest and Legislative Effectiveness Score (ILES) within the health policy area for each member of the U.S. House of Representatives in each Congress from 1973 to 2001. The score captures the share of all law-making activities beginning in the House that could be attributed to each member based on the bills that he or she sponsored.[10] More specifically, we traced each health policy bill that was sponsored in the House, including whether it received action in committee (hearings, votes, markups), action beyond committee (gaining access to a legislative calendar ahead of floor voting), passed the House, and became law. Later stages were weighted more heavily than earlier stages, and bills were downgraded if commemorative and upgraded if more substantive and significant (receiving mention in the *Congressional Quarterly Almanac*).[11]

These scores then allowed us to assess the importance of various personal characteristics and institutional considerations in advancing members' health policy proposals. Additionally, they helped us to identify major policy entrepreneurs in the health policy arena. For example, in Figure 2.2, we illustrate the highest Health-ILES achieved by any lawmaker for each Congress since the early 1970s. As the figure reveals, two members stand out as prominent health policy advocates in the House. First, Paul Rogers (D-FL) was so significant a figure in bringing about health policy change in the 1960s and 1970s that he was referred to as "Mr. Health" by other lawmakers. He is known for facilitating the passage of everything from the National Cancer Act to the Health Maintenance Organization Act. His *lowest* score on the Health-ILES was more than 150 times the normalized average score of 1.00 for our measure.

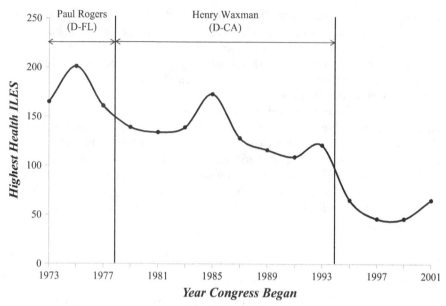

FIGURE 2.2: Identifying policy entrepreneurs
Note: The figure shows the highest value among all members of the House on their Health Policy Interest and Legislative Effectiveness Score (ILES) in each Congress. Based on these scores, we identify Paul Rogers (a.k.a. "Mr. Health") and Henry Waxman as health policy entrepreneurs. Relative to the average value of 1.00 for this measure, they consistently scored above 100, whereas no other member scored above 100 across our time period.

When Rogers retired from the House, Henry Waxman (D-CA) took his place as the most prominent health policy entrepreneur. As Chair of the Subcommittee on Health within the Energy and Commerce Committee, Waxman used his legislative prowess and institutional position to bring about the Orphan Drug Act, the Safe Medical Devices Act, and the Safe Drinking Water Act Amendments, among many others. In most cases, he acted in the realm of entrepreneurial politics, facilitating such laws on behalf of the widely distributed American public, often taking on special interests along the way. When Republicans gained control of the House in the 1994 elections, their most prominent health policy leaders did not score above the 100 Health-ILES level that Waxman had achieved in each and every Congress since the mid-1970s.

To test the Entrepreneurial Politics and Policy Gridlock Hypothesis, however, we need measures beyond just the area of health policy. Therefore, we constructed ILES for each of the nineteen policy areas specified by the Policy Agendas Project of Baumgartner and Jones (2002).[12] In each area, we tracked the bills sponsored by each member of the House, again focusing on how far they move through the law-making process and whether they are commemorative or substantive, as well as their significance. Using the same approach as described earlier for health, then, each member is given a score. And the highest scores are used to identify the most prominent policy entrepreneurs in each issue area in each Congress.

The highest ILES members are useful not only in identifying entrepreneurs but also in identifying areas and eras of entrepreneurial politics. For our purposes, we initially use the average value across Congresses for the highest-performing member in each policy area to identify the areas in which entrepreneurs are prominent. In contrast, for example, client politics would be associated with lower scores, with effective policy making much more spread out across members. This is because many lawmakers wish to act on behalf of powerful clients who can help them in a variety of ways, including in their reelection goals.

On such a criterion, our scores seem to comport well with common views and expectations. For example, as shown in Figure 2.2, the average value for the highest Health-ILES across Congresses is 120.5, consistent with an important role of policy entrepreneurs. The greatest level of entrepreneurship across all policy areas is found in Macroeconomics, an issue area often dealing with promoting economic growth, which offers widely distributed benefits. For example, in the 100th Congress (1987–88), Dan Rostenkowski's (D-IL) Macroeconomics-ILES was 285.2, indicating that he was responsible for *more than half* of all of the major legislative action in this area. Most notably, Rostenkowski shepherded through the Omnibus Budget Reconciliation Act of 1987, taking on organized interests through the closing of corporate loopholes and limiting the powers of large defense contractors, all for the purposes of lowering the budget deficit, another broadly distributed goal.

Scoring much lower on our measure of Entrepreneurial Politics are issue areas such as Public Lands, Defense, Banking and Commerce, and Government Operations. Each of these areas features many "client politics" policies that advance the interests of concentrated groups such as the banking industry. We are therefore quite confident that our approach to identifying policy entrepreneurs through their ILES ratings is also useful in finding the areas featuring entrepreneurial politics.

MEASURING POLICY GRIDLOCK

Our main argument is that entrepreneurial politics is highly associated with policy gridlock, and that such a relationship can be understood broadly across issue areas, rather than merely on a proposal-by-proposal basis. By generating issue-specific ILESs and averaging their highest values across Congresses, we have a measure that we believe accurately characterizes the issues that are most prone to entrepreneurial politics. Using these same issue areas and Congresses, we next turn to the development of a measure of policy gridlock.[13]

Upon looking at the details of lawmaking in these issue areas, at least two possibilities for measures of policy gridlock emerge. First, one could merely focus on the number of laws produced in each issue area in each Congress, either overall or in terms of a limited set of landmark laws (e.g., Mayhew 1991). We believe that such an approach is limited in its usefulness due to its inability to establish a baseline of *demand* for policy action. As Binder (2003) argues, some policy areas face more pressing challenges and greater needs for policy change than do others, in ways that vary over time.

We therefore turn to a second possibility, measuring the percent of bills introduced that become law. Here, once again, to be consistent with our measure of entrepreneurship, we limit our attention to the House of Representatives. Based on information available in the THOMAS database of the Library of Congress, we capture the number of bills introduced in each issue area in each Congress as well as the number of laws produced. Greater law production by this measure is consistent with lower policy gridlock.

Such a measure may be limited in a variety of ways. For instance, members may introduce bills for a large variety of reasons, not just because they believe their proposals stand a significant chance of becoming law. Legislators are focused on reelection, and therefore are often concerned with position taking (Mayhew 1974), a goal that is perhaps easily advanced through bill sponsorship. From our point of view, however, such low-cost introductions serve our purposes quite well. Members wish to take positions on issues important to their constituents, and therefore the number of sponsored bills serves as a useful proxy for public demand for change in a particular issue area. And passage into law is definitely the best way to consider which of these bills has overcome policy gridlock. If a large percentage of the sponsored bills become law, then Congress is able to overcome its deadlock in that particular area, in contrast to those in which few or none of the bills become law.

Table 2.1 shows all nineteen issue areas that Congress confronts, as well as the number of bills introduced and laws enacted between 1973 and 2002. Based on those numbers, we calculate the Success Rate, which shows which policy areas are more gridlocked than are others. Social Welfare clearly stands out as among the most gridlocked, with only 1.33 percent of the sponsored bills in this area becoming law. Also noteworthy for less than a 2 percent success rate are Civil Rights and Liberties; Health; Housing and Community Development; Labor, Employment, and Immigration; and Macroeconomics. On the other end of the spectrum is the issue area of Public Lands, with more than 10 percent of sponsored bills becoming law. Also above a 6-percentage-point success rate are Government Operations and International Affairs.

Earlier we mentioned Health and Macroeconomics as being areas featuring entrepreneurial politics, whereas Public Lands and Government Operations are more likely to exhibit client politics. That the former appear among our list of most gridlocked and the latter appear as least gridlocked therefore provides preliminary support for the Entrepreneurial Politics and Policy Gridlock Hypothesis. Further details of such a relationship can be gleaned from Table 2.1, where the final column shows the Entrepreneurial Politics Score by

TABLE 2.1 *Gridlock Rates and Entrepreneurial Politics across Issue Areas*

Issue Area	Bills Introduced	Laws Enacted	Success Rate (%)	Entrepreneurial Politics Score
Agriculture	4,062	126	3.10	107.9
Banking and Commerce	7,665	230	3.00	51.7
Civil Rights and Liberties	2,715	51	1.88	96.9
Defense	7,446	331	4.45	57.9
Education	4,200	98	2.33	93.9
Energy	5,125	129	2.52	83.9
Environment	5,262	197	3.74	79.7
Foreign Trade	5,354	124	2.32	87.9
Government Operations	13,658	952	6.97	32.2
Health	9,740	154	1.58	120.5
Housing and Community Development	2,800	49	1.75	125.1
International Affairs	2,739	177	6.46	84.3
Labor, Employment, and Immigration	6,987	131	1.87	71.1
Law, Crime, and Family	7,185	186	2.59	74.9
Macroeconomics	5,295	102	1.93	146.3
Public Lands	8,693	905	10.41	36.4
Science and Technology	2,126	93	4.37	132.3
Social Welfare	6,305	84	1.33	80.0
Transportation	5,746	224	3.90	96.4

Note: The table shows the aggregate numbers of bills introduced and laws produced by issue area from the 93rd through 107th Congresses (1973–2002), as well as the overall success rates in each area. Success rates range from a low of 1.33% of Social Welfare bills becoming law to 10.41% for Public Lands, showing some policy areas to be much more gridlocked than others. The Entrepreneurial Politics Score is based on the highest ILES score across members within the issue area averaged across all fifteen Congresses examined.

issue area, which is simply the average value across Congresses for the highest ILES among members in the given issue area.

A more systematic measure of the relationship between entrepreneurial politics and policy gridlock can be generated by calculating the correlation coefficient between Success Rate and Entrepreneurial Politics Score across the nineteen issue areas in the table. Consistent with the hypothesis, this correlation is negative (-0.57) and statistically significant $(p = 0.01)$. The negative correlation indicates that policy areas with more entrepreneurial politics tend to have lower success rates (or more gridlock). The statistical significance indicates that this correlation was unlikely to have occurred merely due to the two variables taking higher or lower values in random ways across issue areas.[14] This correlation therefore supports the Entrepreneurial Politics and Policy Gridlock Hypothesis.

ENTREPRENEURIAL POLITICS AND POLICY GRIDLOCK OVER TIME

Just as we believe that examining each policy proposal separately may offer too thin a brush with which to paint a portrait of entrepreneurial politics, so too might classifying each major policy area as a whole be an inappropriately broad brush. Indeed, the nature of the politics of issues changes substantially as problems are redefined over time. As illustrated in Figure 2.2, political entrepreneurs are more prevalent in some Congresses than in others. Such is true also of policy gridlock, with some issues being more gridlocked than are others at specific points in time.

Figure 2.3 illustrates how our measure of gridlock, based on bill success rates, varies substantially over time, both overall and in the policy areas of Health and of Foreign Trade. Overall, about 5 percent of all introduced bills became law in the 1980s and 1990s. In contrast, health bills were always more gridlocked, rising above 3 percent success rates only in the Congresses that began in 1983, 1989, and 1995. Trade bills found a great deal of success in the 95th Congress (1977–78) when health bills foundered and in the 104th Congress (1995–96) when health bills performed relatively well.

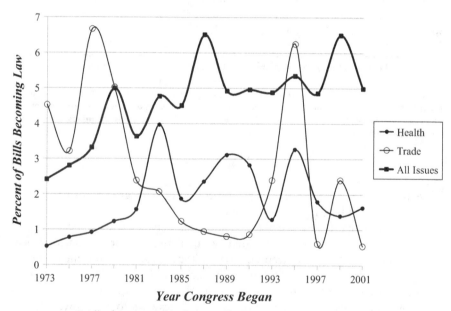

FIGURE 2.3: Gridlock rates vary substantially over time within issue areas
Note: The figure shows the percent of bills that become law overall (squares and thick line) and in the Health (closed circles) and Foreign Trade (open circles and thin line) issue areas, for each of the 93rd through 107th Congresses (1973–2002), revealing substantial variance in policy gridlock across issues over time.

These examples are representative of a broader pattern (or lack thereof) across all issue areas. Namely, each faces periods of feast and of famine that seem to correlate strongly neither with one another nor with the overall rate of success across all issues. This degree of disaggregation over time, therefore, offers a more difficult testing ground upon which to assess the Entrepreneurial Politics and Policy Gridlock Hypothesis. Can entrepreneurial politics, as we have defined and measured it here, help explain such broad swings in success across issues?

To answer this question, we explore the same data as earlier, used to generate Success Rates and Entrepreneurial Politics Scores, although this time allowing such measures to vary not only across issues but also over time. Specifically, we now examine the success rate of each issue area in each of the fifteen Congresses from 1973 to 2002. And, in terms of entrepreneurial politics, we subdivide each issue area in each Congress into one of two groups. We label as highly entrepreneurial issues those policy areas in specific Congresses wherein the highest ILES is above the median value for the highest ILES across all issues and all Congresses. The remaining half of the issue Congresses are labeled as low entrepreneurial issues. Such a subdivision allows us to extend our analysis beyond mere correlations, in order to identify broader patterns over time.

In particular, in Figure 2.4, we graph the average success rates for low entrepreneurial issues and for highly entrepreneurial issues in each Congress.[15] If the Entrepreneurial Politics and Policy Gridlock Hypothesis is correct, we should see much higher success rates among the low entrepreneurial issues than among the highly entrepreneurial issues. This is exactly what we find. For each Congress since the early 1970s, the success rate is lower among the issues featuring entrepreneurial politics than among those without such an entrepreneurial presence.[16]

Perhaps most strikingly, the gap in success rates between the two lines in the figure increases substantially over time. From the late 1970s through mid-1980s, there is about a 1-percentage-point gap between the highly entrepreneurial issues and the low entrepreneurial policies. Throughout the late 1980s and early 1990s, this gap expands to more than 2 percent. And it widens even further heading into the 21st century. Indeed, in the 107th Congress (2001–02), low entrepreneurial policies have more than *triple* the success rate of highly entrepreneurial policies.

That such a gap is opening up precisely during the time period when the parties have become more polarized (e.g., Bartels 2008; Hetherington 2009; McCarty, Poole, and Rosenthal 2006) leads us to question whether claims about partisan-based gridlock may be overstated. Many of the prominent examples of the inability of Congress to address major issues fall squarely in areas of entrepreneurial politics. For example, proposals to restrict handgun access in response to school shootings offer widely distributed benefits set against well-organized opposition of the NRA and other gun-rights groups.

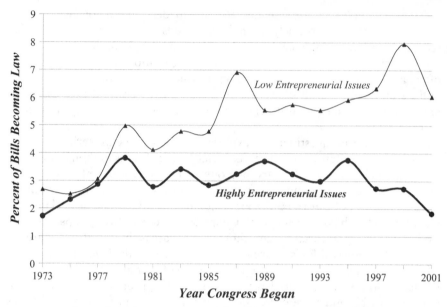

FIGURE 2.4: Issues featuring entrepreneurial politics are more gridlocked
Note: The figure shows the percent of bills that become law, among highly entrepreneurial (thick line) and low entrepreneurial (thin line) issue areas, for each of the 93rd through 107th Congresses (1973–2002), revealing greater gridlock among issues featuring greater entrepreneurial politics. Entrepreneurship is characterized by the highest ILESs among all lawmakers in the given issue and given Congress. Each issue in each Congress is then labeled highly entrepreneurial if its highest ILES value is above the median such value for all issues and all Congresses.

Proposals to reduce deficits and the national debt for the benefit of future (unorganized) generations are countered by those who pay the costs immediately, whether those who lose their tax breaks or those who see their health benefits reduced. That is, none of these policies clearly map into the majoritarian politics cell in the Wilson typology, which is often the category of policies over which political parties embrace two distinct sides. The same holds true for many other gridlocked policy areas discussed throughout this volume, whether on the environment or on immigration policy.

Thus, whether we narrow our focus to prominent individual policy proposals or broaden it to entire issue areas across decades of congressional policy making, the gridlock associated with entrepreneurial politics is profound. The importance of entrepreneurial politics in explaining policy success has been increasing in recent years, as evident in Figure 2.4. Therefore, perhaps the effect of entrepreneurial politics is best understood *in conjunction with* the recently polarized nature of congressional policy making. As alluded to earlier (and stated explicitly in Chapter 3), one might expect that the job of policy entrepreneurs has become more difficult in such settings, with coalition members harder to secure, especially across party lines. But, whether linked to polarization, to partisanship, or simply to more intractable public policy problems, the need to focus on entrepreneurial politics as a source of policy gridlock is particularly clear in the early 21st century.

DO POLICY ENTREPRENEURS HELP OVERCOME GRIDLOCK?

Given such a high level of gridlock associated with issues of entrepreneurial politics, with only 2–3 percent of sponsored bills becoming law in these areas, are the entrepreneurs themselves still important in generating policy success? On the one hand, perhaps there is little that any lawmaker can do in the face of such extreme odds. On the other hand, perhaps policy entrepreneurs are even more necessary and valuable than ever before. Calculating the exact value of such entrepreneurs in the lawmaking process is beyond the scope of our goals for this chapter.[17] Instead, before concluding, we here highlight the entrepreneurial activities undertaken by two prominent lawmakers who emerged from our analysis of issue-by-issue ILESs. These vignettes offer a sense of how policy entrepreneurs overcome even the thorniest issues of entrepreneurial politics. They point to how a focus on individual lawmakers in Congress is valuable (and perhaps even necessary) to understanding the public policies arising from the institution as a whole.

Henry Waxman as Health Policy Entrepreneur

In considering our first example, it should be fairly uncontroversial to label Henry Waxman (D-CA) as a health policy entrepreneur. First elected to Congress in 1974, Waxman served in the House until retiring at the conclusion of the 113th Congress (in 2014). It is not an understatement to claim that Waxman had his hand in virtually every major piece of health-related legislation that passed the House since the early 1980s. Indeed, President George W. Bush's Medicare director once argued that "fifty percent of the social safety net [in the United States] was created by Henry Waxman when no one was looking" (McManus 2014); and his involvement in the passage of the Nutrition Labeling and Education Act of 1990 was no exception to this rule.

As noted in the vignette from our introduction to this chapter, the status of food labeling in the mid-1980s was a confusing (and sorry) state of affairs; and concerns about the efficacy of labeling drew the attention of potential entrepreneurs in both parties. In March 1990, President George H. W. Bush's Secretary of Health and Human Services (Louis Sullivan) had gone so far as to refer to the American grocery store as a "Tower of Babel" due to completely confusing food labels and the lack of common standards in labeling (Specter 1990). Sullivan announced that his department would be proposing rules for food labeling to be promulgated over the coming year; yet such rulemaking would clearly feature fierce industry opposition.

Even before Secretary Sullivan had made his announcement, however, Waxman had already begun to take action. The bill that would ultimately become the Nutrition Labeling and Education Act of 1990 was introduced by Waxman into the House in July 1989 (as the Nutrition Labeling and Education Act of 1989), whereupon it was referred to the House Committee on Energy and Commerce, and then sent to the Health Subcommittee (which Waxman chaired). As it was initially introduced, the bill required that all processed foods have labels that clearly identified various quantities of interest that are now commonplace on products (e.g., calories, saturated and unsaturated fat, cholesterol); and it also established specific definitions for various terms of art, such as "light" and "low fat." Moreover, the bill also required that food producers and manufacturers only post health-related claims on their packaging if such claims could be justified by an objective consideration of the extant scientific evidence.

As soon as it was introduced, the bill ran into significant opposition from food industry trade groups such as the Grocery Manufacturers of America and the National Food Processors Association who argued (publicly) that the new law would be too costly to implement. These same interests expressed concerns in private that the law would constrain their abilities to make various health claims about their products.[18] Such concerns had successfully contributed to the demise of previous attempts at food labeling laws. In this case, however, the political calculus had changed. More specifically, many Republicans favored some change to the status quo vis-à-vis food labeling, and Ed Madigan (R-IL), the ranking member of the Health Subcommittee of the Energy and Commerce Committee, in particular, was in favor of the bill. Hence, the legislation was likely to succeed in some form, at least in committee, contrary to the wishes of food industry advocates.

As a result of this perceived inevitability, the industry shifted its focus away from trying simply to kill the bill, to rather shaping the bill in such a way so that it served their needs. In this case, they wished to ensure that the federal standards that were created by the bill would effectively preempt more stringent existing state regulations over food labeling, such as California's Proposition 65, which mandated that any foods containing any carcinogens be labeled as such.

While Waxman had significant support within his subcommittee for food labeling legislation in general, there was less support for the more nuanced aspects of such labeling (including whether or not the federal law would preempt state standards). Moreover, Madigan had expressed his intention to support the industry's preemption goals by proposing to amend Waxman's bill when it was ultimately considered by the full Energy and Commerce Committee. Given that such an amendment would likely pass, Waxman engaged in a series of subtle parliamentary maneuvers to ensure that any such amendment would be deemed as nongermane to the bill (and hence, it could not be added to the bill) by Committee Chairman John Dingell (D-MI). Waxman was ultimately successful in this regard, and the bill was reported from the full committee without the Madigan amendment.

Even though the bill had survived the committee process, Waxman was cognizant of the numerous potential roadblocks that the bill might encounter in the broader House and the Senate – especially given that any Senator could potentially put a hold on the measure. To sidestep any potential landmines, Waxman sat down with all relevant skeptical parties to negotiate agreements and compromises before the bill came up for a vote in the House. For example, not only were there still concerns about the preemption of state law, but a wide range of sector-specific concerns emerged, such as the labeling requirements for small vegetable stands, and what, precisely, constituted "maple syrup." In each of these matters, Waxman was a central player, and did whatever he could to facilitate compromise. In the end, the bill was brought up and passed under suspension of the rules in the House. The Senate passed a slightly altered form just before the 1990 elections, and Waxman scrambled to ensure House passage of the Senate version on Halloween. President Bush signed the bill on November 8, 1990, and Henry Waxman had one more piece of health policy legislation that he could add to his long list of accomplishments.

Phil Crane as Trade Policy Entrepreneur

Putting aside matters of health policy, the crucial role of entrepreneurs can also be observed in numerous other policy areas, such as foreign trade. In the late 1990s, a new school of thought began to emerge that advocated a different approach for trying to address poverty in Africa. Rather than embracing conventional forms of foreign aid, such as direct cash transfers between nations or multinational lending, a collection of scholars and practitioners argued for the cancellation of Africa's foreign debt and the opening up of markets through the reduction of trade barriers, which together were intended to stimulate economic growth and facilitate self-sufficiency (Passell 1997). Such sentiments were embraced by the Clinton Administration, which supported decisions of the World Bank and IMF to write off debt obligations from African nations in exchange for domestic political reforms in those countries. Such sentiments were also embraced by several members of Congress – most notably Phil Crane (R-IL), who introduced the African Growth and Opportunity Act (H.R. 1432) into the 105th Congress in April 1997.[19]

Similar in substance to legislation that he had introduced during the dwindling days of the 104th Congress,[20] the African Growth and Opportunity Act essentially created a free-trade zone between the United States and Sub-Saharan Africa. Among other features, the proposed bill explicitly eliminated quotas on textile and apparel imports from Kenya and Mauritius, if those countries provided for a mechanism to prevent the transshipment of fabrics through their jurisdictions (such as from China) and into the United States. Crane's measure drew support from a diverse coalition of interests including liberal Democrats,

such as Charles Rangel (D-NY), who thought that the bill was a plausible tool
for alleviating African poverty, as well as free-market conservatives, such as
House Speaker Newt Gingrich (R-GA).

While Crane's bill had the explicit backing of the Clinton Administration,
support among its diverse legislative coalition started to fracture as the measure
moved through the House. Several members of the Congressional Black Caucus
(CBC) expressed concerns that the legislation failed to provide adequate protections for American jobs (Woellert 1998a). Additionally, Maxine Waters (D-
CA) argued against provisions of the legislation that might significantly compromise African governmental autonomy. Another Democrat, Jesse Jackson,
Jr., (D-IL) was even more vocal in his opposition to the measure, arguing that
the insistence on African political and market reforms as requirements for
favorable trading status was analogous to the policies that facilitated the slave
trade in the 17th century (Woellert 1998b).

The concerns of the members of the CBC, however, were nothing compared
with those being voiced by the U.S. textile industry and various labor unions,
who feared that the legislation would essentially lead to Sub-Saharan Africa
becoming a pass-through stop for textiles from other parts of the world that
sought to penetrate the American market, duty- and quota-free. In many ways,
the opposition to the legislation was representative of a classic case of entrepreneurial politics. Any change to the status quo (i.e., liberalizing trade) would
impose concentrated costs on a relatively small number of interests, while the
benefits from the proposed change would be widely dispersed. As a result, one
would expect that there would be significant status quo bias in the absence of
an effective political entrepreneur, and the legislation would ultimately die.
Indeed, this is precisely what occurred. Despite passing the House by a
237–186 margin in March 1998, the bill spent the remainder of the 105th
Congress bottled up on the Senate Legislative Calendar in light of the opposition raised by labor and the textile industry, and due to a controversy pertain-
ing to "fast track" trade policy authority.

Despite, or perhaps because of, its fate in the previous Congress, Crane
introduced similar legislation into the 106th Congress on February 2, 1999,
and marked up the legislation in his subcommittee the very next day. Once
again, Crane's measure provided for the establishment of a free-trade zone with
Sub-Saharan Africa and included provisions that aimed to eliminate duties and
quotas related to textile and apparel that had been imported from Kenya and
Mauritius. This time, Jesse Jackson, Jr., stepped up his opposition, introducing
competing legislation (Selinger 1999) and launching an aggressive
"cyberlobbying" campaign against Crane's measure (Muwakkil 1999).

In spite of these concerns, Crane's bill passed the House by a 234–163
margin and it advanced to the Senate, where it received an initially friendly
welcome from the Republican leadership. Unfortunately for advocates of free
trade, however, the legislation quickly became a lightning rod for controversy,
as labor and textile-industry activists lobbied the Senate aggressively to kill or

water down the bill. The Senate was unable to pass an identical bill as the House. The chambers were also unable to agree on amendments to the legislation, which led to the Senate requesting a conference committee in November 1999. In the subsequent months, a contentious series of negotiations occurred between members of the House and the Senate (before a conference committee formally convened). The prospects of the legislation's success dimmed further when Phil Crane, the bill's sponsor and most vocal advocate, had to take a leave of absence in March 2000 to enter rehab for alcohol abuse.

While extricating himself from the direct negotiations over the trade measure during his twenty-four days in rehab, Crane was still a passionate observer of the discussions, requesting regular status reports on legislative bargaining during his time away from Congress (Zeleny 2000). Emerging from rehab in early April, Crane inserted himself directly into the legislative process, and was widely acknowledged with brokering the crucial compromises that facilitated its passage through the conference committee (and both chambers).[21] President Clinton signed the final bill into law on May 18, 2000; and the Trade and Development Act of 2000 was widely viewed as a major legislative accomplishment for Crane. It was a clear example of an entrepreneurial legislator engaging a policy area that was rife with gridlock and producing policy change through bargaining and tenacity, even in the face of immense personal struggle.

CONCLUSION

The public policy challenges facing the United States in the 21st century are immense, ranging from security issues to environmental concerns to fiscal crises. It is easy to point to gridlock and to the inability of Congress to solve such problems in a timely manner as evidence of failures of democratic governance and of our system of separation of powers.[22] Moreover, it has not gone unnoticed that current gridlock is coupled with a period of polarization and intense partisanship. With two ideologically distant, but internally aligned parties, there is little middle ground for compromise, apart from during periods of strong unified government (e.g., Chapter 3).

We do not doubt that major policy challenges exist, that Congress struggles to address them, and that partisan polarization is a concern. However, we offer something of an alternative view. In contrast to the characterization of broad policy gridlock, we here establish that some issue areas are much more gridlocked than are others. Such lack of policy success varies across issues over time. But gridlock does not occur randomly. Instead, the nature of the problems and their likely solutions determines the politics surrounding those issues, and some political situations are more difficult to resolve than are others.

Specifically, expanding upon the work of James Q. Wilson, we argue that major issue areas at particular points in time can be accurately characterized as facing entrepreneurial politics. This occurs when the likely solutions to the major policy challenges in those areas are such that the benefits of policy changes are broadly distributed across Americans while the costs are highly concentrated, thus generating intense political opposition. It is such organized opposition to specific policy changes, rather than (or perhaps in addition to) the general ideological leanings of members, that accounts for much of the legislative gridlock seen today.

Moreover, we offer an approach through which to characterize whether issues face entrepreneurial politics and to identify the entrepreneurs important in overcoming the resultant policy gridlock. We argue that scholars of legislative politics would benefit from paying greater attention to the legislative effectiveness of individual lawmakers. Indeed, with increasing ideological polarization across parties, a focus on the ideological ideal points of individual members (e.g., Clinton, Jackman, and Rivers 2004; Poole and Rosenthal 1997) may be less informative and valuable to understanding the workings of Congress than are measures of who can overcome partisan gridlock and get things done in Congress. We illustrate how ILES can be calculated within major issues areas, and how entrepreneurs and entrepreneurial politics can be identified through a focus on the highest performing members based on such scores.

Upon using such measures, we establish that those policy areas featuring outliers as policy entrepreneurs tend to face entrepreneurial politics. Those policies featuring entrepreneurial politics, as identified here, are far more gridlocked than those facing other types of political arrangements, be they client, interest group, or majoritarian. Moreover, the differences in gridlock rates between entrepreneurial politics and other configurations rose steadily from the 1970s through the start of the 21st century, with bills on low entrepreneurial issues becoming law at more than three times the rate of those confronting problems in highly entrepreneurial issue areas.

Beyond classifying policy areas in terms of the likelihood of facing entrepreneurial politics, and beyond linking such categories to policy gridlock, our aim here was to also illustrate the importance of examining individual policy entrepreneurs in Congress, and of therefore treating members as lawmakers rather than merely as partisans or as voters on the floor of the House. While not every potential policy entrepreneur is as able to navigate the law-making process as well as the examples we offer of Waxman and Crane, without their repeated attempts and initial failures, even greater policy gridlock would have ensued.

If the most thorny issues before Congress today are to be resolved, lawmaking entrepreneurs are needed, perhaps more so in the polarized environment of the early 21st century than in less partisan times. Thankfully, each member elected to Congress represents an opportunity for a new policy entrepreneur to emerge. Yet, scholars of Congress are keenly aware that members are responsive to their constituents, to voters who might not always be willing to let them seek out policies that cut across party lines or across the ideological spectrum. To the extent that voters are focused solely on ideological positions and on party voting, the only possible solutions are those that create winners within one party and losers within the other. Even more likely than producing partisan solutions, such an approach by voters will simply produce more gridlock because of polarized preferences, divided government, and numerous ways to stop policy change.

However, to the extent that voters also consider the degree to which their representatives act as effective lawmakers and policy entrepreneurs, there will be a greater chance of generating new solutions for America's pressing policy problems. Moreover, given members' reelection goals, entrepreneurial lawmakers will undoubtedly tailor those solutions to serve not only the country as a whole but also the voters who took a chance on electing such problem solvers.

Notes

1. Quotations in this example come from Specter (1989).
2. Quote from Gladwell (1990).
3. See Chapter 3 for further details.
4. These lawmakers often share many of the qualities of the archetypal "coalition leaders" who are described by Arnold (1990) as being instrumental in bringing about policy change.
5. For an overview of the causes and consequences of party polarization in Congress, see Theriault (2008) and Schaffner (2011).
6. Likewise, increases in party polarization should also have consequences for the resources that party leaders might have to offer to members of their own parties to induce them to vote for measures that they might otherwise find undesirable (i.e., Herron and Wiseman 2008; Jenkins and Monroe 2012).
7. Although with a different focus and terminology, Lowi (1964) likewise works to classify varying policy types. Grossmann (2013) offers a critique of the use of broad policy typologies.
8. The Wilson matrix has proven valuable to a broad array of students, scholars, and practitioners interested in understanding the politics of the public policy process. For example, it plays a significant role in business and public policy courses taught to future business leaders (e.g., Baron 2013).
9. Mintrom and Norman (2009) offer a recent review of the relevant scholarship that engages the role of entrepreneurs in facilitating policy change.
10. Wawro (2001) creates a different set of measures of congressional entrepreneurship, based largely on bill sponsorship activities.
11. For more on the methodology, see Volden and Wiseman (2011).
12. These policy areas are listed in Table 2.1. Bill classifications are made available through the Congressional Bills Project of Adler and Wilkerson (2013). However, they are limited to be through the 107th Congress (2001–02) at the time of this writing.
13. Binder (2011) offers a comprehensive overview of the literature on gridlock in Congress.

14. One may be concerned about the degree to which Success Rates and Entrepreneurial Politics Scores are endogenous to one another and are interrelated. To be sure, neither can be calculated before the completion of the Congress, and both reflect complexities in how the law-making process has played out. Consistent with Wilson, we are not claiming that there is a causal relationship necessarily. Instead, we argue that the nature of policy problems and the politics surrounding them are closely related, and that neither can be well understood without considering the other. Our analyses show that this sort of relationship is indeed a strong one that takes place at an aggregate level in ways consistent with our main hypothesis.

15. Figure 2.4 replicates figure 5.5 from Volden and Wiseman (2014, p. 152).

16. For the earliest years on the figure, the differences are not statistically significant. They gain such significance ($p < 0.05$) in the 96th Congress (1979–80) and maintain such significance thereafter.

17. Indeed, it is even difficult to conceive of the research design needed to answer such a question in a quantitative manner. In one attempt, we (Volden and Wiseman 2014, p. 187) illustrate how highly effective legislative entrepreneurs have built broad bipartisan coalitions across a wide array of issues, even in recent polarized Congresses.

18. Many details regarding the legislative negotiations surrounding the Nutrition Labeling and Education Act of 1990 described in this section are drawn from Waxman and Green (2009, pp. 108–17).

19. A consideration of Crane's Trade ILES scores reveals that he had the highest score in the 104th, 105th, and 107th Congresses, and the second-highest score in the 106th Congress.

20. H.R. 4198, African Growth and Opportunity: The End of Dependency Act of 1996, was introduced by Crane into the 104th Congress on September 26, 1996.

21. Under the terms of the compromise, quota levels would be tied to whether African manufacturers used U.S. yarn. African apparel that was made from local (i.e., African) materials would still be subject to quotas, but the quota would rise each year. According to the Clinton Administration, the policy would boost African shipments of apparel from $250 million to $4.2 billion over eight years (Neikirk 2000).

22. Mann and Ornstein (2006; 2012) offer compelling accounts of Congress as a "broken branch," and of how "it's even worse than it looks."

References

Adler, E. Scott, and John D. Wilkerson. 2013. *Congress and the Politics of Problem Solving*. New York: Cambridge University Press.

Aldrich, John H., and David Rohde. 2000. "The Consequences of Party Organization in the House: The Role of the Majority and Minority Parties in Conditional Party Government." In Jon R. Bond and Richard Fleisher, eds., *Polarized Politics: Congress and the President in a Partisan Era*. Washington, DC: CQ Press.

Arnold, R. Douglas. 1990. *The Logic of Congressional Action*. New Haven, CT: Yale University Press.

Baron, David P. 2013. *Business and Its Environment*, 7th ed. New York: Pearson.

Bartels, Larry M. 2008. *Unequal Democracy: The Political Economy of the New Guilded Age*. Princeton, NJ: Princeton University Press.

Baumgartner, Frank R., and Bryan D. Jones (eds.). 2002. *Policy Dynamics.* Chicago, IL: University of Chicago Press.

Baumgartner, Frank R., and Bryan D. Jones. 2009. *Agendas and Instability in American Politics,* 2nd ed. Chicago, IL: University of Chicago Press.

Binder, Sarah A. 2003. *Stalemate: Causes and Consequences of Legislative Gridlock.* Washington, DC: Brookings Institution Press.

Binder, Sarah. 2011. "Legislative Productivity and Gridlock." In Eric Schickler and Frances E. Lee, eds., *The Oxford Handbook of the American Congress.* New York: Oxford University Press, pp. 641–58.

Brady, David W., and Craig Volden. 2006. *Revolving Gridlock: Politics and Policy from Jimmy Carter to George W. Bush,* 2nd ed. Boulder, CO: Westview Press.

Clinton, Joshua, Simon Jackman, and Douglas Rivers. 2004. "The Statistical Analysis of Roll Call Data." *American Political Science Review* 98 (2): 355–70.

Cox, Gary W., and Mathew D. McCubbins. 2005. *Setting the Agenda: Responsible Party Government in the U.S. House of Representatives.* New York: Cambridge University Press.

Denzau, Arthur T., and Michael C. Munger. 1986. "Legislators and Interest Groups: How Unorganized Interests Get Represented." *American Political Science Review* 80 (1): 89–106.

Gailmard, Sean, and Jeffery A. Jenkins. 2007. "Negative Agenda Control in the Senate and House: Fingerprints of Majority Party Power." *Journal of Politics* 69 (3): 689–700.

Gladwell, Malcolm. 1990. "New Rules to Govern Food Labels, Drug and Medical Devices." *Washington Post,* November 7, 1990, p. A21.

Grossmann, Matt. 2013. "The Variable Politics of the Policy Process: Issue-Area Differences and Comparative Networks." *Journal of Politics* 75 (1): 65–79.

Hansen, John Mark. 1991. *Gaining Access: Congress and the Farm Lobby, 1919–1981.* Chicago, IL: University of Chicago Press.

Herron, Michael C., and Alan E. Wiseman. 2008. "Gerrymanders and Theories of Lawmaking: A Study of Legislative Redistricting in Illinois." *Journal of Politics.* 70 (1): 151–67.

Hetherington, Marc J. 2009. "Putting Polarization in Perspective." *British Journal of Political Science* 39 (2): 413–48.

Jenkins, Jeffery A., and Nathan A. Monroe. 2012. "Buying Negative Agenda Control in the U.S. House." *American Journal of Political Science* 56 (4): 897–912.

Kingdon, John W. 2011. Agendas, Alternatives, and Public Policies, *updated* 2nd ed. Boston: Longman.

Krehbiel, Keith. 1993. "Where's the Party?" *British Journal of Political Science* 23 (2): 235–66.

Krehbiel, Keith. 1998. *Pivotal Politics: A Theory of U.S. Lawmaking.* Chicago, IL: University of Chicago Press.

Krehbiel, Keith, Adam Meirowitz, and Alan E. Wiseman. 2015. "A Theory of Competitive Partisan Lawmaking." *Political Science Research and Methods* 3 (3): 423–48.

Lebo, Matthew J., Adam J. McGlynn, and Gregory Koger. 2007. "Strategic Party Government: Party Influence in Congress, 1789–2000." *American Journal of Political Science* 51 (3): 464–81.

Leech, Beth L. 2011. "Lobbying and Interest Group Advocacy." In Eric Schickler and Frances E. Lee, eds., *The Oxford Handbook of the American Congress*. New York: Oxford University Press, pp. 598–617.

Lowi, Theodore J. 1964. "American Business, Public Policy, Case-Studies, and Political Theory." *World Politics* 16 (4): 677–715.

Mann, Thomas E., and Norman J. Ornstein. 2006. *The Broken Branch: How Congress Is Failing America and How to Get It Back on Track*. New York: Oxford University Press.

Mann, Thomas E., and Norman J. Ornstein. 2012. *It's Even Worse Than It Looks: How the American Constitutional System Collided With the New Politics of Extremism*. New York: Oxford University Press.

Mayhew, David R. 1974. *Congress: The Electoral Connection*. New Haven, CT: Yale University Press.

   1991. *Divided We Govern: Party Control, Lawmaking, and Investigations 1946–1990*. New Haven, CT: Yale University Press.

McCarty, Nolan, Keith T. Poole, and Howard Rosenthal. 2001. "The Hunt for Party Discipline in Congress." *American Political Science Review* 95 (3): 673–87.

   2006. *Polarized America: The Dance of Ideology and Unequal Riches*. Cambridge, MA: MIT Press.

McManus, Doyle. 2014. "Tougher Than a Boiled Owl." *Los Angeles Times*, February 2, 2014, p. A22.

Minozzi, William, and Craig Volden. 2013. "Who Heeds the Call of the Party in Congress?" *Journal of Politics* 75 (3): 787–802.

Mintrom, Michael, and Phillipa Norman. 2009. "Policy Entrepreneurship and Policy Change." *Policy Studies Journal* 37 (4): 649–67.

Muwakkil, Salim. 1999. "Jesse Jr. Challenges the Status Quo." *Chicago Tribune*, May 24, 1999, p. 15.

Neikirk, William. 2000. "House OKs Trade Breaks for Africa, Caribbean Bill Cuts Apparel Tariffs; Senate Approval Likely." *Chicago Tribune*, May 5, 2000, p. A3.

Passell, Peter. 1997. "Economic Scene; New Ideas go Beyond Handouts in the War on African Poverty." *New York Times*, March 13, 1997, p. D2.

Poole, Keith T., and Howard Rosenthal. 1997. *Congress: A Political-Economic History of Roll Call Voting*. Oxford: Oxford University Press.

Rohde, David. 1991. *Parties and Leaders in the Postreform House*. Chicago, IL: University of Chicago Press.

Schaffner, Brian N. 2011. "Party Polarization." In Eric Schickler and Frances E. Lee, eds., *The Oxford Handbook of the American Congress*. New York: Oxford University Press, pp. 527–49.

Selinger, Marc. 1999. "Free-Trade Opponents Attack Clinton Policies." *The Washington Times*, February 3, 1999, p. B6.

Snyder, James. 1991. "On Buying Legislatures." *Economics and Politics* 3(2): 93–109.

Snyder, James M., Jr., and Tim Groseclose. 2000. "Estimating Party Influence in Congressional Roll-Call Voting." *American Journal of Political Science* 44 (2): 193–211.

Specter, Michael. 1989. "Food Labels Often Light on Nutrition Information: FDA Seeks to Improve Voluntary System." *The Washington Post*, July 23, 1989, p. A1.

1990. "Uniform Food Labels Proposed by HHS: Nutrition Information Called Inadequate." *The Washington Post*, March 8, 1990, p. A1.

Theriault, Sean M. 2008. *Party Polarization in Congress*. New York: Cambridge University Press.

Truman, David B. 1951. *The Governmental Process: Political Interests and Public Opinion*. New York: Alfred A. Knopf.

Volden, Craig and Alan E. Wiseman. 2011. "Breaking Gridlock: The Determinants of Health Policy Change in Congress." *Journal of Health Politics, Policy and Law* 36 (2): 227–64.

2014. *Legislative Effectiveness in the United States Congress: The Lawmakers*. New York: Cambridge University Press.

Wawro, Gregory. 2001. *Legislative Entrepreneurship in the U.S. House of Representatives*. Ann Arbor: University of Michigan Press.

Waxman, Henry, and Joshua Green. 2009. *The Waxman Report: How Congress Really Works*. New York: Twelve (Hachette Book Group).

Wilson, James Q. 1980. *The Politics of Regulation*. New York: Basic Books.

Wiseman, Alan E. 2004. "Tests of Vote-Buyer Theories of Coalition Formation in Legislatures." *Political Research Quarterly* 57 (3): 441–50.

Woellert, Lorraine. 1998a. "Black Caucus Divided on Africa Trade." *The Washington Times*, February 26, 1998, p. 4.

1998b. "Fast Track Echoes Threaten Africa Bill." *The Washington Times*, March 11, 1998, p. 1.

Wright, John R. 2003. *Interest Groups and Congress: Lobbying, Contributions and Influence*. New York: Longman.

Zeleny, Jeff. 2000. "Sober Crane Has Life, Clout Back, Friends Say." *Chicago Tribune*, October 27, 2000, p. 2C.1.

3

Partisan Polarization and Congressional Policy Making

Barbara Sinclair

Early twenty-first-century American politics is characterized above all by partisan polarization, so understanding polarization's impact on Congress's capacity to make public policy is imperative. To do so, I argue, we need to recognize that the impact has both a direct and an indirect component. If the political parties become more internally ideologically homogeneous and more distant from each other, the character of the feasible winning coalitions is affected. Polarization as a concept implies a spatial understanding of the distribution of policy preferences and, within that framework, a winning coalition can be formed only if a policy change that is preferred by all its members to the reversion point can be found.

Thus the best-known models attempting to explain policy gridlock and policy change assume a spatial distribution of stable, exogenously determined policy preferences (Krehbiel 1998; Brady and Volden 1998). A policy is said to fall within the "gridlock interval" if there is no policy preferred to it by a coalition able to effect change; that is, there is no policy that can – based on preferences alone – muster a majority in both houses, overcome a Senate filibuster, and not fall to a presidential veto (Brady and Volden 1998, 14–20). Keith Krehbiel, David Brady, and Craig Volden show that such a single-dimensional model predicts that any policy within the "gridlock interval" will not be changed while any outside the interval will quickly be changed.

I contend that, in addition to this direct effect, polarization has had an indirect effect through the changes in internal chamber organization and distribution of power it has spawned. In particular, polarization has made possible stronger party leadership, especially in the House of Representatives (Bach and Smith 1988; Rohde 1991; Sinclair 1983; 1995; 2006). Stronger party leadership and greater internal rewards for acting as team members amplify the behavioral effects of externally based polarization and thereby amplify the impact of partisan polarization on policy. I argue, in essence, that in the

48

preferences versus party debate, Cox and McCubbins (1993) (and Rohde 1991; Sinclair 1995; Smith 2007; and a large number of other scholars) have it right; policy outcomes cannot be explained solely by stable, exogenously determined member preferences as Krehbiel contends. As I demonstrate in the body of the chapter, the indirect effect of polarization is a party effect and is crucial to understanding contemporary politics and policy making.

The character of the effect of partisan polarization on policy consequently depends on whether partisan control of the branches and chambers is unified or divided. I illustrate my argument by examining policy making in the highly polarized early 21st century, particularly in the 111th (2009–10) and 112th (2011–12) Congresses.

The increase in partisan polarization in voting in both chambers has been so well documented that little is needed here (see Poole 2015). Figure 3.1, showing the difference in the parties' median DW-NOMINATE first dimension scores from the 1950s to the present, should suffice as a reminder. Several points do require emphasis. First, polarized parties are not monolithic parties; although the parties have become considerably more ideologically homogeneous internally, each still has internal differences, and both homogeneity and the distance between the parties' centers of gravity vary across issues. Second, voting is public behavior and is a function of a member's personal policy preferences *and* of his or her electoral calculations, as are the member's other policy-related behaviors. Consequently, while we may assume members' own policy preferences change only slowly if at all, alterations in the political environment may alter members' electoral calculations over the short run. Third, as Figure 3.1 makes clear, polarization is not a recent phenomenon; it has developed over several decades and so its impact on internal congressional organization and processes has had time to develop as well.

This paper examines the impact of polarization in the early 21st century with special emphasis on the 111th Congress, the first of the Obama presidency and one in which Democrats controlled both chambers by substantial margins, and the succeeding 112th, in which Republicans controlled the House and Democrats' margin in the Senate was significantly reduced. Putting a lie to the journalistic platitude that polarization inevitably leads to gridlock, the 111th was one of the most legislatively productive congresses of the post-World War II period. It enacted landmark health care reform legislation, the Dodd-Frank financial services regulation reform, the stimulus bill, and much other significant legislation including the Lilly Ledbetter Fair Pay Act, a major change in the student loan program to free up more money for loans, food safety and child nutrition bills, a credit card regulation bill, legislation to allow the FDA to regulate tobacco, an expansion of the hate crimes covered by federal law, and the repeal of "Don't Ask Don't Tell." The 112th, in contrast, struggled to enact even the most essential of "must pass" legislation. In brief, my argument is that high partisan polarization can facilitate the enactment of landmark legislation when control of the branches and chambers is unified but, when control is

Barbara Sinclair

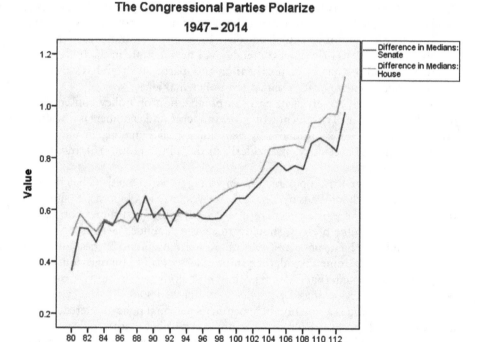

FIGURE 3.1: The congressional parties polarize, 1947–2012.
Source: data from Keith Poole's VoteView site, http://voteview.com.

divided, it may well result in near stalemate and public policy that is "bad" from the perspective of all the major actors.

MAKING NONINCREMENTAL POLICY CHANGE IN A POLARIZED ERA

The Patient Protection and Affordable Care Act (ACA) of 2010 is the archetypal case of landmark, nonincremental legislation that passed during this current period of high partisan polarization and so deserves special attention for what it can tell us about the impact of polarization on such policy making. Although no precise definition of nonincremental policy change is attempted here, agreement that the ACA belongs in the category is near universal. By any reasonable definition, landmark legislation makes big changes in policy and consequently is difficult to pass. That passage is discretionary only adds to the difficulty; the reversion point is the status quo, not some calamity, as is the case for the "must pass" legislation to be considered later.

How did the ACA manage to pass? The Democratic party's considerable ideological homogeneity and strong and skillful congressional party leadership were key, I argue. That is, both the direct and the indirect impacts of polarization were, on balance, favorable in this case.

Considerable agreement on policy objectives among a party's elected officials and candidates across offices clearly makes reaching an intraparty accord on legislation easier. Presidential candidate Barack Obama and congressional Democrats ran on quite similar issues in the 2008 elections, and the election results could be read as an endorsement of – if not a clear mandate for – that agenda. Health care reform was central to the Democratic agenda. Obama, like all the other major Democratic presidential candidates, had strongly advocated health care reform throughout the lengthy presidential campaign; it figured prominently in the campaigns of many Democrats running for Congress and a great many incumbent Democrats had been working on the issue for years. With congressional Democrats having been in the minority for most of the 1995–2006 period and then having their policy objectives frustrated by President George W. Bush, when they did win back majorities in the 2006 elections, pent-up demand for policy change among Democrats was immense.

Significantly, since the failed Clinton health care reform effort, the health care reform policy community – the health care reform academic experts and advocacy groups – had reached substantial agreement on a policy approach that would be politically feasible as well as substantively effective (Skocpol 2013, 24–25). The consensus was that policy approaches like a public single-payer system that entailed remaking the entire system were not politically feasible.

As important as these circumstances were to policy success, strong and skillful congressional party leadership was also essential. Of course legislative bodies of any size require some sort of leadership to coordinate member activities in order pass legislation. Reforming the health care system presented an enormous challenge; the system is highly complex so effective reform could not be simple – or simply explained. The economic stakes for major industries are huge and pressure from interest groups would be intense. The impacts of reform proposals were likely to vary by region, by urban versus rural area, and by income, with the result that divergent interests and views within the Democratic congressional membership were inevitable.

For all their increased ideological homogeneity, Democrats were not monolithic. The 111th Congress House majority of 257 included 49 members from districts that Republican John McCain carried in the 2008 presidential election. These members tended to be moderates and most felt electorally vulnerable. The Blue Dogs, a grouping of moderate Democrats who could be expected to resist the more sweeping proposals, included a number of 2006 and 2008 freshmen. On the other end of the spectrum was a large group of liberal Democrats, many organized in the Progressive Caucus, who would have preferred a more radical approach than any that was likely to be on the table.

The party leadership is responsible for various coordination tasks, especially scheduling legislation for floor consideration. It is also now centrally involved in putting together and holding together winning coalitions on major bills. What that entails varies across issues and also differs in the House and Senate because of the chamber's different rules and memberships.

House rules allow a reasonably cohesive majority to work its will. As the parties became more ideologically homogeneous, this gave majority party members an incentive to give the speaker, their party leader, significant powers and resources and to allow him or her to use them aggressively, because the legislation the speaker would use them to pass was broadly supported in the party. Reciprocally, stronger leadership with more control over resources gives members a greater incentive to act as team members. By the mid-1980s, majority party members – Democrats at that point – had given their party leadership new authority and the leadership did, in fact, employ it assertively to pass legislation the members wanted. With the Republican take-over of the House in the 1994 elections, the trend only accelerated (Sinclair 1999b; 2008). Certainly, by the 2000s, when major legislation was at issue, the House majority was expected to act as the "shock troops, the first on the beach."

How, then, did leaderships' strength and skill make a difference in passing the ACA? Three House committees have jurisdiction over health care legislation. To avoid the turf fights that had hindered President Clinton's health care reform effort, Speaker Nancy Pelosi asked the chairmen of the three House committees to negotiate a single bill that then could be introduced in all their committees. The chairmen complied because they all wanted to pass reform legislation, they wanted the new president of their party to succeed, and, in any case, committee chairmen lack the sort of independence their predecessors of the prereform era had; that is, the chairmen's policy, electoral, and power interests all led them to act as team players as they would throughout the process.

The three chairmen and their staffs would do most of the technical substantive work, but at every stage in the process party leaders were engaged in the coalition-building process: Pelosi and her leadership team undertook an intensive campaign of consulting, educating, and negotiating with their members and Pelosi herself made the tough calls. When the bill produced by the three chairs and fine-tuned by the leadership ran into trouble in the Energy and Commerce Committee, the party leadership stepped in to craft a compromise and Obama helped out as well. Enough Blue Dog Democrats on the committee opposed the bill as written to deny Committee Chairman Henry Waxman a majority to report the bill out. Their concerns included the form of the public option and what they believed were insufficient cost controls. In a pattern that would repeat itself throughout the process, Pelosi and Majority Leader Steny Hoyer held a series of meetings with all the groups that had concerns. Obama called Energy and Commerce Democrats to the White House for a meeting and a "verbal agreement" on the cost issue was reached. Finally on July 29, "after two weeks of very long and intense negotiations" as one Blue Dog said, a deal was reached (O'Connor and Brown 2009).

In fall 2009, when the bills from the three committees had to be reconciled and readied for floor consideration, the House leadership again took the lead; the aim, of course, was to create a bill that could pass the chamber. No Republican had voted for the bills in committee so the leaders knew they could expect no Republican votes at the floor stage; consequently they could lose at most thirty-nine Democrats, which meant getting a considerable number of moderate to conservative Democrats on board. The core House negotiating group included the top party leaders and the three chairmen. But Pelosi made it clear that a number of voices would be involved in healthcare discussions.

Several major disputes needed to be settled. Whether or not the bill would include a public option and, if so, what its form would be received the most media attention. Progressives, including Pelosi herself, strongly favored the so-called "robust" public option, a public insurance plan that would pay providers at the Medicare rate plus 5 percent. Many Blue Dogs preferred no public option at all; some were, however, willing to support the version contained in the Education and Commerce compromise; that called for a public insurance plan with rates negotiated by the secretary of Health and Human Services. The cost of the bill and how to pay for it were contentious issues. Blue Dogs worried about the total cost; junior Democrats from wealthier suburban districts opposed the Ways and Means bill's surtax on the wealthy to pay for a good part of the cost. When Obama in his September 7 speech called for a bill with a maximum cost of $900 billion dollars, the Democratic leaders knew they would have to reduce the price tag on their bill but doing so created other problems, including assuring that subsidies for the middle class remained high enough to make coverage affordable. Anti-abortion Democrats insisted on strong language to prohibit any federal funds from being used for elective abortions; pro-choice Democrats were outraged, claiming that this was an effort to make anti-abortion language more draconian than at present. In August, the "tea party" protesters and right wing bloggers claimed that the Democrats' health care bill would provide benefits to illegal aliens; Republican Joe Wilson's infamous exclamation of "you lie" at Obama during his health care speech was in response to the President's assertion that this was not the case. Latino Democrats were concerned that, in attempting to assure that undocumented workers would not receive benefits, the bill would place onerous conditions on legal immigrants. Each of these controversies threatened, if not adeptly handled, to drain away crucial votes.

Based on innumerable meetings, whip counts, and her own well-honed sense of where the vote stood, Pelosi made the final tough decisions. The votes for the robust public option were not attainable; the weaker form would go into the bill. Bart Stupak, a fervently anti-abortion Democrat, would be allowed to offer a stringent anti-abortion amendment on the floor; the U.S. Conference of Catholic Bishops opposed the bill without the amendment and that would doom it. On both decisions, Pelosi came down against the position of her strongest supporters, the liberals, and against her own policy preferences. But as leader of her party in the House, she did what was necessary to pass a bill.

The cooperative relationship between the House leadership and the president that agreement on the agenda fostered was also crucial. Obama had not submitted a detailed plan to Congress; he laid out general principals and depended on congressional Democrats to fill in the details, calculating that members who had a major role in shaping legislation would have a much greater stake in its enactment. Clinton, it was generally agreed, had made a mistake by drafting his plan in the White House without much member input. It was possible for Obama to rely on congressional Democrats because there was strong agreement on the goal and considerable agreement on the means. This strategy did not represent a hand-off approach. The Office for Health Care Reform (OHCR) that Obama created shortly after he became president "acted as liaison between the executive and the legislative branches. Its purpose was to relay White House positions and priorities to Congress and try to influence the direction the bill was taking but not to write the bill itself" (Beaussier 2012, 775). Initially the OHCR met with the relevant committees weekly but by summer 2009 meetings with committees and the party leadership were taking place daily. Nancy-Ann DeParle, who headed the office, became an almost continuous presence on the Hill.

Congressional Democrats' primary criticism of the president's role centered on what they saw as his feeble efforts to sell the enterprise to the public. Obama was considered an exemplary orator and members of Congress, like the Washington political community generally, have inordinate faith in the efficacy of the "bully pulpit." Obama had promoted health care reform publicly through statements and appearances. Yet the consensus was that he had failed to convey a "clear and coherent" message. After the August recess proved to be a public relations debacle for Democrats, criticism reached a crescendo. Opponents had staged rowdy protests at a number of Democratic House members' town hall meetings and the media gave the most disruptive demonstrations enormous play. Republican leaders endorsed the protests and slammed the entire Democratic reform endeavor as an outrageously expensive big-government power grab. The "tea party" movement had become a force in national politics and especially in the politics of health care reform. By the time the recess ended, the media were declaring health care reform on life support if not completely dead.

At the behest of the congressional Democratic leadership, Obama delivered a speech on health care reform to a joint session of Congress on September 9. His three goals, he emphasized, "were providing security and stability to individuals who already have coverage, extending coverage to those who don't, and slowing the growth of health spending" (CQ Weekly 9/14/2009). The plan would cost $900 billion over ten years and, he promised, would be entirely paid for. The speech was well received by Democrats; "everybody in the Caucus loved the speech," a moderate Democrat reported. "He made people feel a lot better."

Why did the reform effort survive the tea party protests when the Clinton reform effort succumbed to the much less grassroots-based and less virulent "Harry and Louise" public relations attack? Certainly no speech, however good, could by itself accomplish that. To be sure, during the spring and summer Obama and his closest aides had repeatedly talked privately to various groups of members in an effort to keep the process moving forward and he would continue to do so. Before the bill was finally enacted, he also would go to the Hill numerous times to deliver pep talks to the Democratic membership at crucial stages.

Furthermore and critically, early in the process Obama had made a deal with the pharmaceutical industry that resulted in the Pharmaceutical Research and Manufacturers of America (PhRMA), the drug companies' powerful trade association, becoming something of an ally in passing a bill. All of the major industry groups had fought the Clinton bill and that wall of opposition had killed the effort. Obama decided he would attempt to preempt the opposition by drawing the major interest groups into the process; getting and keeping those groups at the table and negotiating deals when possible was a major administration aim from the beginning. Although some congressional Democrats believed the pharmaceutical deal specifically was too generous, the White House's deal-making did prevent monolithic opposition from industry groups.

Presidential persuasion and, more crucially, the White House's success in at least neutralizing some of the key industry groups certainly were important in making it possible for the reform effort to survive the "tea party" onslaught and its poor polling results. But more essential was that many congressional Democrats – probably a large majority – sincerely wanted to pass health care reform and knew that their strongest supporters fervently favored reform and expected them to pass a bill; local unions, consumer groups, and community groups, organized in a coalition Health Care for America Now (HCAN), made sure members were kept aware of their supporters' expectations (Skocpol 2013, 38–44). Furthermore, almost all Democrats believed that their electoral fate was inextricably linked to the Democratic president's success and that the reform effort's demise, especially at this late stage, would assure his failure.

The bill passed the House on the evening of November 7 on a vote of 220–215; 39 Democrats voted against the bill; of those, 31 represented districts McCain had won in 2008; 29 of 53 Blue Dogs voted for the bill (New York Times 11/08/09). One Republican cast a vote for the bill, but only after its passage was assured.

The postreform House party leadership's single most powerful tool for facilitating passage of legislation in its preferred form is its control over the special rules governing when and how legislation is considered on the House floor. The rule for the ACA specified that the "manager's amendment" and a "perfecting" amendment to it "shall be considered as adopted"; that is, adopted without a separate vote by virtue of the rule being adopted. The manager's amendment consisted of changes the leadership had made to pick up votes of various subsets of members and the perfecting amendment consisted of last-minute changes the leaders had negotiated. Only two amendments were made in order: the Stupak abortion amendment and a Republican substitute. As is now routine, the Rules Committee had required the Republicans to submit their substitute to the committee, thus depriving them of any element of surprise. Thus the rule allowed the leadership to incorporate deals into the bill until the last minute, bar votes on potentially coalition-splitting amendments, and keep the number of votes and thus uncertainty as low as possible.

A special rule does need to be approved by a House majority. The current strong presumption that members will support their party on these procedural votes allowed the leadership to win both of the necessary votes easily; the previous question on the rule was moved successfully by a vote of 247–187; then the rule was approved 242–187; on the first vote, 10 Democrats voted with all the Republicans in opposition; on the second, 15 did so.

When the vote on passage reached 218 "yea" votes, a cheer went up from the Democratic side of the chamber. Pelosi, however, had one more chore to perform; she went to a room off the floor to persuade Loretta Sanchez to come in and cast the 219th vote. With more than a bare majority, vulnerable Democrats could not be attacked as having cast the decisive vote. Toward the end of the voting period, Republican Joseph Cao, who had defeated disgraced Democrat William Jefferson in a majority black district, voted for the bill, but only after passage was assured.

To pass health care reform in the Senate, Majority Leader Harry Reid had the advantage of a membership more ideologically homogeneous than that during the Clinton attempt but also confronted a minority that was more cohesive and more willing to use Senate rules to stymie the majority. With much less procedural control than the House majority leadership possesses, Reid faced the barrier of amassing a supermajority of sixty to pass a bill. Under those circumstances, the size of the Democratic Senate majority was crucial; by midsummer, with the seating of Al Franken and the party switch of Arlen Specter, Democrats numbered sixty. Reid's strategy was dictated by the imperative that he either gain some Republican votes or get the vote of every Democrat. Reid – and Obama – deferred to Finance Chairman Max Baucus as he attempted for months to reach a bipartisan compromise on his committee; if he had succeeded, passage in the Senate would have been immeasurably easier though the price in terms of substance might have been high. Baucus failed and it became clear that no Republican votes were likely on passage. Senators have much more capacity for effective independent action than House members do and Senate individualism is still evident; yet a senator who defects on a high-visibility, defining interparty battle will pay a significant price within his or her caucus.

In the fall, Reid coordinated the crafting of a single bill to take to the floor with a core negotiating group consisted of Baucus; Chris Dodd, representing the HELP committee which had also reported a bill; for the White House, Chief of Staff Rahm Emanuel; and Nancy-Ann DeParle. Reid kept the group small with the hope that that would speed action. Nevertheless, the need for sixty votes required Reid to consult widely with his members. He, Baucus, and Dodd held daily meetings with various Democratic senators (Roll Call 10/22/09). Reid repeatedly had to make painful deals necessary to keep every Democrat on board. The public option was dropped and a possible substitute allowing people between fifty-five and sixty-four to buy into Medicare was also abandoned. Special Medicaid and Medicare provisions for Louisiana and Nebraska, respectively, helped obtain the votes of Mary Landrieu and Ben Nelson. Nelson also extracted a last-minute deal on abortion language.

The Senate majority leader's procedural tools are limited but he does command the initiative in floor scheduling. Reid decided when the bill would be brought to the floor and kept it on the floor until, after twenty-five days and five successful cloture votes, it passed on Christmas Eve morning by a vote of sixty to thirty-nine. Republicans, believing that the longer they could delay passage the more likely could kill the bill, used every parliamentary right available to drag out the process. Reid countered by keeping the Senate in on Saturdays and Sundays and often late into the night. Of course, he was able to maintain such a grueling schedule only because he had the support of his members. Like their House party colleagues, a large majority of Senate Democrats sincerely wanted to pass health care reform and almost all believed that their electoral fate was inextricably linked to the Democratic president's success and the failure of health care reform would doom the Obama presidency.

The greater the investment of time and resources in passing health care reform, members understood, the more the president and the Democratic Congress would be judged by whether they succeeded. Without that perception, Republican Scott Brown's winning Ted Kennedy's Senate seat on an anti-health care reform platform in mid-January 2010 would certainly have killed health care reform. Most of the features of an agreement between the House and Senate were in place when that special election outcome sent shockwaves through Washington and came close to provoking panic among Democrats. Democrats now lacked the crucial sixty votes in the Senate and seemingly even the people in deep blue Massachusetts opposed the reform effort. Many commentators and Washington insiders declared health care dead.

Prodded by Speaker Nancy Pelosi, who was determined to complete the task, President Obama decided to double down on passing comprehensive health care reform. The health care summit to which he invited congressional Republicans as well as Democrats put the focus back on the issue and away from the congressional maneuvering and deal-making that had soured the public on the effort and it provided some breathing room for the congressional leaders to work with their members.

Without sixty votes in the Senate, Democrats could not hope to pass a House–Senate compromise through any of the customary procedures. The Obama Administration and the House Democratic leadership had insisted that the 2009 budget resolution include the option of using the reconciliation procedure for health care reform and that now became the only feasible route to passage. The House would pass both the Senate bill and a reconciliation bill that "fixed" it with the essential compromises. The Senate would then pass the reconciliation bill, which is protected from a filibuster by the Budget Act and so only requires a simple majority. The reconciliation procedure was not used to pass the health care bill initially because Senate rules, specifically the Byrd rule, restrict what can be included in such a bill (Gold 2004, 149–152); the "fixes" had to be carefully drawn so as to pass the Byrd rule test.

Republicans attempted to make it as hard as possible for Democrats to finish enacting the bill. They argued that using the reconciliation procedure was outrageously illegitimate. Obama traveled around the country and met with innumerable groups of Democrats at the White House promoting the effort; House and Senate Democratic leaders and senior White House staff worked out the actual language of the reconciliation bill in a long series of meetings. The House leadership, talking to members individually, in small groups, and in the frequent Caucus meetings, argued on substance and on politics, emphasizing that failing to pass health care reform would inflict "severe damage" on the Democratic party; they worked out individual, often constituency-related problems that certain members had with the legislation to the extent they could and coordinated their efforts with allied interest groups. The White House political operation also went into high gear, gathering information and tracking member voting intentions, working with allied groups, and getting influential constituents to lobby their members. Obama involved himself deeply in the effort, spending countless hours on the telephone and at face-to-face encounters at the White House attempting to persuade Democrats to vote for the bill. On Saturday, March 20, with a House vote scheduled for the next day, President Obama came to the Hill to speak to the Democratic Caucus. "Every once in a while a moment comes where you have a chance to vindicate all those best hopes that you had about yourself, about this country," he said. "This is one of those moments" (New York Times 3/21/10). On Sunday evening the House passed the Senate bill on a vote of 219–212; the reconciliation bill passed a little later on an almost identical vote of 220–211. In the Senate, Republicans stretched out the debate and offered a stream of amendments that, many Democrats charged, were crassly political: an amendment by Tom Coburn would have prohibited prescription coverage of erectile dysfunction drugs for child molesters and rapists. The reconciliation bill finally passed unamended on March 25 by a vote of 56–43; 56 of 59 Democrats voted for the bill, no Republicans did.

The health care reform effort survived the near-death experience of Scott Brown's Senate victory, in part because of the smart decisions and enormous efforts of Democratic leaders. Nancy Pelosi's iron-willed determination to complete the task was crucial, as was the insistence of the Obama

Administration and the House Democratic leadership that the 2009 budget resolution include the option of using the reconciliation procedure for health care. But Democratic leaders cannot lead if they lack reasonably willing followers.

The constituency-based increase in ideological homogeneity was key to producing those "reasonably willing followers." The deals that leaders made, the side payments they agreed to, would simply not have been sufficient had those members not been desirous of "getting to yes." The change in the parties within Congress that greater ideological homogeneity fostered contributed to members' desire to "get to yes" as well. Not only do leaders have more carrots and sticks, but being in the good graces of one's party colleagues is important to advancement within the chamber (and to a pleasant Hill life as well), and that requires sticking with the team whenever possible.

The same logic applies, however, to the members of the minority party. Even in the 111th Congress, with its healthy majority party margins, the ideological homogeneity of the Republican party created significant problems for majority Democrats, especially in the Senate. Since the mid-1990s, the Senate minority party had aggressively used its prerogative of extended debate to block or extract concessions from the majority; from the mid-1990s through the mid-2000s on average 51 percent of major measures subject to a filibuster, in fact, confronted some sort of filibuster-related problem; in the newly Democrat-controlled 110th the figure was 76 percent (Sinclair 2012). Both the direct and indirect effects of polarization make it much easier for the Senate minority leader to keep his members unified in opposition to majority party attempts to impose cloture; seldom was it possible during these years for the majority party to entice enough minority party senators to vote for cloture to get to sixty without striking a deal with and so making concessions to the minority leader.

Passing the ACA required Democrats to win five cloture votes; the stimulus bill, Dodd-Frank, and most of the other major legislative achievements had to overcome minority party blocking tactics. In the 111th Democrats confronted filibuster-related problems on 73 percent of major measures and on a number of nominations as well. In a number of cases, getting the sixty votes to impose cloture required significant concessions – to more conservative Democrats on the ACA, as discussed earlier, and also to Republicans on the stimulus and Dodd-Frank. Some important legislation failed enactment despite commanding a majority – most notably the Dream Act. Yet, because the Democrats had such a large majority – from fifty-eight to sixty at various points during the congress – they were able to pick off enough Republicans – three each on the stimulus bill and on Dodd-Frank – to get to sixty. Getting those votes required concessions, but the minority party was not able to kill or gut via concessions these signature bills. Clearly, however, an unusually large Senate majority was essential.

MUST-PASS LEGISLATION UNDER CONDITIONS
OF DIVIDED CONTROL

It is the character of the reversion point that makes legislation "must pass"; when a consensus or near consensus exists that doing nothing is too costly to bear, the legislation is perceived as "must pass." Some catastrophic change in the environment – the near collapse of the financial system in the wake of the failure of Lehman Brothers, for example – may create that perception. More frequently it is the result of legislation that expires at a certain date, leaving not the status quo ante but some much less preferred and possibly catastrophic outcome – default on the national debt, no funding for most government functions, most prominently.

Such drastic reversion points make reaching intraparty agreement easier for the majority party even when ideological homogeneity is not at its height; many possible compromises will be preferred by most party members to doing nothing. And the greater the ideological homogeneity, the easier reaching intraparty agreement should be. However, if some degree of interparty agreement must be achieved to enact legislation, high partisan polarization presents real challenges. High partisan polarization makes picking off even just a few opposition party members – to break a filibuster, for example – much more costly as even those minority party members closest to the majority party in policy preferences are likely to be relatively distant. Furthermore, the high cost – in terms of life and advancement within the party – of defecting when the parties are polarized is likely to make even minority party members closest to the majority party in policy preferences think long and hard before doing so. A real threat to a member's electoral prospects is much more likely than any feasible side payment to induce defection and that is seldom under majority party control.

The stronger party leadership that partisan polarization fosters means that deals most often have to be made at the peak level – leader to leader. But the leaders themselves are constrained by their own members in their deal-making. Bypassing the party leadership when any of the party's votes are needed will often be impossible; even minority leaders may in effect have veto power and the majority leadership, especially in the House, almost always does. Yet the leaders cannot deliver their members' votes for just any deal; although leaders do have more carrots and sticks than they used to, they cannot command the members who, after all, elect them.

The great ideological distance between the parties makes it likely that an agreement will require one or both parties to make major concessions, giving both a strong incentive to play chicken, to hold out as long as possible hoping the opposition will cave. Perhaps circumstances will change in one's favor; maybe a party PR campaign can actually produce such a shift. Perhaps the opposition will come to believe that they will bear the blame for not reaching agreement and thus for potential catastrophe. Such circumstances provide considerable room for maneuver, strategy, and misjudgment. The parties may misperceive the strength of each other's hands. Differences of opinion and misperceptions about how costly not reaching an agreement would be in terms of policy consequences, future electoral prospects, and party reputational effects may arise at the leadership and at the membership level, within a party as well as between them.

PASSING CRISIS-INDUCED MUST-PASS LEGISLATION

How all these considerations play out in practice is best seen by examining a number of examples. Passage of the legislation establishing the Troubled Asset Relief Program (TARP) (the Emergency Economic Stabilization Act of 2008) illustrates how a crisis can lead to a "must pass" situation and yet how difficult passage can nevertheless be. With a financial crisis looming menacingly after the failure of Lehman Brothers and the near failure of the American International Group (AIG), Secretary of the Treasury Henry Paulson on September 19, 2008, called on Congress to pass rescue legislation immediately. The legislation Paulson proposed was so cursory – three pages long – and gave him so much untrammeled authority that congressional leaders and members on both sides of the aisle balked. Still the pressure to act quickly was intense and the regular legislative process would take far too long. So a small bicameral and bipartisan group of congressional party and committee leaders and White House negotiators hammered out a bill in closed-door meetings over the course of a week.

On September 18, when Paulson and Chairman of the Federal Reserve Ben Bernanke had met with a bipartisan and bicameral group of party and committee leaders to brief them on the severity of the crisis – the real possibility of another Great Depression if nothing was done – the leaders had responded positively. The "rally round the flag" effect that crises often produce seemed to promise bipartisanship. "This is a national crisis," said House Republican Leader John Boehner. "We need to rise above politics and show the American people we can work together" (Kaiser 2013, 22).

Boehner soon discovered that many of his members disagreed. Spearheaded by the Republican Study Group, made up of the most hard-line conservatives, many House Republicans vociferously objected to "bailing out" the big banks. President George W. Bush lobbied members to vote for the bill but found that his views carried little weight; he was deeply unpopular and a lame duck besides. On September 29, the bill failed on the House floor by a vote of 205–228, with Republicans voting against it 133 to 65. With Republicans unwilling to support what was a highly unpopular bill, Pelosi was unwilling and perhaps unable to deliver the votes to pass the legislation; 140 Democrats supported the bill but 95 voted against it. As has often been the case when a high visibility, unpopular, must-pass bill is at issue, the agreement was that the parties had to share the blame by a majority of each of its members voting for the bill. Boehner had not delivered; as leader of her party, Pelosi could not ask her members to bear the cost alone, especially for a crisis brought on by Republican policies.

The vote triggered a massive sell-off on Wall Street with the Dow losing 777 points. Reid and McConnell, the Senate leaders, then took over. They agreed on a package that added to the bailout language a number of "sweeteners" – provisions extending various popular tax breaks, expanding incentives for renewable energy projects, limiting the reach of the alternative minimum tax for a year, requiring insurance companies to offer mental health coverage on par with what they offered for other health problems and increasing to $250,000 from $100,000 the bank account amount insured by the FDIC (CQ Weekly Oct 6. 2008, 2692–9). Reid had insisted that Republican presidential candidate Senator John McCain vote for the bill and Democratic candidate Senator Barack Obama was on board. Thus provided with cover and alarmed by the stock market free fall, the Senate passed the bill 74–25 on October 1. On October 3, the House approved the bill by a vote of 263–171. Under extreme pressure from local notables and party-allied interest groups and from the administration as well, Republicans split 91–108 and Democrats 172–63. For the members who switched their votes, the sweeteners, for Republicans especially the tax cuts, made switching their votes a bit easier, but fear of the economic consequences of the legislation's failure appears to have been decisive.

Certainly electoral considerations factored into the "no" votes that initially sank the bill on the House floor. Public opinion was running overwhelmingly against bailing out greedy banks, seen as responsible for the financial mess, and phone calls and e-mail messages to Capitol Hill were running strongly against the bill – particularly before the stock market dive. Additionally, even though the president was a member of their party, a majority of Republicans felt no responsibility for governing now that they were in the minority. But, probably more importantly, many Republicans did not believe catastrophe loomed; they largely dismissed the conclusions of the Republican Secretary of the Treasury, a Republican-appointed chairman of the Federal Reserve who was also a distinguished academic economist, and numerous other highly credentialed experts. That such expertise would carry so little weight was a sign of how far the Republican party had moved outside what had been the broad mainstream of American politics. That would become more evident and the impact greater when Republicans again controlled the House of Representatives.

PASSING MUST-PASS LEGISLATION WITH A REPUBLICAN HOUSE

Republicans won big in the 2010 off-year elections, reducing the Democratic majority in the Senate to 53 and handily taking control of the House of

Representatives. Given divided control and the high partisan polarization so evident in the previous two years, little major new legislation could be expected to pass. David Mayhew (1991) contends that divided control has no significant impact on the production of major legislation (see Binder 2003; Edwards et al. 1997); however, the empirical research on which his conclusion rests focuses on periods of lower polarization. The Krehbiel–Brady–Volden-type models, in contrast, predict that as polarization increases so will the gridlock interval and thus the likelihood of major policy change will decrease.

In fact, lawmaking in the 112th proved to be a sequence of Perils-of-Pauline episodes centering on must-pass measures. At its core, the problem was the one that had become evident in fall of 2008 with TARP. One party had moved far out of what had been the mainstream of American politics. Not only had the Republican party's median policy preferences migrated far to the right, but many of its members were suspicious of mainstream expertise and took their cues from different sources; consequently many really did not believe that the reversion point if must-pass measures were allowed to lapse was as catastrophic as the former consensus posited.

Playing chicken with an opponent who believes going over the cliff is "no big deal" puts one at a major disadvantage, as President Obama and congressional Democrats soon discovered. For the Republican leadership, such a membership proved to be far from an unalloyed advantage. On the one hand, Speaker Boehner's bargaining hand was strengthened by the hard core; when he pushed for more concessions on the basis that they were necessary to sell a deal to his right flank, his opponents had to take him seriously. On the other, Boehner and McConnell did not believe that going over the various cliffs that the 112th faced was "no big deal." Leaders are changed with guarding their party's reputation and they feared that letting any of the various catastrophes happen would severely damage the Republican party's image. They somehow needed to satisfy their members' policy goals to the extent necessary to prevent outright rebellion yet still in the end enact must-pass legislation.

The 112th Congress's first order of must-do business was passing appropriations to fund the government's operations. The Democratically controlled 111th Congress had failed to pass the regular appropriations bills by October 1, the beginning of the fiscal year, and had passed short-term stop-gap legislation instead. During the lame duck session, Senate Republicans blocked legislation appropriating funds through the remainder of the 2011 fiscal year; GOP candidates had promised to cut hundreds of billions of dollars from federal spending and intended to start delivering early in 2011. In December, the outgoing 111th managed only to pass a continuing resolution maintaining funding at current levels until March 4, 2011.

Speaker Boehner and Republican appropriators unveiled their initial proposal in early February. The proposal itself and the reaction presaged the difficulty of the road ahead. The Obama administration and congressional Democrats condemned the severity of the cuts while hard-line conservatives organized in the Republican Study Committee (RSC) objected that they were not nearly enough. The party had promised to cut at least $100 billion in nonsecurity discretionary spending in the 2011 fiscal year and anything less was a betrayal, they argued. Their leaders' contention that, since only seven months of the fiscal year remained, the amount should be prorated did not persuade them. In the face of this resistance, Boehner sent his appropriators back to find more cuts. The House passed the still more draconian HR1 on February 19 with only Republican votes.

Clearly neither Senate Democrats nor the While House would accept the House bill, but the hard-line House Republicans were unwilling to comprom- ise. Boehner very much wanted to avoid a government shutdown, which going beyond the March 4 deadline without a bill would entail. The government shutdown in late 1995 and early 1996 had grievously wounded then-Speaker Newt Gingrich and congressional Republicans (Sinclair 1999a). Many of Boehner's members, however, did not believe shutting down the government would have deleterious policy or electoral effects.

Senate Majority Leader Reid attempted to draw Boehner into negotiations and the White House made clear it was open to some cuts. Two short-term CRs were negotiated and passed, each on the eve of the drop-dead date. The true ideological chasm between the parties and the bargaining advantage of playing chicken made reaching even these interim agreements difficult. It was clear to all participants that Boehner could not get the votes to pass any CR without spending cuts, and both short-term CRs included cuts – the first $4 billion and the second another $6 billion. Still, these were relatively easy cuts, ones that had been included in the president's budget, for example. In early March, after the first short-term CR passed, negotiations on the long-term CR began in earnest. Vice President Joseph R. Biden Jr. headed the administration's team in talks with Speaker Boehner, Senate Majority Leader Harry Reid, Senate Minority Leader Mitch McConnell, and House Minority Leader Nancy Pelosi.

Talks behind closed doors and dueling PR efforts finally culminated in an agreement two hours before the shutdown deadline at midnight April 8. During the final days, Obama had called senior leaders to the White House for meetings several times a day. The deal entailed $39 billion in cuts; most of the policy riders House Republicans had added that Obama and Democrats abhorred were dropped. Although the omnibus appropriations bill passed handily in both chambers, fifty-nine House Republicans refused to vote for it, convinced their leaders had compromised too much. And Boehner had gotten votes by promising that the party would hang tougher on the upcoming debt ceiling fight. He would continue to be forced to mortgage the future in each battle to come.

To forestall an even more dangerous fight over raising the debt ceiling, President Obama redoubled his efforts to strike a grand bargain to restrain the deficit. Despite the continuing weakness of the economy, an official Washington consensus that the deficit was the greatest problem in the United

States had emerged. Speaker Boehner was the indispensable partner in any deal since he controlled access to the House floor where legislation embodying such a deal would need to pass. Even if Obama could have found enough House Republicans willing to vote with minority House Democrats to make a majority, an extremely unlikely prospect, getting legislation to the floor without Boehner's assent would be nearly impossible. Obama worried that even a threat of default would hurt the economy; a bipartisan deal, on the other hand, would likely give the economy and his job approval ratings a boost. But Boehner too had much to gain from striking a deal; he knew that Republicans could not refuse to raise the debt ceiling and consequently be seen as responsible for the U.S. government defaulting on its debts and the financial turmoil that would follow.

Negotiations between Obama and Boehner in the summer of 2011 – and again in late 2012 – never reached fruition. Especially in 2011, Obama had considerable leeway on the character of the deal he could agree to. Even though many Democrats would have detested cuts to entitlement programs by increasing the age for Medicare eligibility and by switching to a less generous cost-of-living adjustment (COLA) formula for social security, a majority of Democrats would have voted for such a deal had he struck one. Extreme polarization gives members of a party a huge investment in the reelection of a president of their own party; both their own electoral fortunes and their policy goals are at stake. Boehner, however, had much less leeway. His members believed the 2010 elections had given them a mandate for policies that Obama – and congressional Democrats – could never accept. For Obama and congressional Democrats, significant new revenue was a bottom-line condition; for most House Republicans – and many Senate Republicans as well – it was deal breaker. During the fight over the omnibus appropriations bill, the House GOP leaders had urged their members to vote for a bill they disliked by promising them a big win on the debt ceiling. Furthermore, a considerable number of House Republicans did not believe the lack of a debt limit increase was "a big deal"; again, they simply did not believe mainstream experts. Many more Republicans in both chambers believed they had by far the stronger hand and so were quite willing to play chicken, holding the debt ceiling increase hostage to extract much greater concessions from Obama.

Once again, on the eve of disaster, a Perils-of-Pauline process yielded an agreement. The Budget Control Act (BCA) passed on August 1, just before the August 2 deadline. It allowed the president to raise the debt limit by up to $2.5 trillion in two steps and subject to disapproval by Congress by a two-thirds vote. The immediate increase in the debt ceiling was to be accompanied by $1 trillion in cuts in defense and domestic discretionary spending over ten years. A Joint Select Committee on Deficit Reduction was to be appointed by the four party leaderships and charged with agreeing on another $1.5 trillion in cuts, with Congress required to vote for the committee's recommendations as a package. If the committee did not agree or Congress did not approve its package, automatic cuts (called sequestration) would take effect. Half the cuts would come from defense and half from domestic spending but Medicaid, Social Security, veterans' programs, and many programs targeted to low-income Americans would be largely exempt. Medicare was also mostly protected (CQ Weekly, 8/8/2011, 1761–62).

The final deal was struck only after stalemate appeared imminent. Boehner had managed with great effort to craft a plan his members would pass; it was, however, so draconian that Obama issued a veto threat and the Senate quickly killed it. Reid could kill anything that the House sent over but could not amass sixty votes to bring his own plan to an up-or-down vote. McConnell, Reid, and the White House in the end came up with the convoluted plan that passed. Many hard-line Republicans were unhappy with the agreement, as were many progressive Democrats. Nevertheless the House passed the bill 269–161; Republicans were split 174 to 66, Democrats 95 to 95. The next day, the Senate passed it 74–26, with 6 Democrats and 19 Republicans voting against it.

Other must-pass measures in the 112th Congress also tended to be excruciatingly difficult to enact. The FAA reauthorization and the transportation bill, not ordinarily highly ideological bills, consumed enormous amounts of time and ran up against multiple deadlines. The FAA authorization actually lapsed for two weeks, resulting in furloughs, suspended airport construction projects, and a cost of at least $25 million a day to the government in fees not collected. House Republicans insisted on a provision making it more difficult for airline and railroad employees to unionize and included in a short-term reauthorization a cut to subsidies for small and rural airports, a program much beloved by key senators. When Senate Commerce Committee Chairman Jay Rockefeller and ranking Republican Kay Bailey Hutchinson attempted to pass a compromise, Orrin Hatch objected and insisted on adding the House labor language; Rockefeller then objected to Hatch's unanimous consent request to pass the bill with the labor language. The next day, Environment and Public Works Chair Barbara Boxer asked unanimous consent to pass a clean short-term bill; Tom Coburn objected and when he then asked unanimous consent to pass the House bill, Boxer objected (CQ Weekly 8/ 8, 2011, 1759). Thus the standoff.

House Republican leaders were never able to pass a long-term transportation bill. The conservative bill reported by the Transportation and Ways and Means Committees by partisan votes was still too "bloated" for the hard-line conservatives and its elimination of trust fund funding for mass transit projects threatened the support of many suburban Republicans. All Boehner's attempts to modify the bill enough to cobble together a majority failed; attempting to mollify hardliners for whom "stimulus" was a dirty word, he, at one point, even asserted that the bill would not create jobs: "we are not making the claim that spending taxpayer money on transportation projects creates jobs," he said (CQ Weekly 2/6/2012, 244).

The Senate passed a longer-term transportation bill on March 14, 2012; although it had garnered considerable bipartisan support in committee, floor passage was nevertheless a long and difficult process. Hard-line conservative GOP senators opposed the level of spending, many more Republicans objected to the Finance Committee's funding provisions, and most saw the must-pass bill as a great opportunity to force votes on their agenda items. After three cloture votes, two of which failed, a vote on contraceptive coverage in the ACA, two on the Keystone XL pipeline, and numerous other amendments, germane and nongermane, the bill passed on a 74–22 vote. The House leadership did manage to pass a three-month extension of the transportation authorization and that allowed House and Senate to go to conference on the bill. On Friday June 29, two days before the gas tax was set to expire, both chambers passed the conference report that largely followed the Senate bill. Like the Senate bill but unlike the more typical five-year reauthorizations in recent decades, the bill was for only twenty-seven months.

The final, enormous showdown over must-pass legislation of the 112th Congress was over the "fiscal cliff." The Bush tax cuts were set to expire at the end of 2012 and the big sequestration spending cuts were scheduled to go into effect on January 1, 2013. Economists argued that the double hit would wreck the economy, precipitating another recession. The Obama administration and most congressional Democrats were deeply concerned with the impact on the economy and also with the damage the across-the-board spending cuts would do to many government programs. Republicans strongly opposed letting any of the tax cuts lapse. Democrats insisted that a fair debt reduction deal should include higher taxes on wealthier Americans.

After the 2012 elections, Obama and Boehner attempted to reach a deal but failed. The elections had not much changed the partisan balance in either chamber nor had Obama's reelection persuaded Republican hard liners to soften their stance. Thus, as in 2011, there was no deal that both sides could agree to. Boehner's troops would not vote for any tax increases. And whether Obama could induce most Democrats to support significant cuts in entitlements was open to question; they no longer needed to worry about his reelection. Boehner pulled out of the talks and then failed to induce his members to vote for a bill raising taxes on those with incomes over $1 million that he hoped to use as basis for negotiations.

At that point, Boehner withdrew and left it to Senate Minority Leader Mitch McConnell to work out an agreement with the White House. Both Boehner and McConnell realized that they could not allow taxes to go up on all Americans by objecting to any increase on the wealthy; the Republican party's reputation required preventing that. Boehner's members made it impossible for him to make the concessions necessary; McConnell's members gave him more leeway. The Senate Republican membership included fewer extreme hard liners and more pragmatists and their being in the minority removed some of the pressure of satisfying the base.

An agreement was reached on New Year's Eve and approved by both chambers the next day. It made permanent the Bush tax cuts for everyone with an income below $400,000, made some other changes in tax law that increase taxes on the well-off, and extended benefits for the long-term unemployed. It also postponed the sequester until March 1. The Senate passed the bill by 89 to 8. The House vote was a comfortable 256–171, but, while Democrats supported the compromise by 172 to 16, Republicans opposed it 151 to 85. Majority Leader Eric Cantor and Majority Whip Kevin McCarthy voted "no."

The 113th Congress began without the now-typical fireworks on must-pass financial legislation but, by fall of 2013, it climaxed with a sixteen-day government shutdown. In early 2013, Speaker Boehner persuaded his members to suspend the debt ceiling for three months and pass a continuing resolution to fund the government without holding it hostage to cuts beyond those due to sequestration, but only by promising them a budget that balanced in ten years without any new tax revenue. Still other problems emerged. In June, hard liners defeated the farm bill on the House floor. Just before the August recess, House leaders were forced to pull the transportation appropriations bill from the floor for lack of votes. Appropriations Committee Republicans had written a bill that abided by the draconian strictures of the budget resolution. The result was that suburban Republicans opposed the bill because of the impact of the harsh cuts on their districts, yet those members for whom no cuts were ever severe enough refused to relent and vote for the bill.

Increasingly frustrated with their inability to force policy change on a president with very different policy preferences than theirs, Republican hard liners attempted to use the continuing resolution necessary to fund the government after October 1 to defund the ACA. The leadership's frantic attempts to head off a shutdown failed when the Senate refused to go along and Obama refused to cave; a government shutdown began. As the shutdown stretched on, Republicans' favorability ratings with the public sank to all-time lows and eventually they were forced to accept a deal that yielded them nothing.

In December, a bipartisan budget deal that relaxed sequestration for two years passed. Although Republican majorities in both chambers voted in opposition, the agreement made possible a relatively peaceful, if exceptionally unproductive, 2014. Even the most hard-line Republicans had learned that with the presidency and the Senate in the control of a Democratic party with policy preferences far distant from theirs, they could not hope to force major policy change. Under pressure from their leadership and from more pragmatic members, they were willing to wait until after the next elections to try again.

ENTREPRENEURS, PARTIES, AND POLICY CHANGE

In Chapter 2, Volden and Wiseman present "something of an alternative view," one that focuses on the role of individual policy entrepreneurs in policy making. How does my approach and theirs differ and how are they congruent? Attempting to answer that question should shed some light on the choices political scientists make when studying policy change and the consequences of those choices.

Volden and Wiseman argue that "given the complex legislative organization of Congress, the strategic choices of policy entrepreneurs are crucial in bringing about significant change." Their emphasis on strategic choices within the legislature is congruent with my argument; my mini-case study of the ACA clearly shows how important such choices were to success. The conditions may be favorable to major policy change, but the decisions legislators (and the president) make affect whether the potential is realized. In contrast, modelers such as Krehbiel tend to deemphasize strategic choice within the legislature and emphasize one specific condition – exogenously determined member preferences.

My research shows, I believe, that, with polarization, the "policy entrepreneurs" most often are or work closely with the party leadership on major legislation. That was clearly true in the case of the ACA, in which both the party leadership, especially Speaker Nancy Pelosi, and Henry Waxman played important roles. Of course, at no time have individual policy entrepreneurs actually brought about policy change by themselves; legislating is a collective enterprise and many actors have to at minimum acquiesce for a bill to become a law. With so much of the most visible and most important legislation now splitting the parties and with the greater powers and resources that have accrued to party leadership, those party leaders are now very frequently central actors. Even committee leaders – and all of the entrepreneurs Volden and Wiseman mention were committee or subcommittee chairs – now have limited ability to act on their own on major legislation.

My analysis conceptualizes preferences in spatial terms; Volden and Wiseman rely on an interest-based schema. These differences lead to somewhat different predictions about when policy change can occur. Whether the benefits and costs and so the support and opposition are concentrated or widely distributed are the key variables in Volden and Wiseman's schema of four types of politics. When benefits and thus support are highly concentrated and costs and so potential opposition are highly dispersed the result can be described as distributive politics and policy change is easy. The opposite configuration – dispersed benefits and concentrated costs – makes policy change most difficult and so requires an entrepreneur for policy change. In contrast, I posit a spatial distribution of member policy preferences that is in part the result of interest group pressure, both constituency-based and party-aligned, but also of the member's own policy views and those of his or her activist supporters. When these variables result in members' preferences being polarized along coinciding partisan and ideological lines, organizational and behavioral changes within the chamber lead to stronger party leadership and greater rewards for members acting as team members and so amplify the effects of exogenous polarizing forces. My conceptualization thus predicts that policy change occurs on the major issues that divide the parties when control of the chambers and the presidency is unified and is much less likely when control is divided.

Unsurprisingly, I believe that my approach is more illuminating for periods of high partisan polarization such as the early 21st century. The Volden and Wiseman approach does bring an important emphasis on legislator behavior within the legislature. We need to remember that no matter what the configuration of member preferences on an issue is, laws do not make themselves; legislators make laws.

POLARIZATION AND POLICY

Spatial models have proved themselves to be extremely useful for explaining policy gridlock and policy change, yet their explanation of the policy consequences of polarization is incomplete and in some ways misleading because it only captures what I have labeled the direct effect of polarization. Polarization's impact on how the chambers function internally is missing. Thus its explanations of the high productivity of the 111th and the gridlock of the 112th (and 113th) are incomplete. The 2008 election results, by bringing in a president with different preferences and enlarging the pro-leftward-change majority in the Senate, significantly expanded the opportunity for policy change in the 111th Congress. And, in fact, the 111th was one of the most legislatively productive congresses of the post-World War II period.

The process of enacting this major legislation was, however, by no means frictionless and strong and skillful congressional leadership was essential to success. The preferences of members of Congress are considerably more complex than the model portrays them; members have multiple preferences – for policy, reelection, influence in the chamber, and retention or attainment of a chamber majority and of the presidency for their party. As the parties became more ideologically homogeneous from the late 1970s forward, this gave majority party members an incentive to give the Speaker, their party leader, significant powers and resources and to allow him or her to use them aggressively, because the legislation the Speaker would use them to pass was broadly supported in the party for both policy and electoral reasons. Reciprocally, stronger leadership with more control over resources gives members a greater incentive to act as team members. Stronger party leadership and greater internal rewards for acting as team members amplify the behavioral effects of externally based polarization and thereby amplify the impact of partisan polarization on policy. Yet even so the political parties are not monolithic and, as the ACA case study showed, leaders had to use their procedural tools and their resources to construct and hold together the winning coalitions.

The simple spatial model can explain why the 112th (and the 113th) Congresses produced little major new discretionary legislation; with a much more conservative House membership, the "gridlock interval" expanded as policies preferred to the status quo by the House majority, the president, and sixty senators became vanishingly small. Yet must-pass legislation confronts every Congress and the series of Perils-of-Pauline episodes that characterized the

112th again demonstrated the incompleteness of the model's explanations. The complexity of preferences – of leaders as well as members – is one missing element. Most important for the short-term future of policy making at the national level is, however, the quite stark differences between the parties' understanding of how the polity and the economy operate. Not only are Democrats and Republicans highly polarized in their policy preferences, but many Republicans, office holders as well as activists, are suspicious of mainstream expertise and take their cues from different sources. Consequently their leadership, though possessing more powers and resources than their predecessors, can not persuade them to agree to deals that might benefit the party in the medium run but require them to compromise their policy preferences.

Many commentators have argued that the policy results of the high partisan polarization have been "kick the can down the road" deals or complete gridlock on major problems. Certainly the last few years have seen considerable gridlock; when Congress allows the FAA authorization to lapse for two weeks, when it refuses to fund the government for sixteen days, that is gridlock. And certainly the deals that have been struck have tended to kick the can down the road in the sense that no grand bargain has really come close to being consummated. Less often highlighted is that the legislation that is enacted often is or leads to inferior if not downright "bad" policy – often from all the actors' points of view. A transportation bill that extends for only two rather than the usual five years makes planning big projects difficult and inefficient. Funding government through continuing resolutions makes it impossible for departments and agencies to respond to new information and new challenges. And sequestration, even with the bits of discretion Congress gave some departments and agencies, is mindless.

References

Bach, Stanley, and Steven S. Smith. 1988. *Managing Uncertainty in the House of Representatives*. Washington, DC: The Brookings Institution.

Beaussier, Anne-Laure. 2012. "The Patient Protection and Affordable Care Act: The Victory of Unorthodox Lawmaking." *Journal of Health Politics, Policy and Law*, June 14.

Binder, Sarah. 2003. *Stalemate: Causes and Consequences of Legislative Gridlock*. Washington, DC: Brookings Institution Press.

Boehner, John. 2013. "Memo to House Republicans." March 28.

Brady, David, and Craig Volden. 1998. *Revolving Gridlock*. Boulder, CO: Westview Press.

Cox, Gary, and Mathew McCubbins. 1993. *Legislative Leviathan: Party Government in the House*. Berkeley: University of California Press.

Edwards, George C. III, Andrew Barrett, and Jeffrey Peake. 1997. "The Legislative Impact of Divided Government." *American Journal of Political Science* 41 (2) (April): 545–63.

Gold, Martin. 2004. *Senate Procedure and Practice*. Lantham, NY: Rowman & Littlefield.

Highlights of Budget Control Act. 2011. *Congressional Quarterly Weekly*, August 8.

Kaiser, Robert G. 2013. *Act of Congress*. New York: Alfred A. Knopf.

Krehbiel, Keith. 1998. *Pivotal Politics: A Theory of U.S. Lawmaking*. Chicago, IL: University of Chicago Press.

Mayhew, David. 1991. *Divided We Govern*. New Haven, CT: Yale University Press.

O'Connor, Patrick, and Carrie Budoff Brown. 2009. "Henry Waxman Wins Breakthrough on Health Bill." *Politico*, July 29.

Poole, Keith. 2015. "The Polarization of the Congressional Parties." http://voteview.com/political_polarization.asp.

Rohde, David. 1991. *Parties and Leaders in the Postreform House*. Chicago, IL: University of Chicago Press.

Skocpol, Theda. 2013. "Naming the Problem: What It Will Take to Counter Extremism and Engage Americans in the Fight against Global Warning." Paper prepared for the Symposium on The Politics of America's Fight Against Global Warming, February 14.

Sinclair, Barbara. 1983. *Majority Leadership in the U.S. House*. Baltimore, MD: Johns Hopkins University Press.

1995. *Legislators, Leaders, and Lawmaking*. Baltimore, MD: Johns Hopkins University Press.

1999a. "The President as Legislative Leader." In Colin Campbell and Bert A. Rockman, eds., *The Clinton Legacy*. Chatham House Publishers.

1999b. "Transformational Leader or Faithful Agent? Principal Agent Theory and House Majority Party Leadership in the 104th and 105th Congresses." *Legislative Studies Quarterly* 24 (August).

2006. *Party Wars: Polarization and the Politics of the Policy Process*. University of Oklahoma Press.

2008. "Orchestrators of Unorthodox Lawmaking: Pelosi and McConnell in the 110th Congress." *The Forum* (Issue 3).

2012. *Unorthodox Lawmaking*, 4th ed. Washington, DC: CQ Press.

Smith, Steve S. 2007. *Party Influence in Congress*. Cambridge: Cambridge University Press.

PART II

CONGRESS AND SOCIETY

4

Making a Rainbow Military

Parliamentary Skill and the Repeal of "Don't Ask, Don't Tell"

Rick Valelly

When the Department of Defense was born in the late 1940s it arrived inside the cabinet with a significant prohibition: gay and lesbian citizens were not welcome to serve in America's armed forces[1] (Bérubé 1990, 261). The United States then went on to operate an officially "straight" military well into the 21st century. Congress contributed greatly to such longevity. In 1993, after initial opposition from President Bill Clinton, Congress enacted the "Don't Ask, Don't Tell" statute (DADT). It codified the proscription on gay and lesbian service – and thus gave it new life. Congress indeed formalized the idea of a military closet. This 1993 statute recognized that many thousands of gays and lesbians bore arms but it held that their sexual orientation was inherently a threat to an effective military. Non-straight orientation was best kept secret. If a non-straight soldier were outed then the disclosure would lead to discharge.

After 1993 only a statute enacted by both houses of Congress and signed by the president could truly recast the status of non-straight personnel in the U.S. military. The road to a "rainbow" military ran through Congress. That road would be difficult to traverse. Members of Congress would have to instruct the military that the criteria for service were flawed. But recent research has shown that members of Congress respond to pro-gay opinion in their districts only when it is exceptionally high and vocal (Krimmel et al. 2012). The number of House districts and states that fit these criteria is small.

Not only would an unlikely congressional coalition for the repeal of DADT have to form, but repeal would also require a president willing and able to promote DADT repeal. Congress imposed DADT on an unwilling Commander-in-Chief, to be sure, but Congress would never dictate the reverse – that is, the repeal of DADT – to an unwilling president.

Thus lifting the statutory ban on gay and lesbian military service also depended on the Democratic party hitting the Madisonian jackpot – that is, on unified control of the federal government. Of the two parties Democrats were much more likely to respond to demands for repeal from LGBT advocacy groups. DADT was enacted during the previous instance of unified Democratic control, 1993–1995, and a Southern Democrat, Sen. Sam Nunn (D-GA), led the enactment. But Democrats soon turned against Nunn's handiwork and committed themselves to repeal, even as Republicans became strong supporters of the policy.

Unified control Democratic control returned in 2009. DADT repeal became one of many policy possibilities that were opened up by public reaction to the administration and policies of President George W. Bush and to the rapidly worsening economy in 2008. DADT repeal was not high on the Democratic party's agenda, though, as Democrats regained unified control of Congress and the White House. Democrats turned first toward fiscal stimulus, health care reform, and stronger financial regulation.

Not until the latter half of the 111th Congress – in a process that spilled over into the December 2010 "lame duck" session – did congressional majorities in the House and Senate act. When they did, they authorized a self-repeal process inside the armed forces that finally led to formal cessation of the historic ban on September 20, 2011.

To paraphrase a famous comment by Vice President Joe Biden, was this a big deal? Clearly it was. Given the inertia behind the old policy, and the structural impediments to its reversal, the authorization of DADT repeal marked a milestone in American political evolution. In doing that congressional majorities *bettered* the civic status of gays and lesbians. That was a historic "first" for Congress.

It was also a "first" for gay rights advocates. They and their legislative, partisan, and military allies ended the last remnant of official federal discrimination against gays and lesbians. More broadly, on September 20, 2011, gays and lesbians formally won the "right to fight" *as themselves,* and not as closeted men and women who had to constantly live on the lookout against the discovery and dishonoring of their identity. "Not satisfied with rights alone, the end gays sought was honor, the honor of serving their country's military" (Hirshman 2012, 333).

WHY DADT REPEAL IS NOTEWORTHY
FOR CONGRESS SCHOLARS

DADT repeal thus richly merits the attention of Congress scholars. President Harry Truman's famous effort to desegregate the military, and the follow-on determination of his successor, Dwight D. Eisenhower, shape how we think about "right to fight" politics (James 1995; Krebs 2006; Nichols 2007, 42–50). Congressional–military relations, in contrast, are pictured as turning on distributive issues, such as base closing and weapons procurement; good housekeeping, that is, budgetary servicing of an essential governmental function; or, of course, the conduct of war (Kriner 2010; Rundquist and Carsey 2002; Stevenson 2006). This is a major and "least likely" case of congressional–military collaboration over social values and the civic status of an identity-based minority.

Moreover, in 2010 Congress carved out a role in a markedly more polarized ideological and legislative context relative to 1993. Between 1993, the 103rd Congress, and 2007, the 110th Congress, the distance between party means in left–right issue space in the House grew 33.5 percent (as indexed by DW-NOMINATE.) In the Senate, the same "spatial" distance changed only half as much – 16 percent. But the Senate divergence was associated with quite remarkable changes in how the Senate conducted its business. There was a 74 percent increase in the number of cloture motions filed between these two Congresses (103rd through 107th), a 143 percent increase in votes on cloture, and a 335 percent increase in cloture being invoked.

Majority rule in the Senate – always an elusive phenomenon – seemed to metamorphose into supermajority rule by the 111th Congress. This change – the advent of a sixty-vote requirement for legislation – turned the Senate into a major battleground for DADT repeal.

The House repeal process played out in straightforward majoritarian fashion. In the House, Democrats had increased the majority that they had regained in the 2006 elections, and they enjoyed a 257–178 margin in the 111th Congress. But Democrats enjoyed a sixty-vote majority in the Senate only very briefly, during summer 2009, between the arrival of Al Franken of Minnesota, after the settlement of the disputed senatorial election there, and the incapacitation of two highly effective and influential Democrats, Sen. Edward Kennedy (D-MA) and Sen. Robert Byrd (D-WV) (Burden 2011; Hulse 2009). By the time DADT repeal was on the Senate agenda in 2010, Senate Democrats not only needed to hold their majority but they also needed to attract Republican votes.

Sheer legislative ability in framing DADT repeal so that it garnered bipartisan support thus mattered greatly in the Senate phase of the repeal. So did simple capacity to avoid mistakes and adeptness in quickly recovering from blunders. DADT repeal pivoted, in the end, on how adroitly Senate Majority Leader Harry Reid (D-NV) – and the caucus of which he was the agent – operated in the harsh political environment of the 111th Congress. The pressures to deliver before the 112th Congress grew, in fact, over the course of 2010. By mid-summer, 2010, the shadow of Republican resurgence in the 2010 elections hung ominously over the Democrats (Baker 2010).

The case of DADT repeal offers lessons, then, in how parliamentary skill cemented an unusual congressional policy intervention. Many think of Congress as the "sick man" of the separation of powers (Zelizer 2013). But here members of Congress displayed strength. They proved quite capable of effectively interacting with the military and the presidency about large matters of justice and inclusion. As a result Congress was present at the historic creation of the "rainbow" military.

OVERVIEW OF THE ANALYSIS

To flesh out a dramatic story, this chapter proceeds by first applying John Kingdon's well-known conceptualization of the policy process (Kingdon 1984). Classic theoretical frameworks survive in large part because they perform well in illuminating new cases. Kingdon's elegant scheme nicely captures the fleeting nature of the opportunity for DADT repeal in the 111th Congress. (This is the section entitled "Three Streams Toward the Repeal Window.")

To recall, Kingdon posits that there is a *problem* stream – by which he means the process that leads to public or elite recognition (or both) that there really is a policy problem that needs debate. There is a *political* stream – such as a favorable set of electoral results that empowers politicians to act on such recognition. Finally, there is a *policy* stream – think here of the learning that proponents for a policy change undergo as they float ideas and puzzle through what successful change will require.

When these three streams "couple" – connect temporally – then a "policy window" opens. By emphasizing such low-probability confluence in the politics of problem solving, Kingdon warns us that lots of societal problems can go unresolved for long periods of time. Over time democracies address important problems disjointedly. Indeed, there is no guarantee at all that they will fix problems that, arguably, *ought* to be fixed. No coupling, no policy window. No policy window, no *chance* of problem solving.

Policy windows, moreover, have a "use them or lose them" quality. The opportunity may disappear. As Kingdon writes, "In space shots, the window presents the opportunity for a launch.... Similarly, windows open in policy systems. These policy windows, the opportunities for action on given initiatives, present themselves and stay open for only short periods.... If the window passes without action, it may not open again for a long time" (Kingdon 1984, 174, 178). The 111th Congress was just that sort of policy window. If DADT repeal did not happen then, DADT might today still be in effect.

As we will also see ("Obama Reconfigures the Policy Window"), the political action on repeal shifted markedly when President Obama weighed in on the issue in early 2010. In particular, Obama and the Pentagon complicated congressional use of the policy window. They did so by explicitly ignoring the congressional and electoral calendar. The Pentagon would report *its* views on repeal on its own timetable, in late 2010. How Congress would work with the new executive timeline was entirely up to Congress.

In "Congressional Response: Formal Delegation to the Pentagon; Hitching a Ride on the NDAA," I trace the facets of repeal politics that followed from what the president and the Pentagon did in the first few months of 2010. First, in spring 2010, congressional Democrats bargained with the White House and the Pentagon with an eye toward assuring DADT repeal no matter what happened to Democratic majorities in Congress after the 2010 elections. In particular, they negotiated terms of repeal that formally *delegated* the process to the Pentagon. Congress embraced what Obama and the Pentagon had stipulated – but also created Pentagon accountability to Congress. By announcing that Congress accepted the Pentagon process, and getting the Pentagon's express agreement to this announcement, Congress subtly moved what Obama and the Pentagon had proposed closer to a principal–agent relationship.

Second, the actors favoring DADT repeal unveiled a clever strategy for getting such delegation through the Senate gauntlet during the 111th Congress: they placed DADT repeal into the National Defense Authorization Act (NDAA). The NDAA was must-pass legislation, particularly at a time when the United States was engaged in two wars.

Yet here in the discussion ("If Skill Matters, So Does Miscalculation") we also get to the contingency of DADT repeal. Even though – perhaps because – the NDAA was must-pass legislation, congressional Democrats attached more than one controversial measure to it and simultaneously sought to procedurally shield it from GOP amendment. Sen. Reid (presumably acting on behalf of his caucus) refused to bargain with friendly GOP colleagues – such as Sen. Susan Collins (R-ME) – over amendments to the NDAA, even though she was a member of the Senate Armed Services Committee. Democrats placed a bet that they could hitch DADT repeal onto the NDAA on their terms and win.

In thus procedurally shielding the NDAA so that it could be used to repeal DADT, Democrats squandered the possibility of garnering the necessary Republican votes. What looked like legislative skill was overplaying their hand. In an unusual turn of events, NDAA 2011 was successfully filibustered by a bipartisan coalition. A cloture vote on September 21 failed.

In "Action-Forcing Failure," I zero in on the *second* failed cloture vote. This happened on December 9 – and as we will see, it seemed to draw the curtain down on DADT repeal. The policy window of the 111th Congress, to all appearances, slammed shut.

In fact, the failed cloture vote actually speeded up repeal. The second failed cloture vote was a "faux failure." Sen. Reid instead used it to satisfy immigration policy advocates that Senate Democrats had tried to enact the Development, Relief, and Education for Alien Minors (DREAM) Act (an immigration measure that benefited children of undocumented immigrants who were not natural-born citizens). This had also been tucked into the NDAA. The vote's outcome also sharply raised the pressure on those working for DADT repeal to quickly devise a way toward their goal.

And it was suddenly easy to do just that. By December 9, the road forward was in view. By then, the Department of Defense and the Joint Chiefs of Staff vocally asked for repeal before the conclusion of the 111th Congress. (The details are treated in "The Top Brass Gets Drawn In.") Also, Sen. Joe Lieberman and Sen. Susan Collins had identified a sixty-vote coalition in favor of a stand-alone repeal, separated from NDAA 2011. That coalition's emergence revealed a broad willingness in the Senate to work with military leaders.

In the wake of the December 9 failed vote, Lieberman, Collins, and Senate Majority Leader Reid certified to House leaders and repeal advocates in that chamber that the Senate would quickly match a House vote for a stand-alone repeal. "All The Pieces Suddenly Fall Into Place" sketches the deft mechanics of getting a bill to the president to sign – and the bill signing itself.

"Lessons of DADT Repeal" attends to how the case study can reframe how we think about congressional problem-solving and representation in a polarized age. It also underscores the continuing relevance of Kingdon's "policy windows" framework. The key contribution of this chapter both for congressionalists and for policy scholars who are seeking to assess the utility of the policy windows approach is that we need to incorporate parliamentary skill into our analyses. This is not an original point: Volden and Wiseman emphasize this for the House (Volden and Wiseman 2014). What I add here is a focus on its role in the Senate's dynamics, in bargaining with the White House, and in bargaining with the military.

Three Streams Toward the Repeal Window

When President Bill Clinton signed "Don't Ask, Don't Tell" in 1993, it was not obvious that the statute would mutate into a policy problem. Clinton called it a reasonable compromise between what the military wanted, which was the retention of an existing ban on gay and lesbian service, and his own proposal that gays and lesbians serve openly (Frank 2009, 58–136). The very name – devised by the military sociologist Charles Moskos – suggested a workable middle ground (Holley 2008). The idea was to stop inquiry into sexual orientation at the time of enlistment ("Don't Ask") but require that sexual orientation remain private thereafter ("Don't Tell").

But in fact this arrangement was not a Solomonic compromise. The statute clearly described homosexuality as a threat to military order. Also, sexual orientation was and is discernible over the course of frequent interactions in any work environment. As Diane Mazur wrote in a critique of the policy, "People have private lives apart from their professional military lives, but they generally don't have secret lives" (Mazur 2010, 150). Although the policy never kicked out more than a very small fraction of the gays and lesbians in service it did create a difficult – sometimes extremely difficult – work environment for all non-straight service members and officers (Burrelli 2010; Gates 2004; GAO 2005). There were reports of physical and psychological harassment of lesbians and gays. A horrific murder occurred at Fort Campbell, Kentucky. In that incident a gay soldier successfully fought off a straight soldier. The man whom he bested took revenge by clubbing the gay soldier to death while he slept (Frank 2009, 192–96).

Toward the end of his second term President Clinton told CBS News that the policy was not working. Soon after he left office he repudiated it. Its main architects, Gen. Colin Powell and former Sen. Sam Nunn (D-GA), also eventually turned against it (Frank 2009, 276, 289).

Once the United States went to war in Afghanistan and Iraq – and the news that it was throwing out valuable personnel became widely reported – DADT metamorphosed into a perverse policy. DADT became the center of – in Kingdon's language – a "problem stream." Editorial opinion, military opinion, and public opinion shifted against it. A full study of editorial opinion in print newspapers is unavailable. But Aaron Belkin found that editorial attitudes among the roughly 200 newspapers that editorially supported President George W. Bush's reelection in 2004 were far from opposed to repeal. As for the major national newspapers with generally liberal editorial stances, these were openly calling for repeal (Belkin 2008).

Within the military, a 2004 Annenberg National Election Survey found considerable (though not majority) disagreement with the policy among service members. A *Military Times* survey from 2003 similarly found that support for the policy decreased as one's rank in the armed forces decreased (Belkin 2008). (*Military Times* is a Gannett online product that polls regularly and reports results for the previous two years at http://projects.militar ytimes.com/polls.)

Moreover, among the officer corps some reaction to the policy was evident. Patrick Murphy, an Iraq War veteran and later a congressional leader of repeal, reported in his 2008 campaign biography abut his experience in teaching public law at West Point: "When I started teaching my segment on Don't Ask, Don't Tell, I'd always take a poll and find that only about one or two cadets opposed it. By the end of my lectures on equality, usually only one or two still supported the policy" (Murphy 2008, 54–5). Such anecdotal evidence dovetails with Aaron Belkin's observations of genuinely critical discussion of DADT within the service academies (Belkin 2012).

In fact, in 2007, at his Senate confirmation hearing, the new chairman of the Joint Chiefs of Staff, Admiral Michael Mullen, openly invited Congress to revisit DADT. At his confirmation hearing he said, "'I really think it is for the American people to come forward, really through this body, to both debate that policy and make changes, if that's appropriate." He went on to say that, "I'd love to have Congress make its own decisions 'with respect to considering repeal'" (OutServe-SLDN 2008).

Among the public at large, gay and lesbian service was no longer controversial. A full treatment of the survey evidence is beyond the scope of this chapter. But the *Washington Post*–ABC News poll is suggestive. In late May, 1993 – when the issue was in the news – the poll asked, "do you think homosexuals who do NOT publicly disclose their sexual orientation should be allowed to serve in the military or not?" Sixty-three percent said yes, and 35 percent said no. When the 1993 respondents were asked "Do you think homosexuals who DO publicly disclose their sexual orientation should be allowed to serve in the military or not?" only 44 percent said yes and 55 percent said no. Fifteen years later, in mid-July 2008, 78 percent of the public favored closeted service – *and 75 percent favored open service.*

One way to read these results is that the public was happy either way, with closeted *or* open service. It is doubtful that the American public was indignant about DADT's unfairness, its administrative costs, and the loss of personnel eager to serve. But the polling evidence around this time does suggest that the public would not oppose repeal of DADT (*Washington Post*–ABC News Poll July 2008).

In addition to the evolution of the "problem stream," there was a "political stream" that affected the politics of DADT repeal. As noted in the sketch of repeal politics with which I began this chapter, the political stars aligned just a few months after this *Washington Post*–ABC News poll. The Democratic Party platform that year had promised a repeal of DADT. At the 2008 nominating convention the delegates adopted a platform plank calling for repeal of DADT:

We will ... put national security above divisive politics. More than 12,500 service men and women have been discharged on the basis of sexual orientation since the "Don't Ask, Don't Tell" policy was implemented, at a cost of over $360 million. Many of those forced out had special skills in high demand, such as translators, engineers, and pilots. At a time when the military is having a tough time recruiting and retaining troops, it is wrong to deny our country the service of brave, qualified people. We support the repeal of "Don't Ask Don't Tell" and the implementation of policies to allow qualified men and women to serve openly regardless of sexual orientation (Democratic Party Platforms 2008).

That plank would have been in the Democratic Party platform no matter which candidate, Sen. Hillary Clinton (D-NY) or Sen. Barack Obama (D-IL), won the Democratic presidential nomination. By 2008, the Democratic Party had become the party of gay rights. As David Karol has stressed, political parties attract "intense policy demanders" (Karol 2009). Although there are important pro-GOP gay rights organizations, such as Log Cabin Republicans, most LGBT "policy demanders" long ago moved into the Democratic Party – bringing congressional Democrats along (Karol 2012; Krimmel et al. 2012).

During the race for the nomination Obama sought to please LGBT activists. To them, he was a devout black Christian whose commitment to LGBT policy concerns was unknown (Wolff Interview 2011). Yet over the course of the nomination struggle Obama reassured LGBT activists. Obama issued an "open letter" in February 2008 in which he called, among other promises, for a repeal of DADT.

The results of the 2012 elections further heightened the prospect of change. Sen. Obama defeated Sen. John McCain 52.9 percent to 45.7 percent. In the House, Democrats increased the majority they had regained in the 2006 elections, with a 257–178 margin. The Senate Democratic majority was the largest it had been since 1993–95, during the 103rd Congress – and it was augmented by the support of two Independents who leaned Democratic, Sen. Joseph Lieberman (I-CT) and Sen. Bernard Sanders (I-VT).

Expectations rose yet more before the president's inauguration. On January 9, 2009, Robert Gibbs, the president-elect's Press Secretary, was asked if the president-elect planned to end DADT. Gibbs replied, "You don't hear politicians give a one-word answer much. But it's 'yes'" (Frank 2013, 167).

But what policy vehicle would become the basis for repeal? DADT was a statute. A repeal would also have to be a statute. The "policy stream" inevitably came to be about statutory design.

Here we get to the first materialization of statutory DADT reform. This was the Military Readiness Enhancement Act (MREA, pronounced "Maria" by the players in the policy domain). It emerged only in the House of Representatives, not the Senate. Legislative action in the Senate, even though Democrats in the 111th Congress organized it, only came *after* the president's 2010 State of the Union address calling for repeal of DADT.

Rep. Martin Meehan (D-MA) introduced the first MREA bill in 2005 and it gained 122 cosponsors. Meehan reintroduced it in the 110th Congress, and the number of cosponsors climbed to 149. The House Armed Services Military Personnel Subcommittee held hearings on MREA and the policy in July 2008. Tellingly, the Pentagon sent no one to defend the policy (Frank 2010, 286).

By then, Rep. Meehan had resigned his seat in Congress to lead the University of Massachusetts-Lowell campus. Stepping in, Rep. Ellen Tauscher (D-CA) introduced the bill in the 111th Congress. When Rep. Tauscher resigned *her* seat – to accept a State Department position – the lead sponsor became Rep. Patrick Murphy (D-PA).

As the first Iraq War veteran elected to Congress, Murphy was an ideal lead sponsor of MREA. Murphy punctuated his takeover of leadership on the bill by joining a mid-summer, 2009, rally for repeal that was held in Philadelphia by Servicemembers United, a new gay veterans group (Benen 2009; Nicholson 2010, 89–90). Also, the number of cosponsors grew some more (and eventually reached 192).

The bill that Murphy now shepherded was H.R. 1283, introduced earlier in March, 2009. The bill announced that its purpose was to "to institute in the Armed Forces a policy of nondiscrimination based on sexual orientation." It then read:

The Secretary of Defense, and the Secretary of Homeland Security with respect to the Coast Guard when it is not operating as a service in the Navy, may not discriminate on the basis of sexual orientation against any member of the Armed Forces or against any person seeking to become a member of the Armed Forces.

DISCRIMINATION ON BASIS OF SEXUAL ORIENTATION. – For purposes of this section, discrimination on the basis of sexual orientation is –

(1) in the case of a member of the Armed Forces, the taking of any personnel or administrative action (including any action relating to promotion, demotion, evaluation, selection for an award, selection for a duty assignment, transfer, or separation) in whole or in part on the basis of sexual orientation; and

(2) in the case of a person seeking to become a member of the Armed Forces, denial of accession into the Armed Forces in whole or in part on the basis of sexual orientation.

The bill defined "sexual orientation" as "heterosexuality, homosexuality, or bisexuality, whether the orientation is real or perceived, and includes state- ments and consensual sexual conduct manifesting heterosexuality, homosexuality, or bisexuality." The bill gave the Secretary of Defense ninety days after enactment of the statute to revise Defense Department regulations and issue new, implementing regulations, and provided that the Secretary "further direct the Secretary of each military department to revise regulations of that military department ... not later than 180 days after the date of the enactment of this Act" (United States Congress 2009: H.R. 1283).

In sum, the bill was a straightforward prohibition on discriminatory treat- ment. It equated – *and*, as a matter of status within the military, it *equalized* – the sexual orientation of straights, non-straights, and bisexuals. And change would happen quickly. The military, including the Coast Guard, would become orientation-neutral, as it were, within six months.

Obama Reconfigures the Policy Window

Obama kept his own counsel. Repeal activists filled the silence, hoping to draw him into action. The Palm Center, a research and advocacy nonprofit institute in California, issued a report making a persuasive case that the president had the authority to suspend DADT. This idea generated considerable interest and press attention (Frank 2013; see Henning 2009).

Seizing on the publicity around the idea, Rep. Alcee Hastings (D-FL) and seventy-six other members of the House issued a call for the president to use this authority:

We urge you to exercise the maximum discretion legally possible ... until Congress repeals the law ... [and] that you direct the Armed Services not to initiate any investi- gation of service personnel to determine their sexual orientation, and that you instruct them to disregard third party accusations that do not allege violations of the Uniform Code of Military Justice.... Under your leadership, Congress must then repeal and replace Don't Ask, Don't Tell with a policy of inclusion and non-discrimination (Hast- ings et al. 2009).

By September, the Senate Majority Leader, Harry Reid, followed suit, sending letters to the president and to Secretary of Defense Gates asking for their views on repeal: "'Your leadership in this matter is greatly appreciated and needed at this time'" (Frank 2013, 183).

The president's caution was understandable. Obama hardly wanted to make the same mistakes that President Bill Clinton made. In fact, the stakes were higher than that. With the national security situation and military posture of the United States utterly different from 1993, Obama could not afford poor relations with the Pentagon and the services. Clinton's famously strained relationship with the Pentagon had been brought on, in part, by military resistance to his proposed executive order on military service by gays and lesbians (Desch 1999, 29–33).

But with his first State of the Union Address in January, 2010, the president finally responded. It was a memorably contentious event. A South Carolina Republican congressman loudly called the president a liar. An angry Associate Justice Samuel Alito mouthed disagreement with the President's characterization of the *Citizens United* campaign finance decision. Amid the tension in the chamber came the following: "This year, I will work with Congress and our military to finally repeal the law that denies gay Americans the right to serve the country they love because of who they are. It's the right thing to do" (see Nicholson 2012, 106).

Sitting at home watching the speech, Alex Nicholson, the director of Servicemembers United, the pro-repeal veterans' group, noticed a crucial ambiguity in the statement: the President was not clear on precisely *when* he saw repeal taking place. This was the first glimmer of what soon came into focus: the president and the Pentagon were ignoring the congressional and electoral calendar (Nicholson 2012, 106). They would set in motion a separate process. The subtext was: Congress was on its own. How it would connect to the executive timeline was up to Congress.

On February 2, Secretary of Defense Gates and Chairman of the Joint Chiefs of Staff Adm. Mullen went to Capitol Hill to back up the president at a hearing of the Senate Armed Services Committee. Gates testified first, and he announced his full support for the president's position. "We have received our orders from the Commander in Chief and we are moving out accordingly." But Gates also underscored the need for a deliberate pace: "I am mindful of the fact, as are you, that unlike the last time this issue was considered by the Congress ... *our military is engaged in two wars that have put troops and their families under considerable stress and strain*" (emphasis added). He immediately added that

attitudes toward homosexuality may have changed considerably ... in the military ... over the intervening years.... To ensure that the department is prepared should the law be changed ... I have appointed a high-level working group ... that will immediately begin a review of the issues associated with properly implementing a repeal of the "Don't Ask, Don't Tell" policy.

Gates acknowledged that "our approach ... will take the better part of a year" but "[a]n important part of this process is to engage our men and women in uniform and their families ... since ... they will ultimately determine whether or not we can make this transition successfully" (Gates 2010).

Admiral Mullen, in seconding Gates, noted that "[t]he Chiefs and I are in complete support of the approach that Secretary Gates has outlined." He stressed that he personally opposed DADT because it "forces young men and women to lie about who they are in order to defend their fellow citizens" and he believed that the military could adapt to a repeal. But he did not know for a fact how we would best make such a major policy change in a time of two wars ... I also recognize the stress our troops and families are under ... we need to move forward in a manner that does not add to that stress.... What our young men and women and their families want – what they deserve – is that we listen to them.... What the citizens we defend want to know ... is that their uniformed leadership will act in a way that absolutely does not place in peril the readiness and effectiveness of their military ... balance and thoughtfulness is what we need most right now. *It's what the president has promised us* [emphasis added], and it's what we ask of you in this body. Federal News Service 2010, 47–8.

One month later, Secretary Gates issued a March 2 memorandum for the general counsel to Gen. Carter Ham, Commander, U.S. Army, Europe, calling for the establishment of what later became known as the Comprehensive Review Working Group (CRWG.) This "high-level working group" would deliver its report to the secretary on December 1, 2010 (Lee 2013).

Alex Nicholson of Servicemembers United later wrote, "the administration had made a deal with the Pentagon. In exchange for senior defense leaders' support ... the President would allow the Pentagon to spend all of 2010 doing an extensive and expensive study to help build both cover and consensus" and then the White House would "pursue legislative repeal in 2011" (Nicholson 2012, 127; see Frank 2013, 188–9).

The president's plan made sense from his perspective and from the Pentagon's point of view. But it had an obviously implausible premise: that Democrats would continue to control both houses of Congress with the same majorities that they had in the 111th Congress. The president assumed away the recurrence of a regular pattern in American politics – the significant loss of support for the president's political party during off-year elections.

Congressional Response: Formal Delegation to the Pentagon; Hitching a Ride on the NDAA

Congressional partners in the repeal process faced a problem: how to lock in the certainty of a repeal *despite* the open-ended nature of the executive part of the process – and despite Secretary Gates' demand that Congress not act until the Pentagon's report was ready. Evidently seeking a way around this problem, Sen. Joe Lieberman introduced S. 3065 the day after Gates issued his memorandum establishing the CRWG. His bill, S. 3065, updated MREA by adding language that recognized the existence of a working group and envisioning a generously delayed implementation of the repeal (United States Congress 2010, S. 3065). This idea strongly resembled what Servicemembers United called for in a plan that it dubbed SE/DI: Set End Date/Delayed Implementation (Eleveld 2010). Congress would repeal DADT on the basis of MREA during the 111th Congress – and *later* the Pentagon would implement the repeal in conjunction with the administrative recommendations of the CRWG.

Repeal proponents would thus trust the Pentagon to end DADT but to do so under congressional instruction. In principle, the Pentagon review was open-ended. Whether the armed forces were ready for repeal awaited serious investigation and internal debate. But S. 3065 essentially told the military, "make the debate come out the way that we want it to." As we will see, this message grated on Secretary Gates.

Over in the House, Rep. Patrick Murphy proposed that the language of S. 3065 be incorporated into the NDAA for 2011. But, in response, the Missouri Democrat chairing the House Armed Services Committee (HASC), Rep. Ike Skelton, asked for a statement of the Secretary's preference – and he got it. Skelton was opposed to DADT repeal. He assumed, correctly, that Gates opposed a plan that boxed Gates, Mullen, and the CRWG process into a recommendation of repeal.

Skelton was right. The secretary did *not* want Congress to act – and he wrote a public letter to Skelton saying that. On the basis of Gates' letter, Skelton and HASC reported the NDAA to the floor – *without* Murphy's amendment.

Still, Secretary Gates also unilaterally acted in a way that signaled good faith. In late March, 2010, he effectively halted further operation of "Don't Ask, Don't Tell" by instituting two adjustments to the discharge procedure. First, only a general or admiral could initiate discharge procedures. Second, the evidentiary standard for "telling" was changed. Any third party "outing" of a gay or lesbian service member would subject the person who exposed someone's orientation to testimony under oath and also special scrutiny with regard to motivation. In other words, DADT died administratively (Shanker 2010; U.S. Naval Institute n.d.). Gates thus signaled that he was willing to act as *something* like an agent of repeal proponents but without formal statutory instruction.

Gates got what he wanted. In late May, NDAA was amended on the House floor without the command that S. 3065 contained. By then all the major principals in the process – the White House, the Pentagon's senior leadership, the leaders of the repeal proponents in the House and Senate, and staff from the repeal advocacy groups – had agreed on language that ultimately became the basis for repeal. In effect, they wrote a contract.

The public signals of the deal over new repeal language came in an exchange of letters among Sen. Lieberman, Rep. Murphy, the chair of the Senate Armed Services Committee, Sen. Carl Levin (D-MI), and Peter Orszag, the Director of the Office of Management and Budget, who issued a May 24 letter in response to a letter made public earlier that day (Donnelly and Anderson 2010; O'Keefe 2010).

The three members of Congress wrote to the President,

We applaud the pledge in your State of the Union Address. . . . We further commend the Secretary and the leaders of the working group. . . . Given the important efforts of the working group, we have developed a legislative proposal for consideration by the House and Senate that puts a process in place to repeal "Don't Ask, Don't Tell" once the working group has completed its review and you, the Secretary of Defense, and the Chairman of the Joint Chiefs certify that repeal can be achieved consistent with the military's standards of readiness, effectiveness, unit cohesion, and recruiting and retention. We ... request the Administration's official views on our legislative proposal.

In response, Peter Orszag wrote to each of the three that same day:

While ideally the Department of Defense Comprehensive Review on the Implementation of Repeal of 10 U.S.C. § 654 would be completed before the Congress takes any legislative action, the Administration understands that Congress has chosen to move forward with legislation now and seeks the Administration's views on the proposed amendment ... the Administration is of the view that the proposed amendment meets the concerns raised by the Secretary of Defense and the Chairman of the Joint Chiefs of Staff. The proposed amendment will allow for completion of the Comprehensive Review, enable the Department of Defense to assess the results of the review, and ensure that the implementation of the repeal is consistent with standards of military readiness, effectiveness, unit cohesion, recruiting and retention. The amendment will also *guarantee that the Department of Defense has prepared the necessary policies and regulations needed to successfully implement the repeal* [emphasis added] ... such an approach recognizes the critical need to allow our military and their families the full opportunity to inform and shape the implementation process. ... The Administration therefore supports the proposed amendment (O'Keefe 2010).

This new language – that is, "the proposed amendment" – responded to the interbranch political problem posed by the content of S. 3065 (i.e., that Congress explicitly mooted the comprehensive review and any surprises or information that it might contain). Instead, there was new, very opaque language. Critically, this language *dropped* the explicit prohibition of sexual orientation discrimination that was the heart of MREA (and in the end, repeal went forward in 2011 without such a prohibition).

The new language authorized completion of an internal military review of the administrative feasibility of the military's response to abrogation of Section 654 of Title 10 of the United States Code. When complete, the President would submit a memorandum to (in the statute's words) "the congressional defense committees." The Secretary of Defense and the Chairman of the Joint Chiefs of Staff would also sign that memorandum. It would certify "[t]hat the implementation of necessary policies and regulations pursuant to the discretion provided by the amendments ... is consistent with the standards of military readiness, military effectiveness, unit cohesion, and recruiting and retention of the Armed Forces." The amendments to the U.S. Code (which presumably would be written by the military) "would take effect 60 days after the date of the memorandum's transmittal." If there was no transmittal then "section 654 of title 10, United States Code, shall remain in effect" (United States Congress 2010, S. 3454, 203–7).

Congress would not be ordering the Pentagon around. Any member of the House who voted for repeal simply authorized the Pentagon to proceed with its plans. In fact, if the Pentagon changed its mind, then the statute said – on its face – that DADT stood and would *not* be repealed. If there was no transmittal of a certification that the military had prepared itself for non-straight service members being open about their sexual orientation then *"section 654 of title 10, United States Code, shall remain in effect"* (emphasis added).

This change evidently converted House Democrats who were uneasy with MREA's explicit prohibition of sexual orientation discrimination.

In the House, several Blue Dog Democrats said they were still weighing their unease with the initial proposal against the compromise. Rep. Henry Cuellar (Texas), for example, said he has received a blunt directive from those serving on the Randolph Air Force Base in his district: "Don't repeal, don't repeal, don't repeal." But Cuellar said the go-ahead from Gates and Mullen is compelling him to rethink his position. "If they were not on board, it'd be hard to even consider it," he said (Newmyer and Dennis 2010).

As R. Douglas Arnold has pointed out, congressional delegation is politically very useful. Because members of Congress want to get reelected they often cannot vote sincere policy preferences. They instead carefully manage what their roll-call record will say about them. On the other hand, members of Congress also devise the procedures for making policy. They can therefore often collude to find a procedure that blurs the "traceability" of the *consequences* of yeas or nays.

If congressional leaders devise a policy design that will not *later* make its supporters electorally or politically vulnerable then members of Congress act responsibly. But policy design must blur traceability (Arnold 1990). It is hard to imagine a better way to blur traceability in the repeal of DADT than the self-certification plan that was devised in late spring, 2010.

What about those who preferred the *explicit* prohibition? To them the self-certification design seemed trustworthy. Speaking for this point of view, the chairman of the Senate Armed Services Committee, Sen. Carl Levin (D-MI), said,

there is *very little risk* [emphasis added] that the "don't ask, don't tell policy" would be re-established under a future administration. "We've already got the Secretary of Defense and the chairman of the Joint Chiefs favoring ending the ban," Levin said. And once it is repealed, the odds of reinstating it are "so remote it's a little bit like whether or not we're going to repeal the Civil Rights Act of 1964" (Newmyer and Dennis 2010).

This last comment by Sen. Levin is fairly suggestive. One might interpret it as revealing the core of the Pentagon promise – and why it was trustworthy. The internal review required a significant investment of bureaucratic resources. It did so, first, by assessing the extent of internal *administrative* change. Second, such administrative change would be implemented across the entire range of military bureaucracies both within and without the United States and all over the world. That process would require truly extensive education and training. When the process ended, formal certification and transmittal occurred. And by then the policy would be "locked in." Any *subsequent* legislative–executive coalition that was bent on repealing the repeal would have to do something very politically costly, if not impossible: order the military to undo the administrative process that repealed DADT. Reverse engineering the repeal would repudiate a great deal of good faith work. Would Republicans and conservative Democrats really disrupt the military in this way? In other words, the chance of an ex-post veto was small.

Also, it may be the case that repeal proponents understood that they had subtly transformed what Obama and the Pentagon proposed. They turned it into a "report-to-Congress" process locked inside military funding. Repeal proponents in Congress thereby made the Pentagon *their* agent as well as the president's agent. But they did this in a way that made the new principal–agent relationship rather opaque.

In the end, the May 27, 2010, vote in the House to add the repeal language to NDAA 2011 was 229 Democrats and 5 Republicans in favor (234) against 26 Democrats (mostly Southern Democrats) and 168 Republicans (194). The vote on the rule for NDAA 2011 had been 241–178, with only 11 Democrats defecting on that vote. The next day, the vote on final passage of NDAA was 246 (with 26 Democrats defecting) to 169 (with 9 Republicans voting for final passage).

The Senate Armed Services Committee reported NDAA 2011 with identical repeal language that had been added to the markup by Sen. Joe Lieberman. The vote there on May 27 was 16–12, with Sen. Jim Webb (D-VA) voting against the amendment in committee, and Sen. Susan Collins voting for it. The final vote of approval for NDAA 2011 in committee was 18–10 (Donnelly and Anderson 2010).

The congressional actors favoring DADT repeal thus unveiled a clever strategy for getting through the Senate gauntlet. By 2010, the Senate had become the battlefield where Republicans fought President Obama and the Democratic party's highly activist policy agenda. That change had origins in the previous Congress. When Democrats regained control of the Senate in 2007 during the 110th Congress, the number of cloture votes scheduled by the majority jumped sharply. When the next Congress, the 111th, opened for business, the shift to a sixty-vote threshold for legislation was the premise for how the Senate operated. Yet the Democrats really did not have a sixty-vote majority (Burden 2011; Koger 2012).

And they faced Republican opposition. The fact that a majority of House Republicans voted against NDAA 2011 was actually startling. Voting against the NDAA during a time of two wars clearly was *not* bad politics, if the point of the vote was to stop the repeal of DADT.

The 2008 Republican platform on which Sen. John McCain (R-AZ) ran for president supported the retention of DADT: "Military priorities and mission must determine personnel policies. Esprit and cohesion are necessary for military effectiveness and success on the battlefield. To protect our servicemen and women and ensure that America's Armed Forces remain the best in the world, we affirm the timelessness of those values, the benefits of traditional military culture, *and the incompatibility of homosexuality with military service"* (emphasis added) (Republican Party Platforms 2008).

Also, two major veterans groups that were organized across states and House districts reinforced the GOP position. These were the Veterans of Foreign Wars and the American Legion. The Legion stated in February, 2010, "Now is not the time to engage in a social experiment that can disrupt and potentially have serious impact on the conduct of forces engaged in combat." A spokesman for the Veterans of Foreign Wars also said, "The VFW is fully aware that societal norms regarding homosexuality have changed since the 1993 passage of [the ban], but what is considered acceptable by civilians must not be blindly imposed on a military institution that the great majority of society chooses not to join" (Scarborough 2010).

Repeal opponents, both within and without Congress, considered their case fairly weighty. The United States was engaged in two major and protracted wars, the Iraq war and the Afghanistan war. Because the armed forces were an all-volunteer force, they had been stretched thin. It was bad policy, the thinking went, to significantly change how the military ran its own house. As one GOP member of Congress later anonymously responded to a *National Journal* Congressional Insiders Poll, "The military has its hands full fighting terror. *Doesn't need the distraction of social engineering"* (emphasis added) (Cohen and Bell 2010).

Given the Senate gauntlet and Republican opposition, legislative vehicles that could attract at least a few Republicans became very attractive. The NDAA fit the bill. A NDAA had never failed to pass in the previous forty-eight years. The NDAA was a strong congressional institution, less likely to get mired in partisan conflict and the growing polarization of Congress. And this particular defense authorization contained a 1.4 percent pay raise for troops and increases in housing and subsistence allowances (Donnelly and Oliveri 2010; Shogan 2012).

If Skill Matters, So Does Miscalculation

But then – despite repeal being primed for success – the effort fell apart. Until this point the leading proponents of repeal on Capitol Hill – Sen. Carl Levin, Sen. Joe Lieberman, and Rep. Patrick Murphy – displayed considerable skill. They finessed how the president and the Pentagon had abruptly turned repeal into an open-ended process. In doing that they subtly changed the relationship between the Pentagon and congressional advocates of repeal. They embedded the formal delegation to the Pentagon inside must-pass military funding – all the more urgent because the United States was fighting two wars.

To be sure, the NDAA did not have special "fast-track" protection against filibusters – in the way, for instance, that free trade legislation does. But did it need such protection? Looking around the Senate, Sens. Levin and Lieberman could see relatively moderate Republican Senators who seemed sure to vote for NDAA 2011, including their Armed Services Committee colleague, Sen. Susan Collins (R-ME).

Yet Senate Democrats overloaded the NDAA with nongermane provisions. Also, they procedurally overplayed their hand, causing Sen. Collins to abruptly walk away from the repeal. On September 21, 2010, the Majority Leader presided over a cloture vote for NDAA 2011. By then the NDAA had two additional items tacked onto it, in addition to DADT repeal (which was perfectly germane, since DADT had been initially enacted through NDAA 1994). NDAA 2011 (the Senate version) had immigration legislation in the form of the DREAM Act, a bipartisan bill that provides a way for minors brought by undocumented parents into the United States to become citizens. Also, the bill had a prohibition on secret holds that had been developed by Sen. Ron Wyden (D-OR) and Sen. Claire McCaskill (D-MO), and that seemed to enjoy wide support in the Senate.

Thus NDAA 2011 at this point – that is, September 2010 – had a mix of germane and nongermane, controversial and seemingly uncontroversial provisions. To protect this legislative contrivance, so that it might all work, the Senate majority leader "filled the amendment tree." This is a maneuver in which the majority leader exploits the majority leader's right of first recognition to unilaterally fill in all of the available amendment opportunities that are attached to the measure that is up for a cloture vote. Filling the tree has many tactical uses. One of them is to make the most of an anticipated supermajority in favor of cloture (Rybicki 2010).

But filling the tree was polarizing – and Sen. Reid surely knew that. Why did Reid risk the polarization? One possibility is that he simply had less time to do his leadership job. He faced a very arduous reelection fight in his home state, Nevada. A Tea Party candidate, Sharon Angle, was putting him to a severe test. Reid no longer had the same time and energy to give to quiet bargaining that he had enjoyed earlier in the 111th Congress (Friel 2010). So Reid and his Senate colleagues took the risk that they could get what they wanted from NDAA 2011 without time-consuming bargaining that they really could no longer afford.

But no sooner than Sen. Reid called the cloture vote than he received bad news straight from the floor. Sen. Susan Collins stated that she very strongly supported DADT repeal. She had been the only Republican on the Armed Services Committee to vote for NDAA 2011. But filling the tree deprived her of opportunities for amendment votes that she wanted (and presumably thought that she needed, either to mend fences with her colleagues, or for credit-claiming in her state, or both).

Perhaps, too, Sen. Collins was irritated by a widely publicized pro-repeal rally in her home state of Maine. The national spotlight shone on Collins thanks to the celebrity singer, Lady Gaga, who appeared in Portland on September 20. Lady Gaga called on Collins and her similarly moderate Republican colleague, Sen. Olympia Snowe (R-ME), to vote for repeal. It seems safe to assume that Collins or Snowe hardly wanted the appearance, among Maine Republican and conservative Democratic voters, of doing Lady Gaga's bidding.

If Collins would not vote for cloture then certainly *other* possible swing votes – Sen. Scott Brown (R-MA) and Sen. Snowe – would not vote for it either. Sen. Levin sought to persuade the moderate Republicans that nothing would be lost by voting for cloture – politically useful changes could be made to the bill later (presumably in conference). But in the end, two Arkansas Democrats, Mark Pryor and Blanche Lincoln, joined Sen. Collins and all of the other Republicans. The cloture vote failed 56–43 (Donnelly 2010, 2232). Sen. Reid was among the 43. (Murkowski was not present.) This tactic – available to Reid as Majority Leader – saved NDAA 2011 for later, presumably the lame-duck session after the elections, since Reid's "no" vote meant that he reserved the right to hold another vote on the motion for cloture. But the prospects of DADT repeal – seemingly bright before the cloture vote – now were much dimmer. Richard Socarides, former President Clinton's adviser for gay rights, called the failed cloture vote "a political train wreck" (Bangor Daily News 2010).

Action-Forcing Failure

Then came the shock of the 2010 off-year elections. They were a historic triumph for Republicans. The *Wall Street Journal* reported that "The drive in Congress to repeal the military's 'don't ask, don't tell' policy appears all but lost for the foreseeable future."

Asked what the White House priorities are for the coming congressional session, press secretary Robert Gibbs named four issues – tax cuts, a nuclear-arms treaty with Russia, a child nutrition bill and confirmation of Jack Lew as White House budget director. Asked why he wouldn't put gays in the military on the list, Mr. Gibbs said it looked like Republicans would block action (Meckler 2010).

Such an assessment was plausible. But it also underestimated how legislative expertise might function in the lame duck session. Majority Leader Reid could now devote *all* of his time to his Senate leadership role: he had defeated Sharon Angle in the Nevada Senate election. The Senate would also remain in Democratic control in the next Congress. Reid was hardly a lame duck majority leader.

Nonetheless, DADT repeal was competing with a very full agenda: (1) the expiration of lower income tax cuts and the estate tax repeal; (2) the expiration of the continuing resolution funding the federal government; (3) an impending 23 percent cut in Medicare physician reimbursement rates; (4) the expiration of unemployment insurance; (5) the defense authorization itself; (6) Senate ratification of a nuclear arms reduction treaty with Russia (New START); (7) renewal of an assortment of expired tax breaks, such as the research and development credit; (8) renewable energy standards for the electric grid; (9) wage parity for women; (10) food safety legislation; (11) a child nutrition bill; (12) action on the recommendations of the president's fiscal commission; (13) the DREAM act for children of undocumented immigrants; and (14) campaign finance legislation (*CQ Weekly* – In Focus 2010). That was a lot of competition. Sen. John Kerry (D-MA) was reported as saying, "I think we're going to have to kind of come to grip with the realities of how much time is left and what's real and what can really pass" (Stanton and Hunter 2010).

Given such a truly crowded agenda, what happened next was quite shocking. But it might well be seen as a clever move by Sen. Reid to force action. Several strong signals informed Reid that DADT repeal would happen in the lame duck session *even if* a second cloture vote on NDAA 2011 failed.

To be sure, there is no direct evidence of such tactical sophistication. But there is nonetheless a plausible case that Reid grasped the subtle uses of apparent failure. If he went ahead with the cloture vote he and his colleagues would get political credit for trying one last time to enact the DREAM Act, which was still attached to NDAA 2011. Also, everyone invested in DADT repeal would grasp that the repeal really had to be hived off from the NDAA and enacted as a separate bill – and thus they would pour themselves into that task. Since there were other controversial items in the NDAA (such as funds for abortions at military hospitals), NDAA would also be quickly adjusted in committee, in negotiation between Sen. Carl Levin and Sen. John McCain, the ranking member. The 111th Congress would thus end with a successful NDAA as well.

On December 9, Sen. Reid sought to break the filibuster of NDAA 2011 a second time, and again he procedurally shielded the bill from amendment. Startled by the news that Reid was doing this, Sen. Collins rushed to the chamber and pleaded with Reid to postpone the vote. She pointed to the progress that had been made by both sides on what amendments would in fact be allowed. There was no need to risk failure. Reid, in response, said that it was time to act given how full the overall agenda of the lame duck session was. He had a point. Collins's plan for amending NDAA would have to be adjusted in the House or conferenced.

But the cloture vote failed *again*, 57–40 (although this time Collins voted for cloture despite her open frustration with Reid.) *Stars and Stripes* reported the bad news on December 9: "*gay rights advocates ... may have to wait years for another chance* [emphasis added] ... House Republicans, who will take over as the majority party next month, have already voiced their opposition to allowing openly gay troops to serve in the ranks, and Senate Republicans will also see their numbers increase next year" (Shane 2010b).

Gay rights advocates and sympathetic observers were now deeply uncertain about the quest for military reform. Ari Shapiro, NPR White House reporter, recalled, "everybody I talked to – from activists to Capitol Hill staffers – can describe the moment they knew 'don't ask, don't tell' would never be repealed" (NPR Weekend Edition 2010). The director of Servicemembers United, Alex Nicholson, wrote in his memoir of the DADT repeal struggle, "We were finally at the end of our rope. The following week was the only week left in the year before the week of Christmas, and if it didn't get done that week, it just wasn't going to happen" (Nicholson 2012, 242). Even Sen. Collins was downbeat. "'I'm sad to say I think the chances are very slim for getting it through,' Ms. Collins acknowledged an interview after the vote" (Steinhauer 2010).

But in fact a stand-alone repeal was quickly forming. Anticipating the scheduled release of the Defense Department report on readiness for repeal, Sen. Lieberman and Sen. Collins called for the report's release on November 15 (Brady 2010b). On November 18, Lieberman announced that he had identified a sixty-vote majority for repeal (Brady 2010c). Then, on November 30, the Defense Department issued its much-anticipated report. The report led to an early-December bout of intense engagement by military leaders with the legislative process.

The Top Brass Gets Drawn In

The report that the Pentagon released on November 30, 2010, resulted from an unprecedented internal effort by America's military leaders to assess whether – in the midst of two wars – the U.S. armed forces could transition into what I have called a "rainbow" military. The assessment was clear: all of the evidence gathered by the CRWG showed that the services could adjust to repeal.[2]

The Senate Armed Services Committee convened a public hearing on December 2 to discuss the report and its implications. At it Secretary Gates called for DADT repeal before the end of the year. Admiral Mullen was actually eloquent in his call for the repeal of DADT: "Back in February when I testified ... I said that I believed the men and women of the armed forces could accommodate ... a change, but I did not know it for a fact. Now I do. *So what was my personal opinion is now my professional opinion*" (emphasis added) (Lee 2013, 305). Thus the process that congressional Democrats, the White House, and the Pentagon set in motion in May led by December to a strong pro-repeal signal. Everyone knew that a report would come during the lame duck session – and many suspected that it would break any legislative log jam. As *CQ Weekly*'s reporter, John Donnelly, wrote after the failed September cloture vote:

there are ... reasons to think the Senate will find a way to pass the measure later this year ... By December, the Pentagon will have completed its review of the effect that a repeal of 'don't ask, don't tell' would have on the military. If the review finds no serious obstacles, it would strengthen Democrats' position (Donnelly 2010, 2232).

When the report actually came it sent a very clear message – that the Pentagon is ready – and that signal in turn was strongly amplified by Secretary Gates and Admiral Mullen.

In the wake of the December 2 hearings key Republicans began to speak in favor of repeal. Just after the Gates-Mullen testimony, it was clear that Sen. Scott Brown would eventually vote for repeal:

I pledged to keep an open mind about the present policy on Don't Ask Don't Tell. Having reviewed the Pentagon report, having spoken to active and retired military service members, and having discussed the matter privately with Defense Secretary Gates and others, I accept the findings of the report and support repeal based on the Secretary's recommendations that repeal will be implemented only when the battle effectiveness of the forces is assured and proper preparations have been completed (Sargent 2010b).

Sen. Lisa Murkowski (R-AK) also expressed support,

After reviewing the DOD report and the testimony before the Senate Armed Services Committee by Defense Secretary Gates and Chairman of the Joint Chiefs of Staff Admiral Mullen, I have concluded that it is time to repeal the "Don't Ask, Don't Tell" law ... under current law gay and lesbian service members may speak about their sexual orientation only at the risk of being discharged from performing the duties they have trained hard to carry out. ... I agree with Defense Secretary Gates' view that the military can successfully implement a repeal of the "Don't Ask, Don't Tell" law provided that proper preparations are implemented (Sargent 2010a).

Similarly, Sen. Olympia Snowe stated, "After careful analysis of the comprehensive report compiled by the Department of Defense and thorough consideration of the testimony provided by the Secretary of Defense, the Chairman of the Joint Chiefs of Staff and the service chiefs, I support repeal of the 'don't ask, don't tell' law" (Metzler 2010).

When the cloture vote failed seven days after the December 2 SASC hearing, the Secretary of Defense publicly requested repeal before the end of the 111th Congress. Secretary Gates seized on the remote possibility of DADT's *judicial* invalidation to urge that Congress assure that the Pentagon's own process would continue to proceed smoothly.

Here the clock needs to be turned back just a bit to appreciate what Gates was doing. On September 9, a pro-GOP gay rights group, Log Cabin Republicans, succeeded in winning a constitutional ruling against "Don't Ask, Don't Tell" from the federal district court for the central district of California. The judge then enforced the ruling worldwide on October 12 – and for a few days, until October 20, DADT was actually abolished by judicial fiat until the Ninth Circuit Court of Appeals stayed the order in response to an emergency appeal by the federal government (Garamone 2010; Miles and Garamone 2010).

Thus, in December, there was a possibility in the air: the famously liberal Ninth Circuit *might* uphold the district court injunction. This prospect hung over the lame duck session – and had implications for Congress failing to act.

Gates used this contingency to reinforce his earlier testimony to the Senate Armed Services Committee:

I believe this is a matter of some urgency because, as we have seen this past year, the federal courts are increasingly becoming involved in this issue. Just a few weeks ago, one lower-court ruling forced the Department into an abrupt series of changes. ... It is only a matter of time before the federal courts are drawn once more into the fray, with the very real possibility that this change would be imposed immediately by judicial fiat – by far the most disruptive and damaging scenario I can imagine, and the one most hazardous to military morale, readiness and battlefield performance. Therefore, it is important that this change come via legislative means – that is, legislation informed by the review just completed. What is needed is a process that ... carries the imprimatur of the elected representatives of the people of the United States. *Given the present circumstances, those that choose not to act legislatively are rolling the dice that this policy will not be abruptly overturned by the courts* [emphasis added] (Capehart 2010).

All the Pieces Suddenly Fall Into Place

On the heels of the second failed cloture vote of December 9, "Sen. Joseph Lieberman (I-Conn.) and Collins called a news conference and announced they would introduce stand-alone 'Don't Ask, Don't Tell' legislation – a move seen by many as a 'Hail Mary' pass to make repeal happen before the end of the year" (Johnson 2010). But their effort was hardly a "Hail Mary" pass – that is, a long shot lofted high on a wing and a prayer. Sen. Brown, Sen. Murkowski, and Sen. Snowe had already revealed that they supported DADT repeal. Moreover, the Senate Minority Leader, Sen. Mitch McConnell (R-KY), was quietly releasing any Republicans who wanted repeal. He would not whip a stand-alone bill. Finally, a small business bill was available in the House for quick passage. It had been conferenced but not revoted. Therefore, its original language could be stripped out and the DADT repeal language from NDAA 2011 added to the bill in its place. The procedural benefit of this maneuver was that no conference on the DADT repeal language would be necessary as a result. Majorities in both chambers could pour the wine of DADT repeal into the identical small business bottles that were available (Titus 2011–12; Science Business 2010; GovTrack.us).

The House votes took place on Wednesday, December 15 – over Republican protests about the amendment procedure and the wisdom of acting to repeal DADT during two simultaneous wars. Here the GOP could point to testimony that came immediately after the December 2 testimony before the Senate Armed Services Committee. The Secretary of Defense and Admiral Mullen called on December 2 for repeal. But on December 3, the service chiefs, when they went to Capitol Hill, revealed that they worried about frictions among personnel, despite the CRWG report. Also, on December 14, the Marine Corps Commandant spoke out against repeal. This difference in military views provided the GOP with talking points. Nonetheless, the vote on the rule passed comfortably, 232–180. Later that day, after a second impassioned debate, the vote on final passage was 250–175. The Pentagon promptly issued a statement calling on the Senate to act.

On Saturday, December 18, on the other side of the Capitol, Senate Majority Leader Reid called for a cloture vote on the identically amended small business bill that now carried DADT repeal. That vote passed 63–33. The Republicans voting with Sen. Susan Collins to proceed to a final vote on the stand-alone repeal bill were Sens. Scott Brown (R-MA), Mark Kirk (R-IL), Lisa Murkowski (R-AL), Olympia Snowe (R-ME), and George Voinovich (R-OH). Then, on final passage later in the day, Sen. Richard Burr (R-NC) and Sen. John Ensign (R-NV) joined these Republicans. That vote was 65–31.

Although he did not speak on the floor, Sen. Kirk issued a statement:

I very carefully read the Joint Chiefs of Staff report [sic] and met at length with Chief of Naval Operations, Admiral Gary Roughead. Following their exhaustive and considered military judgment, I support the Joint Chief's recommendation to implement the repeal of the current policy once the battle effectiveness of the forces is certified and proper preparations are complete . . . the Constitution charges the Congress with setting military policy and the Executive branch with implementing it. The legislation containing the recommendations of the Joint Chiefs of Staff will remove the various orders of conflicting and uncertain court litigation from our military, allowing uniformed leaders to once again effectively manage our national defense. As a 21-year Navy Reserve officer, I believe it is important for military leaders, not federal judges, to run our armed forces (*Illinois Review* 2010).

Sen. John Ensign's vote on final passage had been foreshadowed by a mid-November statement that he would be guided by the CRWG report (Johnson 2010). Burr, also a final passage vote for repeal, released a statement just after Christmas saying that he had concerns over "timing" but that repeal was "the right thing to do" (Burr 2010). Only Voinovich kept quiet altogether; he was retiring from the Senate once the 111th Congress adjourned.

On December 22, President Obama signed the repeal at a jubilant ceremony at the Department of the Interior, with Sen. Susan Collins standing prominently by his side. Obama then gave extended and moving remarks on the bill's significance. The president sketched vignettes of exceptional combat bravery by gay soldiers. Indeed, soldiers with non-straight sexual orientation had fought for America since the Revolution: "There can be little doubt there were gay soldiers who fought for American independence, who consecrated the ground at Gettysburg, who manned the trenches along the Western Front, who stormed the beaches of Iwo Jima. Their names are etched into the walls of our memorials. Their headstones dot the grounds at Arlington" (Parrish 2010).

Lessons of DADT Repeal

Observers of the DADT repeal process have been struck by how much it went down to the wire (Frank 2013, 203; Nicholson 2012, 242). Given that the prospect of failure seemed so palpable in the aftermath of the December 9 cloture vote, what made the legislation salvageable? Why did the principals in the drama redouble their efforts and throw themselves into a stand-alone bill? They might have given up and concluded, with varying degrees of resignation, regret, or remorse, that they would bide their time until a "policy window" opened again at some point. But they did not. Why?

One subtle lesson of the case is that parliamentary skill induces further displays of such skill – and it can dissolve legislative obstructionism just enough for remarkably difficult reform to happen. Repeal proponents in Congress showed great flexibility in responding to the very strong procedural preferences of the Pentagon and the president. By May, 2010, through bargaining with the White House and the Pentagon, they locked in a process that was certain to deliver a very strong pro-repeal signal from the military.

Parliamentary skill was not smoothly supplied, error-free, as the tale of overloading NDAA 2011 shows. But skill and dexterity were essential to the forging of the congressional partnership with the Pentagon – and that partnership, in turn, was so attractive during the lame duck session that it induced a final, decisive supply of yet more finesse. The timely ramping up of energy and ingenuity made repeal happen before the policy window really finally snapped shut. The imposing alliance that had been forged with the Pentagon also critically weakened the solidity of GOP opposition in the Senate, and brought over Republican senators willing to place policy goals ahead of party cohesion and discipline.

To be sure, many other factors were at work in the repeal of DADT. The story is just as conjunctural as all "Congress makes a law" stories. Also, the lame-duck session of the 111th Congress was unusually productive; members of Congress were in a mood to get things done (Franke-Ruta 2010).

But this case study does underscore that congressional problem-solving and good public policy are perfectly possible in a polarized age *so long as Congress continues to attract political talent.* Congress's attraction for ambitious and talented professional politicians is not likely to decline so long as it provides careers and is not hampered by term limits. Moreover, as Mayhew has shown, the separation of powers underwrites the attractiveness of Congress for adroit and determined politicians (Mayhew 2000, chs. 1 and 6).

As for Kingdon's "policy windows" framework, it has an inarticulate predicate which this case study has made explicit. Again, it is the supply of legislative skill at a fairly high baseline level. So long as Congress has enough people in it with such skill, and 'a subset with very high levels of it, then Kingdon's approach will continue to have analytic value.

Notes

1. Aaron Belkin of The Palm Center (www.palmcenter.org/), Nathaniel Frank (www.un friendlyfire.org/), and Matt Gagnon (http://pinetreepolitics.bangordailynews.com/

author/mattgagnon/) kindly discussed the politics of DADT repeal with me. Charles Stevenson taught me much about the history of congressional stances toward military personnel policies, as did David Burrelli of the Congressional Research Service. Craig Volden raised a very useful question about one of the critical roll-call votes described here. None of them, however, is responsible for any mistakes in this analysis. One further acknowledgement: in addition to the references listed at the back, the Congressional Record, GovTrack.us, Congress.gov, Thomas.gov and Wikipedia were essential resources. (On Wikipedia as an "open source" data source, see Brown 2011.) So were http://dadtarchive.org/, built by the now defunct Servicemembers United but still under maintenance, the OutServe-Servicemembers Legal Defense Network (SLDN) site, www.sldn.org/pages/about-dadt1, and the Defense Department website, www.defense.gov/home/features/2010/0610_dadt/.

2. This assessment is based on Hillman 2013; Lee 2013.

References

Arnold, R. Douglas. 1990. *The Logic of Congressional Action*. New Haven, CT: Yale University Press.

Bailey, Beth. 2013. "The Politics of Dancing: 'Don't Ask, Don't Tell,' and the Role of Moral Claims." *Journal of Policy History* 25 (Winter): 89–113.

Baker, Peter. 2010. "'Gibbs-Gate': 16 Words Can Be a Big Issue in Politics." *New York Times*, July 17. www.nytimes.com/2010/07/18/weekinreview/18baker.html?_r=0.

Bangor Daily News. 2010. "Collins Says No, and 'Don't Ask' Stalls in Senate." September 21. http://bangordailynews.com/2010/09/21/politics/collins-says-no-and-dont-ask-stalls-in-senate/.

Barnes, James A. 2010. "Insiders Split on Prospects for Deficit Reduction, DADT Repeal." *National Journal/Hotline on Call*, December 2.

Belkin, Aaron. 2008. "'Don't Ask, Don't Tell' – Does the Gay Ban Undermine the Military's Reputation?" *Armed Forces & Society* 34 (January): 276–91.

   2012. *How We Won: Progressive Lessons from the Repeal of "Don't Ask, Don't Tell."* revised ed. New York: Huffington Post Media Group.

Benen, Steve. 2009. "Political Animal: Patrick Murphy Steps Up on DADT." *Washington Monthly*, July 8. www.washingtonmonthly.com/archives/individual/2009_07/018984.php.

Bérubé, Allan. 1990. *Coming Out Under Fire: The History of Gay Men and Women in World War Two*. New York: The Free Press.

Brady, Jessica. 2010a. "DADT Hits Senate Roadblock." *Roll Call*, December 9. www.rollcall.com/news/-201349-1.html.

   2010b. "Lieberman, Collins Urge Early Release of DADT Review." *Roll Call*, November 15. www.rollcall.com/news/-200554-1.html.

   2010c. "Lieberman Predicts DADT Repeal in Lame Duck." *Roll Call*, November 18. www.rollcall.com/news/-200755-1.html.

Brown, Adam R. 2011. "Wikipedia as a Data Source for Political Scientists: Accuracy and Completeness of Coverage." *PS: Political Science & Politics* 44 (April): 339–43.

Burden, Barry C. 2011. "Polarization, Obstruction, and Governing in the Senate." *The Forum* 9 (4), Article 4.

Burr, Richard Senator. 2010. "Burr Statement on Repeal of Don't Ask Don't Tell." December 28. www.burr.senate.gov/public/index.cfm?FuseAction=PressOffice.Press Releases&ContentRecord_id=2de886cf-a3f5-b63a-85b2-c6a8f50ecd2a.

Burrelli, David F. 2010. "'Don't Ask, Don't Tell': The Law and Military Policy on Same-Sex Behavior." CRS Report for Congress. Congressional Research Service. October 14.

Burstein, Paul. 2003. "Is Congress Really for Sale?" *Contexts* 2 (3): 19–25.

Capehart, Jonathan. 2010. "Post-Partisan: Sec. Gates's Blunt Message to the Senate and Sen. McCain." *Washington Post*, November 30. http://voices.washingtonpost.com/postpartisan/2010/11/sec_gatess_blunt_message_to_th.html.

Cohen, Richard E., and Peter Bell. 2010. "Congressional Insiders Poll." *National Journal Magazine*, February 13.

CQ *Weekly* – In Focus. 2010. "Lame Duck Outlook: Many Issues, Little Resolution." CQ *Weekly*, November 15, p. 2654.

Democratic Party Platforms. 2008. "Democratic Party Platform." August 25. Online by Gerhard Peters and John T. Woolley, The American Presidency Project www.presidency.ucsb.edu/ws/index.php?pid=78283.

Desch, Michael C. 1999. *Civilian Control of the Military: The Changing Security Environment*. Baltimore, MD: Johns Hopkins University Press.

Donnelly, John M. 2010. "Authorization, 'Don't Ask' Repeal Blocked." CQ *Weekly*, September 27, p. 2232. http://library.cqpress.com/cqweekly/weeklyreport111-000003740702.

Donnelly, John M., and Joanna Anderson. 2010. "Hill Advances 'Don't Ask' Repeal." CQ *Weekly*, May 31, pp. 1338–39. http://library.cqpress.com/cqweekly/weeklyreport111-000003675755.

Donnelly, John M., and Frank Oliveri. 2010. "Defense Authorization May Be Doomed." CQ *Weekly* – Weekly Report/Defense, December 13, p. 2869.

Eleveld, Kerry. 2010. "Daily News." Advocate.com, February 10. www.advocate.com/news/daily-news/2010/02/10/gay-group-pushes-new-repeal-plan?page=0,1.

Federal News Service. 2010. Hearing of the Senate Armed Services Committee. February 2. www.defense.gov/qdr/HEARING_OF_THE_SENATE_ARMED_SER VICES_COMMITT1.pdf.

Frank, Nathaniel. 2009. *Unfriendly Fire: How the Gay Ban Undermines the Military and Weakens America*. New York: St. Martin's Griffin/Thomas Dunne Books.

——— 2013. "The President's Pleasant Surprise: How LGBT Advocates Ended Don't Ask, Don't Tell." *Journal of Homosexuality* 60 (February): 159–213.

Franke-Ruta, Garance. 2010. "The Most Productive Lame Duck since WWII – and Maybe Ever." December 22. www.theatlantic.com/politics/archive/2010/12/the-most-productive-lame-duck-since-wwii-and-maybe-ever/68442/.

Friel, Brian. 2010. "Senate Battles Become Reid's Game of Inches." CQ *Weekly* – In Focus. August 2, p. 1852.

GAO. 2005. United States Government Accountability Office. Report to Congressional Requesters. "Military Personnel: Financial Costs and Loss of Critical Skills Due to DOD's Homosexual Conduct Policy Cannot Be Completely Estimated." February.

Garamone, Jim. 2010. "Department Abides by 'Don't Ask, Don't Tell' Injunction." Armed Forces Press Service. October 14. www.defense.gov//News/NewsArticle .aspx?ID=61279.

Gates, Gary J. 2004. *Gay Men and Lesbians in the Military: Estimates from Census 2000*. Washington, DC: Urban Institute. September 28.

Gates, Robert M., Secretary of Defense. 2010. "Statement on Don't Ask, Don't Tell." February 2. www.defense.gov/speeches/speech.aspx?speechid=1419.

GovTrack.us. H.R. 2965 (111th): Don't Ask, Don't Tell Repeal Act of 2010. www.gov track.us/congress/bills/111/hr2965/text.

Hastings, Rep. Alcee, et al. 2009. Letter to the Honorable Barack H. Obama, The President of the United States. June 22. http://alceehastings.house.gov/index.php? option=com_content&task=view&id=348&Itemid=98.

Henning, Charles A. 2009. "U.S. Military Stop Loss Program: Key Questions and Answers." CRS Report for Congress. Congressional Research Service. July 10.

Hillman, Elizabeth J. 2013. "Outing the Costs of Civil Deference to the Military." *Journal of Homosexuality* 60 (February): 312–26.

Hirshman, Linda. 2012. *Victory: The Triumphant Gay Revolution – How a Despised Minority Pushed Back, Beat Death, Found Love, and Changed America for Every- one*. New York: HarperCollins.

Holley, Joe. 2008. "Charles Moskos, 74; Created the Military's 'Don't Ask, Don't Tell.'" *Washington Post*, June 4. http://articles.washingtonpost.com/2008-06-04/ news/36861032_1_military-draft-military-issues-sociology.

Hulse, Carl. 2009. "Congressional Memo: What's So Super about a Supermajority?" *New York Times*, July 1. www.nytimes.com/2009/07/02/us/politics/02cong.html? _r=0.

Illinois Review. 2010. "Don't Ask Don't Tell Passes Senate Cloture Vote; Il's Kirk and Durbin Support." December 18. http://illinoisreview.typepad.com/illinoisreview/2010/ 12/dont-ask-dont-tell-passes-senate-cloture-vote-ils-kirk-and-durbin-support.html.

James, Scott C. 1995. "A Theory of Presidential Commitment and Opportunism: Swing States, Pivotal Groups and Civil Rights under Truman and Clinton." Paper pre- sented at the Annual Meeting of the American Political Science Association.

Johnson, Chris. 2010. "Sen. Ensign to Support 'Don't Ask' Repeal." *Washington Blade*, November 18. www.washingtonblade.com/2010/11/18/sen-ensign-to-support- dont-ask-repeal-source/.

Karol, David. 2009. *Party Position Change in American Politics: Coalition Manage- ment*. New York: Cambridge University Press.

    2012. "How Does Party Position Change Happen? The Case of Gay Rights in the U.S. Congress." http://themonkeycage.org/wp-content/uploads/2012/08/Party-Position- Change-on-Gay-Rights1.pdf.

Kingdon, John W. 1984. *Agendas, Alternatives, and Public Policies*. Boston: Little, Brown.

Koger, Gregory. 2012. "The Rise of the 60-Vote Senate." *Extensions*, Winter. www.ou.edu/ carlalbertcenter/extensions/winter2012/Koger.pdf.

Korb, Lawrence J., and Alexander Rothman. 2013. "Formalizing the Ban: My Experience in the Reagan Administration." *Journal of Homosexuality* 60 (February): 273–81.

Krebs, Ronald R. 2006. *Fighting for Rights: Military Service and the Politics of Citizen- ship*. Ithaca, NY: Cornell University Press.

Krimmel, Katherine L., Jeffrey R. Lax, and Justin H. Phillips. 2012. "Gay Rights in Congress: Public Opinion and (Mis)Representation." Unpublished ms. http://kather inekrimmel.files.wordpress.com/2012/08/gay-rights-in-congress.pdf.

Kriner, Douglas L. 2010. *After the Rubicon: Congress, Presidents, and the Politics of Waging War.* Chicago, IL: University of Chicago Press.

Lee, Jonathan L. 2013. "The Comprehensive Review Working Group and Don't Ask, Don't Tell Repeal at the Department of Defense." *Journal of Homosexuality* 60 (February): 282–311.

Mayhew, David R. 2000. *America's Congress: Actions in the Public Sphere, James Madison Through Newt Gingrich.* New Haven, CT: Yale University Press.

Mazur, Diane H. 2010. *A More Perfect Military: How the Constitution Can Make Our Military Stronger.* New York: Oxford University Press.

Meckler, Laura. 2008. "Drive to Repeal 'Don't Ask' Policy All But Lost for Now." *Wall Street Journal*, November 8. http://online.wsj.com/article/SB100014240527 48703856504575600851961320666.html?mod=wsj_valettop_email.

Metzler, Rebekah. 2010. "Snowe pledges support for 'don't ask' repeal." *Maine Sunday Telegram*, 15 December. www.pressherald.com/Snowe-pledges-support-for-dont-ask-repeal.html.

Miles, Donna, and Jim Garamone. 2010. "Appeals Court Issues Stay on 'Don't Ask' Order." Armed Forces Press Service. October 21. www.defense.gov//News/News Article.aspx?ID=61359.

Murphy, Patrick J., with Adam Frankel. 2008. *Taking the Hill: From Philly to Baghdad to the United States Congress.* New York: Henry Holt and Company.

Neff, Christopher L., and Luke R. Edgell. 2013. "The Rise of Repeal: Policy Entrepreneurship and Don't Ask, Don't Tell." *Journal of Homosexuality* 60 (February): 232–49.

Nichols, David A. 2007. *A Matter of Justice: Eisenhower and the Beginning of the Civil Rights Revolution.* New York: Simon & Schuster.

Nicholson, Alexander. 2012. *Fighting to Serve: Behind the Scenes in the War to Repeal "Don't Ask, Don't Tell."* Chicago, IL: Chicago Review Press.

NPR Weekend Edition. 2010. "Obama Closes Lame-Duck Session with Victories." December 25. www.npr.org/2010/12/25/132324254/Obama-Closes-Lame-Duck-Session-With-Victories.

O'Keefe, Ed. 2010. "Federal Eye: Obama's Letters Supporting 'Don't Ask, Don't Tell' Repeal." *Washington Post*, May 24. http://voices.washingtonpost.com/federal-eye/2010/05/obamas_letters_supporting_dont.html.

OutServe-SLDN. 2008. "Chairman of the Joint Chiefs Tells Cadets Military Ready to Accept Gay Service Members." May 6. www.sldn.org/news/archives/chairman-of-the-joint-chiefs-tells-cadets-military-ready-to-accept-gay-serv.

Parrish, Karen. 2010. "Cheers, Applause Accompany 'Don't Ask' Repeal Signing." American Forces Press Service. www.defense.gov/news/newsarticle.aspx?id=62216.

Pilkington, Ed. 2011. "Sailors Share U.S. Navy's First Official Gay Kiss." *The Guardian*, December 23. www.guardian.co.uk/world/2011/dec/23/sailors-us-navy-gay-kiss.

Republican Party Platforms. 2008. "Republican Party Platform." September 1. Online by Gerhard Peters and John T. Woolley, The American Presidency Project. www.presidency.ucsb.edu/ws/index.php?pid=78545.

Rybicki, Elizabeth. 2010. "Filling the Amendment Tree in the Senate." www.apsanet.org/~lss/Newsletter/jan2010/Rybick.pdf.

Rundquist, Barry S., and Thomas M. Carsey. 2002. *Congress and Defense Spending: The Distributive Politics of Military Procurement.* Norman: University of Oklahoma Press.

Sargent, Greg. 2010a. "The Plum Line: Lisa Murkowski's Statement on DADT." *Washington Post,* December 8. http://voices.washingtonpost.com/plum-line/lisa-murkowskis-statement-on-d.html.

———. 2010b. "The Plum Line: Scott Brown Comes Out in Favor of DADT Repeal." *Washington Post,* December 3. http://voices.washingtonpost.com/plum-line/2010/12/scott_brown_comes_out_in_favor.html.

Scarborough, Rowan. 2010. "Veteran Groups Resist 'Don't Ask' Repeal." *Washington Times,* February 4. www.washingtontimes.com/news/2010/feb/4/veterans-groups-rap-push-to-end-military-gay-ban/#ixzz2TBkTXAQn.

Schickler, Eric. 2001. *Disjointed Pluralism: Institutional Innovation and the Development of the U.S. Congress.* Princeton, NJ: Princeton University Press.

Science Business. 2010. "Small Business Research Grants Reauthorized in DADT Bill." December 27. http://sciencebusiness.technewslit.com/?p=2568.

Shane, Leo III. 2010a. "DADT Repeal Clears Last Major Hurdle." *Stars and Stripes,* December 18. www.stripes.com/dadt-repeal-clears-last-major-hurdle-1.129205.

Shane, Leo III. 2010b. "'Don't Ask, Don't Tell' Repeal Effort Dies in Senate." *Stars and Stripes,* December 9. www.stripes.com/news/don-t-ask-don-t-tell-repeal-effort-dies-in-senate-1.128126.

Shanker, Thom. 2010. "Military to Revise 'Don't Ask, Don't Tell' Rules." *New York Times,* March 24. www.nytimes.com/2010/03/25/us/25military.html?_r=0.

Shogan, Colleen J. 2012. "Defense Authorization: The Senate's Last Best Hope." In Jacob R. Straus, ed., *Party and Procedure in the United States Congress.* Lanham, MD: Rowman & Littlefield.

Stanton, John, and Kathleen Hunter. 2010. "Still No Agenda for Lame Duck." *Roll Call,* November 30.

Steinhauer, Jennifer. 2010. "Senate Stalls Bill to Repeal Gay Policy." *New York Times,* December 9. www.nytimes.com/2010/12/10/us/politics/10military.html?_r=0.

Stevenson, Charles A. 2006. *Warriors and Politicians: US Civil-Military Relations under Stress.* London and New York: Routledge.

Titus, Herbert W. 2011–12. "The Don't Ask, Don't Tell Repeal Act: Breaching the Constitutional Ramparts." *William and Mary Journal of Women and Law* 18: 115–33.

United States Congress. 2010. 111th Congress, 2nd Session. S. 3453: A bill to authorize appropriations for fiscal year 2011 for military activities of the Department of Defense, for military construction, and for defense activities of the Department of Energy, to prescribe military personnel strengths for such fiscal year, and for other purposes. June 4.

———. 2010. 111th Congress, 2nd Session. S. 3065. A bill to amend title 10, United States Code, to enhance the readiness of the Armed Forces by replacing the current policy concerning homosexuality in the Armed Forces, referred to as "Don't Ask,

Don't Tell," with a policy of nondiscrimination on the basis of sexual orientation. March 3.

U.S. Naval Institute. N.d. "Key Dates in U.S. Policy on Gay Men and Women in Military Service." www.usni.org/news-and-features/dont-ask-dont-tell/timeline.

Volden, Craig, and Alan Wiseman. 2014.*The Lawmakers: Legislative Effectiveness in the United States Congress*. Cambridge University Press.

Washington Post–ABC News Poll. July 2008. www.washingtonpost.com/wp-srv/polit ics/documents/postpoll_071408.html?hpid=topnews.

Wolff, Tobias Barrington. 2011. Interview with LGBT Liaison for Obama for President Campaign, 2008. January 19. Penn Law School. Philadelphia, PA.

Zelizer, Julian. 2013. "Don't Say 'Dysfunctional Congress.'" CNN Opinion. July 15. www.cnn.com/2013/07/15/opinion/zelizer-dysfunctional-congress.

5

Who Votes for Inequality?

Nicholas Carnes[1]

In an age of soaring economic inequality, what good is our Congress? Should we expect law makers to push back against the economic and social changes that are driving wealth into fewer and fewer hands? Or do legislators have incentives to let the broadly shared prosperity America enjoyed a half century ago become the stuff of history books?

Over the last four decades, economic inequality in the United States has grown to levels not seen since the start of the last century (for useful reviews, see Bartels 2008, ch. 1; Jacobs and Skocpol 2005; Kelly 2009, ch. 1). From the 1940s to the 1970s, the incomes of the rich and the poor grew by roughly the same amount. From the 1970s on, however, the vast majority of Americans have endured tepid income growth, while the richest have enjoyed astronomical economic fortunes. Figure 5.1 plots Piketty and Saez's (2003) well-known data on the percentage of income earned by the richest 1 percent of Americans. The mid-20th-century decades of shared prosperity are over. Today, we live in what Bartels (2008) has aptly termed the New Gilded Age.

There are good reasons to be concerned about how unequal America has become: economic inequality usually spells trouble. Although we might disagree about how much inequality is "right" in some moral or normative sense, scholars who study inequality have consistently found that more unequal places are worse off on a host of objective measures of well-being. Cross-nationally, countries that are more unequal tend to have higher rates of obesity, mental illness, homicide, teen pregnancy, incarceration, drug use, and social fragmentation (for another useful review, see Wilkinson and Pickett 2011). Of course, it is difficult to know which way the causal arrow runs – economic inequality might cause other social problems, or widespread social problems might make societies more economically unequal (or both). Either way, *at best* inequality is a symptom of a larger illness; at worst, it is the disease itself. Our New Gilded Age is a serious red flag, a warning sign that

FIGURE 5.1: Income inequality in the United States.
Source: Piketty and Saez (2003); data for 1999–2011 available online from elsa.berkeley.edu/~saez/
(accessed May 20, 2013).

our social fabric is fraying in ways that could have far-reaching consequences
for the well-being of American society.

How has our legislative branch responded to accelerating inequality? For the
most part, it hasn't done much to step on the brakes. To the contrary, in many
instances, Congress has actually punched the gas pedal. It has enacted policies
that relaxed regulations on corporations and banks. It has taxed types
of income unique to the rich – in particular, money from investments and
derivatives – at lower rates than income earned the way most Americans earn
it. And it has done even more by inaction: Congress has allowed the real value
of the minimum wage to plunge to record lows (by not increasing it) and
tolerated the emergence of a quasi-legal "wealth defense industry" that fur-
nishes the super-wealthy with exotic tax dodges (by not policing it; Winters
2011, ch. 5). As economic outcomes have become more and more unequal in
the last few decades, Congress could have embarked on an ambitious reform
program to keep inequality at bay. Instead, law makers often made life easier
for wealthy Americans.

Why didn't Congress do more? Why did our legislative branch allow
inequality to reach record levels? Why didn't law makers prevent the New
Gilded Age?

To date, scholars of Congress have had surprisingly little to say about these
important questions. In general, political scientists have been less interested in

studying economic inequality than scholars in other fields.[2] Within our discipline, moreover, the scholars who have most energetically investigated inequality have seldom been experts on Congress itself.

It is high time for Congress specialists to play more of a role in the conversation. They have a lot to contribute: scholars and activists have highlighted a wide range of factors that might discourage our legislative branch from fighting inequality. Lobbyists have grown more numerous on Capitol Hill. Money has grown more important in congressional elections. Unions have declined. Political participation has become more unequal.

To date, however, there have not been many efforts to document the connections between forces like these and the decisions members of Congress make about economic inequality. Many studies in the larger literature on the politics of inequality have focused on factors such as public opinion on inequality or economic gaps in political participation and simply *assumed* that these factors influence congressional action on economic inequality. Other studies have attempted to link these kinds of inputs to economic outcomes (e.g., showing that declining rates of unionization are associated with worse economic outcomes for workers) without analyzing the legislative missing link that presumably occurs in between (e.g., without pressure from unions, law makers pass fewer pro-worker policies).

The few studies that have focused on how Congress handles economic inequality have been somewhat piecemeal. We know that legislators' class backgrounds are associated with how they voted on the Bush tax cuts (Carnes 2013, ch. 5), that the preferences of pivotal actors relative to the status quo affect the outcomes of law making on the minimum wage (Clinton 2012), and that Democrats are "cross-pressured" in ways that have complicated their positions on tax policies in the last few years (as Hertel-Fernandez and Skocpol show in Chapter 6 of this volume). But are the factors that affect how law makers handle individual issues such as taxes or the minimum wage important when law makers confront the larger set of problems and policies related to inequality? In Congress, is there a broader *politics of inequality*?

The legislative branch should be front and center in research on the role of government in economic inequality. To that end, this essay examines several potential *obstacles* to congressional action on inequality, several factors that could discourage law makers from supporting policies that would reduce the growing rich–poor gap. Most are widely believed to be responsible for Congress's tepid response to rising economic inequality, but many have never actually been shown to be associated with congressional action on this paramount social problem. Scholars and political observers often argue that Congress drags its feet on inequality because citizens don't understand inequality, because unions are weak, because businesses have sophisticated lobbyists, and so on. Activists and reformers often devote their lives to changing these aspects of our political process in the hopes of making our legislative branch more receptive to pro-equality policies. In many cases, however, the empirical evidence in support of these views is surprisingly thin.

Do the factors scholars and activists have identified really affect how legislators think or vote or advocate on issues related to economic inequality? Do they help explain why law makers haven't done more to reduce the rich–poor gap? Who exactly votes for inequality in Congress?

SIX REASONS A MEMBER OF CONGRESS MIGHT NOT CARE ABOUT INEQUALITY

Scholars have identified several social and political phenomena that might discourage law makers from getting serious about economic inequality. As I see it, six stand out as especially important (although my list is by no means exhaustive). Why hasn't Congress done more to fight inequality? There are several potential obstacles:

1. Many Americans don't realize how unequal the United States is, or they don't care.
2. The rich are more likely to participate in public affairs.
3. The rich are better able to advance their goals with organizations and lobbyists.
4. Law makers depend on wealthy campaign donors to finance their elections.
5. The parties are polarized, and Republicans oppose policies that would reduce inequality.
6. Most law makers are from the top economic strata themselves.

Each of these aspects of American political life has been carefully studied by scholars of U.S. politics. In most cases, however, scholars have never directly linked the phenomenon in question to data on how Congress handles economic inequality – they have focused on analyzing the phenomenon itself and assumed that congressional action follows, or they have focused on how the phenomenon affects congressional action on one narrow issue or policy.

Still, the circumstantial evidence is strong. There are good reasons to suspect that these six factors make it difficult for Congress to pass a wide range of policies that might reduce inequality.

1. *Many Americans don't realize how unequal the United States is, or they don't care*

To date, only a handful of scholars have given any serious thought to how legislators' choices might be influenced by the public's confusion about economic inequality. However, most Americans are confused about inequality – and the potential effects on congressional decision making are probably enormous.

In general, most citizens don't pay much attention to politics most of the time (Delli Carpini and Keeter 1996), and many are misinformed about how economic policies affect them (Bartels 2008, ch. 6). Many Americans overestimate their odds of becoming rich some day (DiPrete 2007), which dampens their support for policies that reduce inequality (Benabou and Ok 2001). Racial stereotypes and prejudices can also confound how voters think about inequality and antipoverty policy (Gilens 1999). As a result, many Americans simply don't care about rising economic inequality.

Many don't even realize how unequal the United States has become. In a recent survey, Norton and Ariely (2011) asked a representative sample of citizens to estimate the percentage of wealth that different quintiles of Americans possessed. Although the richest 20 percent of Americans have close to 85 percent of our country's wealth, the average citizen thinks that the top fifth only has around 58 percent of the money. Simply put, most Americans don't realize how wide the gulf between the rich and the poor has grown.

How, then, can they demand that members of Congress take action? Norton and Ariely (2011, 12) make exactly this point, noting that their findings help explain why "more Americans, especially those with low income, [are] not advocating ... greater redistribution of wealth." If most Americans don't know much about economic inequality, don't care much about it, or can't see the connection between inequality and economic policy, should it come as a surprise that members of Congress don't do more to curb inequality?

To date, there are no studies that directly examine the link between public opinion about inequality and how members of Congress behave in office. Public opinion scholars often speculate that mass attitudes on inequality translate into congressional action on the issue, but no study has taken the additional step of demonstrating a link between those attitudes and the choices members of Congress make. In a recent paper on the political views of the very wealthy, for instance, Page et al. (2013, 68) note that "if one accepts, at least for the sake of argument, the notion that the wealthy exert substantial political power, our findings may shed some light on the current state of American politics," but that, "Obviously, our findings regarding the policy preferences of wealthy Americans cannot, in and of themselves, provide any direct evidence that those preferences actually shape public policy." Their approach is typical of the larger literature on public opinion on inequality (e.g., Bartels 2005). Scholars routinely assume that public opinion on inequality drives legislative inaction on the issue, but to date, no one has tested this assumption with hard data on public opinion and legislative action.

Of course, the assumption seems eminently plausible. Scholars of Congress have known for decades that members make choices with an eye to how their decisions might affect them at election time (Arnold 1990; Mayhew 1974). If a legislator's constituents don't know much about inequality or don't care much about how Congress deals with it, the legislator won't have much incentive to take the problem seriously, either. Why don't members of Congress do more to fight inequality? Although it hasn't been directly tested, one of the most obvious possibilities is that their constituents simply don't care.[3]

2. The rich are more likely to participate in public affairs

Another possibility is that their *voters* don't care. Scholars who study political participation have consistently found that people who are better off are more likely to participate in politics, that is, more likely to vote, attend a political rally, keep up with the news about public affairs, and so on (Miller and Shanks 1996; Verba et al. 1995). Summarizing decades of data on numerous forms of political participation, Schlozman et al. (2005, 69) conclude that "those with high levels of income, occupational status and, especially, education are much more likely to be politically articulate." And in turn, they argue, these inequalities in participation have "unambiguous implications for what policymakers hear." As a headline on a *Slate Magazine* blog bluntly put it, "90 percent Of Life Is Just Showing Up, And The 99% Don't" (Yglesias 2011).

The fact that the rich participate more could tilt what law makers hear about economic inequality or how hard they work to address the problem. If the people who show up on election day are the ones who *benefit* from rising inequality, why would we expect members of Congress to do anything about it?

Although this explanation seems intuitive, to date scholars haven't had much luck demonstrating that inequalities in routine forms of political participation have any bearing on what members of Congress do in office. Like the literature on public opinion and inequality, the literature on political participation and inequality has generally focused on participation itself and assumed that legislative action follows, that "a shifting balance among forms of participation has implications for what and from whom the government hears" (Verba et al. 1995, 6).

The handful of studies that have attempted to go further and directly link participation to economic or political equality have produced mixed results. Cross-nationally, countries where voters turn out in larger numbers (and where, presumably, the poor are more likely to vote) tend to adopt more progressive redistributive policies (Lupu and Pontusson 2011; Mahler 2008). In the United States, however, scholars have never demonstrated a link between unequal participation and legislative action. To the contrary, the scholars who have tried have come up empty-handed. In his analysis of voting in the Senate, for instance, Bartels (2008, ch. 9) finds that inequalities in political engagement are *not* responsible for the fact that Senators are more responsive to their rich constituents. Likewise, Gilens (2012) finds that differences in education levels (a strong proxy for routine political engagement) have little bearing on whose voices actually influence public policy.

The case is far from closed, however. Scholars and activists interested in political participation routinely claim that the poor would have more of a voice if they showed up at the polls more often or paid more attention to politics. If we wish to understand why Congress has done so little to stop rising inequality, we cannot ignore the possibility that unequal participation is part of the problem.

3. The rich are better able to advance their goals with organizations and lobbyists

Another obstacle seems to be inequalities in who participates in larger organizational efforts, that is, inequalities in serious forms of collective action like social movements and interest groups (Skocpol 2003). Since the 1970s, interest groups representing corporations and businesses have become increasingly sophisticated and well funded (see Hacker and Pierson 2010). At the same time, organizations representing working people have lost ground at a steady clip. In the 1950s, roughly one in three workers in the United States belonged to a labor union. Today, less than 15 percent of Americans are in unions (Clawson and Clawson 1999; Western and Rosenfeld 2011). Although the landscape of interest group politics in the United States still includes many groups that represent the interests of middle- and working-class Americans, the well-to-do dominate the world of organized political voice. "[T]he heavenly chorus," as Schattschneier (1975, 35) noted a half century ago, still "sings with a strong upper-class accent" (see Grossman 2012; Schlozman et al. 2012).

And that accent seems to affect what law makers do. Of course, interest groups can't simply "buy" legislators' votes (despite what many citizens and advocates think). However, lobbyists and interest groups can mobilize their allies in Congress to take action on a particular bill (Hall and Wayman 1990), can make it easier for members to support certain policies by "subsidizing" the legislative work involved (Hall and Deardorff 2006), and can threaten to alert the constituents who share their views if members get out of line.

These processes probably play an important role in congressional inaction on the issue of economic inequality. Whereas the links between legislative action on inequality and public opinion or political participation have been mostly the subject of speculation, the links between lobbying and congressional inaction on inequality have been the subject of some empirical analysis. Hacker and Pierson (2010), for instance, have vividly illustrated how organized interests representing the wealthy have influenced the legislative process on issues such as tax policy, financial and business regulations, and union rights. Interest groups represent the wealthy more often than they represent the poor – and that seems to help explain why Congress hasn't done more to fight inequality.

4. Law makers depend on wealthy campaign donors to finance their elections

Likewise, the fact that law makers usually need to raise huge sums to finance their reelection campaigns is probably part of the story, too. All told, the 2012 election was the most expensive in history: federal candidates and their outside supporters spent more than $6 billion on campaigns. In the House, the average incumbent raised $1.2 million; in the Senate, incumbents raised roughly $11 million each (Center for Responsive Politics 2013).

Especially since *Citizens United*, activists and journalists have increasingly sounded warnings about how campaign finance practices affect members of Congress. Members often spend hours a day calling wealthy donors to ask for money. They attend countless fundraisers, sometimes for themselves, sometimes for their allies.

Many observers have questioned how members who are forced to raise heaps of money from wealthy donors can make unbiased decisions about the government's role in economic affairs (Lessig 2011). Some have directly implicated campaign finance in rising inequality: As Massey (2007, 185) bluntly put it, "How have policies that so obviously benefit the few been implemented and ratified in an electoral system ostensibly controlled by the many? An obvious answer is that money talks and politicians listen."

The evidence linking fundraising and legislative decision making is rapidly accumulating (e.g., Powell 2014), but to date, no studies have directly examined the claim that fundraising affects legislative action on the problem of economic inequality. However, the argument's logic is easy to understand. If law makers depend on the wealthy – the class of people who have benefited from rising inequality – to fund their campaigns, they may pick up the wealthy's attitudes, or they may underestimate how concerned their larger constituency is about inequality (e.g., Broockman and Skovron 2013). Or they may simply worry that combating inequality might alienate enough big donors to cost them the next election. Why hasn't Congress done more to fight the concentration of resources among the wealthy? One important possibility is that members depend more than ever on campaign donations from the wealthy.

5. The parties are polarized, and Republicans oppose policies that would reduce inequality

Many observers have looked to our party system to explain congressional inaction on economic inequality. In the 1970s – at around the same time that economic inequality began to creep upward – the two major parties began to diverge sharply in Congress. Over the next four decades, the ideological distance between the two parties expanded rapidly, both parties became more internally homogenous, and the dividing lines between the two parties centered more and more on economic issues (e.g., McCarty et al. 1997).

Polarization makes it harder to pass any policy in Congress, especially in the presence of supermajoritarian voting rules in the Senate and other potential choke points that effectively require bills to have large coalitions in order to succeed. The effects of polarization are often exacerbated when issues are complex and require a great deal of expertise (as Volden and Wiseman show in Chapter 2 of this volume). Passing legislation requires careful coordination by party leaders (as Sinclair shows in Chapter 3 of this volume).

Polarization makes this kind of cooperation harder – it gives both parties incentives to play chicken.

Moreover, members of Congress have polarized on economic policies, exactly the kinds of policies law makers would need to pass to respond forcefully to rising inequality. Republicans – who tend to oppose measures that would reduce economic inequality – seem to be especially committed: a small but growing body of research has found evidence of asymmetric polarization, that is, evidence that congressional Republicans have pulled to the right faster than congressional Democrats have pulled to the left (Hacker and Pierson 2006).

On this point, the evidence linking these changes to congressional decision making on inequality is more direct. McCarty et al. (2006) have carefully illustrated how polarization in Congress makes it difficult to pass laws that address economic inequality. They aren't alone in pointing to the importance of parties. As Bartels (2008, ch. 6) illustrates, economic inequality tends to grow under Republican presidents and shrink under Democrats. Why did Congress allow inequality to grow so much? One of the most well-supported hypotheses is simply that Congress is polarized and that GOP law makers are opposed to many policies that would reduce inequality.

6. *Most law makers are from the top economic strata themselves*
Last, law makers might not care much about the growing gap between the rich and the poor because law makers themselves tend to be privileged. Members of Congress have always been considerably better off than their constituents. Today, millionaires make up a majority of all three branches of the federal government – including a majority of the House and a supermajority in the Senate (Carnes 2013, ch. 1). Because law makers are on the winning end of economic inequality themselves, they may not have many personal incentives to tackle the problem in a serious way.

Scholars have long recognized that members of Congress base their choices in office on their own views and opinions, at least some of the time (Burden 2007; Jewell 1982; Kingdon 1981, ch. 10). As a result, the kinds of differences that pollsters see in public opinion – between men and women, whites and blacks, and so on – often play out in a similar fashion in our legislatures. Women tend to have more progressive views on issues related to gender equality; so do women in Congress. Black citizens tend to favor more generous social spending; so do black law makers (e.g., Berkman and O'Connor 1993; Canon 1999; Griffin and Newman 2008; Swers 2002; Thomas 1991; Whitby 1997).

The same seems to be true for class. Legislators from white-collar professions – especially those from profit-oriented jobs in the private sector – tend to vote more conservatively on economic issues, especially compared with law makers who spent time in blue-collar jobs (Carnes 2012b; 2013; see Carnes and Lupu 2013). States with more of these white-collar law makers have higher rates of economic inequality (Carnes 2013, ch. 5). Wealthier legislators are less likely to vote to repeal the estate tax (Griffin and Anewalt-Remsburg 2013). Legislators who are heavily invested in the stock market are more likely to vote to protect it (Grose 2013).

In short, there are good reasons to suspect that legislators sometimes vote with their own economic or class-based interests in mind. And in our white-collar Congress, that poses yet another potential obstacle to serious efforts to reduce economic inequality.

There are many factors that might help explain why Congress hasn't done more to fight economic inequality. Most haven't been extensively analyzed, however, at least with data on how members of Congress make decisions on a broad range of issues related to inequality. The existing literature points to many factors that *may* be discouraging Congress from dealing with economic inequality in a serious way, but many of these explanations still need to be tested.

Testing them is more than simply an academic exercise. Many activists premise their work on exactly the hypotheses outlined here. Some attempt to educate citizens about how bad inequality has gotten with white papers (Mishel et al. 2012) and viral videos (Klein 2013). Others focus on closing the gap in routine forms of political participation. Still others focus on combating biases in the organized pressure system, getting the money out of politics, or reducing polarization in Congress. A handful of us are even exploring ways to elect more working-class Americans to public office.

In short, a lot of people have a lot riding on the question of what might discourage Congress from taking economic inequality seriously. Many believe that they know the root of the problem, and many consequently invest their time and resources in reform efforts premised on the idea that some factor or set of factors is what *really* prevents Congress from taking economic inequality seriously.

But few reformers have a strong empirical basis for these beliefs. The research on the politics of inequality in Congress is thin. Few activists can say for certain whether members of Congress who *don't* suffer from the problem they are focused on actually take inequality more seriously. As it stands, there simply isn't much research linking several of the obstacles scholars and activists have identified to congressional action on inequality.

WHO SUPPORTS INEQUALITY?

If we want to know why members of Congress support or oppose policies that reduce inequality, the first step is to measure how often they do so. Collecting these data is harder than it might seem, however. Members make lots of decisions that affect economic policy – they cast votes, they sponsor bills, they serve on committees, they do work behind the scenes. Along the way, however, no one keeps track of how their choices affect economic inequality. In principle, most of the substantive legislation Congress considers probably has some effect on the distribution of wealth or income in the United States, even if only indirectly or in some small way. For the vast majority of proposals, however, no one really knows how they affect inequality – no one can really sum up how the bills a member of Congress supports and opposes collectively affect the distribution of income or wealth in this country.

We can, however, study how legislators respond to policies that are likely to significantly and directly affect economic inequality. In the last few decades, advocacy organizations have started paying closer attention to how members of Congress vote and what they do behind the scenes. Many have developed scorecards to determine who their friends and enemies are in the legislative branch. Groups that care about economic inequality are no exception. Since the 1970s, the AFL-CIO has ranked legislators based on how they vote on bills the organization deems important to the well-being of lower-income and working-class Americans.

To determine where members of Congress stood on measures that significantly affect inequality, I analyzed how members scored on a new legislative report card computed by the Institute for Policy Studies (IPS) that focuses exclusively on high-stakes legislation related to economic inequality. In October 2012, the fifty-year-old think tank released a legislative scorecard that ranked House members on how they reacted to twenty-four bills and amendments during the 2011–12 legislative session that "stand out as having tremendous impact (or potential impact) on economic inequality in America" (Anderson et al. 2012, 11). Most of the actions focused on major tax reforms (e.g., a bill to repeal the estate tax, a bill to enact the so-called Buffett Rule, a measure to extend the Bush Tax Cuts, and so on), budget proposals (e.g., the Ryan Budget), jobs and wages bills (e.g., increasing the minimum wage), anti-poverty policy, and other measures with clear implications for economic inequality. The organization also included a few items related to education, housing, and health policy. (For a complete list, see Anderson et al. 2012.) The IPS was not alone in flagging these proposals – a review of other progressive organizations' websites found that other major groups mentioned at least half of the items on the IPS scorecard as important to the future of economic inequality. In short, the IPS seems to have created a useful measure of how law makers responded to proposals that were widely believed to have serious implications for the gap between the rich and the poor.

The procedure the IPS used to compute each legislator's letter grade was fairly straightforward. On recorded votes, legislators were awarded one point for voting for a bill that would reduce inequality (or voting against a bill that would increase inequality) or penalized one point for voting to increase inequality. On bills that didn't reach a floor vote, legislators were awarded one point for sponsoring a bill that would reduce inequality, penalized one point for sponsoring a bill that would increase inequality, and awarded or penalized a half point if they simply cosponsored. The IPS then totaled each legislator's score, divided each chamber into five roughly equal-sized groups, and assigned each legislator a letter grade that reflected how much she supported or opposed economic inequality.[4] These grades did not appear to be motivated by partisan or electoral calculations – although the IPS is a progressive organization, within each party, there was considerable variation in the scores it gave to individual members.

In many respects, the IPS Inequality Report Card is an ideal resource for studying how members of Congress handle policies related to inequality. The IPS measure focused on a broad range of inequality-related policies, not just a single issue such as taxes or the minimum wage. And it focused on legislation with large and immediate implications for economic inequality – not simply economic policy more generally, which might be tapped by other common measures such as first-dimension DW-NOMINATE scores. To study congressional action on inequality, we need a measure that reflects legislators' choices on a variety of important enactments (and excludes legislators' choices on bills that have less immediate relevance to the problem of economic inequality). The IPS's scores seem to fit the bill.

Moreover, the IPS Report Card was created during the 112th Congress, a congressional term when people in and around government were paying close attention to inequality. In 2011 and 2012, the *New York Times* ran Warren Buffet's "Stop Coddling the Super-Rich" op-ed, the Occupy Wall Street protests began, and the president gave a State of the Union Address that focused centrally on economic inequality. During the 112th Congress, policy makers, activists, and citizens were more likely to be thinking about the gap between the rich and the poor – more than usual, law makers were basing their choices on their views about economic inequality.[5]

The IPS Inequality Report Card's other major advantage is that it included not just how legislators voted, but also whether they cosponsored several important bills that never reached a floor vote. Especially in the Republican-controlled 112th House, many bills with the potential to significantly reduce economic inequality never stood a chance of making it to a vote. Instead, many law makers signaled their support by cosponsoring stalled legislation. The bill to enact the so-called Buffet Rule, for instance, was never put to a vote in the House – but was cosponsored by seventy-two representatives. By including data like these, the IPS Inequality Report Card avoided some of the problems associated with simply studying roll call voting, which can miss important actions behind the scenes.[6]

Of course, there are obvious drawbacks to studying the IPS data: They don't account for issues that were never even proposed in Congress (a weightier form of agenda control than keeping a bill from a floor vote), they only cover a narrow time frame (they don't tell us anything about how legislators voted on some of the most important legislation related to inequality, such as the New Deal and Great Society programs, the 1986 Tax Reform Act, or the 2001 Bush tax cuts), and they only allow us to see differences in how members behave on the margin – if there are forces that discourage *every* member of Congress from taking inequality seriously (such as the filibuster or first-past-the-post elections), we won't be able to see them with data such as these.

Even so, the IPS Inequality Report Card gives us a straightforward way to test a variety of hypotheses about the factors that discourage members of Congress from tackling economic inequality. It gives us a valuable window into how today's Congress makes decisions on a broad range of policies that could make our country more or less unequal.

To make it easier to understand the scores, I rescaled and reverse-coded the IPS Report Card so that the values ranged from 0 to 100, with a score of 0 being equivalent to the best grade the IPS gave, an "A+," and a score of 100 being equivalent to an "F" on the IPS Inequality Report Card. I then simply examined whether the law makers who scored higher on this rescaled measure – who were *more likely* to support policies that would *increase* inequality – were also the law makers who had the qualities that scholars and activists think discourage action on inequality. Who supports inequality in Congress? Law makers whose constituents don't care much about the problem? Those who represent districts where the rich participate in public affairs at higher rates? Those who are more tightly connected to business lobbyists and less tightly connected to working-class interest groups? Those who raise more campaign money? Those who are further to the right ideologically? Those who are well-off themselves?

To determine how much each representative's constituents cared about inequality, I used a few somewhat blunt measures. Computing public opinion in congressional districts is still challenging: most nationally representative surveys don't include enough cases to calculate average opinion in such small geographic areas. As such, I relied on the only recent survey that was large enough to generate reliable district-level estimates of public opinion, the Cooperative Congressional Election Study (Ansolabehere 2012). Using the 2010 wave of the survey, I computed the average ideology of each legislator's constituents (using the standard five-point scale), their average partisanship (using the standard seven-point scale), their median household income, and their average response to a question that asked them what percentage of their state's budget deficit should be covered by spending cuts (versus increased taxes).[7] None of these was an exact measure of how much constituents cared about inequality, but they were good proxies: my findings were the same when I replicated my analysis using a question from the 2000 and 2004 National Annenberg Election Study that asked constituents whether they believed the federal government should do more to fight economic inequality. Asking citizens where they stand ideologically or what they think about taxing and spending seems to be a good way to tap into their views about economic inequality.

To test the idea that members of Congress are less concerned about inequality because wealthier Americans are more likely to participate in civic life, I used the CCES to compute the median family incomes of voters in each district and the median incomes of highly engaged citizens, who I defined as those who had done two or more of four items related to political participation in the last year: "attending local political meetings (such as school board or city council)," "put [ting] up a political sign (such as a lawn sign or bumper sticker)," "work[ing] for a candidate or campaign," or "donat[ing] money to a candidate, campaign, or political organization." If the rich participate more, do law makers pay less attention to inequality?

And what if the wealthy are better organized collectively? To determine which legislators had more to gain (or fear) from organizations representing the rich and the poor, I used the CCES to compute the percentage of constituents in each district who lived in union households, and I used data from OpenSecrets (2013) to measure the amount of money each legislator received from labor groups and, separately, from businesses groups.

Likewise, as a simple measure of which legislators raised more money, I collected data from OpenSecrets on the total amount of money each legislator raised during the 2011–12 congressional term. To measure legislators' parties and ideologies, I used Poole and Rosenthal's (2013) DW-NOMINATE data. And to measure law makers' own economic and social class backgrounds, I used data on legislators' net worths from Open-Secrets and data from my Congressional Leadership and Social Status (CLASS) dataset on the occupations legislators had before they served in Congress (Carnes 2012a).[8]

THE POLITICS OF INEQUALITY IN CONGRESS

Why doesn't Congress take rising inequality more seriously? Is it because citizens don't care? Because political activists are wealthy? Because the rich are well-organized and the poor aren't? Because the GOP has moved so far to the right? Because legislators are so rich?

Strikingly, the answer to nearly all of these questions is "yes." In Congress, the political deck is powerfully stacked in favor of economic inequality.

Law makers whose constituents cared less about inequality were less likely to fight inequality in the House. Figure 5.2 plots legislators' rescaled IPS Inequality Report Card scores against measures of how much their constituents preferred cutting government services versus raising taxes ("Constituent Preferences," top left panel), their constituents' average ideologies (top right), their constituents' average party identifications (bottom left), and their constituents' median family incomes (bottom right). In each panel, I have added separate best-fit lines for Democrats (printed dark gray and dashed) and Republicans (printed light gray and solid).

Two patterns immediately stand out in Figure 5.2. First, the two parties were separated by an enormous gulf: the average Republican in the House scored about sixty points higher on this measure of support for inequality than the

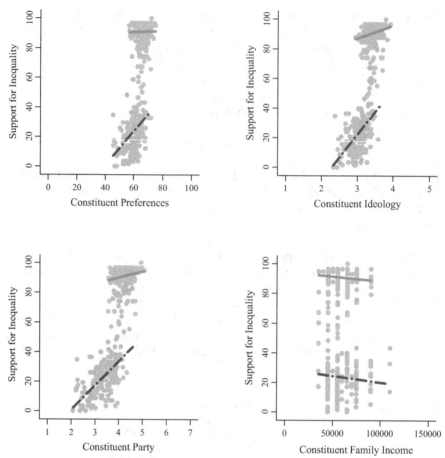

FIGURE 5.2: Support for inequality and public opinion.
Note: This figure plots legislators' Inequality Report Card scores (rescaled to range from 0 to 100, with higher values signifying greater support for policies that would increase economic inequality) against the variables in question. The figure also includes separate linear best fit lines for Democrats (dark gray, dashed) and Republicans (light gray, solid).

average Democrat. Second, within both parties, legislators who represented constituents who cared less about inequality, who were more conservative, or who were more likely to be strong Republicans were more likely to support policies that would increase inequality. This pattern was especially pronounced among Democrats – consistent with the idea that Republicans have moved further to the right and tend to vote cohesively, the Republican representatives in this sample tended to support inequality regardless of where their constituents stood on the issue. Why hasn't Congress done more to fight inequality? Part of the explanation is that the GOP almost always opposes policies that

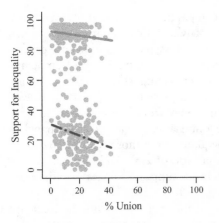
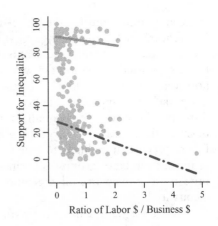

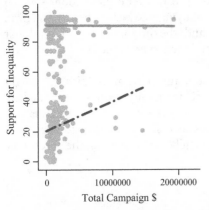

FIGURE 5.3: Support for inequality and organized influence.
Note: This figure plots legislators' Inequality Report Card scores (rescaled to range from 0 to 100, with higher values signifying greater support for policies that would increase economic inequality) against the variables in question. The figure also includes separate linear best fit lines for Democrats (dark gray, dashed) and Republicans (light gray, solid).

would reduce inequality – and congressional Democrats join in when their constituents don't care about the issue.

Data on organized groups and money in politics tell a similar story. Figure 5.3 plots representatives' inequality scores against the percentages of their constituents who live in union households, the relative amount of money they receive from organized labor and business (specifically, the ratio of the two, a simple comparison that accounts for the fact that some legislators raise more money overall[9]), and the total amount of money each legislator raised from any source during the 2011–12 campaign cycle. On most measures, Republicans are at the ceiling: regardless of who lobbies them or how much they receive, more than 90 percent of the time, the typical Republican representative supported legislation that would increase inequality. Among Democrats, however, organized influence seems to matter. Congressional Democrats are more likely to support inequality when they represent less heavily unionized districts. Those who receive half as much money from labor as they do from business (i.e., a ratio of 0.5 on the horizontal axis in the top right panel of Figure 5.3) are more likely to vote for inequality than those who receive twice as much from labor groups as businesses (a ratio of 2.0). And Democrats who raise more money overall are more likely to support policies that increase inequality.[10]

Like Figure 5.2, the data summarized in Figure 5.3 underscore the challenge pro-equality reformers face in Washington. In Congress, one party is staunchly opposed to policies that would reduce inequality, and the other party's support varies with the relative strength of grassroots pro-worker organizations – which are declining – the balance of organized lobbying – which is heavily tilted in favor of businesses and the wealthy – and the importance of high-dollar campaign donors – who are more influential than ever as the costs of congressional campaigns spiral upward.

In addition to the electoral, interest group, and partisan politics that might discourage law makers from taking economic inequality seriously, law makers also appear to have personal incentives that discourage them from taking action. Figure 5.4 plots representatives' rescaled IPS Inequality Report Card scores against data on how they earned a living before Congress (the percentage

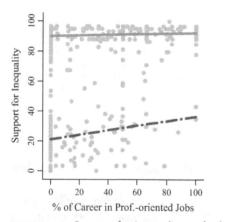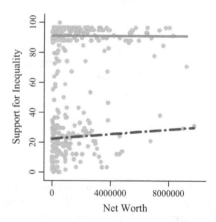

FIGURE 5.4: Support for inequality and who governs.
Note: This figure plots legislators' Inequality Report Card scores (rescaled to range from 0 to 100, with higher values signifying greater support for policies that would increase economic inequality) against the variables in question. The figure also includes separate linear best fit lines for Democrats (dark gray, dashed) and Republicans (light gray, solid).

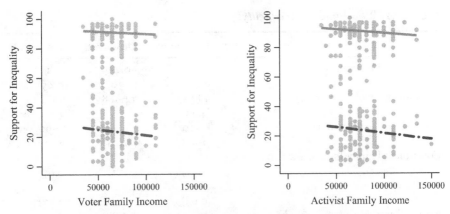

FIGURE 5.5: Support for inequality and political participation.
Note: This figure plots legislators' Inequality Report Card scores (rescaled to range from 0 to 100, with higher values signifying greater support for policies that would increase economic inequality) against the variables in question. The figure also includes separate linear best fit lines for Democrats (dark gray, dashed) and Republicans (light gray, solid).

of their career spent in profit-oriented white-collar jobs, such as running a business) and how much of a living they earned in the process (their net worth). Again, among Democrats, those who spent more of their careers running businesses and (to a lesser extent) those who made more money doing so were more likely to support legislation that would make inequality worse. Fighting inequality in Congress is truly an uphill battle: only one party will even consider laws that reduce inequality, and among those law makers, there are many factors – both external and personal – that might discourage them from taking a stand against the widening gap between the haves and the have-nots.

If there is good news in these data for people who care about reducing economic inequality, it is that gaps in routine forms of political participation seem not to be a culprit. Figure 5.5 plots rescaled IPS scores against the median family incomes of the voters and highly engaged citizens in each legislator's district. There is essentially no relationship. Although scholars often worry that unequal participation spells unequal political voice, law makers tend to vote for inequality at roughly the same rates regardless of whether lower-income citizens make up a large or small share of voters or engaged citizens. There are many factors that might discourage members of Congress from taking economic inequality seriously. The social class gap in routine political participation doesn't seem to be one of them.

Of course, many of the factors that are associated with support for inequality are correlated with one another: Republicans tend to represent more conservative districts, receive more money from business lobbyists, and spend more of their precongressional careers in profit-oriented professions. Are any of

TABLE 5.1 *Who Votes for Inequality?*

	Full Sample	Democrats	Republicans
Constituent Preferences (0 to 100)	−0.145	−0.459	−0.121
	(0.15)	(0.30)	(0.15)
Constituent Ideology (1 to 5)	9.835[*]	14.888[*]	4.902
	(4.23)	(7.06)	(4.20)
Constituent Party (1 to 7)	8.410[**]	11.042[**]	0.990
	(2.33)	(3.44)	(2.27)
Constituent Family Income (in $10k)	−1.037	−1.648	−0.916
	(0.72)	(1.23)	(0.69)
Voter Family Income (in $10k)	0.743	0.627	1.204[*]
	(0.68)	(1.19)	(0.57)
Activist Family Income (in $10k)	−0.133	0.051	−0.563[+]
	(0.34)	(0.63)	(0.32)
Unionization Rate (0 to 100)	−0.031	−0.096	−0.077
	(0.06)	(0.10)	(0.07)
Ratio of Labor $ / Business $	−4.437[**]	−5.142[**]	−2.356
	(1.47)	(1.89)	(1.59)
Total Campaign Receipts (in $1M)	0.949[**]	2.278	0.187
	(0.24)	(1.39)	(0.14)
Pct. of Career in Profit-oriented Professions	0.030[*]	0.067[+]	0.017
	(0.02)	(0.04)	(0.01)
Net Worth (in $1M)	0.003	0.019	0.000
	(0.01)	(0.05)	(0.00)
Republican (indicator)	54.677[**]	—	—
	(1.98)		
Intercept	−22.954[**]	−26.347[*]	80.068[**]
	(8.76)	(11.91)	(10.41)
N	396	169	227
R^2	0.9396	0.4635	0.1106

[+] $p < 0.10$,
[*] $p < 0.05$,
[**] $p < 0.01$, two-tailed.

the factors that seem to discourage law makers from dealing with inequality simply proxies for other important factors? Can we rule out any of these factors as duplicates of the others?

As a simple test, Table 5.1 reports the results of three regression models that relate legislators' inequality scores to the variables in Figures 5.2, 5.3, 5.4, and 5.5. In the first model, I have included the entire sample and simply added an indicator variable for Republican members. In the second and third models, I have limited my attention to Democrats and Republicans, respectively.

Nothing washes out. Each of the individual factors that seem to be associated with congressional action on inequality in Figures 5.2 through 5.5 still seems to matter when we control for all of the factors at once. Of course, big regression models like this one are risky (Achen 2005). However, in a fairly hard test – with a relatively small sample and a large number of explanatory variables – most of the patterns summarized in the figures are still evident (and at least marginally significant) in these models. The party a law maker comes from is by far the best predictor of her or his inequality score: the estimated gap between Republicans and Democrats in the first model in Table 5.1 was more than half of the possible range of the variable. However, there seems to be more to the politics of inequality in Congress than just the GOP. Law makers who worked in profit-oriented white-collar jobs tend to be less concerned about inequality, especially compared with those who worked in blue-collar jobs (a gap I omit here but explore in more detail elsewhere; see Carnes 2012b; 2013). Likewise, law makers who represented more conservative districts and who received more money from businesses and other campaign donors were more likely to support policies that would increase inequality. Of course, just as in Figures 5.2 through 5.5, these associations were generally confined to Democrats. Across the board, Republicans tended to score high on the inequality support measure.

To check the robustness of these findings, I also carried out a series of auxiliary analyses (available on request). I computed a version of the IPS scores that excluded sponsorship data (and focused only on roll-call voting) and re-ran the models in Table 5.1. I re-ran them using the IPS's raw scores (not their letter grades). I re-ran the models in Table 5.1 with additional controls for the legislator's race and gender. And to check that my findings were not somehow driven by the time period I studied – to check, for instance, that these results are not limited to periods of Republican control in the House – I analyzed how the legislators in this sample who also served during the 110th Congress (when Democrats controlled the House and Senate and a Republican was president) scored on the AFL-CIO's congressional vote scorecard (the closest thing there was to the IPS Inequality Report Card during the 110th Congress). In every case, my findings were essentially the same (though sometimes less precise): Democrats' support for economic equality tended to vary according to the views of their constituents, the strength of unions, the amount of money they raised from campaign donors, and their occupational backgrounds. Republicans tended to oppose efforts to reduce inequality regardless.

The opponents of economic inequality face a bleak outlook in the 21st-century Congress. Figure 5.6 summarizes the challenge. The figure plots the relationship between representatives' inequality scores and their first-dimension DW-NOMINATE scores, a composite measure of legislator ideology based on every vote a law maker casts. On the major legislation affecting economic inequality in the 112th Congress, Republicans of all ideological stripes tended to vote in lockstep against policies that would reduce inequality. Democrats were divided: those further to the ideological left tended to vote to reduce inequality, those further to the right tended to vote to increase it.

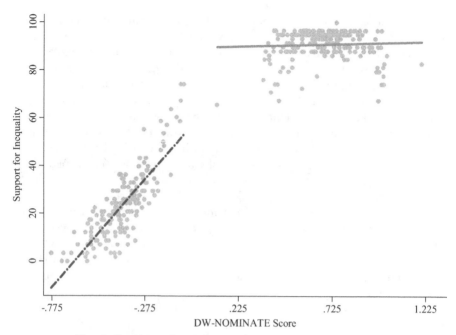

FIGURE 5.6: The challenging politics of inequality in congress.
Note: This figure plots legislators' Inequality Report Card scores (rescaled to range from 0 to 100, with higher values signifying greater support for policies that would increase economic inequality) against the variable in question. The figure also includes separate linear best fit lines for Democrats (dark gray, dashed) and Republicans (light gray, solid).

Why hasn't Congress done more to combat soaring economic inequality? Because those who oppose fighting inequality have a whole party in Congress, and those who want to reduce inequality have only part of one, when the political and personal circumstances are right.

WHAT WOULD IT TAKE TO MAKE CONGRESS CARE ABOUT INEQUALITY?

If we were to design a political institution that would prevent income and wealth from becoming extremely unequal, it probably wouldn't look much like the modern Congress. It wouldn't have ideologically polarized parties; it certainly wouldn't have one party that uniformly opposed efforts to reduce inequality. Its members wouldn't worry so much about constituents who are often confused about the links between public policy and inequality. It wouldn't be surrounded by an organized pressure system dominated by the wealthy. And it wouldn't be packed full of wealthy people itself.

For the most part, the scholars who have sounded alarms about Congress's ability to respond to rising economic inequality have been right to do so.[11] The forces that discourage our legislative branch from taking inequality seriously are considerable, and many of them are getting worse. Legislators whose constituents don't care as much about inequality (and many don't) and who are well-off themselves (and many are) are less likely to take action. Law makers are less likely to oppose inequality when they have close ties to business lobbyists (which are becoming increasingly sophisticated), when they have weak ties to grassroots organizations that represent the working class (which have been dying off for decades), and when they have to raise vast sums to fund their reelection campaigns (which they have to do more and more often). The scholars who have studied these phenomena have long speculated that they slow Congress's response to rising economic inequality. The evidence presented in this chapter suggests that those assumptions were well-founded: most of the factors scholars have been speculating about for decades are indeed strongly associated with congressional action on economic inequality.

Considered together, this set of factors helps to illustrate why simple ideas about the link between economic inequality and redistributive policy have never been borne out in the United States. In principle, we might expect rising inequality to create pressure for government redistribution (e.g., Melzer and Richard 1981): as the wealthy take home more and more of the pie, shouldn't a government by and for the typical citizen do more to redistribute income? Like many studies before it (for a useful review, see Lupu and Pontusson 2011), the theories and findings summarized in this chapter illustrate that there is more to the story. Public opinion about the link between inequality and redistributive policy is fuzzy. And other forces besides the public sway legislators, including interest groups, campaign donors, and personal motives. Against this back-drop, it is easy to see why simple ideas about how law makers might respond to rising inequality do not pan out in practice.

This isn't to say that legislators who "support inequality" want America to be more unequal. They might, but more likely, they probably simply prioritize other goals (like winning reelection) or think other problems are more import-ant than economic inequality (such as reducing the restrictions on how busi-nesses operate). Law makers have to make trade offs between competing values. Some simply may not value economic equality as much as they value other things. However, law makers probably never think to themselves, "I support economic inequality."

Still, many of them do. As inequality has crept upward over the last few decades, federal law makers have often stood by. Sometimes, the policies they have enacted have pushed inequality even higher.

Of course, Congress isn't entirely to blame. Soaring economic inequality is largely a result of changing economic circumstances: deindustrialization, glob-alization, the information revolution, and so on (Frank and Cook 1995; Free-land 2012). And Congress probably would have done more to address these forces if the political circumstances had been different. If more constituents demanded action on inequality, Congress would probably do more to reduce inequality. If more middle-and working-class Americans were engaged in collective action on behalf of their economic interests, Congress would probably do more to reduce inequality. If legislators didn't have to raise huge sums of money to hedge against the possibility of a super PAC attack – hardly a congressional creation – Congress would probably do more to reduce inequality. Most of the factors that discourage Congress from taking steps to reduce economic inequality don't originate within Congress itself.

In that sense, there is a silver lining for those who care about reducing economic inequality. Our legislative branch itself isn't the problem – it's the *inputs* into the legislative process that make it difficult for Congress to deal with inequality.

Most of the problems reformers are trying to tackle are right on the money. Americans need to understand economic inequality better. They need to organize more effectively to press their demands on their representatives. Big donors need to play a smaller role in elections. Middle- and working-class Americans need to play more of a role in government. Even groups that are working to encourage routine forms of political participation probably aren't off base: if voting or putting up yard signs are steps toward participating in larger grass-roots movements, encouraging less affluent Americans to do those things is a step in the right direction.

However, there almost certainly isn't a silver bullet – no single reform will transform Congress into an institution that works to keep inequality under control. Even if Congress were less polarized, if Americans don't care about inequality, Congress probably won't do much about it. Even if a social movement coalesces around the problem of economic inequality, Republicans in our polarized Congress probably still won't support proposals to reduce inequality. Even if we get all of the money out of Washington, if most members of Congress are millionaires, the Millionaire's Tax probably doesn't stand much of a chance. No single reform will work by itself: when there are so many factors that discourage members of Congress from addressing economic inequality, solving any one or two of them probably won't completely solve the problem. If we want Congress to get serious about inequality, we need to reduce party polarization, revive middle- and working-class civic organizations, control business lobbying, reign in big money in congressional elections, *and* transform our white-collar government into one that looks more like the country it represents. Reformers are working hard on each of these problems. If they want Congress to keep inequality in check, they'll probably have to work together.

Notes

1. I'm very grateful to Indira Dammu for research assistance, to Noam Lupu for feedback on an early draft of this essay, to the other participants in the "Congress and Public Policy in the 21st Century" conference, and to the conference's organizers, Jeffery A. Jenkins and Eric M. Patashnik.

2. For instance, from 1999 to 2011, the *American Journal of Political Science, The Journal of Politics*, and the *American Political Science Review* published just nine articles that mentioned economic inequality in their titles or abstracts (Andersen and Fetner 2008; Garand 2010; Golden and Londregan 2006; Kelly 2005; Kelly and Enns 2010; Lupu and Pontusson 2011; Solt 2008; 2011; Wallerstein 1999). During the same period, more than five times as many articles on inequality ran in the *American Economic Review, Econometrica*, the *Journal of Political Economy, The Quarterly Journal of Economics*, and *The Review of Economic Studies*.

3. This observation is consistent with Kelly's (2009) finding that macro-level shifts in the public mood engender changes in public policy related to inequality – that as the public becomes more liberal or conservative on economic issues, economic policy becomes more or less redistributive.

4. This last step did not affect the findings I report in this chapter. When I replicated my analyses using the IPS's raw scores – not their letter grades – my findings were virtually identical. For additional details about the IPS's methodology, see Anderson et al. 2012, Appendix 4.

5. Though as I note below, my findings were similar when I analyzed a similar measure – the AFL-CIO's congressional report card – during a different timeframe – the 110th Congress, when Democrats controlled both chambers, a Republican was in the White House, and inequality was far less central to the political agenda in Washington.

6. As a validity check, I also re-ran the analysis in Table 5.1 using an alternative measure based only on roll-call voting. The results – which are omitted here but available on request – were similar but somewhat less precise.

7. The question asked, "If your state were to have a budget deficit this year it would have to raise taxes on income or sales or cut spending, such as on education, health care, welfare, and road construction. What would you prefer more, raising taxes or cutting spending? Choose a point along the scale from 100% tax increases (and no spending cuts) to 100% spending cuts (and no tax increases). The point in the middle means that the budget should be balanced with equal amounts of spending cuts and tax increases. If you are not sure, or don't know, please check the box below."

8. Roughly 120 of the representatives who held office in the 112th Congress were not included in the CLASS dataset, which covers the 106th through 110th Congresses. For those legislators, I collected occupational data from the online Congressional Biographical Directory and equally weighted each type of job each legislator had before holding office. This approach doesn't seem to have affected my findings: I reached the same basic conclusions when I excluded these 120 legislators and focused only on the law makers in the CLASS dataset, for whom I have detailed, multiple-source-verified, time-weighted occupational data.

9. The results are essentially the same when I separately analyze the percentage of a legislator's total campaign receipts that come from labor groups and the percentage that come from business groups.

10. Of course, we have to be careful when interpreting results like these; the causal arrow could run both ways. The relationship between interest groups and legislators is probably more like a feedback loop: interest groups give to their allies in the legislature, who in turn remain allies – and remain in office.

11. Of course, when it comes to *non*-economic equality – issues of social and legal
equality – Congress often does better. Vallely's work in this volume on the repeal of
"Don't Ask, Don't Tell" is a case in point. And although the deck is stacked against
congressional action on economic inequality, Congress nonetheless passes pro-
equality measures from time to time. The Affordable Care Act, for instance, has
the potential to be one of the most economically equalizing bills in a generation. As
Oberlander notes in this volume, the Affordable Care Act was a rare and remarkable bill – but rare and remarkable pro-equality bills sometimes pass, even though
the deck is stacked against them.

Bibliography

Achen, Christopher H. 2005. "Let's Put Garbage-Can Regressions and Garbage-Can
Probits Where They Belong." *Conflict Management and Peace Science* 22: 327–39.
Andersen, Robert, and Tina Fetner. 2008. "Economic Inequality and Intolerance: Atti-
tudes toward Homosexuality in 35 Democracies." *American Journal of Political
Science* 52 (4): 942–58.
Anderson, Sarah, Chuck Collins, Scott Klinger, and Sam Pizzigati. 2012. "A Congres-
sional Report Card for the 99%." Institute for Policy Studies. www.ips-dc.org/files/
5290/Inequality-Report-Card.pdf (May 22, 2012).
Ansolabehere, Stephen. 2012. "CCES Common Content, 2012." http://hdl.handle.net/
1902.1/21447 (May 22, 2013). CCES [Distributor].
Arnold, R. Douglas. 1990. *The Logic of Congressional Action*. New Haven, CT: Yale
University Press.
Bartels, Larry M. 2005. "Homer Gets a Tax Cut: Inequality and Public Policy in the
American Mind." *Perspectives on Politics* 3 (1): 15–31.
  2008. *Unequal Democracy: The Political Economy of the New Gilded Age*.
New York and Princeton, NJ: Russell Sage Foundation and Princeton University
Press.
Bénabou, Roland, and Efe A. Ok. 2001. "Social Mobility and the Demand for Redistri-
bution: The POUM Hypothesis." *Quarterly Journal of Economics* 116: 447–87.
Berkman, Michael B., and Robert E. O'Connor. 1993. "Do Women Legislators Matter?
Female Legislators and State Abortion Policy." *American Politics Quarterly*
21:102–24.
Broockman, David E., and Christopher Skovron. 2013. "What Politicians Believe about
Their Constituents: Asymmetric Misperceptions and Prospects for Constituency
Control." Working paper.
Burden, Barry C. 2007. *The Personal Roots of Representation*. Princeton, NJ: Princeton
University Press.
Canon, David T. 1999. *Race, Redistricting and Representation: The Unintended Con-
sequences of Black Majority Districts*. Chicago, IL: University of Chicago Press.
Carnes, Nicholas [producer and distributor]. 2012a. Congressional Leadership and
Social Status [dataset].
  2012b. "Does the Numerical Underrepresentation of the Working Class in Congress
Matter?" *Legislative Studies Quarterly* 37 (1): 5–34.
  2013. *White-Collar Government: The Hidden Role of Class in Economic Policy
Making*. Chicago, IL: University of Chicago Press.

Carnes, Nicholas, and Noam Lupu. 2013. "Rethinking the Comparative Perspective on Class and Representation: Evidence from Latin America." Working paper.

Center for Responsive Politics. 2013. "2012 Election Spending Will Reach $6 Billion, Center for Responsive Politics Predicts." www.opensecrets.org/news/2012/10/2012-election-spending-will-reach-6.html (May 21, 2013).

Clawson, Dan, and Mary Ann Clawson. 1999. "What Has Happened to the US Labor Movement? Union Decline and Renewal." *Annual Review of Sociology* 25: 95–119.

Clinton, Joshua D. 2012. "Congress, Lawmaking, and the Fair Labor Standards Act, 1971–2000." *American Journal of Political Science* 56 (2): 355–72.

Delli Carpini, Michael X., and Scott Keeter. 1996. *What Americans Know about Politics and Why It Matters*. New Haven, CT: Yale University Press.

DiPrete, Thomas A. 2007. "Is This a Great Country? Upward Mobility and the Chance for Riches in Contemporary America." *Research in Social Stratification and Mobility* 25 (1): 89–95.

Frank, Robert H., and Philip J. Cook. 1995. *The Winner-Take-All Society: Why the Few at the Top Get So Much More Than the Rest of Us*. New York: Penguin Books.

Freeland, Chrystia. 2012. *Plutocrats: The Rise of the New Global Super-Rich and the Fall of Everyone Else*. New York: Penguin Books.

Garand, James C. 2010. "Income Inequality, Party Polarization, and Roll-Call Voting in the U.S. Senate." *Journal of Politics* 72 (4): 1109–128.

Gilens, Marin. 1999. *Why Americans Hate Welfare: Race, Media, and the Politics of Antipoverty Policy*. Chicago, IL: University of Chicago Press.

2012. *Affluence and Influence: Economic Inequality and Political Power in America*. New York and Princeton, NJ: Russell Sage Foundation and Princeton University Press.

Golden, Miriam A., and John B. Londregan. 2006. "Centralization of Bargaining and Wage Inequality: A Correction of Wallerstein." *American Journal of Political Science* 50 (1): 208–13.

Griffin, John D., and Claudia Anewalt-Remsburg. 2013. "Legislator Wealth and the Effort to Repeal the Estate Tax." *American Politics Review* 20 (10): 1–24.

Griffin, John D., and Brian Newman. 2008. *Minority Report: Evaluating Political Equality in America*. Chicago, IL: University of Chicago Press.

Grose, Christian R. 2013. "Risk and Roll Calls: How Legislators' Personal Finances Shape Congressional Decisions." Working paper.

Grossman, Matt. 2012. *The Not-So-Special Interests: Interest Groups, Public Representation, and American Governance*. Stanford, CA: Stanford University Press.

Hacker, Jacob S., and Paul Pierson. 2006. *Off Center: The Republican Revolution and the Erosion of American Democracy*. New Haven, CT: Yale University Press.

2010. *Winner-Take-All Politics: How Washington Made the Rich Richer – And Turned Its Back on the Middle Class*. New York: Simon and Schuster.

Hall, Richard L., and Alan V. Deardorff. 2006. "Lobbying as Legislative Subsidy." *American Political Science Review* 100: 69–84.

Hall, Richard L., and Frank W. Wayman. 1990. "Buying Time: Moneyed Interests and the Mobilization of Bias in Congressional Committees." *American Political Science Review* 84: 797–820.

Jacobs, Lawrence R., and Theda Skocpol. 2005. "American Democracy in an Era of Rising Inequality." In Lawrence R. Jacobs and Theda Skocpol, eds., *Inequality and*

American Democracy: What We Know and What We Need to Learn. New York: Russell Sage Foundation.

Jewell, Malcolm E. 1982. *Representation in State Legislatures.* Lexington: University Press of Kentucky.

Kelly, Nathan J. 2005. "Political Choice, Public Policy, and Distributional Outcomes." *American Journal of Political Science* 49 (4): 865–80.

2009. *The Politics of Income Inequality in the United States.* New York: Cambridge University Press.

Kelly, Nathan J., and Peter K. Enns. 2010. "Inequality and the Dynamics of Public Opinion: The Self-Reinforcing Link between Economic Inequality and Mass Preferences." *American Journal of Political Science* 54 (4): 855–70.

Kingdon, John W. 1981. *Congressmen's Voting Decisions,* 2nd ed. New York: Harper and Row.

Klein, Ezra. 2013. "This Viral Video Is Right: We Need to Worry about Wealth Inequality." *WonkBlog.* www.washingtonpost.com/blogs/wonkblog/wp/2013/03/06/this-viral-video-is-right-we-need-to-worry-about-wealth-inequality/ (May 20, 2013).

Lessig, Lawrence. 2011. *Republic, Lost: How Money Corrupts Congress – And a Plan to Stop It.* New York: Twelve.

Lupu, Noam, and Jonas Pontusson. 2011. "The Structure of Inequality and the Politics of Redistribution." *American Political Science Review* 105 (2): 316–36.

Mahler, Vincent A. 2008. "Electoral Turnout and Income Redistribution by the State: A Cross-national Analysis of the Developed Democracies." *European Journal of Political Research* 47 (2): 161–83.

Massey, Douglas S. 2007. *Categorically Unequal: The American Stratification System.* New York: Russell Sage Foundation.

Mayhew, David R. 1974. *Congress: The Electoral Connection.* New Haven, CT: Yale University Press.

McCarty, Nolan M., Keith T. Poole, and Howard Rosenthal. 1997. *Income Redistribution and the Realignment of American Politics.* La Vergne, TN: AEI Press.

2006. *Polarized America: The Dance of Ideology and Unequal Riches.* Cambridge, MA: MIT Press.

Meltzer, Allan H., and Scott F. Richard. 1981. "A Rational Theory of the Size of Government." *Journal of Political Economy* 89 (5): 914–27.

Miller, Warren E., and J. Merrill Shanks. 1996. *The New American Voter.* Cambridge, MA: Harvard University Press.

Mishel, Lawrence, Josh Bivens, Elise Gould and Heidi Shierholz. 2012. *The State of Working America,* 12th ed. Ithaca, NY: ILR Press.

Norton, Michael I., and Dan Ariely. 2011. "Building a Better America – One Wealth Quintile at a Time." *Perspectives on Psychological Science* 6 (1): 9–12.

OpenSecrets. 2013. MyOpenSecrets: Open Data. www.opensecrets.org/MyOS/bulk.php (May 22, 2013).

Page, Benjamin I., Larry M. Bartels, and Jason Seawright. 2013. "Democracy and the Policy Preferences of Wealthy Americans." *Perspectives on Politics* 11 (1): 51–73.

Piketty, Thomas, and Emmanuel Saez. 2003. "Income Inequality in the United States, 1913–1998." *Quarterly Journal of Economics* 118 (1): 1–39.

Poole, Keith T., and Howard Rosenthal. 1997. *Congress: A Political Economic History of Roll Call Voting.* New York: Oxford University Press.

2013. Voteview. www.voteview.com/ (May 22, 2013).

Powell, Eleanor Neff. 2014. *"Dollars to Votes: The Influence of Fundraising in Congress."* Working Paper.

Schattschneider, E. E. [1960] 1975. *The Semisovereign People: A Realist's View of Democracy in America*. New York: Wadsworth.

Schlozman, Kay Lehman, Benjamin I. Page, Sidney Verba, and Morris P. Fiorina. 2005. "Inequalities of Political Voice." In Lawrence R. Jacobs and Theda Skocpol, eds., *Inequality and American Democracy: What We Know and What We Need to Learn*. New York: Russell Sage Foundation.

Schlozman, Kay Lehman, Sidney Verba, and Henry E. Brady. 2012. *The Unheavenly Chorus: Unequal Political Voice and the Broken Promise of American Democracy*. Princeton, NJ: Princeton University Press.

Skocpol, Theda. 2003. *Diminished Democracy: From Membership to Management in American Civic Life*. Norman: University of Oklahoma Press.

Solt, Frederick. 2008. "Economic Inequality and Democratic Political Engagement." *American Journal of Political Science* 52 (1): 48–60.

2011. "Diversionary Nationalism: Economic Inequality and the Formation of National Pride." *The Journal of Politics* 73 (3): 821–30.

Swers, Michele. 2002. *The Difference Women Make*. Chicago, IL: University of Chicago Press.

Thomas, Sue. 1991. "The Impact of Women on State Legislative Policies." *Journal of Politics* 53: 958–76.

Verba, Sidney, Kay Lehman Schlozman, and Henry E. Brady. 1995. *Voice and Equality: Civic Voluntarism in American Politics*. Cambridge, MA: Harvard University Press.

Wallerstein, Michael. 1999. "Wage-Setting Institutions and Pay Inequality in Advanced Industrial Societies." *American Journal of Political Science* 43 (3): 649–80.

Western, Bruce, and Jake Rosenfeld. 2011. "Unions, Norms, and the Rise in US Wage Inequality." *American Sociological Review* 76: 513–37.

Whitby, Kenny J. 1997. *The Color of Representation: Congressional Behavior and Black Interests*. Ann Arbor: University of Michigan Press.

Wilkinson, Richard, and Kate Pickett. 2011. *The Spirit Level: Why Greater Equality Makes Societies Stronger*. New York: Bloomsbury Press.

Winters, Jeffrey A. 2011. *Oligarchy*. New York: Cambridge University Press.

Yglesias, Matthew. 2011. "90% of Life Is Just Showing Up, and the 99% Don't." *Slate. com*. www.slate.com/blogs/moneybox/2011/12/18/rich_people_are_politically_active .html?fb_ref=sm_fb_like_blogpost&fb_source=home_multiline (May 20, 2013).

PART III

CONGRESS AND ECONOMIC POLICY

6

Congress Makes Tax Policy

Democrats and Republicans at Two Critical Junctures

Alexander Hertel-Fernandez and Theda Skocpol[1]

Clashes over tax policy have moved front and center in U.S. politics in recent years, reaching a crescendo in the 2012 election. That contest featured debates over the number of Americans who paid no federal income tax, scrutiny of Republican presidential candidate Mitt Romney's low effective federal tax rate, and assessments of the distributional implications of tax cuts proposed in the budget championed by Republican vice presidential candidate Paul Ryan. After President Obama was reelected, Democrats and Republicans immediately went to war over the future of big tax cuts inherited from his White House predecessor, Republican President George W. Bush.

Using the unique – and temporary – leverage afforded by the legal expiration at the end of 2012 of those major tax cuts, President Obama and Congressional Democrats managed to force Congressional Republicans to accept some tax rate hikes applicable to the very wealthiest Americans, though most of the top-heavy Bush tax cuts survived. After that, however, Republicans reasserted their adamant opposition to any revenue increases. And taxes have remained a flashpoint of partisan warfare in ongoing Congressional standoffs over budgets, spending sequesters, and proposals for deficit reduction. As Republican House Speaker John Boehner declared shortly after making the deal with President Obama at the end of 2012, the President "got his tax hikes on January 1 ... talk about raising revenue is over" (Politi 2013). Senate Minority Leader Mitch McConnell reinforced the point that, from the GOP perspective, that deal was the "last word on taxes" (Kapur 2013).

How did we get here? In particular, why have Democrats had such a hard time raising revenues or restructuring the politics of tax decisions to fit their preferences for adequately funded government – even when the prevailing political and economic conditions suggest that shifts could occur? This question is especially pressing given the ongoing contribution of the Bush tax cuts to rising income inequality (CBPP 2012). Eliminating the tax cuts for well-off Americans would have been one clear way that Democrats could have weighed in against inequality. Democratic shortfalls are also puzzling in light of Barbara Sinclair's argument in Chapter 3 of this volume that unified partisan control of government makes passage of nonincremental legislation easier in an era of high and rising political polarization. Even though Democrats controlled both Congress and the White House in 2009 and 2010, we did *not* see a repeal of the top-end Bush tax cuts.

To unravel the factors at work, we focus on how Democrats handled tax policy in the first half of President Obama's first term. We contrast Democrats' management of tax policy in these years with Republican tax policy making in the first half of the Bush administration's first term, showing that Democrats failed to capitalize on four kinds of tactics that had been very successfully employed by Republicans. Relevant tactics include careful timing of tax initiatives in relation to economic trends, management of the majority party's Congressional caucus, agenda setting by party leadership, and the mobilization of outside organized interests.

Looking at the 2009–10 juncture adds a useful bookend to the Bush tax cut story. A growing body of literature has examined the reasons why the Bush tax cuts passed in the first place, and has situated these changes in the long-term forward march of a broader conservative effort against taxes (see Bartels 2005; Block 2009; Graetz and Shapiro 2006; Hacker and Pierson 2006; 2010; Martin 2013; Morgan 2007). But little scholarly attention has been paid to the responses of Democratic officeholders and interest groups to conservative efforts in recent times. Most of the literature focuses on tax cut warriors and largely ignores liberal responses and counterinitiatives (see Campbell 2011; Graetz and Shapiro 2006 for two important exceptions). As we move to fill this lacuna, a good place to look is the first juncture after the Bush presidency when Democrats might have been able to push through their own reforms to the tax system. The failure of the Democrats to repeal the Bush tax cuts in 2009 and 2010 is also an interesting "critical" case because broad factors usually stressed by scholars pointed toward a repeal of the top-end cuts that did not happen. This episode thus lays bare some of the subtler mechanisms that drive tax politics within the Democratic orbit in the current era.

The chapter proceeds as follows. We first review the history surrounding the original Bush tax cuts and the subsequent full and partial extensions approved by President Obama. Next, we explain why it was surprising that Democrats were unable to pass their preferred tax policies when they controlled the White House and Congress by even larger margins than Republicans enjoyed in 2001, and we compare GOP and Democratic tactics along major dimensions. Finally, we spell out the implications of our analysis for assessing contemporary party behavior on taxes and redistributive fiscal policy.

THE BUSH-ERA TAX CUTS

As we begin, it is helpful to step back and take stock of the distributional and fiscal consequences of the 2001 and 2003 tax legislation for the incoming Obama administration – and also get a sense of the distributional tweaks Obama and the Democrats settled for when they tackled tax issues in 2010 and 2012.

The major provisions of the Bush-era tax changes passed in 2001 and 2003 included lowering the marginal income, capital gains, and dividend tax rates; providing marriage penalty relief; repealing the personal exemption and itemized deduction phase-outs; and expanding the child tax credit. In addition, Bush-era changes phased in cuts to the estate tax, resulting in its full (but temporary) repeal in 2010. Finally, the legislation included so-called patches to the alternative minimum tax (AMT) to prevent more taxpayers from becoming subject to the AMT, which were necessary in part as a result of the other reductions in tax rates.

In all, the Bush cuts made the tax system less progressive by increasing the after-tax income of the highest-income taxpayers by much more than the incomes of middle- and lower-income taxpayers. The increase in after-tax income for the top 1 percent of households was 6.7 percent in 2010, compared to just a 1.0 percent increase for households in the bottom fifth and a 2.8 percent increase for households in the middle fifth in 2010 (Huang and Frentz 2012). To put these figures in dollar terms, the average tax cut that people making over $1 million received exceeded a staggering $110,000 each year between 2003 and 2012 (Huang and Frentz 2012).

As a result of their size, the Bush-era cuts represented a major fiscal burden and were a substantial contributor to recent budget shortfalls; growing deficits between 2001 and 2008 were due in large part to the tax cuts (Ruffing and Horney 2011). This fiscal drag persisted into the incoming Obama administration (Ruffing and Horney 2011).

The cuts were due to expire at the end of 2010, and presidential candidate Barack Obama had pledged to let the Bush cuts for upper-income earners do just that (Campbell 2011; Fox News 2008). This squared well with public statements from Democrats in general; Obama's party had been vociferously criticizing the high-end Bush tax breaks ever since they were put in place.

But we now know that things turned out quite differently. On December 17, 2010 – just a handful of weeks before the scheduled expiration of the cuts – President Obama signed into law what the *Washington Post* described as the "most significant tax bill in nearly a decade" (Montgomery et al. 2010). The bill extended the top-heavy tax cuts originally enacted by President George W. Bush for two more years. It was described as a compromise with the Republicans – but, if so, the package was a compromise tilted heavily in the Republicans' direction. Figure 6.1 shows just how top-heavy the compromise tax deal was relative to the original proposal offered by President

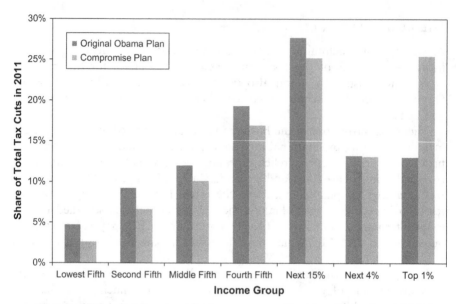

FIGURE 6.1: Shares of total tax cuts by income group, President Obama's original plan and compromise legislation (for 2011).
Source: CTJ 2010.

Obama, with a quarter of the tax cuts in 2011 accruing to the top 1 percent of Americans with the highest incomes. By extending all the cuts, the compromise plan reduced tax revenue and increased the budget deficit by $424 billion in 2011 alone, 40 percent more than the president had originally proposed (CTJ 2010).

President Obama and the Democrats got a second chance to negotiate the terms of the Bush tax cuts at the end of 2012, when the 2010 deal was set to expire. In a vote just hours before the automatic tax increases from the 2010 deal were set to go into effect in the so-called "fiscal cliff," both the House and the Senate approved legislation that preserved the Bush tax cuts on all but the very wealthiest Americans. As part of the deal, the Bush-era individual income cuts ended for household income over $400,000 for individuals and $450,000 for couples – nearly twice the thresholds proposed by Democrats in earlier years.

Although many prominent Republicans criticized the agreement for raising taxes, they were quick to point out that Obama had essentially taken full ownership of the Bush tax cuts. "After more than a decade of criticizing these tax cuts, Democrats are finally joining Republicans in making them permanent. Republicans and the American people are getting something really important, permanent tax relief," said Representative Dave Camp of Michigan (see Steinhauer 2013). Similarly, Ari Fleischer, a White House press secretary for the George W. Bush administration, remarked that "it's fantastic that the Bush tax

TABLE 6.1 *Treatment of Bush-Era Tax Cuts in Fiscal Cliff Deal*

Bush-Era Tax Cut	Fiscal Cliff Deal Outcome
Reduction of the 39.6% Rate to 35%	Made Permanent for Income Up to $450k (Couples)/$400k (Individuals)
Reduction of the 36% Rate to 33%	Made Permanent
Reduction of the 28% and 31% Rates to 25% and 28%	Made Permanent
Introduction of the 10% Tax Bracket (Lowest Bracket was Previously 15 percent)	Made Permanent
Reduction of Rates for Capital Gains in Bottom Four Brackets from 10% and 20% to 0% and 15%	Made Permanent
Reduction of Rates for Capital Gains in Top Two Brackets from 20% to 15%	Made Permanent for income up to $450k/$400k
Reduction of Rates on Stock Dividends in Bottom Four Brackets from Ordinary Rates to Capital Gains Rates	Made Permanent
Reduction of Rates on Stock Dividends in Top Two Brackets from Ordinary Rates to Capital Gains Rates	Made Permanent (Rate of 15% for income up to $450k/$400k, 20% above that Level)
Expansion of Child Tax Credit	Made Permanent
Elimination of "marriage penalty" in the Standard deduction	Made Permanent
Elimination of "marriage penalty" in the 15 percent Rate Bracket	Made Permanent
Reduction in "marriage penalty" in the Earned Income Tax Credit	Made Permanent
Expansion of the Dependent Care Credit	Made Permanent
Repeal of the Personal Exemption Phase-Out (PEP)	Made Permanent for Income Up to $300k/$250k
Repeal of the Itemized Deduction Disallowance ("Pease")	Made Permanent for Income Up to $300k/$250k
Increase in the Exemptions in the Alternative Minimum Tax (AMT)	Made Permanent
Increase in Estate Tax Exemption to $5 million and Decrease in the Estate Tax Rate to 35% (in 2012)	Mostly Made Permanent (Exemption of $5 million, Rate of 40%)

Source: CTJ 2013b.

cuts, which now have to be seen inarguably as overwhelmingly for the middle class, are being made permanent" (see Weisman 2013a).

Table 6.1, from a Citizens for Tax Justice report, shows just how many of the original Bush-era cuts were made permanent by the fiscal cliff deal.

Although Democrats did succeed in getting Republicans to approve an increase in taxes on upper-income households – a victory, to be sure, in an extremely polarized and divided Congress – as well as several other important priorities for their party, such as a temporary extension of unemployment benefits, many on the left were disappointed by both the substance of the deal and the way in which the White House had negotiated. Liberal Democrats, for example, pointed to the fact that the president ultimately agreed to about $600 billion in new tax revenue over the following ten years when House Speaker Boehner had originally promised $800 billion (Weisman 2013a,b). "I just don't think Obama's negotiated very well," lamented Senator Tom Harkin, Democrat of Iowa (see Weisman 2013b).

In all, the deal preserved about 85 percent of the Bush-era income tax cuts, for a total cost of $3.3 trillion over the following decade, and 95 percent of the Bush-era cuts for the estate tax in 2012, totaling $369 billion over ten years (CTJ 2013c). Just as with the previous 2010 compromise, the wealthiest Americans disproportionately benefited from the fiscal cliff deal, even with the higher top rates (CTJ 2013a). The richest 1 percent of taxpayers claimed 18 percent of the fiscal cliff deal's income and estate tax cuts, the same share claimed by the bottom 60 percent of taxpayers. It is clear, then, that President Obama and the Democrats institutionalized a set of Bush-era cuts that were fundamentally slanted toward well-off Americans. In the following section, we discuss why it is so surprising that Democrats failed to take earlier and bolder action on the tax cuts.

WAS IT SURPRISING THAT OBAMA AND HIS PARTY CAVED?

From the perspective of the tax deals negotiated in 2010 and 2012, it is difficult to remember some of the significant advantages that Democrats initially possessed in addressing the Bush tax cuts, especially in the first years of the Obama administration. During the 111th Congress, the position taken by Obama and most Democrats on taxes enjoyed permissive, even supportive, public approbation in national opinion surveys. Democrats also had economic evidence on their side and, most importantly, enjoyed the capacity to set the agenda and frame the politics of critical choices about the expiration of the Bush cuts. There were obvious opportunities to separate decisions about tax reductions for the middle class from decisions about maintaining expensive cuts for the wealthy. With many factors unusually well aligned, many analysts predicted a repeal of the top-end cuts in 2010 (see Fligstein 2010).

Political advantages. When polled in the abstract, Americans generally supported the original passage of the Bush tax cuts in the early 2000s. Still, when presented with policy tradeoffs, most Americans were skeptical of the value of tax cuts relative to other priorities.[2] Crucially, there has always been a slight majority in favor of the repeal of cuts for high-income earners. And a proposal to do just that was included in Obama's presidential campaign policy statements during 2007 and 2008. After President Obama took office, many Americans told pollsters that addressing the Bush tax cuts ought to be an important issue for the new administration. An AP/Gfk Poll conducted in January 2009 found that 61 percent of respondents felt that eliminating the Bush tax cuts for couples earning more than $250,000 a year was either a "top priority" or "an important priority" for President Obama.

Out of ten similarly phrased national polls (extracted from the Roper Center archives) that asked respondents to choose between three options for the Bush tax cuts – extend all cuts, extend cuts for income below $250,000, and let all cuts expire – the original Obama position (letting the cuts expire for high income households) garnered a plurality of support in six polls.[3] Combining respondents who preferred letting all of the tax cuts expire with the White House position produces a majority in all but one of those polls (see Bartels 2013, 64, for similar evidence).

Polling also suggested that a majority of Americans wanted Congress to address the tax cut issue before the 2010 midterm election and that they would hold Democrats, rather than Republicans, responsible for passing a tax deal. In a Fox News poll in the fall of 2010, 65 percent of registered voters reported that they wanted Congress to address the issue before the elections.

To be sure, interpreting public opinion about public policy choices, especially taxes, can be tricky. Political scientist Larry Bartels has argued that early public opinion about the Bush tax cuts was "neither clear nor consistent" and was in many respects ill informed about the implications of the cuts (Bartels 2005). In the years since their original enactment, however, Democratic politicians, journalists, and policy analysts have all focused on the high cost and the top-heavy distribution of the tax breaks. This might explain why in 2010 a majority of Americans favored partial or full repeal of the tax cuts. Overall, the survey evidence we have assembled indicates that American public opinion was at least permissive of the Obama argument to allow the Bush tax cuts to expire for people with very high incomes.

Apart from polling on the specific options available for a redo on taxes, the broader debate offered Democrats a unique opportunity to highlight the class divide between the two parties and capitalize on populist sentiment in the aftermath of the recession and Wall Street bailouts (see Bartels 2013 for a more skeptical assessment). Republicans were trying to make the case to the public that $250,000 represented a moderate middle-class family income, when in fact only about two percent of tax filers stood to be affected by changes at that level – and high-income tax payers would still receive tax breaks on the first $250,000 of their income (Tax Policy Center 2010). Democrats thus had a chance to dramatize the disconnect between Republican priorities and the economic realities faced by the vast majority of Americans.

Economic evidence. Not only was repeal of the Bush tax cuts for top incomes potentially politically advantageous, but most mainstream economists regarded this option as the best course of action to deal with fiscal shortfalls in a sluggish economy. Certainly, it was considered a wiser course than extending *all* of the Bush tax cuts (Marr 2010).

Some proponents of a full extension argued that it would be a mistake to allow the tax cuts for high incomes to expire in an economic downturn, since this could slow economic growth. According to the Congressional Budget Office, however, out of eleven options to stimulate growth and job creation, a full extension of the tax cuts would have been the least effective option; far better would have been targeted measures to aid the unemployed through extensions of unemployment insurance or to promote hiring through job tax credits (CBO 2010). What is more, over the long run a high-income tax cut extension could actually dampen economic growth by swelling deficits and the debt (Marr and Brunet 2010). The fiscally responsible position, then, was to allow some or all of the tax cuts to expire and use the revenue to enact more effective stimulus measures, or at least slowly phase out the top-end cuts, as Republican economic adviser Mark Zandi proposed (Zandi 2010). In short, while the economic crisis certainly constrained the Democrats' position, it would have been possible to repeal the Bush tax cuts for top incomes in a way that would not have hampered the recovery, and if anything, could have facilitated both short- and long-term growth.

Proponents of a full extension also proclaimed that many taxpayers with incomes over $250,000 were in fact small business owners, and thus a repeal of high-end cuts would harm small business growth and job creation. For example, in a press release announcing his opposition to the White House and Congressional leadership position on the tax cuts, Representative Glenn Nye of Virginia, a leader in the House opposition to the repeal of the cuts, claimed that "many of the taxpayers included in this 'upper-income' bracket are successful small business owners ... we should be giving them the support they need to thrive" (Nye 2010). But estimates from the Treasury Department showed that only 2.5 percent of small business owners would have been affected by a repeal of the top-end cuts (Huang and Marr 2012).

In short, the Democrats had a solid economic argument to make, supported by many respected economists and experts. Proponents of repealing some or all of the Bush tax cuts included individuals as varied as former tax cut supporter Alan Greenspan, former supply-sider and Reagan tax cut mastermind David Stockman, and economist Alan Blinder. On this issue, the Democrats occupied the clear fiscal high ground.

THE PARTIES AT CRITICAL TAX JUNCTURES

To analyze the reasons why, despite political support and economic logic, President Obama and Congress flubbed their party's chances to end the top-end Bush tax cuts – and to examine the struggles of Democrats more generally in this issue realm – we dissect developments in two critical periods. We contrast the maneuvers of Democrats around tax cut issues in the first half of

Obama's first term with the original process, back in 2001–03, by which Republicans enacted the original Bush tax cuts in two rounds. Four factors – timing in relation to economic trends, caucus control, agenda-setting, and the mobilization of interest groups – combine to make sense of the successes the GOP had advancing its tax agenda versus the failures of the Democrats to turn tax politics their way.

To be sure, the comparison between the Bush tax cut episodes and the Democrats' effort to raise taxes is inherently asymmetric to a certain degree. All else equal, it is politically easier to cut taxes than to raise them. But within the realm of possible tax increases, we argue that the 2009–10 period looked extremely promising for Democrats for the reasons that we have just described. Similarly, some might consider this comparison unbalanced since Republicans have prioritized tax cutting at all costs in recent decades, while Democrats have pursued a broader agenda aside from tax policy. But this begs the question of *why* tax policy has not been more central to the Democrats' agenda once they controlled the levers of government with the election of President Obama. This is the question we explore in our comparison of the Bush and Obama tax episodes.

Another issue that some may raise with our analysis is that legislators are simply responding to the demands of their constituents; Congressional Democrats did not vote for a repeal of the Bush top-end tax cuts because the voters in their districts preferred to retain the cuts. In response to this concern, we reiterate the observation from the previous section that voters' views of tax policy are poorly defined, and depend heavily on the framing of different policy alternatives. Indeed, as we will document, this was a key insight that Republican leaders understood and exploited in their original campaign for tax cuts in 2001 and 2003, but that Democrats largely neglected in 2009 and 2010. There were opportunities where Democrats could have taken advantage of supportive mass opinion, but chose not to. Individual legislator behavior, then, needs to be assessed against a broader backdrop that recognizes the importance of entrepreneurship and strategizing (or the lack thereof) by party leaders.

Timing in relation to economic trends. Given that the federal deficit had turned to surplus during the years of Clinton's administration, Republican President George W. Bush faced few budgetary reasons not to push forward with the major tax cuts he had promised during the 2000 campaign. With both houses of Congress in their party's control by very slim margins at the start of the session, speed and procedural shortcuts became the GOP order of the day (Rosenbaum 2001; Weisman 2001). Republican leaders in Congress began drafting tax cut legislation even before a budget was passed in 2001, and without many key details of the cuts themselves (see NYT 2001). Although the 2001 tax cuts were first conceived during an economic expansion stretching through the GOP primary and general election, a faltering economy starting in 2001 allowed Republicans to add new arguments, which they used for both the 2001 and 2003 rounds of cuts (Lewandoski 2008).

Years later, a Democratic president arriving in Washington found that economic conditions hampered his ability to carry through immediately on tax promises made in his campaign for office. As he assembled his governing team in late 2008 and moved into the White House in early 2009, Obama was faced with a financial meltdown and a sharp contraction of employment and growth. Forced to first address the rapidly deteriorating economy, Obama temporarily set aside the matter of what to do about the Bush tax cuts and concentrated on passing economic stimulus legislation that included big temporary tax cuts along with additional federal spending and aid to the states. Nevertheless, the Obama Office of Management and Budget projected a repeal of the Bush cuts for high incomes in the first budget released by the administration (Andrews 2009). The president was thus distracted by the economic crisis, but maintained his stated intentions about longer-term tax policy (Calmes 2009; Calmes and Zeleny 2008).

After the passage of the 2009 stimulus, some limited discussion continued within the White House and Congress as to whether Democrats ought to move at once to repeal the tax cuts for high incomes or simply wait for them to expire at the end of 2010 (Calmes 2010b). In retrospect, this was a window of opportunity to do what Bush did back in 2001: make use of a new president's honeymoon period and across-the-board party control to reset tax policies for the longer run. Yet in 2009 so much Democratic attention was directed toward passing health care and financial reform that it was well into 2010 before the Bush tax cuts again claimed much attention (Calmes 2010b). With expiration looming, how might Democrats find a way to continue cuts for the middle class but let them expire for the wealthy?

The Obama White House never quite got its signals straight on their strategy. In early 2010, the White House released a budget that included a permanent extension of the Bush tax cuts, except for the cuts on top incomes (Calmes 2010a). Concurrently, however, aides signaled to Congressional Democrats that the administration might support a temporary extension, with the idea that this could be a good starting point for a comprehensive tax code overhaul (Calmes 2010b). During meetings in mid-summer between the Democratic leadership and the White House, Majority Leader Harry Reid, Speaker Nancy Pelosi, and Senate Finance Chairman Max Baucus all expressed their support for a middle-class-only extension (Bellantoni 2010d).

As the summer unfolded, the Obama White House began increasing the volume of its Bush tax cut messaging, in an encouraging sign for champions of a repeal (Herszenhorn 2010). And in early September, both Pelosi and Reid stated their preference for a vote on the cuts before the midterm elections in a series of conference calls with the White House. But the shepherds were losing strays from their flocks. Soon after the fall recess, moderate members of the Democratic caucus began to express a desire for a full extension of all cuts – even as House Minority Leader John Boehner admitted he would drop the top-end cuts if forced to by Democrats (Bellantoni 2010d; Calmes 2010b;

Herszenhorn 2010). The Senate faced similar divisions, and although Reid was pushed by a small group of progressive Senators to hold a vote, Reid formally announced that the Senate would not take action on the Bush tax cuts before the elections (Beutler 2010c).

By waiting until *after* the 2010 elections – which ended up being a GOP blowout, with Republicans gaining a record sixty-three seats in the House – Democrats were placed in a substantially weakened bargaining position going into the negotiations with Republicans in the lame duck Congressional session. The debate was also pushed quite close to the scheduled expiration of all of the cuts at the end of 2010. Had the economic climate not been so poor, this might have provided additional leverage for the Democrats, because they could have threatened Republicans with a complete repeal of the cuts if no deal was reached. But the economy was still very weak, so it was the Republicans who benefited from the eleventh hour nature of the negotiations.

As it became clear that the incoming GOP-dominated House would make passage of additional fiscal stimulus nearly impossible, the White House began to view the Bush tax cut extension as the only feasible way to pass a last round of stimulus. The pressure of competing economic priorities thus led the Obama White House to drop its call for a repeal of the top end cuts, resulting in a bargain with Republicans that included a one-year payroll tax cut, extensions for unemployment benefits, and a variety of other stimulative tax breaks for individuals and businesses in addition to a two-year extension of the Bush-era cuts (see Stein 2010b).

Party unity and White House coordination with Congress. The enactment of the Bush tax cuts in 2001 and 2003 highlighted the capacities of the GOP to maintain tight partisan discipline. Despite razor thin margins, the Republicans were able to keep strict control of their caucus and sustain remarkable party unity.

During 2009 and 2010, Democrats had commanding margins in both the House and Senate, but Democratic congressional leaders still struggled to herd the cats in their caucuses, and contended with confusing direction from the Obama White House. Nowhere was this more apparent than when taxes were at issue. As we have already seen, there were a number of incidents during the Democrats' struggles over taxes when weak leadership and lack of party discipline were clear culprits.

Like a quarterback unsure what to call in the huddle, the White House stumbled into 2010 sending mixed signals to Congressional Democrats. Although the Obama Office of Management and Budget released a proposed budget for the coming fiscal year that included a permanent extension for the middle-class tax cuts, White House aides simultaneously signaled to Congressional Democrats that they might be open to a temporary extension of *all* the Bush tax cuts, including those at the top end (Calmes 2010b). Later in the year, the outgoing head of the Office of Management and Budget, Peter Orszag, used an OpEd column in the *New York Times* to call on Democrats to compromise with Republicans and extend all the cuts until 2013 (Orszag 2010). Orszag might be speaking for the White House, pundits speculated.

The second – and more important – instance of Democratic disunity occurred shortly after the 2010 Congressional fall recess. Speaker Pelosi and Majority Leader Reid had assured President Obama earlier that summer that they would both attempt to hold a vote on the middle class cuts *before* the November 2010 election. Pelosi brought in pollster Stan Greenberg to regale the House Democratic caucus with survey data showing that tax cuts could be a winning issue for the Democrats in the election – provided Democrats reflected popular preferences to keep tax cuts for the middle class and let them lapse for the rich (Bellantoni 2010d).

But not enough Congressional Democrats got with the program. In spite of the supportive polling data, Pelosi began to hear vocal demands from Democrats that the tax cuts should be extended in full. Shortly after the caucus meeting with Greenberg, a group of thirty-one moderate Democrats publicly circulated a letter to the House leadership stating their explicit support for extending all of the cuts (Bellantoni 2010a). A second letter calling for a full extension not just of the high-end income tax cuts, but also of the cuts for dividend income and capital gains, was circulated soon after by forty-seven members, enough to stymie a vote in the House (AP 2010). It became clear to Pelosi and the House leadership shortly after the release of these two letters that the caucus was too divided to proceed to a formal whip count (Bellantoni 2010b,c).

Although many of the letter signers, in addition to political pundits, would cite competitive races as the impetus for the September revolt in the House caucus, our own quantitative analysis suggests that these representatives did not come from disproportionately competitive races, at least as judged by the Cook Political Report at the time of the circulation of the letters.[4] This was even more apparent once we took other characteristics of the legislators into account (Hertel-Fernandez and Skocpol 2013). The opposition of these Democrats, then, must be explained by other factors, which we explore in a later section.

Dissent from Senate Democrats soon followed, largely from those in vulnerable midterm races, but also from several Democratic senators not up for reelection in 2010. Majority Leader Reid was thus forced to acknowledge in late September that he could not hold a vote before the midterms (Beutler 2010c). Shortly after Reid's announcement, Speaker Pelosi reported optimistically that a vote could still happen in the House before the elections (Lightman 2010). She held one last caucus meeting to convince skeptical members. But the meeting was unsuccessful, so Pelosi, too, was eventually forced to abandon the prospect of a vote before November (Beutler 2010a).

Evidence of divisions within the Democratic ranks continued to pop into public view throughout October. Less than a week after political adviser David Axelrod stated on CNN that the White House would not support extending the tax cuts for the wealthy (Schwarz 2010), Vice President Biden announced that the administration was open to compromises with the Republicans on this matter (Mascaro 2010). Who knew, at that point, what Democrats stood for? Democratic positions ranged from those who supported a continuation, even enhancement of tax breaks for the wealthy, to those who wanted continuing cuts for the middle class but not the wealthy, to those who wanted to see all Bush cuts for both the middle class and the well-to-do fade into the sunset after 2010. Commentators and voters could not have determined a "Democratic" position on the looming expiration of the Bush cuts even if they tried, because there was none.

After the midterms, a chastened President Obama immediately signaled that he would be open to a compromise on the Bush tax cuts (Taylor 2010). The Obama administration feared that letting all of the cuts expire at the end of 2010 would set House Republicans up to pass a bill with a full extension of the Bush tax cuts in early 2011, which would then head to the Senate, where Democrats could not be trusted to oppose the measure (Corn 2012). At the same time, the White House and Congressional leadership were deeply divided over the tactics they might use to negotiate a compromise, especially whether they should start from a higher income cutoff for ending the top-end cuts, such as $500,000 or $1 million, rather than the $250,000 threshold originally used by the Obama campaign (Calmes 2010b).

A final significant division in the Democratic caucus occurred after the White House began negotiations with the Republicans on a tax cut deal. Just days after a long-awaited middle class tax cut-only vote, Obama announced a tentative deal with Congressional Republicans to extend all of the Bush income tax cuts for two more years, along with a number of other provisions to stimulate the economy and extend other Bush-era tax cuts to the estate tax, the capital gains tax, and taxes on dividends. Although the package would benefit nearly all households, it would disproportionately provide benefits to the wealthy (Kocieniewski 2010).

Many progressive members of Congress were up in arms at the top-heavy nature of the deal. Senator Bernie Sanders, for example, promised to stage a filibuster against the proposal (James 2010). Senator Mary Landrieu took a hard stance against the deal as well, a surprising decision given her ordinarily center-right position within the Democratic caucus (Grim 2010). In a powerful symbol of their dissatisfaction with the deal, House Democrats agreed to a nonbinding resolution to not consider the tax cut package in its original form (Beutler 2010b).

Ultimately, the tax cut deal passed both the Senate and House, despite a last-minute effort in the House to change the estate tax provision. At practically every juncture throughout the process, Congressional Democrats were out of sync with each other and with the White House. The disorder that defined the attempted repeal process provides a stark contrast to the discipline of the Republicans in passing the original cuts back in the early 2000s and in flatly opposing any repeal of the Bush tax cuts during the 2009–10 episode.

One can see this dissensus in the Democratic congressional caucus over economic issues reflected in the charts from Nicholas Carnes's Chapter 5 in this volume. What is so striking in Carnes's figures is the variance of Democratic behavior on legislation affecting the distribution of economic resources. While nearly all Republicans tended to vote for inequality increasing bills, including the extension of the Bush tax cuts, Democrats were much more internally divided on these issues.

This dissensus also presents a qualification to Barbara Sinclair's argument (Chapter 3 in this volume) about legislative productivity under unified partisan control of government in an era of polarization. Democrats may have become more ideologically homogenous across many issues (McCarty et al. 2006), facilitating legislative activity when they control the levers of government. But economic policy – and tax policy in particular – presents one area where there is a striking disparity in the cohesion of legislators within the Democratic and Republican caucuses, and this makes Democratic action on taxes much more difficult, even when Democrats control government.

Control of the legislative and political agenda. The previous section established that Democrats suffered from serious divisions in their caucus in contrast to a more unified Republican caucus. But how did Republicans achieve such a high degree of discipline? There are two elements to a possible answer. The first, involving the role of outside interest groups, will be discussed in the following section. The second, discussed in this section, involves ways in which Republicans were able to stack the legislative and political agenda in their favor.

As Jacob Hacker and Paul Pierson outlined in their book *Off Center*, Republicans were able to command party discipline during the passage of the tax cuts through a series of ingenious agenda-setting mechanisms (Hacker and Pierson 2006). First, Republicans framed the issue clearly and compellingly – tax cuts: yes or no. This framing moved the debate away from issues of the size and distribution of the cuts to a simple up or down vote with which legislators would find it hard to disagree.

The Bush White House also used messaging strategies intended to shift the public's attention away from the large cost and top-heavy distributional tilt of the tax cuts. For example, a Bush administration memo explicitly told communications staff to avoid talking about the opportunity cost of the tax cuts, since the public preferred spending on other policies (Hacker and Pierson 2006, 52). Administration officials also frequently conflated the tax cuts for the average taxpayer with the average American, avoiding the fact that one-third of families were too poor to pay income taxes and thus would not receive any benefit from the tax cuts (Hacker and Pierson 2006, 57).

Another technique was aggressive use of institutional and procedural mechanisms to lower the bar for the passage of legislation. For example, the Bush administration used overly optimistic budget projections when calculating the effect of the tax cuts on the long-term fiscal outlook. Republicans also suppressed distributional analyses of the tax cuts that would have shown just how top-heavy the tax cuts really were (Hacker and Pierson 2006, 56). And when it came time for a vote in the Senate, the leadership used the technique of budget reconciliation to pass the tax cuts, which made the legislation immune to the sixty-vote requirement of a filibuster.

Finally, Republicans used negotiations in Congress not as a method to temper their proposals and find middle ground with Democrats, but rather to increase the cost and scope of the legislation compared to their original tax plan. According to House Whip Tom DeLay during the 2001 debate: "[t]he Bush plan is a great beginning, but it's a floor not a ceiling." The same was true for the Senate; a spokesman for Republican leader Trent Lott was quoted as saying "We're negotiating from $1.6 trillion up" (see Rosenbaum 2001).

In contemplating repeal of part of the Bush tax cuts during 2009 and 2010, Democrats used none of these agenda-setting techniques. From the start, Democrats never offered a clear and consistent frame for their effort. Although Obama campaigned on a repeal of the cuts for high earners, the poor economy forced the White House to shift to advocating for an expiration of the high-income tax cuts. Even then, White House aides were signaling that they would be open to a temporary full extension. From the fall to the winter of 2010, the message shifted from a permanent extension of cuts for income below $250,000 (fluctuating between cutoff points of $500,000 and $1 million) to a temporary extension of some of the cuts to a temporary extension of all of the cuts. There was no consistent end goal for the Democrats to rally around or to explain and sell to the American public.

Another crucial messaging opportunity for repeal that the Democrats conceded early on to proponents of a full extension was the conflation of tax cuts for individual households and tax cuts on income. This is a subtle point, to be sure, but it is a distinction that makes an immense difference in the interpretation of how the tax cuts would affect different households. The way the White House and Congressional Democrats initially framed their proposals was that the tax cuts would only flow to families making under $250,000 a year. It seemed that families with incomes above this amount would receive no cuts, when in fact many of these higher income families would have still received substantial tax cuts on their income below the threshold. In fact, a family making over a million dollars a year would have still received a tax cut averaging $6,349 under the original Obama plan (Klein 2010). Although it is likely that the initial confusion between income and individual households was not deliberate and simply stemmed from the complexity of the proposal, the fact remains that the Democrats did not take later steps to clarify their position even when it would have helped their messaging campaign.

Closely related, Democrats were also hindered by the broader absence of a consensus on how to effectively communicate to the public about taxes. While Republicans and conservatives developed a robust messaging apparatus over the past thirty years to sell tax cuts (see Block 2009; Hacker and Pierson 2006),

Democrats have no such equivalent for communicating with the public about tax increases and paying for public priorities.

Democratic fears peaked among moderates worried about being painted by their Republican opponents as "having voted for a tax increase" even when the vast majority of Americans, millionaires included, would have still received a tax break. A senior Democratic House aide explained the position of the Democrats who opposed repealing cuts on high income as follows: "They'll be subject to a 30 second ad saying they raised taxes" (see Sargent 2010c). Representative Jim Matheson, one of the organizers of the pro-full extension letters reiterated this sentiment, stating that even a vote for the middle-class only tax cuts would be portrayed as a tax hike (Sargent 2010a). It is telling that these Democrats did not think that they could win a political battle where they were maintaining lower rates on *all* income below $250,000 a year – even the first $250,000 that millionaires made. That Democrats had no "30 second ad" response to the Republicans' threat is a strong sign of the imbalance between the two parties when it comes to communicating to the public about taxes.

The Democrats did not make creative use of Congressional procedures to pass their tax changes, either. They could not use budget reconciliation to pass tax reform legislation, as the Republicans originally did (Binder 2010). This is in part because Democrats already used the reconciliation process to pass the health care and educational loan reform legislation earlier in 2010 and could not use reconciliation again in the same budget cycle (another consequence of delaying the tax issue until 2010). More generally, they showed no signs of wanting to change the legislative rules in their favor. Indeed, Congressional Democrats had passed legislation in 2007 (and again in 2009) that made it more difficult to use congressional procedures to pass tax changes in response to the Republicans' tactics under the Bush administration (Binder 2010).

Another important strategy that Republicans employed in the passage of the original Bush tax cuts involved the extensive use of phase-ins (cuts that would not fully materialize until many years after the passage of the original bill) and sunsets (cuts that would end after a certain length of time). These features of the Bush tax cut legislation served a number of purposes: reducing the official cost estimate of the tax changes, masking the true distribution of the cuts to different income groups, and setting up future political battles over the tax cuts on more favorable terms to Republicans (Hacker and Pierson 2005, 44–7). Together, these features helped to minimize opposition to passing the cuts and to lock in a durable constituency of tax cut supporters over time.

Given the intricate design of the tax cuts, it is striking that Democrats did not employ an equivalent degree of creativity in their repeal effort, especially before the midterm elections. We have already discussed the fact that Democrats could not settle on a cutoff point for the tax cuts, which was an essential part of the policy design. But equally importantly, Democrats did not pursue phase-outs of the Bush tax cuts. A gradual phase-out of the Bush tax cuts, especially for top earners, might have been one way for the Democrats to address concerns about raising taxes in the middle of a weak economy. But the White House quickly rejected this option after pundits pitched the idea in the media (Stein 2010a).

Mobilization of outside actors and interest groups. Another key to passing the original Bush tax cuts was the mobilization of powerful outside groups that could whip recalcitrant politicians into line to vote for the legislation. In the account presented by Hacker and Pierson (2006), two conservative groups – the Club for Growth and Americans for Tax Reform – were especially important. These small but well-funded groups target Democrats and moderate Republicans for electoral defeat who do not support their tax cut agenda, especially through primary challenges of Republican candidates. In doing so, they help ensure that Congress, and the Republican caucus in particular, will be fully committed to their anti-tax philosophy. According to Representative Jeff Flake, as quoted by Hacker and Pierson: "When you have 100 percent of Republicans voting for the Bush tax cuts, you know that they are looking over their shoulder and not wanting to have Steven Moore [the Club for Growth president] recruiting candidates in their district" (Hacker and Pierson 2006, 54).

The role of these groups, however, extended beyond electoral pressure. These actors, especially Grover Norquist, took a leadership role in coordinating the passage of the tax cut legislation in Congress and in seeking support for the tax cuts from other actors in the conservative movement.

Norquist's Americans for Tax Reform, for example, helped coordinate the passage of pro-tax cut resolutions in a number of key state legislatures, putting pressure on the politicians from those states. "I would call him our field marshal," remarked Horace Cooper, director of coalitions for House leader Dick Armey (see Dreyfuss 2001). In other work we show that this bottom-up pressure helps to explain the votes of legislators on the 2001 Bush tax cuts; wavering legislators from states that had passed these resolutions were more likely to vote in favor of important components of the tax cut package (Hertel-Fernandez and Skocpol 2013).

Norquist was also responsible for coordinating a group of business associations that represented another critical force in ensuring passage of the tax cuts. The so-called Gang of Six – the National Association of Manufacturers, the Business Roundtable, the U.S. Chamber of Commerce, the National Federation of Independent Business, the National Restaurant Association, and the National Association of Wholesaler-Distributers – collectively represent companies that employ more than 22 million people and produce almost half of U.S. GDP (Jensen et al. 2005). Together with Norquist, the Gang of Six spearheaded the formation of a larger coalition – the Tax Reform Action Coalition (now called the Tax Relief Coalition, or TRC) – in conjunction with hundreds of other businesses and business associations. The steering committee of the TRC, as of 2009, consisted of the original Gang of Six, plus Americans for Tax Reform, Associated General Contractors, FreedomWorks, and the International Foodservice Distributors Association.[5]

The TRC and the Gang of Six used their collective clout to push an aggressive tax cut agenda, taking advantage of the fact that they were able to unite business groups that had previously been divided amongst one another. By focusing on broad, probusiness tax measures instead of individual tax breaks for certain sectors or industries (as businesses had typically done before the coalition), the alliance was able to command more power since they spoke for an extraordinarily diverse array of business groups and represented firms from nearly every Congressional district (see Michael Graetz's quote in Jensen et al. 2005).

The TRC was tapped by the Bush White House to be the main group that coordinated the passage of tax cut legislation and the TRC's head, Dirk Van Dongen, managed the tax cut war room within the White House (Birnbaum 2002). For TRC's efforts, President Bush went so far as to personally thank Dongen in a speech promoting the tax cuts, and again after the signing of the legislation (Jensen et al. 2005).

The most significant influence of the TRC is not through campaign donations, according to a reporter who has covered the group's activities extensively, but rather the coalition's ability to mobilize business leaders across the country to talk to their representatives every time taxes appear on the political agenda. TRC is able to get leaders in local communities – for example, prominent auto dealers or franchise owners who are well known and respected – to build relationships with their representatives and use these relationships to ensure that their voice is heard.[6]

This sort of institutional infrastructure and legislative support was notably absent for much of the Democrats' attempt to repeal the high income tax cuts. Left-leaning advocacy groups, such as MoveOn, the Progressive Change Campaign Committee, and labor unions, used votes for the Bush tax cuts sporadically against Republicans in various Congressional elections. However, no coordinated effort was made to systematically turn the Bush tax cuts into a key campaign issue, not even during the 2010 midterms when the issue had the most chance of making a difference in the election results.

Importantly, liberal political groups did not punish dissent from the White House's position in the same way that the conservative groups, such as Americans for Tax Reform and the Club for Growth, did. Unions, perhaps the most obvious, if unequal, counterweight to the business community, did not become visibly involved in the tax cut debate until after the midterm elections (Sargent 2010b). By way of comparison, the NFIB started releasing announcements about the impending expiration of the Bush tax cuts as early as July 2010, citing survey results about the low optimism of small business owners as a key reason to keep tax rates down (NFIB 2010).

Our evidence suggests that this early and aggressive business involvement made a difference. In an analysis of the moderate Democrats who revolted against the Bush tax cut repeal in 2010, we found that one of the best predictors of whether a House Democrat signed a pro-tax cut letter was if they had received National Federation of Independent Business or other Gang of Six business association contributions (Hertel-Fernandez and Skocpol 2013) – even after accounting for the competitiveness of their 2010 race, President Obama's support in that district, the degree to which taxpayers in that member's district stood to be affected by the repeal of the top-end cuts, and legislators' ideologies. In contrast, donations from the Democrats' other major organized supporter, labor, were generally unrelated to whether a House Democrat signed a pro-Bush tax cut letter. These results indicate that even independently of a member's own ideological outlook, electoral imperatives, and district demands, interest group connections play a central role in determining legislative behavior toward taxes within the Democratic caucus.

EXPLAINING DIVERGENT PARTY CAPACITY ON TAX POLITICS

As we have explained, the Democrat-managed tax deal passed in 2010, like the original GOP-sponsored Bush tax cuts, was heavily tilted toward the well-off. Equally important, the full extension in 2010 likely made it more challenging for Democrats to enact a more extensive repeal in 2012, because all the cuts remained in place for a longer period, giving the tax cuts more time to generate supportive constituencies. It was unusual for the federal government to enact such expensive and top-heavy bills in a climate of fiscal austerity. That the Democrats in Congress and the Obama White House extended the top income cuts against public opinion and economic logic is especially remarkable and, we believe, suggestive of several telling conclusions.

In the first place, Democratic struggles in the first half of Obama's first term in office reaffirm findings of previous examinations of the Bush-era tax cuts, namely that some of the most important public policies responsible for the redistribution of massive amounts of public resources are not determined in accord with the concerns of ordinary voters. The broad cross-sections of citizens who reported favoring a repeal of some or all of the Bush tax cuts were not sufficient to ensure that Democrats voted for their repeal in 2010. This is consistent with the work of Martin Gilens (2012), who has shown that even when large proportions of poor and middle-class citizens prefer particular economic policies, such preferences are unlikely to be represented in actual policy, especially if they diverge with the preferences of the very wealthy.

Another conclusion, related to the first, underlines Democratic Party incapacities on tax issues. The repeal muddle put on full display the inability of the Democrats to set agendas, communicate, and devise effective strategies about taxes in competition with the Republicans, even under apparently favorable political and economic circumstances. On the Democratic side of the political spectrum, there are few well-organized activist groups focused on taxes as their primary issue. Even the unions, the member of the Democratic coalition most likely to take on that role, did not put public pressure on the Democrats in the same way that anti-tax groups did during key moments in the 2010 episode. This lack of organized group pressure may go far in explaining the diversity of Democratic positions on taxes, and indeed on other issues of economic redistribution that Carnes documents in the analysis in his chapter.

Linking shifting party positions to the strength, interests, and activities of organized interests fits with the new conceptualization of political parties not as teams of office-seeking politicians (as in the canonical account of Downs 1957) but as coalitions of well-organized policy-demanding groups (Karol 2010). Until the Democratic coalition incorporates policy-demanding groups directly focused on progressive tax policy and greater revenue, it seems likely that the divergence in the capacity of the two parties will persist.

Beyond our substantive findings for this pivotal case, more certainly remains to be learned about how the two parties – and especially the Democrats – have approached tax politics. Several areas of future research seem especially promising. First, even though public opinion may not matter directly for major tax changes, the landscape of preferences and attitudes on taxes may have changed in ways that have disadvantaged those seeking to raise more revenue, or that require those seeking higher taxes to improve the framing of their proposals (see Campbell 2009). Analysts can benefit from better understandings of how public opinion about taxes has shifted – and how the parties strategically use and shape tax attitudes (see Graetz and Shapiro 2006; Jacobs and Shapiro 2000).

Further research on tax politics could usefully focus on health care, too. Although Democrats may have failed in enacting major progressive income tax increases in 2010, the Affordable Care Act contained highly progressive financing mechanisms, prompting *New York Times* analyst David Leonhardt (2010) to characterize it as "the federal government's biggest attack on economic inequality since inequality began rising more than three decades ago" (see Campbell 2011). Why did the Democrats succeed in raising taxes on the wealthy in the context of health reform but not elsewhere? Some of the explanation surely stems from the fact that health care reform promised deficit reduction and contained non-tax provisions attractive to moderate Democrats and business interests (see Jacobs and Skocpol 2012). In addition, this law fits the long-standing pattern wherein taxes earmarked for social benefits are far more popular and politically successful than taxes enacted on their own to raise general revenue (see Skocpol 2000; Zelizer 2000).

Finally, given the centrality of organized interests to the shifting behaviors of the two parties on tax politics, more work is needed to understand the full range of relevant groups and how they have changed over time. Mere snapshots focused on short-term decisions and maneuvers of individual politicians cannot suffice to explain slowly shifting balances of power in critical policy arenas like taxes. Our research suggests that, over many years, anti-tax conservatives and Republicans have proceeded with more focus, persistence, and investment in nimble organizational resources than Democrats and their allies. Interest group agendas and capacities may be evolving around the two major parties, but it remains to be seen whether Democrats and their allies can gain new leverage in the politics of taxation in the months and years to come.

Notes

1. Hertel-Fernandez: ahertel@fas.harvard.edu; Skocpol: skocpol@fas.harvard.edu. We are grateful for the helpful comments we have received on earlier drafts presented at the History, Institutions, and Politics Workshop at Harvard, the Harvard Workshop on Tax Politics and Policy, and the Congress and Policy Making in the 21st Century conference at the University of Virginia. All errors are our own.

2. For an analysis of public opinion on the value of the tax cuts relative to other public policies, see the discussion in Hacker and Pierson 2005. See also the following polls that show increased support for repeal/expiration of the tax cuts when posed in context of the deficit or other public priorities after the passage of the cuts: 59 percent of respondents in a December 2010 Bloomberg poll favored repealing high income tax cuts to reduce the deficit and 54 percent of respondents in an August 2010 Ipsos/Reuters poll reported that reducing the deficit was more important than lowering taxes with the Bush tax cuts.

3. These polls include Gallup/*USA Today* (12/10/10–12/12/10); Pew Research Center (12/1/10–12/5/10; 7/22/10–7/25/10); CBS News (11/29/10–12/1/10); AP/CNBC/Gfk (11/18/10–11/22/10); CNN/ORC (11/11/10–11/14/10); AP/Gfk (11/3/10–11/8/10; 9/8/10–9/13/10; 8/11/10–8/16/10); Allstate/National Journal (8/27/10–8/30/10).

4. We find that these legislators did not come disproportionately from districts with races marked as "competitive" or "toss-up" by the Cook Report. In addition, in a regression analysis with race competitiveness, Obama vote share in 2008, share of affected taxpayers in that member's congressional district, and business group donations, we found that competiveness explained only a small amount of variation in the decision to sign one or both of the letters.

5. Open Letter to Congress from the Tax Relief Coalition, March 17th, 2009.

6. Authors' interview with Bloomberg reporter.

WORKS CITED

Andrews, Edmund. 2009. "Drilling Down on the Budget: Tax Cuts." *The New York Times*, February 26.

AP. 2010. "47 Democrats Side with GOP on Some Tax Cuts." *The Associated Press*, September 28.

Bartels, Larry. 2005. "Homer Gets a Tax Cut: Inequality and Public Policy in the American Mind." *Perspectives on Politics* 3: 15–31.

2013. "Political Effects of the Great Recession." *Annals of the American Academy of Political and Social Science* 650 (1): 47–76.

Bellantoni, Christina. 2010a. "31 Dems to Pelosi: Extend the Bush Tax Cuts for Everyone!" *Talking Points Memo*, September 16.

2010b. "Some Think Reid Is Bowing to Pressure from Dem Candidates." *Talking Points Memo*, September 23.

2010c. "Tax Cut Tick Tock." *Talking Points Memo*, September 24.
Beutler, Brian. 2010a. "Dems Officially Decide to Delay Bush Tax Cut Vote until after Election." *Talking Points Memo*, September 29.
2010b. "House Dems Vote No Confidence in Obama Tax Plan." *Talking Points Memo*, December 9.
2010c. "It's Official: No Bush Tax Cut Fight in Senate til after November Election." *Talking Points Memo*, September 23.
Binder, Sarah. 2010. "Why Democrats Can't Use Reconciliation for Tax Cuts like the GOP Did." *The Monkey Cage*, December 6.
Birnbaum, Jeffrey H. 2002. "The Man in the Middle." *Fortune Small Business*, April 1.
Block, Fred. 2009. "Read Their Lips: Taxation and the Right-Wing Agenda." In Isaac William Martin, Ajay K. Mehrotra, and Monica Prasad, eds., *The New Fiscal Sociology: Taxation in Comparative and Historical Perspective*. New York: Cambridge University Press.
Calmes, Jackie. 2009. "Obama Planning to Slash Deficit, Despite Stimulus Spending." *The New York Times*, February 21.
2010a. "In $3.8 Trillion Budget, Obama Pivots to Trim Future Deficits." *The New York Times*, February 1.
2010b. "Tax Cut Timing Is Proving Problematic for Democrats." *The New York Times*, November 8.
Calmes, Jackie, and Jeff Zeleny. 2008. "Obama Advisers Signal Tax Cuts May Stay." *The New York Times*, November 23.
Campbell, Andrea. 2009. "What Americans Think of Taxes." In Isaac William Martin, Ajay K. Mehrotra, and Monica Prasad, eds., *The New Fiscal Sociology: Taxation in Comparative and Historical Perspective*, eds. New York: Cambridge University Press, pp. 48–67.
2011. "Paying America's Way: The Fraught Politics of Taxes, Investments, and Budgetary Responsibility." In Theda Skocpol and Lawrence R. Jacobs, eds., *Reaching for a New Deal: Ambitious Governance, Economic Meltdown, and Polarized Politics in Obama's First Two Years*. New York: Russell Sage Foundation.
CBO. 2010. *Policies for Increasing Economic Growth and Employment in 2010 and 2011*. Washington, DC: Congressional Budget Office.
CBPP. 2012. *Chart Book: The Bush Tax Cuts*. Washington, DC: Center on Budget and Policy Priorities.
Corn, David. 2012. "The Myth of the Obama Cave-In." *Mother Jones Online*, November 26.
CTJ. 2010. *Compromise Tax Cut Plan Tilts Heavily in Favor of the Well-Off*. Washington, DC: Citizens for Tax Justice.
2013a. *Poorest Three-Fifths of Americans Get Just 18% of the Tax Cuts in the Fiscal Cliff Deal*. Washington, DC: Citizens for Tax Justice.
2013b. *Provisions of the Fiscal Cliff Deal*. Washington, DC: Citizens for Tax Justice.
2013c. *Revenue Impacts of the Fiscal Cliff Deal* Washington, DC: Citizens for Tax Justice.
Downs, Anthony. 1957. *An Economic Theory of Democracy*. New York: Harper.
Dreyfuss, Robert. 2001. "Grover Norquist: 'Field Marshal' of the Bush Plan." *The Nation*, April 26.
Fligstein, Neil. 2010. "Politics, the Reorganization of the Economy, and Income Inequality, 1980–2009." *Politics & Society* 38 (2): 233–42.

Fox News. 2008. "Barack Obama on 'Fox News Sunday.'" *Fox News Sunday*, April 28.

Gilens, Martin. 2012. *Affluence and Influence: Economic Inequality and Political Power in America*. Princeton, NJ: Princeton University Press.

Graetz, Michael, and Ian Shapiro. 2006. *Death by a Thousand Cuts: The Fight over Taxing Inherited Wealth*. Princeton, NJ: Princeton University Press.

Grim, Ryan. 2010. "Mary Landrieu: 'Obama-McConnell Plan' Is 'Almost Morally Corrupt.'" *The Huffington Post*, December 7.

Hacker, Jacob S., and Paul Pierson. 2005. "Abandoning the Middle: The Bush Tax Cuts and the Limits of Democratic Control." *Perspectives on Politics* 3 (1): 33–53.

2006. *Off Center: The Republican Revolution and the Erosion of American Democracy*. New Haven, CT: Yale University Press.

2010. *Winner-Take-All Politics: How Washington Made the Rich Richer – And Turned Its Back on the Middle Class*. New York: Simon & Schuster.

Herszenhorn, David M. 2010. "Next Big Battle in Washington: Bush's Tax Cuts." *The New York Times*, July 25.

Hertel-Fernandez, Alexander, and Theda Skocpol. 2013. "Asymmetric Interest Group Mobilization and Party Coalitions in U.S. Tax Politics." Presented at the Annual Midwest Political Science Association Conference, Chicago, IL.

Huang, Chye-Ching, and Nathaniel Frentz. 2012. *Bush Tax Cuts Have Provided Extremely Large Benefits to Wealthiest Americans over Last Nine Years*. Washington, DC: Center on Budget and Policy Priorities.

Huang, Chye-Ching, and Chuck Marr. 2012. *Allowing High-Income Bush Tax Cuts to Expire Would Affect Few Small Businesses*. Washington, DC: Center on Budget and Policy Priorities.

Jacobs, Lawrence R., and Robert Y. Shapiro. 2000. *Politicians Don't Pander: Political Manipulation and the Loss of Democratic Responsiveness*. Chicago, IL: University of Chicago Press.

Jacobs, Lawrence R., and Theda Skocpol. 2012. *Health Care Reform and American Politics: What Everyone Needs to Know*, revised and updated edition. New York: Oxford University Press.

James, Frank. 2010. "Sen. Bernie Sanders 'Filibusters' Tax Cut Deal." *NPR: It's All Politics*.

Jensen, Kristen, Jonathan Salant, and Michael Forsythe. 2005. "Bush Relies on Corporate Lobbyists to Help Him Push U.S. Agenda." *Bloomberg*, September 23.

Kapur, Salil. 2013. "McConnell to Obama: Fiscal Cliff Was 'The Last Word on Taxes.'" *Talking Points Memo*, January 3.

Karol, David. 2010. *Party Position Change in American Politics: Coalition Management*. New York: Cambridge University Press.

Klein, Ezra. 2010. "Tax Cuts for the Middle-Class Are Also Tax Cuts for the Rich." *The Washington Post: WonkBlog*, September 20.

Kocieniewski, David. 2010. "Tax Package Will Aid Nearly All, Especially Highest Earners." *The New York Times*, December 7.

Leonhardt, David. 2010. "In Health Bill, Obama Attacks Wealth Inequality." *The New York Times*, March 23.

Lewandoski, Mona. 2008. *The Bush Tax Cuts of 2001 and 2003: A Brief Legislative History*. Cambridge, MA: Harvard Law School Federal Budget Policy Seminar: Briefing Paper No. 37.

Lightman, David. 2010. "Pelosi: House May Vote on Tax Cuts before Fall Elections." *McClatchy DC*, September 24.

Marr, Chuck. 2010. *Letting High-Income Tax Cuts Expire Is Proper Response to Nation's Short- and Long-Term Challenges*. Washington, DC: Center on Budget and Policy Priorities.

Marr, Chuck, and Gillian Brunet. 2010. *Extension of High Income Tax Cuts Would Benefit Few Small Businesses; Jobs Tax Cut Credit Would Be Better*. Washington, DC: Center on Budget and Policy Priorities.

Martin, Isaac. 2013. *Rich People's Movements: Grassroots Campaigns to Untax the One Percent*. New York: Oxford University Press.

Mascaro, Lisa. 2010. "Biden Offers Negotiation on Extending Tax Cuts for the Wealthy." *Los Angeles Times*, October 24.

McCarty, Nolan, Howard Rosenthal, and Keith T. Poole. 2006. *Polarized America: The Dance of Ideology and Unequal Riches*. Cambridge, MA: MIT Press.

Montgomery, Lori, Shailagh Murray, and William Branigin. 2010. "Obama Signs Bill to Extend Bush-Era Tax Cuts for Two More Years." *The Washington Post*, December 17.

Morgan, Kimberly. 2007. "Constricting the Welfare State: Tax Policy and the Political Movement Against Government." In Joe Soss, Jacob Hacker, and Suzanne Mettler, eds., *Remaking America: Democracy and Public Policy in an Age of Inequality*. New York: Russell Sage Foundation.

NFIB [National Federation of Independent Business]. 2010. *Don't Raise Taxes on Small Businesses*. Blog Post on NFIB Issue Site.

Nye, Glenn. 2010. "Nye Urging Leadership to Extend Tax Cuts." The Office of Congressman Glenn Nye.

NYT. 2001. "Tax-Cut Fever in the House." *The New York Times*, March 8.

Orszag, Peter. 2010. "One Nation, Two Deficits." *The New York Times*, September 6.

Politi, Daniel. 2013. "John Boehner: 'The Talk about Raising Revenue Is Over.'" *Slate Online*, March 17.

Rosenbaum, David E. 2001. "Republicans, in New Tactic, Offer Increase in Tax Breaks." *The New York Times*, March 15.

Ruffing, Kathy, and James R. Horney. 2011. *Economic Downturn and Bush Policies Continue to Drive Large Projected Deficits*. Washington, DC: Center on Budget and Policy Priorities.

Sargent, Greg. 2010a. "A Blue Dog Dem Explains Why He Doesn't Want Vote on Middle Class Tax Cuts." *The Washington Post Line: The Plum Line*, September 15.

      2010b. "AFL-CIO Calls on Dems to Vote on Just Middle Class Tax Cuts." *The Washington Post: The Plum Line*, November 12, 2010.

      2010c. "Moderates Privately Urge Dem Leaders: No Vote on Middle Class Tax Cuts!" *The Washington Post: The Plum Line*, September 22.

Schwarz, Gabriella. 2010. "Axelrod Won't Budge." *CNN Political Ticker*, October 17.

Skocpol, Theda. 2000. *The Missing Middle: Working Families and the Future of American Social Policy*. New York: Norton.

Stein, Sam. 2010a. "Jared Bernstein, White House Economist, Throws Cold Water on Bush Tax Cuts Compromise." *The Huffington Post*, August 17.

      2010b. "Larry Summers: If Tax Deal Goes Down There's a 'Significant Risk' of a Double Dip Recession." *The Huffington Post*, December 8.

Steinhauer, Jennifer. 2013. "Divided House Passes Tax Deal in End to Latest Fiscal Standoff." *The New York Times*, January 1.

Tax Policy Center. 2010. *T10-0057 – Administration's FY2011 Budget: High Income Provisions; Baseline: Current Policy; Distribution by Cash Income Percentile, 2012.* Washington, DC.

Taylor, Andrew. 2010. "GOP, Obama Embrace Bush Tax Cuts Compromise." *The Associated Press*, November 5.

Weisman, Jonathan. 2001. "Bush's Tax-Cut Hardball Seems to Have Paid Off." *USA Today*, May 28.

2013a. "Lines of Resistance on Fiscal Deal." *The New York Times*, January 1.

2013b. "Senate Passes Legislation to Allow Taxes on Affluent to Rise." *The New York Times*, January 1.

Zandi, Mark. 2010. *The Economic Impact of Tax Cut Proposals: A Prudent Middle Course.* New York: Moody's Analytics.

Zelizer, Julian E. 2000. *Taxing America: Wilbur D. Mills, Congress, and the State, 1945–1975.* New York: Cambridge University Press.

7

The Decline of Regular Order in Appropriations

Does It Matter?

Nolan McCarty*

INTRODUCTION

Political scientists often teach an idealized version of the congressional budget and appropriation process known as the "Regular Order." As codified in the Congressional Budget and Impoundment Control Act of 1974, budgeting and appropriating should unfold in a very precise way. The president initiates the process by presenting a budget request for the following fiscal year on or before the first Monday in February. The action then moves to Congress where the House and Senate pass budget resolutions that contain spending allocations, known as 302(a), for each appropriation jurisdiction. According to the textbook, the House and Senate then use a conference committee to iron out any cross-chamber differences. Following the passage of the budget resolution, appropriation committees formulate 302(b) suballocations for each subcommittee that then produces its own appropriation bill. These proposals come to floor as individual bills that contain only appropriations. Any House–Senate differences in their respective appropriation bills are ironed out in conference. After conference reports are passed, the president signs them into law well before the beginning of the fiscal year on October 1.[1]

But over the past several years, the process is best described as the "Regular Disorder." The president often misses the early February target for his budget request. With increasing frequency, the House and Senate fail to pass a budget resolution. Even when both chambers pass budget resolutions, conference committees are rarely convened so the differences between the two resolutions are never reconciled. Over the past decade, very few appropriations bills have

* Susan Dod Brown Professor of Politics and Public Affairs, Woodrow Wilson School, Princeton University. Email: nmccarty@princeton.edu. I thank Jeff Jenkins, Eric Patashnik, and the participants from the conference on Congress and Policy Making in the 21st Century.

passed before the beginning of the fiscal year. More commonly, governmental activities are funded for many months through continuing resolutions (CRs). Occasionally, all federal spending for an entire year is provided under CRs. When appropriation bills do pass, they are often packaged together as omnibus bills that are negotiated by party leaders and the president, thus circumventing the role of the appropriation committees. These omnibus bills have increasingly become vehicles for legislative initiatives unrelated to appropriations.

In this chapter, I examine trends in what I will call the *procedural fiscal performance* of Congress and the president. In doing so, I evaluate several hypotheses about why the regular order in Congressional budgeting and appropriations has fallen into disuse. While the question has many angles and dimensions, I consider three aspects. First, I consider changes in the use of presidential budgets and congressional budget resolutions. When do presidents make their proposals? Do the House and Senate pass and reconcile resolutions? Then I consider the timing of the passage of appropriations bills and the use of continuing resolutions. Why is Congress more frequently tardy in passing appropriations and to what extent have continuing resolutions and omnibus bills become a substitute for the traditional twelve or thirteen stand-alone appropriations?

Finally, I take up the question of the extent to which the decline of regular order has affected fiscal outcomes. Has the more irregular process undermined the ability of Congress and the president to manage the government's finances? Has it created more policy uncertainty that detracts from government performance and spooks private economic actors?

SOME HYPOTHESES

There has been very little systematic work exploring why adherence to the regular order in fiscal policy making has declined so markedly. Many scholars, however, have noted substantial changes in a wide array of congressional practices that can be attributed to heightened levels of partisanship and ideological conflict in Congress.[2] But most of this work has focused on general legislative procedures and has not focused specifically on budget and appropriations processes.

In fact, there has been relatively little recent work on Congressional budget and appropriation politics. An important exception is Woon and Anderson (2012), who study the determinants of the timing of the passage of appropriation bills. Their focus, however, is on using appropriation delay to test the implications of several policy bargaining models, whereas mine is on how congressional performance has changed over time. Nevertheless, their study is extremely useful in addressing the declining adherence to the regular order. Several of Woon and Anderson's hypotheses suggest plausible mechanisms for the increased propensity of Congress to miss budgetary and appropriation deadlines.[3]

Their basic framework is a bargaining model with incomplete information. Such models predict that bargaining between pivotal actors may fail to produce a timely agreement if the preferences of those political actors diverge significantly.[4] Such a prediction suggests a connection between appropriation delay and rising levels of political polarization. Rising polarization leads to greater divergence between the president and Congress during divided government and greater divergence across chambers and appropriation committees when there is split party control of Congress. Moreover, due to the cloture rule in the Senate, appropriation gridlock may be larger as a result of polarization even during unified party government.[5]

Woon and Anderson also argue that budget enforcement rules such as those contained in the Balanced Budget and Emergency Deficit Control Act of 1985 (the Gramm-Rudman-Hollings bill) and the Budget Enforcement Act of 1990 help facilitate timely completion of appropriation bills. They argue such procedures contain enforced spending caps that reduce the discretion of Congressional majorities and appropriators. With less discretion, there are fewer incentives to engage in the tough negotiation strategies that lead to bargaining failure and delays. In the following I will reexamine these hypotheses and explore whether they help account for changing congressional procedural fiscal performance.[6]

I am unaware of any work in political science that examines whether procedural fiscal performance has a significant impact on fiscal outcomes such as spending levels or deficits. Despite popular concern about the impact of congressional dysfunction, the relationship between appropriation delays and fiscal outcomes is not clear. Because delayed appropriation bills generally lead to continuing resolutions that maintain spending at the previous year's level, delays in the passage of appropriation bills may have a dampening impact on spending and deficits. Alternatively, failures in appropriation bargaining might be symptomatic of strongly divergent spending priorities that can only be reconciled by higher levels of aggregate spending. McCubbins (1991), for example, argues that divided government combined with the clash of Republican priorities of tax cuts and defense spending and Democratic demands for social spending contributed to the large deficits of the 1980s.

A potential effect of budgetary dysfunction is the uncertainty that it creates for the economy. Baker et al. (2014) show that their measure of economic policy uncertainty has grown markedly over the past fifty years, more or less in tandem with increased levels of partisan polarization. They speculate that policy uncertainty and polarization are linked through the effect of polarization on the "capacity of policy makers to address pressing problems." Plausibly, delayed passage of appropriation bills may be one of the links between polarization and economic uncertainty. Unfinished appropriations may result in uncertainty about aggregate government spending and deficits as well as adverse effects for industries that are heavily dependent on government contracts.

I now turn to documenting the trends in procedural fiscal performance, investigating the hypotheses behind its deterioration, and evaluating its consequences.

BUDGET PROPOSALS

In this section, I examine historical trends in the timing of presidential budget proposals and congressional budget resolutions. Currently, presidents are required to make budget proposals before the first Monday in February. That deadline has varied over time, however. The Budget and Accounting Act of 1921 set a deadline of the first day of the regular congressional session.[7] In the 1950s the deadline was changed to be proposed in the first fifteen days of the session. In the 1980s, the deadline was moved up to the first Monday after January 3, but in 1990 the current rule of the first Monday in February was established.

Figure 7.1 demonstrates the timing of presidential budget requests since Fiscal Year 1923 (the first year such a submission was required under the Budget and Accounting Act of 1921). Note that budget submission delays were almost unheard of prior to the late 1970s.[8] In fact, the modal pattern of the 1950s and 1960s was for the budget to arrive on Capitol Hill a few days early except for the initial budgets of new administrations. But late budgets remain relatively rare. Other than the first budgets of new administrations, there have been five late budgets, including the last three. The timing of new administration budgets does not exhibit any clear trend.

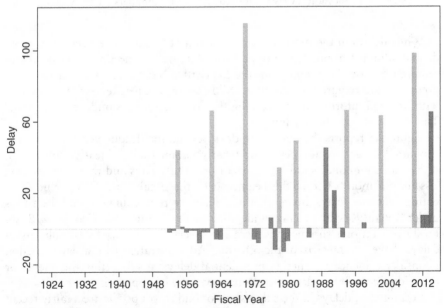

FIGURE 7.1: Each annual observation shows the number of days after the deadline that the president's budget is submitted. Negative numbers are early submissions. The lighter bars are the first budgets of new presidential administrations.

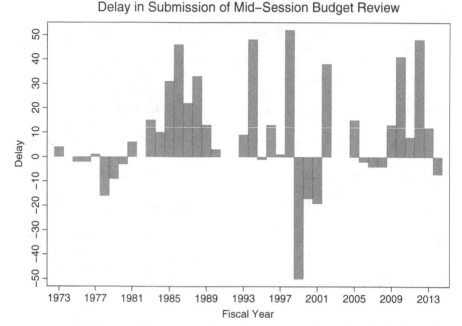

FIGURE 7.2: Each annual observation shows the number of days after the deadline that the president's mid-session review is submitted. Negative numbers are early submissions.

While delays in the presentation of the initial budget have been rare, presidential administrations have not performed as well in meeting other deadlines required by law. Beginning with the Legislative Reorganization Act of 1970, presidents are required to submit a "Mid-Session Budget Review" to Congress with updated information concerning the administration's budgetary request.[9] This report is now due on July 15.[10]

Figure 7.2 reports the number of days beyond the deadline each review was submitted (negative numbers reflect early submissions). Clearly, substantial delays are common, including delays of up to fifty days and therefore arriving less than a month before the beginning of the fiscal year. There is no clear pattern to these delays, however. Long delays were uncommon until the 1980s under Ronald Reagan but rare under George H. W. Bush and George W. Bush. President Clinton's submissions were either very late or very early. Substantial delays have characterized the Obama Administration. In a later section I consider evidence of whether presidential delays in submitting the budget or the midterm reviews delays the ultimate passage of appropriation bills.

In summary, delays in the submission of budget proposals are a fairly recent phenomenon and so are unlikely causes of the longer-term breakdown in the budget and appropriations process. Under the Obama Administration, however, an older pattern of delayed mid-session reviews was revived.

THE BUDGET RESOLUTION

After the president submits a budget, both chambers of Congress go to work on a budget resolution. Under "regular" order, both chambers pass resolutions and the differences are reconciled by a conference committee.

Congressional performance in this stage of the process shows clear deterioration over time. Figure 7.3 plots the number of stages successfully reached for each annual budget resolution. These possible stages are House passage, Senate passage, House passage of conference report, and Senate passage of conference report. From 1976 to 1998, Congress successfully cleared all four of these hurdles. Since then there has been a completed budget resolution in only eight of sixteen years. In 2011, neither chamber passed its own budget resolution.[11]

But other than the obvious time trend, no other clear pattern emerges. Divided or unified party government does not seem to play a role. The perfect success rate up to 1998 covers both divided governments (FY1977, FY1982–FY1993, and FY1996–FY1998) and unified governments (FY1978–FY1981 and FY1994–FY1995). The budget resolution survived split party control of Congress from FY1982 to FY1988. Since 1998, resolutions have both succeeded and failed during divided and unified governments, but have failed more often during unified governments. No split party congress over this period has

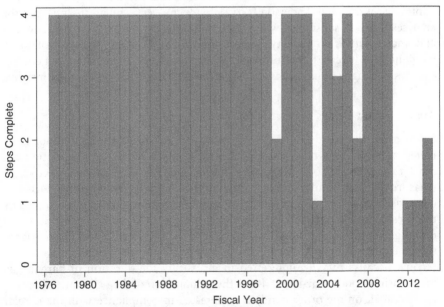

FIGURE 7.3: The progress of each annual budget resolution is scored from zero to four. Passage of an initial resolution by either chamber scores one point and the passage of a conference report by either chamber scores one point.

successfully passed a budget resolution, however. Because the president's signature is not required and budget resolutions are not subject to filibuster, it is somewhat surprising that there are so many instances where single party control of Congress failed to result in a successful budget resolution.

APPROPRIATION BILLS

Under the "regular order," appropriators go to work to allocate funds according to the budget resolution.[12]

If appropriation bills are not passed by the beginning of the fiscal year, Congress and the president must agree to a CR or face a government shutdown such as the ones that occurred in 1995–96 and 2013. Generally, CRs continue the funding levels of the previous fiscal year, but many also include some modifications of spending levels. CRs often contain changes to the authorizing statutes, and because they are often "must" pass legislation, unrelated legislation is often attached.[13]

Consequently, delays in the passage of appropriation bills and the resulting "governing by CR" have drawn wide concern. Late appropriation bills are said to create budgetary uncertainty for government agencies and private actors, reduce the ability to adjust to new spending priorities, undermine the role of committee expertise, and weaken fiscal governance.[14]

In this section, I consider the factors that lead to delayed passage of appropriation bills. Woon and Anderson (2012) conduct a very similar analysis, but the analyses differ in substantial ways reflecting different research concerns. Woon and Anderson (2012) use delay in appropriations to test a general theory of policy bargaining, whereas I am primarily concerned with explaining longer-term changes in congressional behavior. Nevertheless, I draw heavily on their insights.

Appropriation Delays

To measure the trends in the propensity to begin a fiscal year without completed appropriation bills, I compiled data on each regular appropriation bill for FY1974 to FY2014 from http://thomas/loc.gov and www.gpo.gov. To measure delay, I simply compare the date of final passage with the start date of the fiscal year. I consider an appropriation bill to have passed if it is signed by the president as a stand-alone appropriation bill or as a separate title of an omnibus appropriation bill. Thus, I do not count CRs that set funding levels for the remainder of the fiscal year. This is a departure from Woon and Anderson (2012). Because they are interested in measuring the duration of bargaining, they sensibly count year-long CRs as the culmination of the negotiations for the fiscal year. I, on the other hand, am interested in compliance with the regular order. So it is important to draw a distinction between passing appropriation bills and finishing the fiscal year under a CR. There are, however, some difficult coding decisions. In FY1987 and FY1988, omnibus appropriation bills were

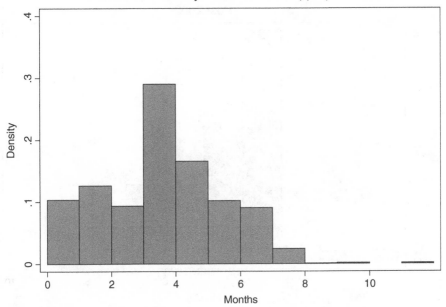

FIGURE 7.4: Distribution of delays in successful appropriation bills: 1974–2014.

passed in the form of a CR so that changes to authorizing legislation could be included. I continue to count these as CRs rather than as successful appropriation bills since the procedures deviated from the regular order.

My data is based on 524 possible appropriation bills from FY1974 to FY2014.[15] Of these, 408 were passed as stand-alone or omnibus appropriation bills. That leaves 95 "failures" – appropriation jurisdictions that were funded by CRs for the entire fiscal year.

Figures 7.4 and 7.5 present the distribution of appropriation delays in months.[16] Figure 7.4 presents the data for the entire sample. Appropriation delays are the norm. Only about 10 percent of all appropriation bills passed prior to the beginning of the fiscal year. The modal month of passage is during the third month of the fiscal year (currently December). But a substantial share of bills pass in months four, five, and six.

Figure 7.5 shows the distribution of delays since 2002. Clearly, delays have become much more common. Very few appropriation bills have been completed on time since 2002 and the frequency of delays exceeding two months has gone up dramatically.

Figure 7.6 presents the trends in appropriation delay in a different way. The figure plots the percentage of the twelve or thirteen appropriation bills that have passed prior to each month since 1984. A lowess line has been added to

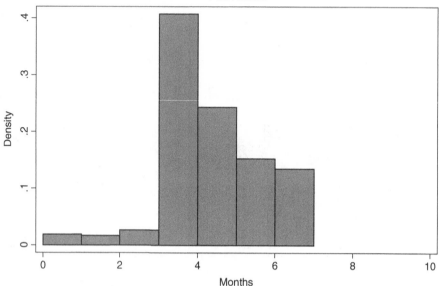

FIGURE 7.5: Distribution of delays in successful appropriation bills: 2002–2014

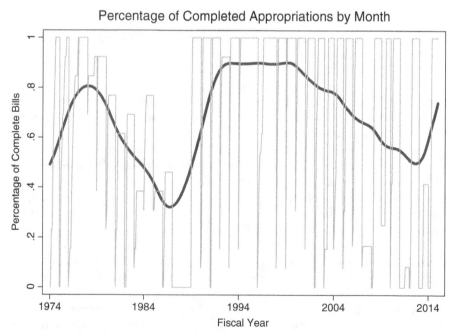

FIGURE 7.6: Completed appropriations by month. The level of the line reflects the proportion of appropriation bills that have been completed in each month of the fiscal year. The darker line is a lowess smoother.

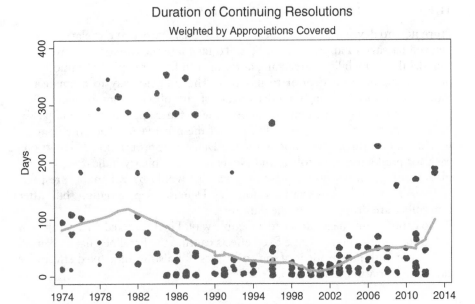

FIGURE 7.7: Duration of continuing resolutions, FY1974 to FY2013.

aid in identifying the short-term trends. There has been an increase in the frequency of spending much of the fiscal year without appropriations. Over the past few years, there have been very few months for which more than 40 percent of the appropriation bills were in effect (although the very recent performance is slightly better). But the figure also demonstrates that the current era of poor performance is not unprecedented. Delayed appropriation bills were also quite common in the 1980s.[17] These nonmonotonic trends suggest that the current difficulties are more than simply a reflection of longer-term trends such as partisan polarization.

Not surprisingly, these patterns of late appropriation bills generate patterns in the usage of continuing resolutions. But as Figure 7.7 shows there are substantial differences in the usages of CRs that are not quite accounted for by delayed appropriation bills. In the 1970s, CRs were less numerous but longer than those of recent years. This reflects the fact that CRs were more often used as a mechanism for crafting omnibus legislation that included appropriation and authorization legislation than as stop-gap measures when appropriation bills were not passed on time. In the 1990s, the low point for appropriation delays, CRs were frequent but very short in nature. But over the past decade, CRs were frequently employed and have increased markedly in duration. From FY1991 through FY2002, the median CR lasted only seven days. Since FY2003, the median has been twenty-one days.

THE CORRELATES OF APPROPRIATION DELAY

I turn now to developing a statistical model of the factors that correlate with the delayed passage of appropriation bills. To facilitate the ease of interpretation, I model the probability of reaching agreement in fiscal month t conditional on not reaching agreement prior to month t. The simplest way to estimate this model is to specify a logit model on all of the observations of incomplete appropriation bills. For example, suppose the Defense appropriation bill passes in November of FY t (the second month of the fiscal year). Then the data set would contain three observations for the Defense appropriation bill at t: one each for pre-October, October, and November. The binary indicator for completing an appropriation for these observations would be 0, 0, and 1, respectively. All monthly observations for the Defense appropriation bill after November are dropped from the data set.

To capture time dependence in a flexible way, I include fixed effects for each month of the fiscal year. These fixed effects capture the baseline "hazard rates" for each month independent of the covariates.[18] I also include fixed effects for each appropriation jurisdiction.[19]

Preference Divergence

Woon and Anderson (2012) present a formal model and evidence that demonstrates that appropriation bills are more likely to be delayed as a result of divergent preferences across those who are negotiating. I will measure preference divergence in two ways. First, I use "common space" DW-NOMINATE to compute measures of the preference differences across chambers and branches.[20] I use four separate measures: the average distance between the House and Senate, the average distance between the House and president, the average distance between the Senate and president, and the maximum of these distances. As a robustness check, I also use partisan indicators for preference divergence using measures such as divided government and split party control of Congress. To capture the possibility that the partisan indicators might represent greater divergence in recent years due to partisan polarization, I interact them with polarization measured as the average distance between the two parties in the House on the common space DW-NOMINATE scores.

Budgetary Enforcement Rules

Budget enforcement rules may also play a role in congressional performance on appropriations. Rules may support prompt action on appropriations in a variety of ways. Rules that reduce the discretion of appropriators may serve to minimize the probability of bargaining failure by reducing the scope of conflict. Internal procedures may also provide incentives for appropriation committees to be first- or last-movers depending on enforcement rules.

I test for the effects of two different budget enforcement regimes. The first is the Balanced Budget and Emergency Deficit Control Act of 1985, better known by the names of its Senate co-sponsors Gramm-Rudman-Hollings (GRH). The key mechanism underlying GRH was specified deficit targets enforced by across-the-board sequester. As a deficit-cutting tool, GRH has generally been deemed a failure, but it did set a precedent for reducing the discretion of appropriators.[21] GRH may also have perversely enhanced the incentives to delay reporting appropriation bills out of subcommittee. Former appropriations subcommittee chair David Obey warned that

so long as Gramm-Rudman is on the books there is an incentive for every committee around here not to bring their bill out to floor, because even if they cut their own bill and meet the spending limitations required under a budget resolution, that does not guarantee that every other committee will perform, and so they can wind up having their bill cut twice.[22]

Therefore, any effect of GRH in reducing the scope of legislative conflict may have been offset by this last-mover advantage. I include an indicator for fiscal years 1985 to 1990 to capture the net effects of GRH.

Following the failure of the GRH mechanisms, Congress passed the Budget Enforcement Act of 1990 (BEA 90). The BEA 90 had three important features: adjustable deficit targets, annual limits on discretionary spending, and statutory "pay-as-you-go" (PAYGO) rules that require offsetting tax increases or spending cuts for measures that increase the deficit.[23] The discretionary spending caps were renewed in 1993 and 1997. PAYGO was extended in 1997, but ended in 2002. Therefore, I include an indicator for the fiscal years 1991 to 2002 to capture the effects of the BEA 90.

Fiscal and Economic Conditions

The timing of appropriation bills may also be influenced by current fiscal and economic conditions. Large deficits may increase the salience of conflicts over spending priorities and contribute to delayed passage. Conversely, periods of economic growth produce more resources for the government and may lessen conflict over spending. To capture these effects, I include two variables: the federal budget deficit from the previous year and the GDP growth rate from the previous quarter. My expectation is that deficits reduce the likelihood of passage in a given month while GDP growth increases it.

The President

I also include a number of controls to capture the presidential impact on the process. As discussed earlier, presidents may be responsible for poor procedural performance by delaying budgetary submissions and reports. So I include two variables measuring the number of days the administration misses the deadline for the initial budget proposal and the number of days the administration misses the deadline for the mid-session review.[24] Clearly, however, one must be careful in interpreting the correlations between these variables and delayed appropriations as causal. Presidents may delay proposals and reports based on expectations of conflict or there may be omitted variables correlated with both delayed presidential action and delayed congressional action.

Presidential transitions may also affect the procedural fiscal performance. Such transitions may be times of greater-than-normal policy change, which may generate more conflict and complexity in fiscal policy making. But transitions may also correspond to presidential "honeymoons" where deference to presidential priorities might facilitate quicker action on appropriations. While I lack a clear prediction about the direction of the correlation, I include an indicator for the first fiscal year of a new presidential administration. For similar considerations, I also include an indicator for the six months prior to a presidential election.

Results

Tables 7.1 and 7.2 report the estimates from the preference- and party-based models, respectively. I begin with the preference model. In model 1, separate coefficients are estimated for the distances between the House and Senate medians, the president and the House median, and the distance between the president and the House median. When all three of these distance measures are included, none is statistically significant. But because all of these distance measures are highly correlated, multicollinearity is clearly an issue. Therefore, models 2 through 4 include a single preference measure. In models 2 and 3, the preference measure has a statistically significant negative coefficient at conventional levels, but the president–Senate difference has a p-value of around 0.2. To gauge the substantive magnitudes of these effects, consider a appropriation bill that would have a monthly conditional probability of passage of 0.5 at the minimum of the distance measure. Model 2 suggests that moving to the maximum value of the House–Senate difference would reduce the monthly probability of passage of that benchmark bill to 0.18. The respective values for the maximum values of the president–House and president–Senate distances are 0.12 and 0.27. In model 5, I replace the individual measures with the maximum of the three distances. The estimate of the maximal difference has an effect almost equivalent to that of the president–House distance.

Table 7.2 presents results from the party model that are quite complementary, although the precision of the estimates is generally lower. In model 6, the presence of a split party Congress or divided government reduces the likelihood of successful passage. If an appropriation bill has a monthly probability of passage of 0.5 under a single party Congress (unified government), it has only a 0.32 (0.35) probability under split party control (divided government). Party polarization is predicted to reduce the likelihood of passage, but the standard

TABLE 7.1 *Preference Models*

	Model 1	Model 2	Model 3	Model 4	Model 5
House–Senate Distance	−1.449	−3.311			
	(1.859)	(1.675)			
Pres-House Distance	−2.255		−2.607		
	(1.659)		(1.079)		
Pres-Senate Distance	0.153			−1.399	
	(1.075)			(1.060)	
Budget Enforcement Act	1.389	1.242	1.482	1.466	1.420
	(0.448)	(0.406)	(0.410)	(0.397)	(0.406)
Gramm-Rudman-Hollings	0.0941	−0.577	0.356	0.103	0.237
	(0.826)	(0.701)	(0.794)	(0.758)	(0.759)
Lagged Surplus	0.0513	−0.00293	0.0711	0.0690	0.0828
	(0.0809)	(0.0736)	(0.0838)	(0.0885)	(0.0854)
Lagged Growth	0.275	0.199	0.277	0.187	0.255
	(0.179)	(0.195)	(0.179)	(0.181)	(0.170)
Presidential Transition	−0.681	−0.193	−0.680	−0.139	−0.579
	(0.994)	(1.101)	(0.990)	(1.087)	(0.989)
Presidential Election	0.760	0.757	0.711	0.598	0.688
	(0.461)	(0.428)	(0.488)	(0.501)	(0.499)
Delay in Budget Submission	0.271	0.175	0.273	0.165	0.253
	(0.257)	(0.273)	(0.260)	(0.279)	(0.260)
Delay in Mid-Session Report	−0.247	−0.180	−0.293	−0.303	−0.276
	(0.131)	(0.125)	(0.125)	(0.123)	(0.122)
Maximum Distance					−2.441
					(0.952)
N	2305	2305	2305	2305	2305
Log-Likelihood	−894.8	−905.8	−897.2	−912.8	−898.3

Standard errors in parentheses.
Logit models of the probability of successful passage of appropriation bill in month t conditional on not passing by end of month t-1. Month and jurisdicion indicators not reported.

error is large. In model 7, I add an interaction between divided government and polarization. This coefficient suggests that polarization has enhanced the negative effect of divided government on procedural performance.[25] Unlike the results using ideological distances, the estimated effects of party control and polarization are not very robust to inclusion of the measures for presidential budget delays (models 8 and 9). This suggests that at least part of the impact of divided government and polarization is produced by the president's behavior on the mid-session review.

I turn now to the findings on budget enforcement rules. Like Woon and Anderson (2012), I find that the GRH procedures have no effect on procedural performance. But I find a large and robust impact of the 1990 Budget Enforcement Act. Based on these estimates, the effects of the BEA are large enough to

TABLE 7.2 *Party Models*

	Model 6	Model 7	Model 8	Model 9
Split Congress	−0.729	−0.694	−0.537	−0.512
	(0.417)	(0.408)	(0.418)	(0.408)
Divided Government	−0.617	0.593	−0.857	−0.0950
	(0.447)	(2.712)	(0.451)	(2.557)
Polarization	−2.260	−1.210	−1.229	−0.585
	(1.690)	(2.800)	(2.012)	(2.797)
Budget Enforcement Act	1.425	1.453	1.611	1.624
	(0.397)	(0.394)	(0.456)	(0.459)
Gramm-Rudman-Hollings	−0.635	−0.653	−0.0529	−0.0782
	(0.733)	(0.731)	(0.814)	(0.814)
Lagged Surplus	0.0536	0.0613	0.0466	0.0518
	(0.0646)	(0.0731)	(0.0750)	(0.0776)
Lagged Growth	0.227	0.233	0.191	0.196
	(0.152)	(0.152)	(0.196)	(0.195)
Presidential Transition	0.377	0.382	−0.496	−0.497
	(0.374)	(0.384)	(1.099)	(1.111)
Presidential Election	0.487	0.524	0.609	0.630
	(0.435)	(0.442)	(0.427)	(0.433)
Polarization × Divided		−1.698		−1.067
		(3.821)		(3.520)
Delay in Budget Submission			0.277	0.277
			(0.274)	(0.275)
Delay in Mid-Session Report			−0.195	−0.191
			(0.136)	(0.134)
N	2305	2305	2305	2305
Log-Likelihood	−899.0	−898.5	−887.4	−887.2

Standard errors in parentheses.
Logit models of the probability of successful passage of appropriation bill in month t conditional on not passing by end of month t-1. Month and jurisdiction indicators not reported.

raise the monthly passage probability from 0.5 to more than 0.8. But we must be concerned about the possibility that the BEA indicator is simply proxying for other unmeasured features of the 1990s. To test this possibility, I consider a number of placebo dates by shifting the twelve-year window forward and backward from the actual dates of FY1991 to FY2002. Based on the estimated log-likelihood and the magnitude of the placebo BEA coefficient, the best-fitting twelve-year window is FY1989 to FY2000. That the improved performance came before the BEA suggests that factors other than the BEA may also have played a role in the procedural performance of the 1990s.[26]

The estimated effects of fiscal and economic conditions are also quite consistent across the preference and party models. I find no evidence that the magnitude of the previous year's surplus or deficit has any impact on the timing of appropriation bills. Economic growth, however, does correlate with good procedural performance. A 1 percent increase in the GDP growth rate from the previous quarter is sufficient to raise the monthly passage probability from 0.5 to 0.57. There is little evidence that performance is either promoted or impeded during the first fiscal year of a new administration. But Congress appears to be somewhat more efficient in the months surrounding presidential elections.

Finally, I turn to the evidence that presidential delays affect congressional performance. Submission delays of the original budget do not slow down the timing of appropriations. In fact, there is a positive probability between the delay in initial submission and the monthly probability of passage (although the standard error of this estimate is large and the effect is not statistically significant). The delay in the mid-session report does have a negative and statistically significant effect. A one-standard deviation increase in the (log) delay is associated with a 0.10 drop in the monthly probability of passage if the baseline is 0.5. But I should repeat the caveat that such estimates may not reflect causal effects if both the president and Congress are responding to some omitted variable.

DOES IT MATTER?

Despite recent concerns about Congress's recent proclivity to "govern by CR," there is little systematic evidence of its consequences on fiscal or economic outcomes. In this section, I provide some preliminary evidence for two possible effects. First, I examine whether procedural performance has any clear impact on Congress's ability to control fiscal outcomes such as spending or the deficit. Second, I consider whether poor procedural performance might create economic uncertainties that affect the broader economy.

Delayed Appropriations, Deficits, and Spending

To evaluate whether procedural performance affects Congress's overall fiscal management, I estimate some simple lagged dependent variable models. Because I am constrained by a relatively short annual time series, I am unable to estimate more complicated dynamic models. I consider three different measures of annual procedural performance: the percentage of appropriations completed by the beginning of the fiscal year and the percent completed by second and third months of the fiscal year. As additional controls, I include the GDP growth rate and an indicator for the Budget Enforcement Act of 1990.

I begin by examining whether there is a connection between fiscal performance and the changes in the government surplus or deficit. Figure 7.8 plots the bivariate relationship between the annual change in surplus and the percentage of appropriation bills completed by the third month of the fiscal year. Clearly,

TABLE 7.3 *Effect of Completed Appropriations on Change in Surplus*

	Start of FY	Month 2	Month 3
Lagged Surplus	−0.241	−0.245	−0.242
	(0.0762)	(0.0765)	(0.0763)
Percentage Complete	0.0750	0.270	0.0979
	(0.570)	(0.602)	(0.556)
Growth Rate	1.231	1.223	1.236
	(0.230)	(0.219)	(0.217)
BEA 1990	0.595	0.496	0.585
	(0.463)	(0.506)	(0.468)
N	40	40	40
R-Squared	0.577	0.579	0.577

Standard errors in parentheses.
OLS estimates of the effects of completed appropriations on yearly change in surplus.
Different models capture completion rates at different points in the fiscal year.

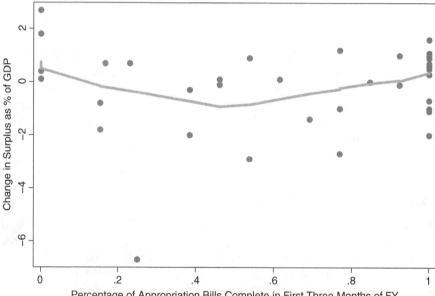

FIGURE 7.8: Complete appropriations and deficits.

there is no strong relationship. Significant deficit reduction coincides with both good and bad procedural performance.

Table 7.3 reports the regression results for the change in government surplus. Controlling for the lagged surplus and economic growth, the coefficient

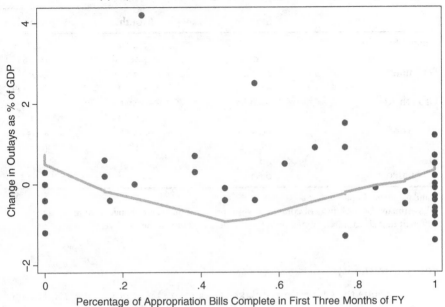

FIGURE 7.9: Complete appropriations and spending.

on completed appropriations is positive, indicating a positive relationship between procedural performance and deficit reduction. But the coefficients are imprecisely estimated and the relationship falls well short of standards for statistical significance.[27]

Of course, surpluses and deficits are functions both of spending and of tax policy. So I now consider whether spending, the area most under the control of the appropriators, correlates with their performance. Figure 7.9 plots the bivarate relationship between annual change in total federal outlays (as a percentage of GDP) and the percentage of complete appropriation bills. Again there appears to be no strong relationship. This is confirmed by the regression results presented in Table 7.4. The coefficient estimates show that spending decreases slightly when more appropriation bills are completed. But the estimates are very imprecise and not statistically significant.

While I do not report the results, the null findings hold even when spending is narrowed to changes in discretionary spending. I also considered whether poor procedural performance led to large changes (positive or negative) to deficits and spending. But there is no systematic correlation between completed appropriation bills and the absolute change in deficits or spending.

In summary, there is very little evidence that procedural performance has a systematic impact on fiscal outcomes (at least at the level of annual spending and deficit levels).

TABLE 7.4 *Effect of Completed Appropriations on Change in Outlays*

	Start of FY	Month 2	Month 3
Lagged Spending	−0.238	−0.236	−0.238
	(0.0652)	(0.0656)	(0.0652)
Percentage Complete	0.0521	0.120	0.0733
	(0.333)	(0.352)	(0.324)
Growth Rate	−0.800	−0.801	−0.797
	(0.134)	(0.128)	(0.127)
BEA 1990	−0.504	−0.543	−0.514
	(0.262)	(0.289)	(0.265)
N	40	40	40
R-Squared	0.633	0.634	0.634

Standard errors in parentheses.
OLS estimates of the effects of completed appropriations on yearly change in total outlays.
Different models capture completion rates at different points in the fiscal year.

Policy Uncertainty

I now examine the suggestion of Baker et al. (2014) that governmental dysfunction contributes to policy uncertainty. To address this question, I use a measure of policy uncertainty developed by Baker et al. (2013) that utilizes media coverage of the economy. Their index is based on search results from ten large newspapers.[28] An article is treated as an indicator of policy uncertainty when it contains the term "uncertainty" or "uncertain," the terms "economic" or "economy," and one or more of the following terms: "congress," "legislation," "White House," "regulation," "federal reserve," or "deficit." Because this policy uncertainty index has been shown to correlate negatively with investment and economic performance, a connection between it and appropriation delays could indicate the macroeconomic costs of poor procedural budgetary performance.

Figure 7.10 plots the monthly policy uncertainty from 1985 to 2014. The figure identifies several periods of high economic uncertainty: the late 1980s and early 1990s, the period around 9/11 and the Afghan and Iraq Wars, and the period since the financial crisis. As we have seen, the first and third of these periods are also periods of procedural dysfunction. So a correlation between delayed appropriations and uncertainty is plausible. Figure 7.11 explores this possibility by plotting the percentage of completed appropriation bills against the policy uncertainty measure. The lowess line shows a slight decline of uncertainty in months with a greater percentage of completed appropriation bills.

To investigate this relationship further, Table 7.5 reports several simple regression models of monthly measures of policy uncertainty on the percentage of completed appropriation bills. Model 1 is the bivariate relationship between uncertainty and completed appropriations. The results indicate that the uncertainty index is about twenty units lower in months where all appropriation bills

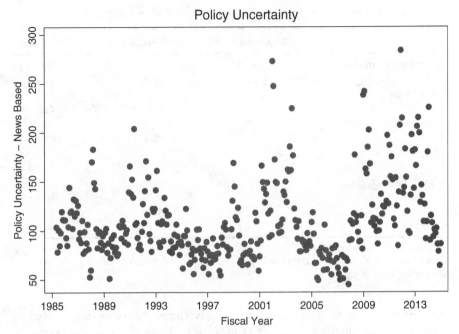

FIGURE 7.10: Policy uncertainty.

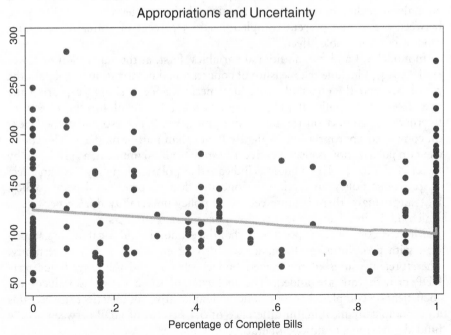

FIGURE 7.11: Uncertainty and complete appropriations.

TABLE 7.5 *Effect of Completed Appropriations on Policy Uncertainty*

	Model 1	Model 2	Model 3
Percentage Complete	−19.92	−21.64	−12.14
	(5.295)	(5.040)	(5.075)
Polarization		109.1	89.11
		(28.13)	(28.46)
International Conflict		43.16	40.49
		(8.327)	(7.890)
Lagged Surplus			−2.937
			(0.696)
Lagged Growth Rate			−18.15
			(3.140)
N	357	357	339
R-Squared	0.0383	0.136	0.258

Standard errors in parentheses.
OLS estimates of the effects of completed appropriations on policy uncertainty.
Data from Baker et al. (2013).

have been enacted than in months where government is completely funded by CRs. Using the findings of Baker et al. (2013), I can quantify the economic magnitude of this effect. Based on results of a vector auto regressive model, they report that a ninety-point increase in policy uncertainty leads to a 2.3 percent annualized decline in GDP. A simple extrapolation suggests that the difference between 0 and 100 percent completion is 0.5 percent of annualized GDP: a modest but noticeable effect.[29]

In model 2, I add two additional variables. First, at the suggestion of Baker et al. (2014), I include the measure of congressional polarization to rule out the possibility that the effect of procedural performance is simply capturing the overall effect of political polarization. Second, I control for the effects of international conflict on the uncertainty measure.[30] The estimated coefficient on completed appropriation is slightly larger than that of model 1. The coefficient on polarization is also negative and statistically significant, as predicted by Baker et al. (2014). These findings indicate that polarization may have an effect on economic policy uncertainty beyond its effect on procedural performance. Not surprisingly, there is more economic policy uncertainty during periods in which the United States is involved in international conflicts.

Model 3 considers the possibility that the economic and fiscal factors associated with procedural performance are driving economic policy uncertainty. Therefore, measures of the lagged budget surplus and the lagged quarterly GDP growth rate are added. The inclusion of these variables reduces the coefficient on completed appropriations significantly, but the effect size remains an economically meaningful difference of 0.3 percent of GDP between a fully funded government and one operating on CRs.

In summary, there is some modest evidence that poor procedural perform-ance enhances economic uncertainty substantially enough to have meaningful economic effects. But given the null results for an effect of procedural perform-ance on objective fiscal policy outcomes, the nature of this uncertainty remains unclear. It may reflect uncertainty about very short-run fiscal outcomes that I cannot capture in the annual time series, or it may be the psychological effect on economic actors of observing apparent government dysfunction.

CONCLUSIONS

Despite the current anxieties over how the Congress and the president are handling their fiscal policy responsibilities, political scientists have focused much less attention on longer-term trends in procedural performance on fiscal policy than they have on the performance of judicial and executive branch nominations and general legislation. The primary goal of this chapter is to lay out some of the trends in procedural performance on fiscal policy and to lay the foundation for future research.

Several of the preliminary findings warrant more intensive future investiga-tion. First, although there is ample evidence that partisan and ideological conflict impedes performance in the budget and appropriation process, my results demonstrate that there must be more to the story. Performance in the relatively less polarized 1980s was poor, it was excellent through much of the 1990s (with the notable exception of the 1995 government shutdown), and it has rapidly deteriorated over the past decade. Second, while the timing of the improved performance of the 1990s does not align exactly with the Budget Enforcement Act of 1990, the evidence is plausibly consistent with the beneficial effects of spending caps and PAYGO rules. Clearly, more work is needed to isolate these effects. Third, this chapter raises the crucial question of whether the propensity to govern by CR has significant effects on outcomes. While there are limitations to my analysis of the effects of appropriation delay on annual deficit and spending figures, the results do seem to rule out first-order effects on major fiscal aggregates. At the same time, I present some evidence consistent with an effect of procedural performance on the expectations of economic actors.

Notes

1. The fiscal year began on July 1 until 1977. See Tollestrup (2013) for a thorough discussion of these procedures.
2. Mann and Ornstein (2006), McCarty, Poole, and Rosenthal (2006), McCarty (2007), Smith (2010), and Sinclair (2006).
3. In a recent paper, Hanson (2014) argues that the Senate leaders of weak majority parties will depart from the regular order by combing several appropriation bills into an omnibus package. Such a maneuver helps insulate the package from minority party amendments. He does not, however, connect his theory to the central concern of this paper – delayed passage of appropriation bills.

4. See Cameron (2000) and Cameron and McCarty (2004) for a discussion and other applications of policy bargaining with incomplete information.

5. See Krehbiel (1998) and McCarty (2007).

6. Another possible reason for the congressional tendency toward governing by CR is that the use of very short-term spending bills may increase congressional leverage over agencies. This was clearly the rationale behind the so-called "crominbus" (CR + omnibus) passed by the Republicans in 2014 where all agencies received annual appropriations except the Department of Homeland Security, which was funded by CR. This was an attempt to prevent the implementation of President Obama's executive order on immigration. This rationale for CRs has almost identical observable implications as the bargaining failure story – CRs rise when interbranch conflict rises. It does have a somewhat more benign normative implication in that Congress may benefit from the strategy. It is not clear that the strategy is an effective one, however. CRs will also maintain presidential leverage through the veto, and thus it is not clear that it produces net gains from Congress.

7. Before the passage of the 20th Amendment, regular congressional sessions typically began in December. So the budget request for fiscal year 1923 was due in December of 1921.

8. The only exception was FY1955, when President Eisenhower missed the deadline by a single day.

9. P.L. 91-510, 84 Stat. 1140.

10. Prior to the change of the start of the fiscal year from July 1 to October 1 in FY1977, the deadline for the mid-session review was June 1.

11. See Lynch (2013) for a discussion of the FY2011 budget politics.

12. If a chamber has not passed its budget resolution, it may pass a "deeming resolution" that contains temporary 302(a) allocations. See Lynch (2013). In 2011, the Senate passed neither a budget nor a deeming resolution.

13. See Tollestrup (2013), p. 21, and White (1988).

14. See White (1988), Devins (1988), and Hanson (2013).

15. There were thirteen possible appropriation bills from FY1974 to FY2005 and twelve from FY2006 to FY2014.

16. In both figures, a delay of zero is assigned to any bill passed prior to the start of the fiscal year.

17. The number of months without appropriation bills in the 1980s is clearly increased by my decision not to treat the spending packages of FY1987 and FY1988 as successful appropriation bills. But because those packages were substantially delayed, the figure would not look qualitatively different if I treated those cases as omnibus appropriations rather than as year-long CRs.

18. My approach, therefore, is roughly equivalent to the Cox Proportional Hazard model. I adopt the logit specification because it lends itself to a more natural interpretation – for each month, what is the probability that an outstanding appropriation bill passes? The results using the Cox model are almost identical.

19. The jurisdiction fixed effects help control for how the content and programs in each area may induce more or less conflict in bargaining. See Woon and Anderson (2012).

20. Poole (2000).

21. Schick (2008).

22. 134 CONG. REC. H68-69 (daily ed. Feb. 2, 1988) from Devins (1988).
23. Unlike legislative rules-based PAYGO, which are enforced by points of order, statutory PAYGO measures are enforced by the Office of Management and Budget, which is empowered to employ sequesters to offset violations.
24. Because these variables are highly skewed, I set all 0 and all negative values to 1 and take the natural logs of number of days.
25. Due to the multicollinearity generated by the interaction, the coefficient on the interaction effect is not statistically significant. But divided government, polarization, and the interaction are highly significant jointly.
26. Importantly, when the dates are backshifted two years, they capture the last two years of the GRH regime. So it is also possible that GRH had a lagged effect on procedural performance.
27. Although Figure 7.8 suggests the possibility of a nonlinear relationship between procedural performance and the change in deficit, there is no evidence in favor of a quadratic specification.
28. The newspapers are the *Boston Globe, Dallas Morning News, Los Angeles Times, Miami Herald, New York Times, San Francisco Chronicle, USA Today, Wall Street Journal*, and *Washington Post*.
29. This calculation is simply suggestive. Neither the conclusions of Baker et al. 2013 nor my estimates are clearly causally identified.
30. My conflict measure is coded 1 for the duration of the Gulf War, September through December of 2001 for 9/11 and the Afghanistan invasion, and the first seven months of the Iraq War in 2003.

References

Baker, Scott, Nicholas Bloom, and Steven Davis. 2013. "Measuring Economic Policy Uncertainty." *Chicago Booth Research Paper* (February).

Baker, Scott, Nicholas Bloom, Brandice Canes-Wrone, Steven J. Davis, and Jonathan A. Rodden. 2014. "Why Has U.S. Policy Uncertainty Risen since 1960?" National Bureau of Economic Research Working Paper No. 19826.

Cameron, Charles M. 2000. *Veto Bargaining: Presidents and the Politics of Negative Power*. New York: Cambridge University Press.

Cameron, Charles, and Nolan McCarty. 2004. "Models of Vetoes and Veto Bargaining." *Annual Review Political Science* 7: 409–35.

Devins, Neal E. 1988. "Appropriations Redux: A Critical Look at the Fiscal Year 1988 Continuing Resolution." *Duke Law Journal* (1988) 389–421.

Hanson, Peter. 2014. "Abandoning the Regular Order: Majority Party Influence on Appropriations in the United States Senate." *Political Research Quarterly* 67(3) 519–532.

Krehbiel, Keith. 1998. *Pivotal Politics: A Theory of U.S. Lawmaking*. Chicago, IL: University of Chicago Press.

Lynch, Megan S. 2013. "The Deeming Resolution: A Budget Enforcement Tool." Congressional Research Service.

Mann, Thomas E., and Norman J. Ornstein. 2006. *The Broken Branch: How Congress Is Failing America and How to Get It Back on Track*. New York: Oxford University Press.

McCarty, Nolan. 2007. "The Policy Effects of Political Polarization." In Paul Pierson and Theda Skocpol, eds., *Transformations of American Politics*. Princeton, NJ: Princeton University Press.

McCarty, Nolan, Keith Poole, and Howard Rosenthal. 2006. *Polarized American: The Dance of Ideology and Unequal Riches*. Cambridge: MIT Press.

McCubbins, Mathew D. 1991. "Party Governance and U.S. Budget Deficits: Divided Government and Fiscal Stalemate." In Alberto Alesina and Geoffrey Carliner, eds., *Politics and Economics in the Eighties*. Chicago, IL: University of Chicago Press.

Poole, Keith T. 2000. "Non-parametric Unfolding of Binary Choice Data." *Political Analysis* 8: 211–37.

Schick, Allen. 2008. *The Federal Budget: Politics, Policy, Process*. Washington DC: Brookings Institution Press.

Sinclair, Barbara. 2006. *Party Wars: Polarization and the Politics of National Policy Making*. Vol. 10. Norman: University of Oklahoma Press.

Smith, Steven S. 2010. "The Senate Syndrome." *Issues in Governance Studies* 35.

Tollestrup, Jessica. 2013. "The Congressional Appropriations Process: An Introduction." Congressional Research Service.

White, Joe. 1988. "The Continuing Resolution: A Crazy Way to Govern?" *The Brookings Review* 6 (3): 28–35.

Woon, Jonathan and Sarah Anderson. 2012. "Political Bargaining and the Timing of Congressional Appropriations." *Legislative Studies Quarterly* 37 (4): 409–36.

8

Congress and the Federal Reserve

Independence and Accountability

Sarah Binder and Mark Spindel*

In his last press conference as chairman of the Federal Reserve's Board of Governors in 2013, Ben Bernanke was asked what advice he would offer Janet Yellen, the incoming chair, for dealing with Congress. Bernanke kept it simple: "Congress is our boss" (Federal Reserve 2013, 29). The Federal Reserve's (or Fed's) relationship with Congress is hardly that straightforward. Indeed, Bernanke immediately added: "It is important that we maintain our policy independence in order to be able to make decisions without short term political interference." Bernanke's advice and admonition highlight the inevitable tension for Congress between insulating monetary policy from political pressure and holding the Fed accountable for its policy decisions.

The trade off between independence and democratic accountability is most apparent in the wake of financial and economic crises with interest rates at zero and central banks compelled to break the glass, tapping unconventional tools to ease policy further. Indeed, the recent global financial crisis reveals the limits of central bank independence. In the United States, Europe, and Japan, politicians have renewed their focus on central banks – replacing governors, revamping lending powers, and demanding greater accountability. Heightened oversight of monetary policy contrasts sharply with studies of central bank autonomy: Politicians are said to prefer independent central banks because more independent monetary authorities aim to deliver lower and more stable inflation (Alesina and Summers 1993). Committing in advance to central bank autonomy in theory prevents politicians from interfering with monetary policy to ease conditions for electoral gain.

* We thank Alyx Mark, Douglas Cohen, and Benny Miller-Gootnick for invaluable research assistance.

Why and when do politicians threaten to revise the degree of independence they afford their central banks? And how does the current state of partisan polarization – coincident with the worst financial crisis since the Great Depression – affect how lawmakers react to the Fed's implementation of monetary policy? In this chapter, we focus on Congress's relationship with the Federal Reserve in the postwar period. First, we offer a framework for understanding how lawmakers influence monetary policy given expectations of central bank independence. We argue that Congress and the president largely shape monetary policy *indirectly*: setting goals for the Fed, reforming Fed governance, and imposing greater transparency. Second, we explore the conditions under which lawmakers threaten to change the Fed's goals, governance, or accountability. Examining patterns in the sponsorship of House and Senate bills addressing the powers and governance of the Fed over a sixty-year period, we show that congressional threats flow predictably from both the state of the economy and lawmakers' electoral and partisan interests. Finally, we explore how the Fed's adoption of unconventional monetary policies in the current period of partisan polarization provoked both parties to push for greater accountability at the cost of the Fed's independence. Accountability, we argue, trumps independence when lawmakers seek to blame the Fed for a faltering economy.

THE ACCOUNTABILITY–INDEPENDENCE TRADE OFF

Politicians face a dilemma in designing central banks. Given the impact on output, inflation, and employment, macroeconomic decisions made by central banks are among the most important policy choices rendered in a democracy. Monetary policy affects interest rates, which in turn shape the public's borrowing costs, the availability of credit, and ultimately household wealth. As public demand for goods and services grows, economic growth ensues as businesses increase production and employ more workers. The dilemma arises from politicians' electoral incentives, which lead them to want to stimulate the economy – particularly in the run-up to an election. That short-term strategy, however, has long-term costs: it increases the chances of inflation and brings an inevitable economic recessionary payback.

The solution worldwide has been to try to insulate central bankers from political interference that might otherwise induce monetary policy makers to keep interest rates too loose for too long. That is the root of politicians' dilemma: fully autonomous central banks preclude a role for lawmakers to oversee macroeconomic policy. In short, lawmakers face a trade off between central bank independence and democratic accountability. The trade off was particularly acute and contested in the wake of the Great Recession in late 2008 and 2009 when the Fed lowered interest rates to zero and implemented additional unconventional policies designed to rescue the financial system, prevent an even more dire economic collapse, and spur an economic recovery. Pumping trillions of dollars into the economy, at times via emergency lending programs insulated from congressional oversight, raised the ire of politicians on the left and right – not surprising given how intensely competitive parties become in a period of polarization. Critics on the right charged that the Fed's three rounds of bond purchases (including mortgages and treasuries) on top of an alphabet soup of targeted lending programs amounted to Fed-driven credit policy – crossing the boundary between monetary and fiscal policy and in effect challenging Congress's control of fiscal policy. Critics on the left hit hard against the Fed's refusal to release the names of borrowers from the Fed's emergency lending facilities and against the Fed's lax supervision of large banks and financial institutions. Congress reacted by strengthening the Fed's supervisory powers, as well as by imposing new transparency rules and clipping the Fed's lending powers when it reformed the financial regulatory system in the Dodd-Frank Act of 2010.

Congress and the president generally grant the Federal Reserve free reign to craft monetary policy within constraints set in the Federal Reserve Act (the Act). Those constraints set the terms of the Fed's independence, although Congress periodically revises the Act in ways that alter the balance between Fed independence, centralization, and congressional oversight. Today, statutory features protecting the Fed's independence include fourteen-year terms of members of the Fed's Board of Governors, self-financing of the Fed through its monetary policy operations (including control of the printing press), staggered four-year terms of presidents and Fed chairs, and insulation of a regional reserve system from political control. Most importantly, within the bounds of the Act, the Fed and its monetary policy committee are granted autonomy over the instruments of monetary policy: Congress mandates audits of the Fed's books, but not its policy choices.

In reviewing challenges to the Federal Reserve's independence six years after the onset of financial crisis in 2007, former Vice-Chairman Donald Kohn (2013) identified three elements of the Fed as potential targets of Congressional activity: the Fed's statutory goals, governance, and accountability. These three elements are central in examining why and when Congress addresses the Fed's conduct of monetary policy. None of the three is itself an *instrument* used by the Fed to shape monetary policy. However, each of them provides lawmakers with a mechanism for influencing how monetary policy is made – enabling the legislature to adjust the level of Fed independence.

Three examples are instructive. First, to influence the broad objectives of the Fed, Congress and the president must amend the Act, which establishes the goals of the Fed. These statutory mandates define the Fed's broad aims in managing the economy. Discussions of the Fed's autonomy typically distinguish between "goal" and "instrument" independence, suggesting that changes to the Fed's goals fall squarely within the province of lawmakers. For example, some lawmakers periodically call for stripping the Fed of its "dual mandate," the twin goals stipulated by Congress in 1977 that require the Fed to pursue both price stability and maximum employment. By setting the Fed's broad objectives (or by threatening to change them) Congress indirectly influences the conduct of monetary policy. The Federal Reserve's adoption of the "Evans Rule" in 2012 – which committed the Fed to keep short-term interest rates near zero so long as unemployment remained above 6.5 percent and future inflation no higher than 2.5 percent – illustrates how Congress can indirectly influence monetary policy: The Fed's adoption of the Evans Rule was justified by the Federal Open Market Committee (FOMC) on the grounds of the Fed's statutory mandate to pursue both employment and low inflation.[1]

Second, Congress has the authority to influence the internal governance structure of the Fed. Since the early 1930s, the structure of the FOMC has been stipulated in the Federal Reserve Act. Legislators periodically seek to revamp the makeup of the FOMC, at times proposing to strip the regional Federal Reserve Bank presidents of their voting rights within the FOMC. Other reforms aimed at Fed governance entail changes to the rules of appointment, such as altering selection and confirmation rules for regional reserve bank presidents or aligning the terms of the chairman of the Federal Reserve and the president. If adopted, such changes grant lawmakers indirect influence over monetary policy and adjust the Fed's degree of independence. Revamping the FOMC empowers Congress to alter the set of central bankers endowed with voting rights, while aligning presidential and chairman terms theoretically could increase a chair's responsiveness to the policy views of the administration.

Third, lawmakers can alter transparency requirements for the Fed. In the late 1970s, such efforts took the shape of compelling semiannual testimony from the Federal Reserve chairman before the Hill's banking panels. More recently, such moves seek to require more disclosure by the Fed about the conduct of monetary policy. Consider, for instance, Rep. Ron Paul's (R-TX) "Audit-the-Fed" plan that was significantly weakened and then incorporated into Dodd-Frank. Paul's original plan would have extended existing GAO audits of the Fed to cover FOMC decision making about monetary policy; the amended provisions in Dodd-Frank imposed new transparency requirements. The Fed was directed to release the identity of borrowers from the Fed's emergency credit facilities during the height of the Great Recession, as well as the identity of future borrowers from the Fed's regular discount window and other emergency lending programs. Such targets do not give lawmakers a direct shot at setting interest rates. But the Fed still strongly opposed the new disclosure requirements, and fought a corollary effort by Bloomberg News to impose transparency through legal action (Zumbrum 2012). The Fed's opposition suggests that higher levels of transparency affect how the Fed weighs the costs and benefits of competing policy choices. That, of course, is why lawmakers favor greater transparency: By constraining Fed independence, such reforms empower Congress to indirectly shape the course of monetary policy.

One exception to these indirect mechanisms for influencing monetary policy merits review. Reaching back to the 1930s, Congress has alternately created, restricted, and restored emergency lender of last resort powers for the Fed, commonly known as 13(3) powers (Fettig 2008), in reference to the section of the Federal Reserve Act that governs lending during "unusual and exigent circumstances." In response to the financial crisis in 2007 and 2008, the Fed relied on its 13(3) authority to set up several novel emergency facilities that ultimately lent over three trillion dollars to commercial and foreign banks, as well as to other types of financial institutions and individual corporations (Torres and Lanman 2010). In Dodd-Frank, Congress reined in 13(3), requiring the consent of the treasury secretary for future emergency lending and prohibiting emergency lending to individual firms. Changes to 13(3) limit Fed independence (by making emergency lending contingent on approval by the treasury) and allow Congress to directly influence the Fed's instruments for pursuing monetary policy. Lawmakers' move to limit the use of the Fed's lender of last resort authority highlights congressional limits on Fed autonomy. As former Federal Reserve chairman Paul Volcker inartfully put it, "Congress created us and Congress can un-create us" (see Greider 1989, 22).

LAWMAKERS' INCENTIVES TO REFORM THE FED

Why do lawmakers pursue potential reform of the Fed? Prominent theoretical treatments of the relationship between Congress and the Federal Reserve argue that legislators have little electoral incentive to care about the conduct of monetary policy. As Woolley (1994, 78) argues, even when Congress is particularly upset with the course of monetary policy, "the Congressional response has almost never taken the form of trying to bring about institutional reforms that would reduce the probability of the same thing happening again." Woolley (1994) argues that legislators either believe that their interests are well served by existing arrangements or disagree about appropriate reforms. As Morris (2000) argues, even if legislators have an incentive to punish the Fed for its policy choices, in equilibrium we are unlikely to see Congress do so: Fear of being punished should motivate the Fed to comply with congressional preferences.

To be sure, the Fed's central macroeconomic role complicates legislators' efforts to credibly claim credit for positive economic news. Taking credit for a robust economy can be thorny because monetary policy is not typically delivered in the form of geographically concentrated benefits. A lawmaker can tout his or her efforts to fund a new bridge or highway interchange in his or her state or district. In contrast, because economic benefits are felt regionally and nationally, lawmakers will struggle to convince voters that they are specifically responsible for an economic boom. The Fed's regional reserve banks provide loans to banks via their discount windows. Theoretically, lawmakers could take credit for such actions by the Fed. In practice, before enactment of Dodd-Frank, the regional banks operating the discount windows did not publicly identify their borrowers. Even with Dodd-Frank's new transparency rules for discount window lending, the long lag between lending and disclosure undermines congressional credit claiming.[2] Concentration of power in the hands of recent Fed chairs further undermines the credibility of legislators' efforts to claim credit for the state of the economy. These considerations should deter "single-minded seekers of re-election" (Mayhew 1974) from investing time or resources in influencing monetary policy, even if they do try to take credit for good economic times.

Still, lawmakers periodically invest energy, time, and resources in efforts to reform the Fed. The same elements of the Fed that complicate credit claiming offer perfect opportunities for blame avoidance. The Fed's independence and prominent leadership complicate voters' efforts to blame lawmakers when the economy sours. With central bankers at least partially responsible for economic conditions, lawmakers can freely scapegoat the Fed for whatever ails the economy. Lawmakers might seek to alter the Fed's goals, governance, or accountability. Or they might simply threaten to do so. It might not matter which route they take: either strategy would require the Fed to anticipate and possibly accommodate Congressional views. In short, when the economy sours, we should expect legislators to introduce more bills targeting the powers and structure of the Fed.

Since lawmakers' electoral incentives underlie their attention to the Fed, we should expect congressional parties' electoral and policy interests to also drive legislative attention to the Fed. Given that Democratic voters might tolerate inflation more readily than higher-income Republican voters, we might expect Democratic lawmakers to pounce on the Fed when unemployment is high. In contrast, Republican lawmakers might be more likely to take aim at the Fed when inflation rises. Of course, since the dual mandate forces the Fed to attend to both inflation and unemployment, Democrats might quell their criticism of the Fed after creation of the dual mandate. In contrast, Republican attention might increase after adoption of the dual mandate if GOP lawmakers thought that the dual mandate put the Fed's commitment to low inflation at risk.

Like most national institutions, the Federal Reserve has been caught in the crosshairs of contemporary partisan polarization. Democratic party leaders were generally quiescent about the Fed's unconventional policies when interest rates hit the zero lower bound, compared with GOP leaders and presidential candidates, who excoriated the Fed, its former chairman Ben Bernanke, and its three rounds of large-scale asset purchases in the wake of the financial crisis and recession. Polarization (which breeds legislative deadlock) may undermine the credibility of lawmakers' threats to reform the Fed. Still, the Fed is vulnerable to congressional intervention on those issues on which the parties agree. In the wake of financial and economic crises starting in 2007, the two parties agreed on a fair amount – including greater accountability of the Fed to Congress.

In short, during particularly bad economic times, we should expect both parties to threaten to reform the Fed. Such attacks could call for clipping the Fed's wings or for endowing the Fed with more power. Given the political value of holding the Fed accountable for declines in the economy, granting the Fed more power after bad economic times could be a rational strategy for blame-averse lawmakers. (It might also reflect the lack of other regulators with sufficient expertise or prominence to share the Fed's responsibilities.) Rather than threatening to retrench central bank authority and autonomy in the wake of financial disaster, politicians might have a strong incentive to expand it. In the following, we explore such possibilities in our analysis of the bill introduction data.

LEGISLATIVE ATTENTION TO THE FED, 1947–2014

We capture lawmakers' attention to monetary policy by tracking the introduction of bills between 1947 and 2014 that address the power, structure, and governance of the Federal Reserve. Following Schiller (1995), Sulkin (2005; 2011), and Volden and Wiseman (2014), we treat lawmakers' bill portfolios as statements of their issue agendas: Regardless of whether legislators' efforts become law, sponsoring a bill signals a lawmaker's policy and political priorities. After identifying the set of relevant bills, we code the content of each bill along several dimensions, including whether the bill seeks to constrain or empower the Federal Reserve, increase or decrease its independence, centralize or decentralize power within the Federal Reserve System, or alter the makeup of the Federal Reserve's Board of Governors.[3] Overall, 879 bills were introduced in the House and Senate over these six and half decades, representing the legislative efforts of 333 House and Senate lawmakers.

Bill sponsorship. We start by examining trends in bill sponsorship. Figure 8.1 shows the number of bills introduced each year. We overlay a smoothed misery index[4] on the data to demonstrate the relationship between attention to the Fed and the state of the economy. The data suggest that legislative attention rises and falls coincident with economic conditions, particularly with the onset of recession in the late 1950s and early 1960s, the mid-1970s and early 1980s, and most recently during and after the Great Recession. Conversely, Congressional attention drops precipitously with the onset of the so-called Great Moderation under Fed chairman Alan Greenspan by the middle of the 1980s.

Bill sponsorships also provide a window into the two parties' relative interest in the Fed, as shown in Figure 8.2's display of the relative annual proportion of Federal Reserve bills introduced by Democrats and Republicans. For most of the postwar period before stagflation set in in the 1970s, Republicans seemed disinterested in monetary policy. Granted, there were typically fewer Republicans than Democrats in the House and Senate over this long period of Democratic control of Congress. Still, Republicans' interest in the Fed began to grow (as Democrats' interest waned) after creation of the dual mandate in 1977, long before the onset of GOP majorities in the 1994 elections. Once Democrats achieved a major change to the Fed's monetary policy mandate compelling attention to rates of unemployment and inflation, their incentives to seek further changes in the powers of the Fed receded.

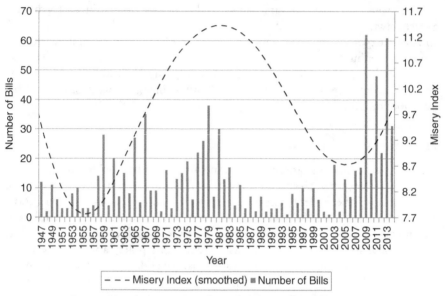

FIGURE 8.1: Congressional attention to the Fed (bills sponsored, 1947–2014).

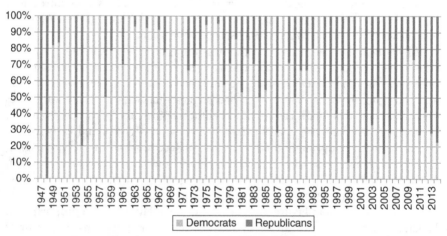

FIGURE 8.2: Congressional attention to the Fed, by party (1947–2014). Figure shows the relative percentage of Federal Reserve bills introduced each year by Democrats and Republicans.

With the onset of the Great Recession and the adoption of unconventional monetary policy tools (after the Fed had already lowered interest rates to near zero), the parties appeared to care equally about the central bank and its policies. Between 2007 and 2012, Democrats and Republicans introduced roughly the same number of bills, although Republicans' legislative activity climbed markedly in 2013 and 2014. Partisans often differed in their prescriptions for the Fed. Democrat Barney Frank of Massachusetts proposed stripping reserve bank presidents of their FOMC votes, a move that would empower presidential Fed appointees and centralize power considerably within the Fed's Board of Governors; Republican Kevin Brady of Texas wanted all twelve reserve bank presidents to vote at each FOMC meeting (rather than the current rotating scheme that limits reserve bank presidents to five votes each meeting). District bank presidents tend to be more hawkish than the DC-based board members, making it tougher on the board to monopolize monetary policy. Still, on some issues – particularly related to transparency – coalitions sported odd bedfellows: Liberal Bernie Sanders (D-Vermont) advocated with conservative David Vitter (R-Louisiana) audits of the FOMC.

Substantive focus. A clear pattern also emerges when we examine the content of the bills. First, we examine bills that would directly empower or constrain the Fed. Empowering bills provide the Federal Reserve System with new authority, for example extending the Fed's authority to purchase obligations directly from the treasury. Constraining bills limit the Fed's authority, for example by preventing the Fed from purchasing certain obligations from foreign governments or mandating new action by the Fed (such as requiring the Board of Governors to establish monthly targets for interest rates).[5] To determine the net sentiment across lawmakers sponsoring bills each year, we tally the total number of constraining and empowering bills each year, and subtract empowering from constraining bills.

Figure 8.3 captures lawmakers' sentiment for reining in the powers of the Fed over the postwar period (with the smoothed misery series overlaid).[6] Congressional attitudes about the powers of the Fed appear to vary predictably with the state of the economy. Lawmakers support more authority for the Fed when the economy is expanding; when the economy slips, lawmakers advocate more oversight and control. Granted, these are proposals, not laws. Others report that Congress and the president are likely to respond to financial crises by legislating new powers for the Fed (Irwin 2013). That said, in the aftermath of the global financial crisis, Congress both endowed the Fed with new regulatory powers and clipped its lending authority. Regardless of how lawmakers *legislate* in times of crisis, congressional sentiment clearly favors punishing the Fed by curtailing its autonomy during economic recessions.

Second, we chart variation in the number of bills that would increase oversight of the Fed, such as bills to shorten the term of governors on the board or to expand government audits of the FOMC. Increasing oversight limits independence without explicitly changing the powers of the Fed. We see a now familiar, countercyclical pattern in Figure 8.4. Efforts to impose greater oversight increase when the economy falters. The trend is most noticeable in the early 1980s. Lawmakers from both parties reacted to Fed chair Paul Volcker's push to markedly increase interest rates in an attempt to induce a deep recession as a means to tame inflation. Democrats advocated changes to the Fed's

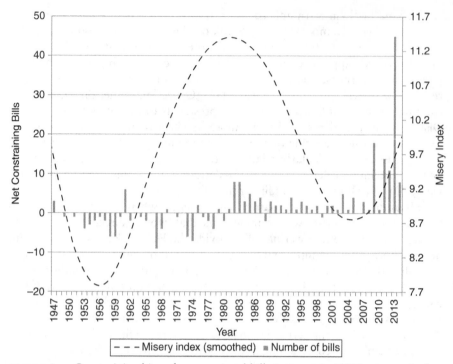

FIGURE 8.3: Constraining bias of congressional bills (1947–2014). "Net constraint" represents the number of bills constraining the Fed minus the number of bills empowering the Fed.

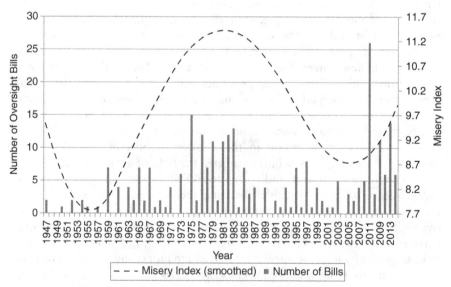

FIGURE 8.4: Bills increasing political oversight of the Fed (1947–2014).

organization and powers, including the expansion of the Fed's Board of Governors. By "packing the court" with additional president-appointed, Senate-confirmed governors to the board, whose members would then dominate the FOMC, Congress would weaken the influence of reserve bank presidents and potentially dilute the chair's influence over monetary policy. Republicans pushed for more audits and for allowing presidents to nominate their own Fed chairs – likely a GOP rebuke to the independent-minded Volcker whose recession contributed to the GOP's 1982 midterm election losses.[7]

EXPLAINING PATTERNS IN CONGRESSIONAL ATTENTION

How do we account for variation in congressional attention to the Fed? What forces shape the parties' varying interest in the nation's central bank? And why do some lawmakers (but not others) take stands on monetary policy by sponsoring bills targeted at the powers and governance of the Fed? In the models that follow, we use patterns in lawmakers' bill sponsorship to probe the forces that shape legislators' interest in the Fed.

Countercyclical congressional attention. Earlier, we suggested that lawmakers' interest in the Fed should increase when lawmakers want to avoid blame for a poor economy. In Table 8.1 (column 1), we model the total number of sponsored bills each year as a function of the inflation and unemployment rates, including lagged versions of both.[8] When both parties' legislative measures are combined, we find initial evidence that lawmakers' interest in the Fed is countercyclical. Although we find no effect for the inflation rate on the quantity of measures introduced, legislators introduce more bills that address the powers of the Fed as the unemployment rate rises. Separating lawmakers' sponsorship patterns by party offers a more nuanced view of congressional interest in the Fed. As shown in column 2, economic conditions help to shape Democratic lawmakers' priorities: Democrats pay more attention to the Fed when the unemployment rate is higher (even after controlling for the rate in the previous year). This suggests that blame avoidance for a poor economy might shape Democrats' focus on the Fed since they turn their attention elsewhere as the economy improves. That said, after a Democratic Congress gave the Fed its dual mandate in 1977, Democrats' interest in the Fed appears to have waned. Legally mandating that the Fed maximize employment while maintaining price stability might have lessened Democrats' perceived need to empower or constrain the Fed through legislative threats. In short, both electoral and policy goals might drive Democrats' attention to the Fed.

In contrast, as shown in column 3, Republican lawmakers' interest in legislating change seems divorced from the state of the economy. We do find that GOP activism rises markedly after the dual mandate was created in the 1970s. We see spikes in GOP bills in the late 1970s (in response to runaway inflation during the Carter administration) and again just before and after the Great Recession. Interestingly, recent commentators have noted that

TABLE 8.1 *Variation in Congressional Attention to the Fed (1947–2014)*

Independent Variables	(1) Total number of bills	(2) Democratic bills	(3) Republican bills
Inflation Rate	0.032	0.059	−0.018
	(0.63)	(1.12)	(0.24)
Inflation Rate (Lagged)	−0.041	−0.026	−0.043
	(0.74)	(0.44)	(0.57)
Unemployment Rate	0.256	0.332	0.235
	(2.40)*	(3.04)**	(1.45)
Unemployment Rate (Lagged)	0.008	−0.035	−0.034
	(0.08)	(0.33)	(0.22)
Dual Mandate	−0.137	−0.764	1.091
	(0.55)	(2.94)**	(2.84)**
Constant	1.056	0.574	−0.234
	(2.48)*	(1.28)	(0.37)
Observations	67	67	67

Notes: Negative binomial regression estimates (generated by Stata 11.2's *nbreg* routine). Absolute value of z-statistics in parentheses.
*significant at p<.05; **p < .01 (2-tailed tests).

Republican views about monetary policy are "stuck in the late 1970s.... To judge from the rhetoric of most Republican politicians, you would think we were again suffering from galloping inflation" (Ponnuru 2013). Perhaps GOP misperceptions – worrying about inflation in the absence of evidence – weaken any relationship between economic conditions and their party's activism more broadly. Low levels of GOP attention to the Fed before the late 1970s might also explain the broken link, shortening the period over which we can detect the impact of economic misery. Finally, we observe that the recent rise in GOP attention to the Fed largely reflects the party's effort to repeal Dodd-Frank. Republicans' recent legislative activism might be driven more by their desire to unravel Democrats' regulatory gains than by GOP concerns about the state of the economy.

Variation across lawmakers. We can also test for the relevance of lawmakers' electoral incentives by examining variation in sponsorship behavior at the individual level. In Table 8.2, we model bill introduction behavior in the 112th (2011–12) House and Senate. Given an economy and labor market still struggling to recover, the time seems ripe for Fed-bashing by electorally vulnerable incumbents seeking to blame the Fed for the weak recovery. If so, we would expect more electorally vulnerable legislators to be more likely to introduce bills addressing the Fed. We also control for factors that typically shape legislators' bill portfolios. For example, lawmakers with the best

TABLE 8.2 *Who Pays Attention to the Fed? (112th Congress, 2011–12)*

Independent Variables	(1) House Democrats	(2) House Republicans	(3) All senators
Freshman	0.735 (.57)	0.012(.02)	1.022(1.24)
Ideology	−5.999 (3.70) ***	1.922 (1.40)	0.998(1.39)
Electoral Vulnerability	1.441 (.2.63) **	0.028 (.967)	–
Running in 2012	–	–	1.22(1.66)*
District Bank in State	0.450 (.90)	0.177 (.29)	−0.148 (.17)
Financial/Banking panel	1.039 (2.49)**	2.367 (5.20)***	1.367(2.42)**
State Unemployment Rate	–	–	−0.090 (.57)
Constant	−6.381 (5.78)***	−3.813 (5.63)***	−1.989 (1.47)
N	191	238	101
Wald Chi2	19.29**	41.91***	10.52[a]

Logit estimates (generated by Stata 11.2's *logit* routine). Absolute value of z-statistics in parentheses
[a]$p<$ .1, *$p<$.05, **$p<$.01, ***$p<$.001
(one-tailed tests, except for two-tailed Wald Chi2 test).

institutional vantage point for influencing policy are more likely to introduce relevant bills. In this case, we should see more legislative activity directed to the Fed by lawmakers who serve on the House Financial Services or Senate Banking panels. Greater legislative activity from these lawmakers might reflect their committee-shaped interests in monetary and financial regulatory policy. Or lawmakers might seek out service on a banking panel if the financial industry is particularly important to their state or district. We also control for each lawmaker's ideological views and freshman status.[9] Finally, we control for whether a lawmaker hails from one of the eleven states hosting a Federal Reserve district bank; such legislators might be particularly attentive to the powers of the Fed.

We model the sponsorship behavior of House Democrats in the first column of Table 8.2. As expected, lawmakers with closer electoral margins are more likely to sponsor bills: the Fed offers an attractive target for vulnerable members seeking to deflect blame for a struggling economy. Members of the House Financial Services panel are also more likely to address the Federal Reserve, as are more liberal Democrats. The results lend little support for the other hypothesized relationships. In contrast, as shown in column 2, Republican attention to the Fed seems divorced from electoral circumstance; only GOP members of the House financial services panel are disproportionately more likely to single out the Fed in their legislative agendas. Such attention could reflect panel members' stronger interests in monetary policy or their districts' greater reliance on the financial industry. If the latter, sponsoring measures addressing the Fed might still be electorally driven, as attention to district interests could be electorally valuable for committee members.

We find similar dynamics underlying senators' legislative attention to the Fed. In Table 8.2, column 3, we pool all lawmakers and model variation in bill sponsorship. Again, electoral considerations matter: senators who were due to face voters in 2012 were slightly more likely to introduce bills affecting the Fed compared to their colleagues who were earlier in their electoral cycles. Institutional position also matters: senators serving on the chamber's banking panel were disproportionately more likely to sponsor bills targeting the Fed. When we control for each state's average unemployment rate over the course of the congress, we find no evidence that state-specific economic conditions motivated senators' legislative agendas. Nor are freshman senators or those from reserve bank states more likely to target the Fed in their bill portfolios.

On balance, the results suggest that electoral and partisan considerations drive legislators' attention to the Fed – contrary to theoretical accounts that dismiss lawmakers' systematic interests in monetary policy. At the individual level, we find strong evidence that the timing and competitiveness of elections – as well as legislators' policy interests – mold lawmakers' activism regarding the Fed. Perceptions of Fed independence do not constrain lawmakers from signaling the need to reform the Fed. At the aggregate level, we see similar dynamics at work in shaping broader trends in lawmakers' attention to the Fed. True, the parties vary in their attention to the Fed over the postwar period: Democrats' interest initially falls off after creation of the Fed's dual mandate in 1977, while Republican interest rises with the Fed-induced recession in the early 1980s. But overall, economic conditions drive lawmakers' prescriptions for the Fed. When the economy is sound, lawmakers propose stronger powers for the Fed; when the economy falters, lawmakers suggest constraining the Fed. Politicians' countercyclical attention to the Fed suggests that lawmakers' instinct for avoiding blame shapes legislative activity on monetary policy: Congress focuses on the Fed only after the horse has been let out of the barn.

CONGRESS AND THE FED WHEN THE PARTIES ARE POLARIZED

As the other chapters in this volume make plain, today's political parties have reached century-high levels of electoral competition and ideological polarization. The intersection of polarization and financial crisis allows us to evaluate oversight of the Fed when the parties hold conflicting views about fiscal and monetary policies. In assessing Congressional oversight during and after the crisis, we note that lawmakers' interactions with the Fed have taken place in an environment of near zero interest rates. This "zero lower bound" was consequential politically because once rates hit zero, the Fed could no longer use conventional tools to stimulate the economy by lowering rates. Instead, the Fed innovated with new, largely untested unconventional monetary policies to rescue and restore the economy. Even Bernanke would later quip after leaving office that the Fed's key unconventional tool worked in practice, but not in theory (Brookings Institution 2014). As we explore in the following, such policies proved controversial on Capitol Hill and far beyond.

By definition, monetary policy becomes more complicated at the zero lower bound. For example, the Fed's large-scale asset purchases (also known as quantitative easing, or QE) that were intended to lower long-term borrowing rates entailed the purchase of both treasuries and mortgage-backed securities, assets underwritten by the housing finance giants Fannie Mae and Freddie Mac. QE supporters argued that because housing finance was at the heart of the financial crisis, bolstering housing markets by reducing long-term rates was essential. Critics, including the president of the Federal Reserve Bank of Richmond, Jeffrey Lacker, countered that "when the central bank buys private assets, it can tilt the playing field toward some borrowers at the expense of others, affecting the allocation of credit" (Lacker and Weinberg 2014). Unconventional monetary policies, in other words, blurred the line between monetary and fiscal policy and put the Fed in the politically fraught position of choosing economic winners and losers. Many argued that distributional issues were better left for politicians to sort out.

Democrats and Republicans reacted differently to the Fed's conduct of monetary policy at the zero bound. As a congressional minority starting in 2007, Republicans (occasionally joined by Democrats skittish about reelection) lobbed sharp attacks on the Fed. For example, Senate Republicans repeatedly blocked confirmation of President Obama's selection of Peter Diamond, a Nobel Prize-winning economist, for a seat on the Fed's Board of Governors. Nearly two dozen Republican economists, money managers, and former GOP officials penned an unprecedented letter to Bernanke criticizing the FOMC's plan for large-scale asset purchases, arguing that the Fed's proposal risked debasing the dollar and stoking inflation ("Open Letter to Ben Bernanke" 2010). One Republican presidential hopeful threatened Ben Bernanke with treason should he step foot in Texas, while other Republicans spearheaded efforts to impose new audits on the Fed or to end the Fed altogether.

In contrast, most Democrats supported the Fed's conduct of QE after the crisis. As Senator Charles Schumer (D-NY) put it in 2012, the Fed was the "only game in town" to restore the economy, given GOP opposition to more aggressive fiscal policy (Menza 2012). To be sure, some Democrats argued that given its mandate, the Fed could do more to address the needs of American workers in the wake of the recession: *Times* columnist Paul Krugman, for instance, wondered about the Bernanke conundrum: "the divergence between what Professor Bernanke advocated and what Chairman Bernanke has actually done" (Krugman 2012). Moreover, some Democrats rallied with the "Occupy the Fed" movement, charging that the Fed had made rescue of Wall Street, not Main Street, its top priority. Protesting both the Fed's role in precipitating the financial crisis as well as its subsequent policy choices, eleven Democrats joined eighteen Republican senators to oppose Bernanke's confirmation for a second term as chair of the Federal Reserve Board of Governors. Democrats on the left (such as Senator Bernie Sanders of Vermont) agreed with more conservative Republicans (such as Richard Shelby of Alabama) that the Fed before and after the financial crisis catered too strongly to Wall Street interests at the expense of Main Street (Andrews 2009).

With control of both chambers and the White House, Democrats did more than question the extent of Bernanke's commitment to the Fed's unemployment mandate. Democrats exploited their congressional majorities in 2009 and 2010 to legislate in the Dodd-Frank Act several new restrictions on the Fed's future use of its powers. Granted, Dodd-Frank also enlarged the scope of the Fed's authority by giving it new supervisory powers to regulate important financial institutions. But Congress also curtailed the Fed's authority. It imposed greater transparency on the Fed's lending programs, limited the scope of future emergency lending and the Fed's autonomy to conduct it, and attempted to reduce conflicts of interest in the selection of reserve bank presidents by tweaking selection procedures for the heads of the reserve banks. Near uniform party lines prevailed in passing the final conference report, with only three GOP defectors joining most House and Senate Democrats in support of the bill.

Although partisans disagreed about the efficacy of QE and how to reform the Fed, congressional efforts by both parties to hold the Fed accountable likely limited Fed independence. Bernanke often reminded his audiences that policy independence was critical for making the right decisions for the economy, and that the Fed always made its decisions immune from short-term political influence. Still, Congress's aggressive oversight of the Fed sent strong signals to the Fed that it would have to become more transparent about its policies and more responsive to its critics if it hoped to forestall stronger limitations on its powers. As Bernanke has acknowledged, "I learned in the crisis that transparency served broader purposes, including maintaining the right relationship with Congress and explaining the Fed's policy choices to the public" (Bernanke 2014). Bernanke responded by reaching out to Main Street: he explained and defended monetary policy choices in college lectures, town hall meetings, and national televised interviews. A truly autonomous central bank might have felt little compulsion to explain itself to the public. Polarized parties in the wake of the crisis made clear to the Fed that its precarious political standing required greater responsiveness to the (often conflicting) demands of its congressional overseers.

CONCLUSIONS

> The decisions made by the central bank are not just technical decisions; they involve trade-offs, judgments about whether the risks of inflation are worth the benefits of lower unemployment. These trade-offs involve values.... The fact that monetary policy involves trade-offs ... has one clear implication in a democratic society. The way those decisions are made should be representative of those that comprise society.
>
> Stiglitz 1998, 216, 218.

Stiglitz's address – a full decade before the Great Recession – highlights the tradeoff democratic governments face in maintaining independent central banks. More autonomous central banks are more likely to deliver lower and more stable inflation than less autonomous ones – and certainly lower and more stable inflation than if politicians directly control the money supply. At the same, politicians have electoral and other incentives to hold the Fed accountable for its policy decisions – particularly in times when a commitment to price stability generates or sustains higher unemployment. Tougher congressional oversight, greater transparency, and new selection mechanisms for Federal Reserve Board and other appointees – these and other reforms provide targets for lawmakers dissatisfied with the effects of the Fed's monetary policy choices.

Congressional views about the appropriate balance between accountability and independence vary across members and over time. Lawmakers' attention to the Fed rises and falls with the state of the economy, a dynamic driven by lawmakers' electoral and partisan incentives. The notion that monetary policy should be divorced from politics is especially hard to sustain in times of economic and financial crisis when monetary policy plays a central role in rebooting the economy. Higher rates of unemployment in particular attract the attention of lawmakers, historically more so Democrats than Republicans. Legislators then propose changes to the Federal Reserve Act to rein in the Fed's powers or to alter its governance structure or transparency rules. Only in the past decade, and especially in the aftermath of the Great Recession, have both Democratic and Republican lawmakers squarely focused their ire on the Fed.

How does the Fed react to countercyclical congressional interest? At least anecdotally, central bankers worry about potential congressional reactions to their monetary policy choices. Consider, for example, the concerns noted in October 2006 by then-president of the Federal Reserve Bank of Chicago, Michael Moskow, when the FOMC discussed whether to adopt a numerical inflation target (FOMC 2006, 131):

For me the biggest issue is the dual mandate responsibility and our relationship to the Congress. Clearly, a persuasive case must be made that we will continue to fulfill our dual mandate responsibilities. The challenge is how to make an explicit numerical specification of price stability operationally compliant with the dual mandate, and to do so, we need to clarify the flexibility of the time period for bringing inflation back to its target, as [Federal Reserve Bank of Richmond president] Jeff [Lacker] just talked about. The amount of time to do this would depend on the size of the current inflation deviation and the deviations from maximum sustainable growth and employment. So I think the intermediate step of explaining longer-term forecasts would help us learn how to communicate these difficult dual mandate issues more effectively.

Governor Frederic Mishkin picked up on Moskow's concerns, warning FOMC colleagues not "to get too far ahead of the Congress on this" (FOMC 2006, 138). As Cathy Minehan, then president of the Federal Reserve Bank of Boston, put it, "we do need to consider the likely interaction with the Congress as we set

a target for one of our goals but not another. . . . What else might that interaction with the Congress provoke? The possibility for unintended consequences
is clear" (FOMC 2006, 153). Two years later, then Fed vice chair Donald Kohn
voiced a similar concern about adopting an inflation target without consulting
first with Congress: "Having an inflation target won't have any effect if it is
repudiated by the Congress. As soon as we make it, it could have a negative
effect" (FOMC 2008, 68).

We also have at least anecdotal evidence that the threat of transparency can
make central bankers more cautious in making policy. Consider the perspective
offered by the president of the St. Louis Federal Reserve Bank, William Poole,
in September 2007 during a meeting of the Federal Open Market Committee. In
discussing potential moves by the Fed to increase liquidity in the financial
system, Poole encouraged his FOMC colleagues to think carefully about how
lawmakers might perceive the beneficiaries of emergency lending:

I just say that I think there's a transparency issue here that might have to be explained. . . .
There is certainly a risk that this facility will not be . . . available to small banks, and the
large banks would be getting access to discount window funds at a rate potentially well
below that available to small banks. If this were to become a political controversy with
some of those who are less friendly to us in the Congress than others, it would complicate the value of this. FOMC 2007.

Such debate during the crafting of monetary policy, especially in the midst of a
financial crisis, raises the possibility that imposing more accountability offers
Congress an avenue for indirectly influencing the Fed's policy choices. Concern
about how a program will be viewed seems to generate a moment's pause
amongst the Fed's ostensibly independent central bankers. Granted, it is hard
to generalize from a single instance. But recent imposition of new transparency
rules – and the Fed's concerted opposition to them – suggests that increased
accountability forces the Fed to take greater stock of congressional preferences
in making policy.

More generally, such comments – embargoed for five years – suggest that
central bankers worry about legislative reaction (even during robust economic
times). The Fed eventually adopted an inflation target in 2012 without formal
congressional consent, having previously considered ways to communicate
policy choices to lawmakers that would keep legislative opposition at bay. In
the words of Janet Yellen (then-president of the Federal Reserve Bank of San
Francisco), the Fed was seeking to not "cause [the FOMC] to respond more
strongly to inflation and less strongly to unemployment" (FOMC 2006), a
move that would have challenged congressional objectives established in the
Fed's dual mandate. The furor against the Fed in the wake of the financial crisis
and Congress's subsequent imposition of more transparency rules suggests that
the Fed pays a cost for failing to anticipate Congress's views. Still, perhaps no
amount of consultation can forestall legislative action when lawmakers' electoral motives are at play.

Indeed, as we observed earlier, Democrats were able to secure a set of reforms in the Dodd-Frank Act in 2010 that partially clipped the Fed's wings (even while endowing the Fed with new supervisory responsibilities for the health of the financial system). Granted, Democrats had a nearly filibuster-proof majority in that Congress and controlled the White House, reducing their need for GOP votes to enact Dodd-Frank. Still, the enactment of significant reforms in a period of persistent gridlock likely signaled to the Fed that public and congressional anger was sufficient to mobilize a coalition to limit Fed autonomy. Politicians' attention to the Fed only rarely yields legislative action. But the Fed seems attuned to the threats it receives from the Hill. Congressional attention to the Fed may be episodic and politically motivated. But as Stiglitz (1998) argues, macroeconomic decisions "are … among the most important of the collective decisions made by any society." Even imperfect congressional attention can provide a means of bringing democratic values to bear on the making of monetary policy.

Notes

1. Of course, the dual mandate has been in place since 1977, and the FOMC only adopted the Evans Rule several years after the onset of the (2008–09) recession. On the rationale for linking employment and interest rates, see Evans (2012).
2. Judging from Irwin's (2013, 193) account of an interaction between the president of the Dallas Federal Reserve Bank and a local member of Congress, we cannot assume that lawmakers understand the lending activity of the reserve banks. According to Dallas reserve bank president Richard Fisher, the member seemed shocked to learn that the Dallas Fed could make loans to banks in his congressional district.
3. For the period 1947–2008 (80th–110th Congresses), we rely on the Congressional Bills Dataset maintained by Adler and Wilkerson (1947–2008) to identify bills that would amend the Federal Reserve Act. For the period 2009–14, we locate relevant bills via Thomas.loc.gov. The content of each bill can be determined from Thomas. For the period before 1973, we consult bill text available in CIS Congressional Bills, Resolutions & Laws on Microfiche (1933–2008).
4. The "misery index" sums up the unemployment and inflation rates. We obtain annual inflation rates (change in the CPI-U maintained by the Bureau of Labor Statistics) from McMahon (2014). Annual unemployment rates are available at Bureau of Labor Statistics (2014): http://data.bls.gov/timeseries/LNU04000000?years_option=all_years&periods_option=specific_periods&periods=Annual+Data.
5. If a given bill includes provisions that both constrain and empower the Fed, we code the provisions separately and determine whether, on net, the bill constrains or empowers the Fed. The drawback of the method is that we treat each provision equally, regardless of substantive significance. The benefit of the method is that we avoid subjective determinations of the relative importance of provisions in a single bill.
6. When the bars rise above zero on the Y-axis, lawmakers on balance favor constraining the Fed; when the bars fall below zero, lawmakers prefer to empower the Fed.

7. Volcker was appointed by Democrat Jimmy Carter, but served well into Ronald Reagan's second presidential term.
8. We estimate a negative binomial regression given the count nature of the data. We reject the alternative Poisson model, given that the overdispersion parameter (alpha) is significantly greater than zero. We also control for the creation of the dual mandate, since requiring the Fed to care about both jobs and inflation should reduce at least Democrats' attention to the Fed's conduct of monetary policy.
9. Ideology is measured via DW-NOMINATE scores made available by Keith Poole at www.voteview.com. Higher scores represent more conservative legislators.

References

Adler, E. Scott, and John Wilkerson. 1947–2008. *Congressional Bills Project*. National Science Foundation 00880066 and 00880061.

Alesina, Alberto, and Lawrence H. Summers. 1993. "Central Bank Independence and Macroeconomic Performance: Some Comparative Evidence." *Journal of Money, Credit and Banking* 25 (2): 151–62.

Andrews, Edmund L. 2009. "Senator Moves to Hold Up Bernanke Confirmation." *New York Times*, December 2. www.nytimes.com/2009/12/03/business/03fed.html, p. B1 (accessed January 20, 2015).

Bernanke, Ben. 2014. Interview with authors, June 13. The Brookings Institution.

Brookings Institution. 2014. "Central Banking after the Great Recession: Lessons Learned and Challenges Ahead." Uncorrected transcript. www.brookings.edu/events/2014/01/16-central-banking-after-the-great-recession-bernanke (accessed January 26, 2015).

Bureau of Labor Statistics. 2014. "Labor Force Statistics from the Current Population Survey." http://data.bls.gov/timeseries/LNU04000000?years_option=all_years&periods_option=specific_periods&periods=Annual+Data.

Committee on Financial Services-Democrats. 2012. Press Release: Barney Frank speaks on the House floor about the Bill to Audit the Federal Reserve. July 24. http://democrats.financialservices.house.gov/press/PRArticle.aspx?NewsID=1484.

Congressional Information Service (CIS). N.d. *Congressional Bills, Resolutions & Laws on Microfiche* (1933–2008). Proquest.

Evans, Charles. 2012. "Some Thoughts on Global Risks and Monetary Policy." Speech delivered on August 27, 2012, at the Market News International seminar in Hong Kong, China. www.chicagofed.org/webpages/publications/speeches/2012/08_27_12_hongkong.cfm.

Federal Open Market Committee (FOMC). 2006–2008. Meetings of the Federal Open Market Committee on October 24–25, 2006; September 18, 2007; December 15–16, 2008. Transcripts. www.federalreserve.gov/monetarypolicy/fomchistorical2007.htm.

Federal Reserve. 2013. Transcript of Chairman Ben Bernanke's Press Conference, December 18. www.federalreserve.gov/monetarypolicy/fomcpresconf20131218.htm (accessed November 15, 2014).

Fettig, David. 2008. "The History of a Powerful Paragraph." The Reserve Bank of Minneapolis. www.minneapolisfed.org/publications_papers/pub_display.cfm?id=3485.

Greider, William. 1989. *Secrets of the Temple: How the Federal Reserve Runs the Country.* Simon and Schuster.

Irwin, Neil. 2013. *The Alchemists: Three Central Bankers and a World on Fire.* New York: Penguin Press.

Kohn, Donald. 2013. "Federal Reserve Independence in the Aftermath of the Financial Crisis: Should We Be Worried?" Remarks delivered at the National Association for Business Economics, January 4. www.brookings.edu/research/speeches/2013/01/04-fed-reserve-independence-kohn.

Krugman, Paul. 2012. "Earth to Bernanke." *New York Times Magazine*, April 24. www.nytimes.com/2012/04/29/magazine/chairman-bernanke-should-listen-to-profes sor-bernanke.html?ref=magazine (accessed January 20, 2015).

Lacker, Jeffrey M., and John A. Weinberg. 2014. "The Fed's Mortgage Favoritism. " *Wall Street Journal.* October 7. www.wsj.com/articles/jeffrey-lacker-and-john-wein berg-the-feds-mortgage-favoritism-1412721776 (accessed January 19, 2015).

Mayhew, David. 1974. *Congress: The Electoral Connection.* New Haven: Yale University Press.

McMahon, Tim. 2014. "Historical Inflation Rate." http://inflationdata.com/inflation/Inflation_Rate/HistoricalInflation.aspx.

Menza, Justin. 2012. "With Congress in Gridlock, 'Fed's the Only Game in Town.'" CNBC, July 17. www.cnbc.com/id/48210558 (accessed January 20, 2015).

Morris, J. Irwin. 2000. *Congress, the President, and the Federal Reserve: The Politics of American Monetary Policymaking.* Ann Arbor: University of Michigan Press.

"Open Letter to Ben Bernanke." 2010. Reprinted in *Wall Street Journal*, Real Time Economics blog, November 10. http://blogs.wsj.com/economics/2010/11/15/open-letter-to-ben-bernanke/ (accessed January 19, 2015).

Ponnuru, Ramesh. 2013. "Reaganism after Reagan." *New York Times*, February 17. www.nytimes.com/2013/02/18/opinion/updating-reaganomics.html.

Schiller, Wendy J. 1995. "Senators as Political Entrepreneurs: Using Bill Sponsorship to Shape Legislative Agendas." *American Journal of Political Science* 39 (1): 186–203.

Stiglitz, Joseph. 1998. "Central Banking in a Democratic Society." *De Economist* 146 (2): 199–226.

Sulkin, Tracy. 2005. *Issue Politics in Congress.* New York: Cambridge University Press.

Sulkin, Tracy. 2011. *The Legislative Legacy of Congressional Campaigns.* New York: Cambridge University Press.

Torres, Craig, and Scott Lanman. 2010. "Fed Emergency Borrowers Ranged from GE to McDonald's." *Bloomberg News*, December 1. www.bloomberg.com/news/2010-12-01/fed-crisis-borrowers-ranged-from-bank-of-america-to-mcdonald-s.htm.

Volden, Craig and Alan Wiseman. 2014. *Legislative Effectiveness in the United States Congress.* New York: Cambridge University Press.

Woolley, John. 1994. "The Politics of Monetary Policy: A Critical Review." *Journal of Public Policy* 14 (1): 57–85.

Zumbrun, Joshua. 2012. "Fed Audit Bill Opposed by Bernanke Approved by U.S. House." *Bloomberg News*, February 25. www.bloomberg.com/news/2012-07-25/fed-audit-bill-opposed-by-bernanke-approved-by-u-s-house.html.

PART IV

CONGRESS AND DOMESTIC POLICY DILEMMAS

9

The $40 Trillion Question

Can Congress Control Health Care Spending?

Jonathan Oberlander

Congress faces few challenges as daunting as health policy. Health care is an issue that touches all Americans, triggering intense emotions as policy choices are framed as matters of life and death. It raises fundamental philosophical questions about the balance between government and markets, individualism and community, and rights and responsibilities. Partisan and ideological divisions on health policy are common, making agreement on remedies difficult. An array of powerful interest groups and constituencies inhabit the health politics arena, aggressively protecting their respective slices of the status quo. The United States has a fragmented nonsystem of health care that comprises a major portion of the American economy, with myriad entrenched public and private programs, further complicating the prospects for reform. Many Americans like their current insurance arrangements, are apprehensive of change, and are fearful of the specters of rationing and socialized medicine.

No wonder, then, that Congress's record in health policy making during the 20th century was mostly dismal. Campaigns to enact universal health insurance repeatedly died in the "Congressional graveyard" (Peterson 2005), as the United States gained the dubious distinction of being the only rich industrialized country with a large uninsured population. The 1965 enactment of Medicare and Medicaid did establish the government's role in providing health insurance to select populations, setting the stage for further expansions in subsequent years. Yet securing coverage for Americans who did not fit into sympathetic demographic categories proved difficult (Blumenthal and Morone 2009; Hacker 2002; Hoffman 2012; Starr 1982; 2011). Even as the uninsured population grew, American health policy oscillated between inaction and incrementalism, and efforts to break that cycle with comprehensive reform – such as the ill-fated Clinton health care plan of 1993–94 – ended badly (Hacker 1997; Skocpol 1996; Starr 1995). Gridlock ensnared Congressional health policy making, with health care bills more likely to fail than legislation from most other policy areas (Volden and Wiseman 2011). Widening partisan polarization in Congress meant that even efforts to reauthorize incremental, popular programs such as the Children's Health Insurance Program (CHIP) sparked controversy and partisan conflict (Oberlander and Lyons 2009).

Given this sobering history, the success of the Obama administration and Congressional Democrats in securing passage of the 2010 Patient Protection and Affordable Care Act (ACA, a.k.a. Obamacare) is all the more remarkable. The ACA represents the most important health care legislation in nearly half a century, and its grandiose ambitions encompass everything from substantially expanding insurance coverage and overhauling the regulation of private insurance to transforming how we deliver and pay for medical care, and much more. Congress – or at least its leaders, Nancy Pelosi and Harry Reid, and the Democrats who voted for the law – can deservedly take a bow for its role in crafting and passing the ACA. Indeed, the Obama administration's health reform strategy rested in no small part on deferring to Congress. If the demise of the Clinton health plan symbolized the failings of America's system of government and politics (Johnson and Broder 1996) and vividly illustrated the institutional biases towards inaction, the passage of Obamacare is vindication that the system can, against extraordinary odds, work, and shows that transformative legislation occasionally survive the Congressional gauntlet (Altman and Shactman 2011; Brown 2011; Cohn 2010; Daschle and Nather 2010; Hacker 2011; Jacobs and Skocpol 2010; McDonough 2011; Oberlander 2010; Starr 2011).

Still, America's health reform journey is far from over. Having made it through Congress, the ACA's implementation has run into other serious obstacles as the law has proven more vulnerable to legal challenges and engendered more state resistance than its advocates anticipated. Even if the ACA survives intact into 2017 and beyond, many health policy challenges remain. None is more formidable than controlling health care spending. The stakes are enormous. The United States currently spends nearly $3 trillion a year on medical care, amounting to over $9,000 per person, and, even after a recent slowdown, is projected to spend a total of $40 trillion during the next decade (Hartman et al. 2015). Health care accounts for over one-sixth of gross domestic product in the United States and expenditures on Medicare and Medicaid comprise 23 percent of the federal budget. Medicare spending is expected to increase substantially in coming years due in large part to population aging – as the Baby Boom generation retires, the Medicare population will grow from 50 million today to nearly 80 million by 2030. Another Medicare funding crisis – the program's trust fund for hospital insurance is projected to be insolvent in 2030 – looms ahead.

Meanwhile, all government insurance programs, including Medicaid and Obamacare, must grapple with the rising costs of medical care and spread of expensive new technologies and therapies. During the last six decades spending on medical care has, on a per capita basis, exceeded growth in the national economy by an average of 2.4 percent a year. Health care consequently increased as a share of gross domestic product from 4.4 percent in 1950 to 17.9 percent in 2011 (Fuchs 2013). Although spending increases on new treatments have helped produce substantially better outcomes for persons with medical conditions ranging from heart disease to depression (Cutler 2004), many experts believe that much of what the United States spends on medical care is wasteful. The high U.S. health care bill reflects significant sums spent on low-value, ineffective care, as well as on administrative costs and service prices much higher than those paid by the health systems of other rich democracies (Aaron and Ginsburg 2009; Berwick and Hackbarth 2012; Laugesen and Glied 2011; Pozen and Cutler 2010; Smith et al. 2012; Wennberg 2010; White 2013). An expert panel convened by the prestigious Institute of Medicine concluded that "there is evidence that a substantial proportion of health care expenditures is wasted, leading to little improvement in health or in the quality of care" (Smith et al. 2012, 12). The panel estimated that in 2009 alone there were a staggering $765 billion of excess costs in the American health care system, encompassing unnecessary services, inefficiently delivered care, forgone prevention opportunities, fraud, and high administrative costs and prices. Such estimates should be taken with a large grain of salt. But they do reflect the consensus in the health policy community about the prevalence of wasted spending and inefficiency in American medical care – a consensus that in turn underlies the case for cost containment.

There is also a compelling fiscal case for restraining health care costs. Health care spending is the most important cause of projected future deficits in the United States (CBO 2013). The nation's budgetary fortunes and economic health are viewed as resting largely on policy makers' ability to hold down increases in health care expenditures (Aaron 2010). Recent plans to reduce the long-term federal deficit – from President Obama; the National Commission for Fiscal Responsibility and Reform, chaired by Erskine Bowles and Allan Simpson; and Republican Congressman and Chair of the House Budget Committee Paul Ryan – have all proposed substantial health care savings (Kaiser Family Foundation 2013). A grand, or even not so grand, budget bargain is difficult to imagine without reducing the rate of growth in spending on Medicare and other federal health programs. In a 2009 speech, President Obama implored Congress to act because "If we do nothing to slow these skyrocketing costs, we will eventually be spending more on Medicare and Medicaid than every other government program combined. Put simply our health care problem is our deficit problem. Nothing else even comes close. Nothing else" (Obama 2009).

Is Congress up to the job? This chapter explores the role of Congress in health care cost control, past, present, and future. I begin by examining the political forces that make controlling medical care spending difficult. Next, I explore past Congressional (in)action on cost control and explain what that history tells us more broadly about Congress's health policy making capacity. I then discuss the 2010 ACA as a crucial case study in Congressional efforts at cost control, including its establishment of a new board outside the normal legislative process charged with curbing Medicare spending and designed to circumvent Congressional inertia and incapacity in health policy making. Finally, I look at what's ahead, how Obamacare could transform the politics of health care cost containment, and the dynamics of health care policy in an era of partisan polarization.

BARRIERS TO CONGRESSIONAL ACTION

There are many reasons to anticipate that Congress will have a hard time controlling medical care spending, not least of which is the widely held view that such spending produces better health and thereby achieves an important societal priority. The starting point, though, for understanding the politics of cost control is an axiom of medical economics: a dollar spent on medical care is a dollar of income for someone. In other words, national health expenditures constitute the money that the medical care industry – doctors, hospitals, drug companies, insurers, nursing homes, medical device manufacturers, and all other suppliers and providers of medical care services – earns. Their organizations – the American Medical Association, the American Hospital Association, America's Health Insurance Plans, PhRMA, and many more – have a concentrated interest in health policy debates. As a consequence, serious attempts at cost control produce a battle with stakeholders who have resources, political clout, and strong incentives to oppose measures that reduce the rate of medical spending growth and their income (Marmor et al. 2009).

It is in the economic interests of such groups to secure policies that increase national health care spending and maximize the flow of government dollars to the medical care industry. Provider organizations can reward politicians who aid them (campaign contributions being one key reward). They also possess the knowledge and resources necessary to monitor and shape arcane rules and regulations impacting their bottom lines. For example, in Medicare an obscure committee of physicians, sponsored by the American Medical Association, plays an influential role in adjusting the values attributed to different medical procedures as part of Medicare's payment formula (Laugesen et al. 2012). Critics charge that because specialist physicians have more representation on the committee than primary care doctors, it sets values that produce higher price increases for specialty services (Edwards 2013; Mathews and McGinty 2010).

In addition to working the policy process, such groups can go public, exploiting Americans' ideological ambivalence about government to influence policy makers through advertising campaigns. The medical industrial complex can frame their quest for more money as promoting the national interest through greater innovation, improved care, and better health outcomes. And they can define cost-control measures as threatening that innovation, and the access to and quality of medical care enjoyed by insured

Americans. Those arguments resonate strongly in a country where fear of government is in the political DNA, where cries of socialized medicine have echoed against health reform proposals for nearly a century, and where well-insured patients are accustomed to relatively unfettered access to medical services (Morone 1990).

Moreover, health care spending, which varies significantly across the country (Wennberg 2010), has important geographic implications that shape health politics (Vladeck 1999). States that receive high payments from Medicare want them maintained, while states whose medical care providers receive comparatively lower reimbursements from Medicare want more funds. Health care spending, after all, creates jobs. Between 1990 and 2011, the share of the American workforce in health sector employment grew from 7.3 percent to 10.7 percent (Roehrig 2011). During the economic downturn of 2007–09, the health care industry proved to be relatively recession-proof, adding jobs as other sectors imploded. In fact, during 2007–13 the health care sector added 1.85 million jobs, while all other industries lost 3.85 million jobs (Wright 2013). Over one in eight Americans employed in the private sector now works in health care.

States, as well as cities, have a strong stake in ensuring that their local medical industries receive favorable treatment in any legislation. This geographic particularism is one-sided: organized geographic interests lobby for more, not less, medical care spending and health employment in their area, and the politics of distributing higher payments is more appealing than the pain that occurs when redistributing money away from areas currently benefiting from the status quo. Thus the major political impact so far of identifying wide geographic variations in health care expenditures has not been to reduce Medicare spending in high-cost areas but to give representatives from low-cost areas more leverage to pursue enhanced federal payments for their regions (White 2011).

Members of Congress seeking reelection have, then, ample reasons to promote medical interests from their districts or states. What politician does not want to take credit for a new or expanded hospital, clinic, or factory producing advanced medical equipment? Or for more medical research funding that promises to save lives? In short, Congress can see medical care spending as generating both health benefits and a formidable jobs program.

Then there are the electoral advantages of currying favor with Medicare beneficiaries. Between 1982 and 2010, Americans over age sixty-five voted in off-year Congressional elections at an average rate of 58.5 percent; only 41 percent of those between the ages of 25 and 44 voted on average during the same period (U.S. Census Bureau n.d.). Given seniors' comparatively high voting levels, as well as the political resources of AARP and other senior advocacy organizations, and the tendency to see any slowdown in the rate of growth in program expenditures as a dangerous benefit cut, spending more to provide greater Medicare benefits seems like a sound political investment. In sum,

Congress's crude electoral calculus (Mayhew 1974) would appear to favor enacting and sustaining policies that produce more spending on medical care.

In contrast to the robust electoral benefits available to members of Congress who support more spending, the political benefits of pursuing health care cost control are not clear. There is no organized group rivaling the medical care industry that lobbies to contain costs. Employers conceivably could be such a force and at times some businesses and business coalitions have advocated for reform. But the business community is also divided, large segments of it are ideologically opposed to government regulation, and firms can respond to rising costs by shifting the burden to workers, reducing benefits, raising premiums and cost-sharing, lowering wages, or ceasing to offer coverage (Brown 1993).

Workers who are worried about their premium costs are another potential constituency for cost control. Yet they have little organization, the power of private sector unions is weak, and some unions are more concerned with preserving the private welfare state and protecting health care benefits for their members than they are with securing nationwide cost containment (Gottschalk 2000). Moreover, many American workers do not understand how much their health insurance costs or that the employer's share of their rising premiums is coming out of forgone wages. One of America's most expensive social programs – the tax subsidy for employer-sponsored private health insurance, whose benefits disproportionately accrue to higher-income earners – is not understood or even recognized as a government policy by many Americans (Havighurst and Richman 2006). The negative implications of rising health care spending and even the major sources of government spending on health insurance are thus obscured.

Medicare and Medicaid generally enjoy strong public support, so cutting spending on these programs may not produce any electoral payoff. Indeed, in opinion polls most Americans usually favor more, not less, government spending on medical care (Blendon et al. 2006). In the case of Medicare, policy makers have to worry about the political fallout from any proposals that Medicare enrollees will view – perhaps as a result of medical industry or partisan messaging – as benefit cuts. In addition, many policies to slow spending are sufficiently technical that the voting public will not be able to detect their presence let alone impact, depriving legislators of a credit-claiming opportunity (Arnold 1990). And if opponents successfully arouse public anxieties by equating cost-saving reforms with rationing medical services or worse ("death panels"), members of Congress supporting such policies risk alienating voters. Recent controversies over new guidelines regarding screening for breast and prostate cancer underscore just how controversial policies can become that are seen as limiting medical services – even if the policies are based on evidence and do not actually limit services.

Health policy analysts regularly talk about the difficulty of simultaneously maximizing goals of high quality, broad access, and restrained costs (Carroll

2012). Given the dynamics described here, it always will be tempting for politicians to conclude that a trade off that produces more access and better quality but higher costs is much more favorable to their electoral fortunes than the reverse. The benefits from avoiding blame for controversial decisions (Weaver 1986) that are perceived as restricting medical care could easily overwhelm any potential benefits from controlling spending.

The fragmentation of American medical care financing presents another challenge. It makes it more difficult to recognize the magnitude of the spending problem, which is divided across different payers and funding streams. Unlike nations such as Germany, where health insurance is funded through a highly visible system of social insurance contributions, American health care is funded through a byzantine mix of earmarked federal payroll taxes, general revenues, cigarette taxes, state revenues, employer and worker premiums, and individual payments. Further, countries that have national health insurance control spending through centralized budgeting, uniform fee schedules, and supply-side controls on capacity and medical technology (Marmor et al. 2009; White 2013). Since the United States has no national health system, it does not possess the same levers. Congress, for example, can alter Medicare spending, yet as large as it is, the program accounts for only about 20 percent of total spending on medical care in the United States. Much of American health policy is actually made by private-sector employers and insurers, and federal influence over private insurance spending is not as strong as it is over government programs. Each insurer, public and private, has different payment policies and reimburses medical providers different amounts for the same procedure, with no coordination across payers. Because the system does not have uniform payment rules, controlling costs in one area (such as Medicare) can actually result in higher spending in another part of the system (private insurance) if medical providers increase prices to other payers to compensate for lost revenues.[1]

Providers are not the only ones who can cost shift. Congress's perception of the health care cost problem is that it is largely a federal budget issue (Marmor et al. 2009). To the extent that policy action is motivated by budgetary pressures, Congress has an incentive to reduce federal health care spending even if it raises private or state health care spending. A Congress looking to lower the deficit could, for instance, cut the federal share of Medicaid payments, which would shift the burden of funding to the states without actually reducing the level of national health care spending. However, the dynamics of the federal budgetary process creates challenges as well: legislation must be scored by the Congressional Budget Office (White 1995), which traditionally has been skeptical of unproven but politically attractive cost-control measures (e.g., managed competition, pay for performance, electronic medical records).

The challenges of controlling costs in a fragmented health care system are amplified by the all-too-familiar characteristics of Congress and American politics that inhibit effective policy making. Multiple committees have jurisdiction over health insurance programs across the House and Senate, making coherent policy development a struggle (Evans 1995). America's system of electoral representation entrenches geographic particularism into Congress (Lee 2005), as Senator Ben Nelson's so-called Cornhusker Kickback vividly demonstrated (it provided extra federal funding for Medicaid expansion to Nelson's home state of Nebraska in exchange for his vote supporting 2009 health reform legislation). The fragmented institutional structure of American government gives groups representing the medical industry numerous opportunities to block or weaken reforms, and to instead push through provisions that advance their narrow financial interests (Immergut 1992; Peterson 2005; Steinmo and Watts 1995). Critics, including some of its former members (Daschle et al. 2008), believe Congress lacks the political will to stand up to such groups and implement policies that reduce their incomes, and is incapable of making the hard decisions necessary to rein in spending. They also contend that Congress lacks the expertise to grapple with highly technical and complex decisions about health care, and that it relies too little on evidence in making policy (Berenson et al. 2009). Congress cannot adjust policy quickly or nimbly enough to keep up with changes in the health care system, leading to poor outcomes (such as pricing distortions in Medicare payments). Congress is additionally said to engage in too much micromanagement – often at the behest of stakeholder groups – of health policy issues better left to experienced administrators or experts (Aaron 2011). The electoral cycle ensures that Congress has short-term time horizons in health policy, when a coherent long-term vision is required. Finally, the two parties often have divergent ideas about health care reform, and partisan polarization, as well as the increasing use of the filibuster, makes agreement on cost-control policies that much harder.

In sum, a Congress that is said to be too inexpert, too partisan, too short-term in its vision, and too beholden to pressure groups confronts the world's most expensive health care system, which is extraordinarily fragmented, difficult to control, and resistant to change. There seemingly could not be a worse match between the magnitude of a policy problem and the depths of institutional incapacity. When an irresistible force meets a permeable institution, it hardly qualifies as a surprise that the latter gives way. In fact, as I discuss later, many health policy analysts and politicians believe that the limits of Congressional government are so severe, the web of interest groups so dense, and the urgency to control costs so pressing that it is necessary to create a new governance structure for Medicare outside of Congress.

A BRIEF HISTORY OF FAILURE IN HEALTH
CARE COST CONTROL

During most of the 20th century, health care cost control was not a public policy issue. Spending more on medical care, policy makers believed, would ensure that Americans enjoyed the benefits of new therapies and produce a healthier population. Rather, debates focused on what role the government should play in making care affordable and accessible by expanding health insurance coverage (Blumenthal and Morone 2009; Starr 1982; 2011). Proposing universal health insurance in 1945, Harry Truman noted that the United States spent only 4 percent of national income on health services – "We can," he avowed, "afford to spend more" (Truman 1945). Truman's national health plan failed to pass, but Congress did enact legislation funding hospital construction and biomedical research (Starr 1982). The distributive politics of health care spending had begun (Jacobs 1995).

The 1965 enactment of Medicare and Medicaid established the government's role in providing insurance to the elderly and some of the poor. Yet the two programs were adopted with scant regard for their impact on health care spending and without meaningful limits on program expenditures. The Medicare statute explicitly circumscribed federal policy makers' ability to control spending and program administrators, in a quest to assure the program's successful implementation, made decisions on payment policy aimed at conciliating the health care industry (Brown 1983; Derthick 1979; Feder 1977; Marmor 1973; Morone 1990; Oberlander 2003).

Medicare's architects, intent on demonstrating that federal health insurance could work and avoiding the stigma of socialized medicine, had no appetite for a battle with the health care industry. Moreover, in 1965 concern over the amount of national health care spending simply did not exist. But the enactment of Medicare and Medicaid transformed the health policy agenda. As program costs quickly rose and consumed a growing share of the federal budget, policy makers took notice and started to look for ways to restrain medical care spending. By 1972, Richard Nixon was urging resistance to "the relentless inflation of health care costs" (Nixon 1972).

Since then, presidents and Congresses have perennially decried rising medical care costs and grappled with numerous plans to rein in spending. As proposals for national health insurance floundered, cost containment emerged as the dominant issue in health policy making. Enacting and sustaining reforms to restrain medical care inflation, though, proved extraordinarily difficult. The last four decades of American health politics are littered with failed efforts to pass robust cost controls, hyped reforms that did not live up to their promise, and potentially effective policies that were enacted only to be weakened in implementation or discontinued.

In 1971, Richard Nixon imposed wage and price controls on the entire economy, including health care, in order to curtail inflation as part of his Economic Stabilization Program (Altman and Shactman 2011). Medical inflation was a particular concern – between 1967 and 1970 Medicare spending for hospital services increased at an average annual rate of 18 percent. The Nixon administration set, through an executive order, specific caps on hospital price increases and physician fees in 1972. However, efforts to extend the caps required legislation and were defeated in Congress after "strenuous opposition by the hospital industry" (Davis et al. 1990, 16).

Jimmy Carter took on the issue again with a 1977 proposal (subsequently modified and reintroduced in 1979) to limit revenue increases across all hospitals. Once again, the hospital industry lobbied vigorously and Carter's proposals were defeated in Congress. Instead, hospitals offered a "voluntary effort" to restrain spending, which not surprisingly did no such thing. Meanwhile, initial attempts to moderate Medicare spending in the 1970s – including reviewing the appropriateness of Medicare patients' hospital stays – were weakened by opposition from the medical industry and its success at gaming the new regulations that did make it through Congress; these policies proved ineffective (Altman and Shactman 2011; Davis et al. 1990; Oberlander 2003; Starr 1982). Other measures to stem medical inflation – such as requiring medical facilities to request a Certificate of Need before expanding – produced similarly disappointing results.

After Carter's experience with cost containment, no president proposed and Congress did not consider system-wide cost controls again until 1993 as part of the debate over the Clinton health plan (the Health Security Act). Instead, Congress focused more narrowly on Medicare spending and on incremental expansions of insurance coverage that did not address spending limits. More comprehensive policies to limit spending – such as Canadian-style single-payer – went nowhere.

The Clinton plan itself would become the paradigmatic case illustrating the perilous politics of health care cost containment. The Clinton administration proposed a series of ambitious policies to limit spending, including moving Americans into a system of managed competition where they would choose from a menu of private insurance options at varying prices, thereby generating (at least in theory) incentives for consumers to join lower-cost plans and for providers to reorganize health care delivery into a more efficient system. The Health Security Act additionally proposed a cap on how much health insurers could raise their premiums and established a National Health Board that would set and enforce spending targets. It also relied on savings from Medicare and Medicaid to help pay for the expansion of insurance coverage. All together, these measures were projected to substantially reduce the rate of growth in health care spending (CBO 1994).

And that was, in part, the Clinton plan's undoing. While a broad range of stakeholders voiced support for the goal of containing spending, it turned out they were less enthused about actual policies that really would slow the flow of money to the health care industry. The health insurance industry fought tenaciously against the reform plan and its new regulations and price controls. The proposed Medicare cuts cost the administration the support of the hospital industry, which had endorsed universal coverage, and resulted in AARP largely sitting out the fight (Starr 1995). The Clinton plan further alienated many insured Americans who were anxious that health system reorganization would force them into managed care plans and erode the quality of their medical care, a fear that opponents fueled with misleading warnings (Hacker 1997; Jacobs and Shapiro 2000; Johnson and Broder 1996; Skocpol 1996; Starr 1995; Zelman and Brown 1998).

After the debacle, President Clinton never again attempted system-wide cost control. Members of Congress, especially Ted Kennedy, played crucial roles in enacting laws regulating the portability of health insurance in 1996 and creating the State Children's Health Insurance Program for low-income families in 1997. Having learned the painful lessons of the Clinton administration's misadventures, those reforms sought to expand access without controlling costs. Meanwhile, geographic particularism and interest group influence remained prominent features of Congressional health policy making. Writing about the 1997 Balanced Budget Act (BBA), Bruce Vladeck, formerly the chief administrator of the Health Care Financing Administration, the federal agency overseeing Medicare and Medicaid, reported that "the law contains no fewer than half a dozen provisions targeted at individual hospitals, or, at most, a mere handful" (Vladeck 1999). The hospital industry's broader influence also persisted. When Medicare payment cuts enacted in the BBA were deemed too damaging, the industry successfully lobbied Congress to pass "giveback" legislation in 1999 and 2000 (Mayes and Berenson 2006).

Nor did health care cost control emerge as a top issue during the George W. Bush administration. Congress enacted annual limits on growth in Medicare physician payments – known as the sustainable growth rate (SGR) – only to cancel the required payment cuts every year after 2002 (Ginsburg 2011). The 2003 Medicare Modernization Act (MMA), which added an outpatient prescription drug benefit to the program, contained policies aimed at currying favor with insurers, drug companies, hospitals, doctors, and a host of other groups; rural areas also gained higher Medicare payments. Echoing the original Medicare legislation's hands-off attitude toward medical providers, the MMA prohibited the Secretary of Health and Human Services from negotiating prices for Medicare patients with drug manufacturers (Morgan and Campbell 2011; Oberlander 2006). The MMA did, though, advance a cost-control measure outside of Medicare backed by conservatives: high-deductible health insurance and Health Savings Accounts.

Even as federal Medicare spending climbed upward, Congress forbade program administrators from considering costs when deciding to cover new medical technologies – a rejection of cost-effectiveness strongly supported by a medical industry more interested in maximizing income than in comparing therapies (Neumann 2005). Moreover, Congress has pressured Medicare administrators to reverse coverage decisions adversely affecting some companies because of stakeholder pressure. Congress also has interfered with potentially promising demonstrations in Medicare payment and delivery reform (Berenson et al. 2009). A program designed to reduce Medicare spending – allowing beneficiaries to enroll in privately run managed care plans – has instead lost money, largely because reimbursement formulas approved by Congress have ensured that these plans receive excess payments. Nor has

Congress given administrators tools to restrain utilization of medical services by Medicare beneficiaries – such as prior authorization before patients can receive a treatment and selective contracting with some, rather than all, health care providers – commonly used by private insurers (Berenson and Harris 2002). As noted earlier, in a classic case of regulatory capture (Lowi 1969; McConnell 1966; Stigler 1971), substantial control over updating Medicare payment values for physicians has been ceded to the American Medical Association (Laugesen et al. 2012). And despite, or perhaps because of, Medicare's size, Congress has never set a firm annual budget for program expenditures.

In short, the presumption that Congress will not control health care spending, and will resist presidential initiatives to do so, has plenty of empirical support, though America's dismal health care cost-control record leaves plenty of blame for the presidency as well. Congress has often appeared incapable of standing up to interest groups and making the politically difficult decisions necessary to limit spending. Yet the story of Congressional failure in health policy is, in important respects, both incomplete and misleading.

CONGRESSIONAL ACTION IN COST CONTROL

Congress's record in health care cost control is certainly not great, nor is it consistently good, but it is better than commonly assumed. Congress has steered clear of politically treacherous system-wide cost-control actions, instead focusing its energies on the largest federal health insurance program, Medicare. In fact, concerns over excessive Medicare spending were first raised by Congress after program spending rose precipitously by an average annual rate of 40 percent during 1968–69. Russell Long, chair of the Senate Finance Committee, warned in 1969 that Medicare had become a "runaway program." The Finance Committee held hearings and issued reports critical of the Johnson administration's permissive reimbursement policies and solicitous stance toward the health care industry (Oberlander 2003).

As a consequence of Medicare's inflationary beginnings, fiscal policy came to dominate the policy agenda. Despite the political incentives for expansion and more spending, as well as the limited scope of the program's insurance protections, Congress rarely expanded Medicare benefits during 1966–2000. The overriding issue in Congressional policy making for Medicare became how to restrain costs. As noted earlier, initial measures to slow Medicare spending were weak and ineffective. But during the 1980s, Congress enacted a series of laws that transformed Medicare payment policy, including a prospective payment system for hospitals (1983) and a fee schedule for physicians (1989). Those measures gave the government powerful tools to moderate Medicare spending and set prospective limits on what Washington would pay medical providers. Congress played an especially crucial role in developing the new formula for paying physicians (Smith 1992).

During the 1990s, Medicare savings were a regular feature of deficit reduction laws. Budget acts in 1990, 1993, and 1997 contained policies aimed at reducing Medicare spending growth, with the 1997 BBA calling for nearly $400 billion in reductions over ten years. Contrary to conventional wisdom, Congress allowed the vast majority of these savings to go into effect (Horney and Van de Water 2009; Merlis 2010). While the annual theater surrounding canceling scheduled cuts in physician payments strengthened the perception that Congress cannot implement cost controls, that payment formula – the SGR – was badly designed and never expected to generate significant savings (Horney and Van de Water 2009). Preoccupation with the SGR (which was repealed in 2015) obscured the fact that most cost-saving policies from the 1997 BBA were implemented, and even after 1999 and 2000 "giveback" legislation the law produced substantial cost control in Medicare. Moreover, although Congress canceled deep cuts in payment rates triggered by the SGR, Medicare fees to doctors per service did not increase much at all during the 2000s. In 2005, Congress enacted another deficit reduction package with Medicare savings, this time targeting imaging, home health services, and durable medical equipment (White and Ginsburg 2012). The 2010 ACA, discussed at length later, also contained substantial reductions in projected Medicare spending growth.

Put simply, Congress has repeatedly enacted measures to constrain Medicare spending, and most of those measures have endured. The cumulative impact of these policies has been to reduce the annual rate of excess cost growth – defined as costs above per-person growth in the gross domestic product after adjusting for demographic changes – in Medicare over the past three decades. That rate fell "from 5.6% during 1975–1983 to 2.1% during 1983–1997, and to only 0.5% during 1997–2005" (White 2008, 793). In contrast, during that same period excess cost growth increased for the nonelderly population (White 2008). In fact, Medicare spending per enrollee has grown slower than private insurance expenditures over the past four decades, a gap that widened after Medicare instituted payment reforms in the early 1980s (MedPAC 2012). The full history of Medicare policy does not support the conventional wisdom that Congress cannot control health care costs and that it is institutionally incapable of making the politically difficult decisions necessary to restrain spending.

To be sure, Medicare's record of cost containment is mixed and Congress's contributions to reforms aimed at slowing spending growth have been inconsistent. Medicare has been much more successful at regulating prices than restraining the volume and intensity of services delivered to program beneficiaries. While Medicare physician fees barely budged during the 2000s, program physician service payments per beneficiary nonetheless rose at an average annual rate of 5.4 percent during that decade because of increases in the volume of services delivered (Reinhardt 2010). Additionally, slowdowns in Medicare spending growth are sometimes followed by spending increases; after spending controls were adopted in 1997, a benefit expansion, the addition of prescription drug coverage, ensued in 2003. The absence of a firm annual program budget makes Medicare susceptible to such vicissitudes.

None of this, though, changes the facts that Congress has enacted important cost-control measures in Medicare, that "there has been a long-term trend toward tighter Medicare payment policy" (White and Ginsburg 2012, 1074), that these policies have produced substantial savings for the federal budget, and that excess costs in Medicare have been declining over time.

The question is why Congress has defied expectations in pursing policies, albeit inconsistently and imperfectly, to restrain Medicare spending. What political dynamics and institutional features have enabled Congress, on more than one occasion, to overcome the formidable barriers to health care cost control? And what does the Medicare case tell us more broadly about Congress's role in public policy?

LESSONS FROM MEDICARE

The rise of deficit politics is perhaps the most important reason Congress repeatedly adopted policies to contain Medicare spending. As deficit reduction emerged as a prominent political issue in the 1980s and 1990s, Congress increasingly looked to Medicare for savings and embraced more robust reforms. In part, this reflected budgetary math: expenditures for federal health insurance programs were a major contributor to the federal deficit. Moreover, because Medicare and Medicaid's fiscal footprint was so large, substantial savings could be projected from even modest reductions in their growth rates. Finally, resistance to raising taxes made spending reductions more imperative – absent a political commitment to generate more funds for Medicare, balancing program finances required cost controls.

Regardless of the substantive virtues or drawbacks of deficit reduction, policy makers believed that it was in the public interest to reduce federal spending (White and Wildavsky 1989). And that underscores one important lesson from the Medicare experience: members of Congress are not exclusively concerned with reelection but also care about making good policy (Arnold 1990; Kelman 1987). In the case of Medicare, that meant working to moderate program spending growth. In so doing, Congress showed a willingness to take on interest groups representing the medical care industry. The ideology of deficit reduction transformed Medicare politics by giving policy makers cause to regulate spending and restrain the flow of income from federal health insurance to hospitals, doctors, and other providers. A second lesson is thus that interest groups do not always win in health policy, and they do not always succeed in blocking health care cost control.

The budgetary process provided Congress with an appealing political opportunity to adopt cost-containment measures. Most of the reforms to Medicare payment policy were enacted not as standalone laws but as parts of broader budget legislation, reinforcing the connection between Medicare and deficit reduction and making it harder for interest groups to resist the changes (Jost 1999; Oberlander 2003). Additionally, different rules accompanied budget legislation that reduced the normal barriers to enactment, particularly in the Senate, making it easier to push Medicare reforms through.

The structure of Medicare itself also facilitated cost control. Put simply, Congress could slow Medicare spending without cutting benefits. Unlike Social Security payments, which go directly to beneficiaries, Medicare pays medical providers for services used by enrollees. As a consequence, it is possible to constrain program spending by reducing the prices paid to doctors, hospitals, and other providers without reducing program enrollees' benefits. Though some reforms have raised beneficiaries' premiums and cost-sharing, policy makers have achieved the vast majority of Medicare savings over the past three decades through payment reductions to providers. Confronted with a zero-sum game requiring spending reductions, and faced with the choice of alienating seniors or taking on the medical care industry, Congress has preferred the politics of targeting providers (White 1995).

Medicare's structure mattered in a second respect. Medicare relies on earmarked payroll taxes to finance its hospitalization insurance, so it is susceptible to trust fund "crises" when a shortfall occurs (Oberlander 2003; Patashnik 2000; Pierson 1994). That financing structure created opportunities for Congress to adopt cost controls above and beyond deficit pressures. Resistance to raising payroll taxes (Campbell and Morgan 2005; Oberlander 2003) meant that more often than not, Congress responded to those shortfalls by adopting reforms to reduce payments to the medical care industry.

Notably, during the 1980s and the 1990s, Medicare payment reforms often enjoyed bipartisan support. The Reagan administration sponsored the 1983 Prospective Payment System for hospitals, with support from Republicans and Democrats in Congress. The 1989 Medicare Fee Schedule, which overhauled how the program paid doctors, and 1997 BBA, which made substantial cuts in projected Medicare spending growth, similarly had bipartisan support in Congress.

Bipartisanship in Medicare payment policy may have reflected, in part, the institutional realities of divided government that predominated during this period, where presidents of one party had to come to agreement with at least one house and at times both houses of Congress controlled by the other party in order to pass legislation. Divided government did not halt governance (Mayhew 1991). In addition, after programs are enacted, the political dynamics of partisan divisions can change. Medicare emerged following its 1965 enactment as one of the nation's most popular social policies and Republicans accommodated it, seeking to limit its growth rather than pursuing repeal. Meanwhile, rising costs and changes in the political environment defused Democratic plans to expand Medicare, and they focused on preserving the program. Both parties, then, embraced policies to moderate program costs and other incremental changes, a turn to "rationalizing politics" (Brown 1983).

Indeed, that rationalizing impetus and the pull of deficit reduction were sufficiently strong that during the 1980s and 1990s Congressional Republicans supported reforms that strengthened federal regulatory power to set Medicare payments. Republicans, in other words, backed Medicare price controls, though obscured by technocratic language and rhetorics of efficiency and competition, largely because they believed that reducing the budget deficit and Medicare spending required an expansion of federal power (White 1995; Oberlander 2003). The fact that Medicare did not operate under Republican majorities in both the House and Senate until 1995, or unified GOP control of Congress and the White House until 2001, abetted both bipartisanship and the embrace of regulatory reforms.

In pursuing Medicare reform, Congress has defied expectations that health policy is too technical an area for it to handle. Even the most complex formulas for paying medical providers contain highly visible, crude instruments that Congress can use to adjust Medicare expenditures (the update factor for hospital payments is one such device). Further, Congress has more technical capacity than often assumed. Long-serving members of Congress on committees and subcommittees grappling with health policy can become experts on the subject; expertise is one advantage of incumbency. Members have access to committee staff, some of whom are also long-serving, who possess considerable technical knowledge about health policy and federal programs. Underscoring its extraordinary influence on policy making, Congress has at its disposal its own bureaucracy and sources of expertise independent of the executive branch and of stakeholder groups, including the Congressional Research Service, the Congressional Budget Office, and the Medicare Payment Advisory Commission (Oberlander 2003). Congressional government is alive and well in health policy.

In sum, Congress has substantial policy making capacity and it has often, though certainly not always, used it to adopt effective policies to moderate Medicare spending. Congress has at times resisted powerful interest groups to enact reforms perceived to be in the public interest, typically in the name of deficit reduction. The structure of Medicare, which permits costs to be slowed without slashing benefits, and of the budget process, where controversial health care provisions can be attached to omnibus legislation, has enabled Congress to pursue such policies. Perhaps most crucially, Medicare's experience demonstrates that federal health care spending is not simply the inevitable result of technological changes, consumer demand, and other ostensibly immutable forces, but is amenable to public policy (White 2008).

THE AFFORDABLE CARE ACT

Do the lessons of Congressional action in Medicare apply to other sectors of health policy? Can Medicare's partial success at moderating spending be extrapolated to new health care programs? Or is the Medicare story just that, a story about Medicare's singular circumstances? Will future Congresses attempt even more robust cost controls, and can such measures pass Congress given the extraordinary levels of partisan polarization? The ACA provides an opportunity to investigate these questions and explore further the promise and limits of Congressional policy making related to health care cost containment.

The 2010 Patient Protection and ACA represents a breakthrough in American health policy. After decades of incrementalism and inaction, the ACA moves the United States closer to the ideal that every American should have access to health insurance.[2] In addition to expanding insurance coverage, the ACA aims to slow the growth in health care spending. The ACA contains three major policy strategies designed to bend the cost curve (Oberlander 2011). It calls for a significant reduction in the annual rate of growth in Medicare spending, primarily by cutting payments to hospitals and private insurance plans that enroll program beneficiaries. Other measures, including establishment of an innovations center, are intended to facilitate more rapidly the spread of cost-saving innovations in Medicare.

The law also imposes an excise tax on high-cost private health insurance plan – the so-called Cadillac tax. The idea, embraced by many health economists, is that current tax incentives give employees and employers incentives to, respectively, seek and provide overly generous health coverage. Such comprehensive policies are expensive and, according to critics, encourage overutilization of low-value services. Advocates expect that the Cadillac tax will force private plans to become more efficient and employers to offer less expensive coverage so they avoid the tax, which is a steep 40 percent above the threshold specified in the law.

Obamacare additionally aims to transform how medical care services are delivered and paid for through a variety of reforms, including accountable care organizations (ACOs, a modified version of HMOs), medical homes (focused on primary care), bundled payment (an effort to move away from inflationary fee-for-service), and value-based payment (reimbursing for quality rather than quantity). The hope is that by creating new incentives for high-quality care and care coordination, costs can be slowed while improving medical care delivery and health outcomes (White 2013).

Given the formidable barriers to enacting health reform and the law's perilous and nearly fatal journey through Congress it is remarkable that Obamacare contains any meaningful cost containment at all. The 2006 health reform law in Massachusetts that became the model for Obamacare did not attempt to limit health care spending because its architects believed that to do so would have turned the Herculean task of pursing universal coverage into a Sisyphean ordeal (Kingsdale 2009). At the federal level, the pattern has long been, dating back to Medicare and Medicaid's enactment, that coverage expansions are accompanied by weak or no cost controls. The ACA broke the mold: its Medicare provisions, if implemented as scheduled, should achieve substantial savings. Indeed, those provisions are already having a significant impact; Medicare spending in 2014 "was expected to be $1200 lower per beneficiary in 2014 than was projected in 2010" by the CBO after the ACA's passage (Neuman and Cubanski 2014). At the same time, members of Congress have successfully pressed the Obama administration to cancel slated payment cuts to private Medicare Advantage plans, though Medicare spending growth has slowed even with those givebacks. While the precise sources of the Medicare spending slowdown are difficult to quantify, the ACA's cost-control policies appear to be responsible for much of the unanticipated decline in Medicare expenditure growth (White et al. 2014).

That the ACA also contains the Cadillac tax, a controversial provision long desired by many health policy analysts but bitterly opposed by unions among others, and a host of potentially transformative payment and delivery reforms, speaks to the fact that the Obama administration and Congressional Democrats achieved more in cost control than reasonably could have been expected given political constraints (Oberlander 2011).

Yet the ACA's cost containment provisions for Medicare are arguably more robust than those designed to restrain spending in the rest of the health care system. The Cadillac tax does aim to contain the costs of private health insurance and could generate significant savings. But the tax is not scheduled to go into effect until 2018, and that delayed implementation reveals just how controversial and unpopular an idea it is. Given the difficult politics of taxing health insurance, there is no guarantee that a new president and Congress will actually impose the Cadillac tax in 2018. Instead, the tax could become an object of repeal. In addition, it could create more *underinsurance* by leading insurers to raise deductibles and cost-sharing in health plans that are comparatively costly not because they are overly generous, but because they have a disproportionately sicker, expensive insurance pool. Still, its substantial revenue-generating capacity will make retention (and perhaps even strengthening) of the Cadillac tax attractive to budget hawks.

That leaves payment and delivery system reform, the centerpiece of Obamacare's cost containment aspirations. The ACA's answer both to the dilemma that costs can be controlled only through politically painful, centralized measures and to the challenge of restraining the volume of medical services used by patients without invoking fears of rationing is to put its faith in decentralized policies that promise, through innovation, to contain spending while improving quality of care. That framing is crucial to the law's strategy of long-term cost control: improving how we deliver medical services will produce better care, better health outcomes, and cost savings, advocates believe, all without controversial policies such as budgeting and price controls that the American political system is allergic to. Regardless of the rhetorical advantages ACOs, medical homes, and other delivery and payment reforms hold, there is, however, limited evidence to date that any of these reforms can save much money. In many cases they are being rolled out by the ACA on a limited basis through demonstrations. It is not clear that they have enough scope to make a major dent in health care spending, though they could be scaled up in subsequent years. It is impossible to say how far such reforms will spread, how well they will work, or what the interaction of so many different policies will produce. The ACA's delivery and payment system reforms have potential to restrain spending. Yet at present this reflects wishful thinking more than it represents a reliable strategy of cost containment (Marmor et al. 2009; Oberlander 2011).

What is striking about Obamacare is what the law does not do to control spending. Unlike the 1993 Clinton plan, it does not establish a system-wide budget for or caps on national health expenditures. Having witnessed the fierce resistance to the Clinton administration's controls, the Obama administration and Congressional Democrats chose to avoid centralized cost-control measures, eventually abandoning plans for a Medicare-like public insurance option for the uninsured as well (Hacker 2008; Halpin and Harbage 2010). As political strategy the decision to defer stronger spending limits made perfect sense; it is doubtful that Obamacare could have passed Congress with such controls (Oberlander 2011). The reliance on delivery and payment system reform is, in effect, an attempt to work around the political barriers to centralized cost control by betting that decentralized innovations can produce savings without centralized budgeting or federally imposed limits. That strategy, whatever its political attraction, leaves the U.S. health care system without reliable, system-wide cost control (White 2013).

How did the patterns of Congressional health policy making regarding cost control described earlier play out in the debate over and enactment of Obamacare? The ACA's primary focus on controlling Medicare spending – this time in the service of producing CBO-scoreable savings to help defray the costs of expanding insurance coverage – and the willingness to reduce payments to medical care providers are familiar themes. Once again, Congress demonstrated that it can enact legislation to slow health care spending. Still, the furor over mythic "death panels" and "pulling the plug on grandma" and the weakening of provisions designed to promote comparative effectiveness research served as visceral reminders of the political barriers that confront proposals to curb medical care spending in the United States. The absence of reliable, system-wide cost controls in the ACA exposed the limits of Congressional action in health policy. An array of policies to control spending either were not on the agenda (a national health budget and coordinated system of price controls) or failed to survive the legislative process (the public insurance option). In addition, the politics of Obamacare were highly partisan, with no Republicans voting for the ACA's final version. That made the law, including many of its cost-control provisions, a target for a Republican repeal campaign, in contrast to bipartisan Medicare policy making during the 1980s and parts of the 1990s. Rising partisan polarization in Congress (McCarty et al. 2006) shaped and suffused the debate over Obamacare.

In one other respect the ACA broke important ground in health policy. Congress essentially conceded its own limitations in cost containment and, with prodding from the Obama administration, set up a new institution to constrain spending outside the normal legislative process: the Independent Payment Advisory Board (IPAB). In terms of Congressional health policy making, the

IPAB is arguably Obamacare's most compelling innovation, and one of its most misunderstood.

DELEGATED HEALTH POLICY: THE INDEPENDENT PAYMENT ADVISORY BOARD

The ACA established the IPAB as a fifteen-member, nonelected board. Among other duties, the IPAB is empowered to recommend changes to Medicare if projected per-beneficiary spending growth exceeds specified targets. Congress must consider Medicare reforms proposed by the board under special fast-track legislative rules, including limits on debate, designed to ensure speedy action. If Congress does not enact legislation containing those proposals or alternative policies that achieve the same savings, the IPAB's recommendations are to be implemented by the secretary of health and human services (HHS). Other rules make it difficult for Congress to override these procedures (supermajorities are required) or eliminate the board altogether (the ACA allows Congress to do so only in 2017 through a supermajority vote) (Aaron 2011; Ebeler et al. 2011; Jost 2010; Newman and Davis 2010).

The IPAB is modeled after the Base Realignment and Closure (BRAC) process that Congress turned to in the late 1980s to try to overcome "decades of congressional resistance to closing bases and savings billions of dollars" (Mayer 1999) and on the Federal Reserve (Daschle et al. 2008). The aim is to create a nonpartisan board insulated from political pressures that can formulate more rational and coherent Medicare policy. Since it is nonelected and ostensibly independent of political pressures, the board is expected to resist the medical industry's entreaties and make the tough decisions necessary to control spending. Senator Jay Rockefeller (D-WV), one the board's chief sponsors, argued "that Medicare payment policy should be determined by experts, using evidence, instead of by the undue influence of special interests" (Pear 2009).

In 2010, Obama administration officials hailed the IPAB as "the most important institutional change" in the ACA and a crucial component of health care cost containment (Orszag and Emmanuel 2010, 603). The IPAB's supporters praise it as a failsafe that ensures that Medicare spending growth is moderated regardless of congressional inaction. It gives experts a prominent role in Medicare policy and effectively compels Congress to take their recommendations – IPAB represents a new governance structure for Medicare, one that reorders the balance of power between legislators, interest groups, and experts. Like BRAC, the board leverages Congressional inertia; it is premised on the ideas of legislative incapacity and gridlock. If Medicare spending exceeds spending targets and Congress does not act on IPAB recommendations, those proposals become law.

Controversy has followed the IPAB since its inception. Because the board is prohibited by law from making recommendations that raise revenues, increase Medicare beneficiaries' cost-sharing, or restrict benefits and eligibility, it is expected to focus on savings from medical providers. A broad coalition of health care industry groups, fearful that it will reduce Medicare payments, fiercely opposes the IPAB. In addition, Republicans view it as an instrument of rationing and bureaucratic intrusion into medicine – even though the law prohibits the IPAB from recommending proposals to ration care. House Republicans have voted to repeal the IPAB and in January 2013 the GOP adopted a House rule declaring that the IPAB "shall not apply" in the current Congress, thereby rejecting the special procedures that the ACA had established for congressional consideration of IPAB recommendations.

Democrats have also criticized the IPAB. Pete Stark called the Medicare board "an unprecedented abrogation of Congressional authority to an unelected, unaccountable body of so-called experts" (Guadagino 2012). IPAB appeared to have stronger support in the Senate than in the House in 2010, and it is highly unlikely that it could have passed Congress as standalone legislation.

Like BRAC, the IPAB represents "an astonishing delegation of legislative power" (Mayer 1999) and consequently is an intriguing development in Congressional health policy. Yet the IPAB's importance has been exaggerated by both its supporters and detractors (Oberlander and Morrison 2013). It is much more likely to be irrelevant than to become the centerpiece of cost containment. At present, the IPAB's ability to move forward at all is in doubt. Five years after its establishment, the IPAB has no members. Its members – the board is to comprise health policy experts, physicians, and other health professionals, employers, third-party payers, and consumer representatives – are supposed to be nominated by the president for Senate confirmation in consultation with both Democratic and Republican congressional leaders. Republicans, though, have refused to provide any recommendation for board appointees and President Obama has not, as of this writing, nominated anyone. Even if Democrats settle on a slate of nominees, it is not clear that they can make it through the Senate confirmation process given the controversy surrounding the board, though filibuster reform could create a pathway. The Republican majorities that currently govern the House and Senate are likely to continue to target IPAB for repeal.

The Obama administration's difficulties launching IPAB point to a broader problem. The board's appeal lies largely in its aspiration to remove politics from Medicare – to create a policy making process that is informed by experts; insulated from electoral pressures, interest-group demands, and financial considerations; and isolated from partisan divisions. But given Congress's extreme partisan and ideological polarization, the ongoing fight over Obamacare, the legacy of mythic "death panels" and partisan recriminations over Medicare reform, the IPAB's rough start should not be surprising. This is not the sort of a political environment in which an independent board charged with making controversial decisions about one of America's most popular social program is likely to thrive. These dynamics are unlikely to recede soon, which means that the IPAB is stuck in purgatory, neither operational nor canceled – an institution designed to be above politics that cannot escape the political binds and partisan polarization holding it back.

However, if no members are appointed, the power to recommend changes to Medicare when spending targets are exceeded does not disappear: it reverts to the HHS secretary. But Medicare spending is currently projected to grow at a sufficiently moderate clip that the most controversial feature of the IPAB – congressional consideration of IPAB proposals under fast-track procedures – will not come into play any time soon. The CBO currently forecasts no savings from IPAB over the next decade (Oberlander and Morrison 2013). In the end, IPAB's actual effect on health care spending – as opposed to the symbolic value invested in it by both supporters and opponents – is likely to be negligible.

The enactment of IPAB was an extraordinary expression of Congressional recognition of its own limitations as a policy making body and its willingness to cede some control over Medicare policy to another institution. The failure thus far to implement IPAB, though, is a reminder of the more familiar difficulties of realizing such delegation in practice, of the political challenges of health care cost control, and of the crucial influence that partisan polarization now has on Congressional health policy. Delegating responsibility for controversial policy choices to slow health care spending to a nonelected board is an appealing workaround, but it is unlikely to spare Congress from the hard decisions ahead.

CONGRESS AND THE FUTURE OF COST CONTROL

In coming years Congress will have to grapple with the daunting political and policy dilemmas inherent to health care cost control. There is, though, some good news: during 2006–13 the growth rate in national health care spending slowed significantly (see Figure 9.1), a trend visible both in Medicare and private insurance. The reasons for the decline are not fully understood and are in dispute, though the economic downturn, rather than any cost-control measures adopted by Congress, is likely the single most important explanation. The migration of more persons into government health insurance programs, which are less expensive than private plans, and longer-term declines in Americans' real incomes may also have contributed to lower rates of spending growth (Holahan and McMorrow 2013). Other analysts alternatively point to the spread of high-deductible health insurance plans in the private market that require greater patient cost-sharing (Chandra et al. 2013). Where does Obamacare fit into the picture? The ACA has helped to produce a significant slowdown in Medicare spending (White et al. 2014). It is, though, too early to tell how well the ACA's cost-containment measures outside Medicare are working or to credit Obamacare for definitively bending the cost curve, especially since the decline in spending growth started before the ACA's passage. Perhaps the law's enactment, contributed to the slowdown by persuading the health care industry that it must become more efficient in anticipation of

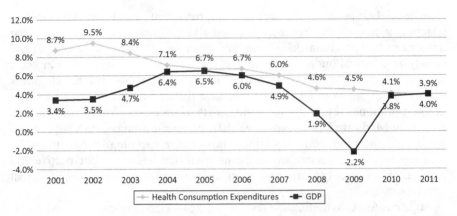

FIGURE 9.1: Annual percent change in health spending and GDP, 2000–11. Estimates of growth in spending and GDP are in nominal terms. Source: Centers for Medicare and Medicaid Services, Office of the Actuary, and National Health Statistics Group.

coming cuts and payment reforms, even as the ultimate effectiveness of those reforms remains uncertain.

Could the health spending slowdown change the policy debate over cost control? A persistent slowdown would reduce projected long-term federal spending on health insurance programs by hundreds of billions of dollars; the health care cost crisis would suddenly appear to be less foreboding. Given the hazardous politics of cost control, any reason to avoid or defer action will be tempting to members of Congress with reelection on their minds. Moreover, in the short term, the shrinking federal deficit may temporarily alleviate pressure to curb health care spending.

Yet the health care cost problem has hardly been solved. Annual increases in spending have declined before only to swell again – talk of a "permanent" slowdown in U.S. health care spending is, to put it mildly, premature. In fact, health care spending increased in 2014 at a faster clip than in recent years as millions of Americans gained insurance coverage under the ACA. And over the next decade spending is projected to grow at a higher rate than it did during 2006–13, though that increase is still expected to be lower than the historical average (Keehan et al. 2015). Moreover, population aging means that Medicare spending will rise significantly during the next two decades and the budget deficit is projected to soon increase again, driven largely by the growth in expenditures on federal health insurance programs. And if congressional Republicans continue their intense opposition to tax increases, that will generate more demands for health care savings in budget legislation as the federal government strains to fund the growing costs of entitlement programs.[3] Controlling health care spending remains central to long-term deficit reduction and budget politics.

While deficit politics will, over the long run, create conditions favorable to enacting additional cost controls, it could also encourage policy remedies that amount to budget gimmicks. Congress's vision of health care spending is still largely as a federal budget problem and that can lead to policies that are cost shifting rather than cost saving. For example, proposals to raise the eligibility age for Medicare from 65 to 67 could save the federal government a modest amount of money, but only by shifting costs to states, employers, and seniors, and since Medicare is less expensive than private insurance, such a proposal actually would increase total national health care spending. It remains to be seen whether Congress can overcome its parochial budgetary perspective and embrace the politically more challenging task of implementing system-wide cost controls.

Still, the ACA, assuming it survives the 2016 elections intact, could transform the politics of health care cost containment. By expanding Medicaid, mandating individuals to obtain health insurance, and providing subsidies for the uninsured to buy coverage, the ACA gives federal policy makers a stronger stake in restraining health care spending. Medicare's history suggests that as the costs of a federal health insurance program mount, the willingness of Congress to adopt spending constraints increases, particularly in the contexts of deficit pressures and resistance to tax increases. Over time, then, even if its experiments in payment and delivery system reform disappoint, the ACA could precipitate much stronger health care cost control in the United States.

Medicare, though, has a constituency that is sympathetic, politically active, and well represented by advocacy groups. It is not clear that the ACA will affect the political participation of its beneficiaries in the same way (Campbell 2003). The ACA is not a single program but a series of programs, policies, rules, regulations, and subsidies that affects different groups of Americans in different ways at different times. That complicates efforts to build a political coalition of Obamacare beneficiaries. Moreover, the ACA's chief beneficiaries – low-income, uninsured adults – are not as sympathetic a group as Medicare enrollees. As a consequence, it is possible that cost pressures could lead to policies that erode the ACA's subsidies, benefits, and insurance protections, rather than to stricter controls on payments to medical care providers.

The uncertainty surrounding future choices between cost control and benefit cuts is mirrored by uncertainty about the future political environment. Who will control Congress and the White House? Ongoing battles over Obamacare and Medicare reform illustrate how partisan the politics of cost control have become, with polarization between Democrats and Republicans in Congress evident across a wide range of health policy issues. There is a broad partisan divide in health policy, as in many other policy areas (McCarty et al. 2006), and the shape of future cost-control efforts depends in no small part on the partisan composition of Congress. While moderating levels of health care spending makes inaction convenient for now, sooner or later more policy interventions will be required. Achieving further health care cost control in a polarized Congress could prove to be a difficult task. Indeed, the fate of health care reform and the ACA itself could hinge on the partisan composition of Congress and which party holds the White House in 2017.

Still, there is perhaps more partisan agreement on health care cost containment than meets the eye. The ACA, which no Republican ended up voting for, reduced Medicare payments to private health plans and hospitals, and increased federal regulatory authority over private insurance. But this Democratic-sponsored health reform also promoted insurance plan competition in its new marketplaces for the uninsured with the aim of ensuring lower premiums, a cost-control idea consistent with GOP health care principles. Both parties, despite recent election rhetoric, also favor slowing the growth in federal health care spending. Republican budget plans authored by Paul Ryan would repeal Obamacare yet keep its Medicare savings – a concession to budgetary realities. Both Democrats and Republicans have supported establishing budgetary targets for Medicare spending, albeit through very different mechanisms.

The alternative to a health policy engulfed by partisan divisions and driven to stalemate is this: fiscal imperatives and the burden of rising health care costs could eventually prove so compelling that Congressional Democrats and Republicans overcome their polarization, rediscover some measure of bipartisanship and compromise in health policy, and commit to additional measures to slow health care spending. That outcome is hardly a certainty and maybe not even likely in this polarized era. But if such bipartisanship happens, the question is will future measures focus only on improving the federal government's balance sheet or will Congress at last broaden its vision to take on national health care spending more aggressively?

Notes

1. While many hospital executives strongly believe that when Medicare reduces payments to hospitals they simply bill private insurers more, the evidence for such cost-shifting indicates that it happens less often than commonly assumed and that when it does occur, its magnitude is limited (Frakt 2011).
2. For more on the Congressional politics of the Affordable Care Act, see Barbara Sinclair's Chapter 3 of this volume.
3. On tax politics, see Alexander Hertel-Fernandez and Theda Skocpol's Chapter 6 of this volume.

References

Aaron, Henry J. 2010. "How to Think about the U.S. Budget Challenge." *Journal of Policy Analysis and Management* 29 (4): 883–91.
    2011. "The Independent Payment Advisory Board: Congress's Good Deed." *New England Journal of Medicine* 64 (25): 2375–7.

Aaron, Henry J., and Paul B. Ginsburg. 2009. "Is Health Care Spending Excessive? If So, What Can We Do about It?" *Health Affairs* 28 (5): 1260–75.

Altman, Stuart, and David Shactman. 2011. *Power, Politics, and Universal Health Care: The Inside Story of a Century-Long Battle*. Amherst, NY: Prometheus Books.

Arnold, R. Douglas. 1990. *The Logic of Congressional Action*. New Haven, CT: Yale University Press.

Berenson, Robert A., and Dean M. Harris. 2002. "Using Managed Care Tools in Traditional Medicare – Should We? Could We?" *Law and Contemporary Problems* 65 (4): 139–68.

Berenson, Robert A., Len M. Nichols, and Tom Emswiler. 2009. "Reforming Medicare's Governance to Enhance Value-Based Purchasing." In Robert A. Berenson and Len M. Nichols, eds., *Making Medicare Sustainable*. Washington, DC: New America Foundation, pp. 21–57.

Berwick, Donald M., and Andrew D. Hackbarth. 2012. "Eliminating Waste in US Health Care." *Journal of the American Medical Association* 307 (14): 513–16.

Blendon, Robert J., Molyann Brodie, John M Benson, Drew E. Altman, and Tami Buhr. 2006. "Americans' Views of Health Care Costs, Access, and Quality." *Milbank Quarterly* 84 (4): 623–67.

Blumenthal, David, and James A. Morone. 2009. *The Heart of Power: Health and Politics in the Oval Office*. Berkeley: University of California Press.

Brown, Lawrence D. 1983. *New Policies, New Politics: Government's Response to Government's Growth*. Washington, DC: Brookings Institution.

    1993. "Dogmatic Slumbers: American Business and Health Policy." *Journal of Health Politics, Policyand Law* 18 (2): 339–57.

Brown, Lawrence D. 2011. "The Elements of Surprise: How Health Reform Happened." *Journal of Health Politics, Policy and Law* 26(3): 419–427.

Campbell, Andrea Louise. 2003. *How Policies Make Citizens: Senior Political Activism in the American Welfare State*. Princeton, NJ: Princeton University Press.

Campbell, Andrea Louise, and Kimberly J. Morgan. 2005. "Financing the Welfare State: Elite Politics and the Decline of the Social Insurance Model." *Studies in American Political Development* 19 (2): 173–95.

Carroll, Aaron. 2012. "The 'Iron Triangle' of Health Care –Access, Costs, and Quality." *JAMA Forum*, October 3. http://newsatjama.jama.com/2012/10/03/jama-forum-the-iron-triangle-of-health-care-access-cost-and-quality/ (accessed December 7, 2013).

Chandra, Amitabh, Jonathan Holmes, and Jonathan Skinner. 2013. *Is This Time Different? The Slowdown in Healthcare Spending*. Washington, DC: Brookings Institution.

Cohn, Jonathan. 2010. "How They Did It: The Inside Account of Health Reform's Triumph." *The New Republic*, June 10, pp. 14–25.

Cutler, David M. 2004. *Your Money or Your Life: Strong Medicine for America's Health Care System*. New York: Oxford University Press.

Congressional Budget Office (CBO). 1994. *An Analysis of the Administration's Health Proposal*. Washington, DC.

    2013. *The 2013 Long-Term Budget Outlook*. Washington, DC.

Daschle, Tom, and David Nather. 2010. *Getting It Done: How Obama and Congress Finally Broke the Stalemate to Make Way for Health Care Reform*. New York: Thomas Dunne Books.

Daschle, Tom, Scott S. Greenberger, and Jeanne M. Lambrew. 2008. *Critical: What We Can Do about the Health-Care Crisis*. New York: Thomas Dunne Books.

Davis, Karen, Gerard E. Anderson, Diane Rowland, and Earl P. Steinberg. 1990. *Health Care Cost Containment*. Baltimore, MD: Johns Hopkins University Press.

Derthick, Martha. 1979. *Policymaking for Social Security*. Washington, DC: Brookings Institution.

Ebeler, Jack, Tricia Neuman, and Juliette Cubanski. 2011. *The Independent Payment Advisory Board: A New Approach to Controlling Medicare Spending*. Kaiser Family Foundation.

Edwards, Haley Sweetland. 2013. "Special Deal: The Shadowy Cartel of Doctors That Control Medicare." *Washington Monthly*, July/August.

Evans, Lawrence. 1995. "Committees and Health Jurisdictions in Congress." In Thomas J. Mann and Norman I. Ornstein, eds., *Intensive Care: How Congress Shapes Health Policy*. Washington, DC: American Enterprise Institute and Brookings Institution Press, pp. 25–51.

Feder, Judith M. 1977. *Medicare: The Politics of Federal Hospital Insurance*. Lexington, MA: D.C. Heath.

Frakt, Austin. 2011. "How Much Do Hospitals Cost Shift? A Review of the Evidence." *Milbank Quarterly* 89 (1): 90–130.

Fuchs, Victor. 2013. "The Gross Domestic Product and Health Care Spending." *New England Journal of Medicine* 369 (2):107–9.

Ginsburg, Paul B. 2011. "Rapidly Evolving Physician Payment Policy – More Than the SGR." *New England Journal of Medicine* 364 (2):172–6.

Gottschalk, Marie. 2000. *The Shadow Welfare State: Labor, Business, and the Politics of Health Care in the United States*. Ithaca: Cornell University Press.

Guadagino, Christopher. 2012. "IPAB Is Medicare's New Hammer for Spending Accountability." *The Hospitalist*, February. www.the-hospitalist.org/details/article/1453379/IPAB_is_Medicares_New_Hammer_for_Spending_Accountability.html (accessed December 7, 2013).

Hacker, Jacob S. 1997. *The Road to Nowhere: The Genesis of President Clinton's Plan for Health Security*. Princeton, NJ: Princeton University Press.

2002. *The Divided Welfare State*. New York: Cambridge University Press.

2008. *The Case for Public Plan Choice in National Health Reform*. Berkeley: University of California, Berkeley, School of Law.

2011. "Why Reform Happened." *Journal of Health Politics, Policy and Law* 36 (3): 437–441.

Halpin, Helen A., and Peter Harbage. 2010. "The Origins and Demise of the Public Option." *Health Affairs* 29 (6): 1117–24.

Hartman, Micah, Anne B. Martin, David Lassman, Aaron Catlin, and the National Health Expenditures Account Team. 2015. "National Health Spending in 2013: Growth Slows, Remains in Step with the Overall Economy." *Health Affairs* 34 (1): 1–11.

Havighurst, Clark C., and Barack Richman. 2006. "Distributive Injustice(s) in American Health Care." *Law and Contemporary Problems* 69 (2): 7–82.

Hoffman, Beatrix. 2012. *Health Care for Some: Rights and Rationing in the United States Since 1930*. Chicago, IL: University of Chicago Press.

Holahan, John, and Stacy McMorrow. 2013. *What Drove the Recent Slowdown in Health Spending Growth and Can It Continue?* Washington, DC: Urban Institute.

Horney, James R., and Paul N. Van De Water. 2009. "House-Passed and Senate Health Bills Reduce Deficit, Slow Health Care Costs and Include Realistic Medicare Savings." Center for Budget Policy and Priorities, December 4. Washington, DC.

Immergut, Ellen M. 1992. *Health Politics: Interests and Institutions in Western Europe.* Cambridge: Cambridge University Press.

Jacobs, Lawrence R. 1995. "Politics of America's Supply State: Health Reform and Technology." *Health Affairs* 14 (2): 143–57.

Jacobs, Lawrence R., and Robert Y. Shapiro. 2000. *Politicians Don't Pander: Political Manipulation and the Loss of Democratic Responsiveness.* Chicago, IL: University of Chicago Press.

Jacobs, Lawrence R., and Theda Skocpol. 2010. *Health Care Reform and American Politics: What Everyone Needs to Know.* New York: Oxford University Press.

Johnson, Haynes, and David S. Broder. 1996. *The System: The American Way of Politics at the Breaking Point.* Boston: Little, Brown.

Jost, Timothy Stoltzfus. 1999. "Governing Medicare." *Administrative Law Review* 51 (1): 39–116.

2010. "The Independent Payment Advisory Board." *New England Journal of Medicine* 363 (2): 103–5.

Kaiser Family Foundation. 2013. *Medicare and the Federal Budget: Comparison of Medicare Provisions in Recent Federal Debt and Deficit Reduction Proposals.* Menlo Park, CA.

Keehan, Sean P., Gigi A. Cuckler. Andrea M. Sisko, Andrew J. Madison, Shelia D. Smith, Devin A. Stone, John A. Poisal, Christian J. Wolfe, and Joseph M. Lizonitz. "National Health Expenditure Projections, 2014-2024: Spending Growth Faster Than recent Trends." *Health Affairs* advanced online article, doi:10.1377/hlthaff.2015.0600.

Kelman, Steven. 1987. *Making Public Policy: A Hopeful View of American Government.* New York: Basic Books.

Kingsdale, Jon. 2009. "Implementing Health Reform in Massachusetts: Strategic Lessons Learned." *Health Affairs* 28 (4): w588–w594.

Laugesen, Miriam J., and Sherry A. Glied. 2011. "Higher Fees to Paid to US Physicians Drive Higher Spending for Physician Services Compared to Other Countries." *Health Affairs* 30 (9): 1647–56.

Laugesen, Miriam J., Roy Wada, and Eric M. Chen. 2012. "In Setting Doctors' Medicare Fees, CMA Almost Always Accepts the Relative Value Update Panel's Advice on Work Values." *Health Affairs* 31 (5): 965–72.

Lee, Frances E. 2005. "Interests, Constituencies, and Policymaking." In Paul J. Quirk and Sarah A. Binder, eds., *The Legislative Branch.* New York: Oxford University Press, pp. 281–313.

Lowi, Theodore. 1969. *The End of Liberalism: Ideology, Policy, and the Crisis of Public Authority.* New York: W.W. Norton.

McCarty, Nolan, Keith T. Poole, and Howard Rosenthal. 2006. *Polarized America: The Dance of Ideology and Unequal Riches.* Boston: MIT Press.

McConnell, Grant. 1966. *Private Power and American Democracy.* New York: Knopf.

McDonough, John E. 2011. *Inside National Health Reform.* Berkeley: University of California Press.

Mann, Thomas E., and Norman J. Ornstein (eds.) 1995. *Intensive Care: How Congress Shapes Health Policy*. Washington, DC: American Enterprise Institute and the Brookings Institution.

Marmor, Theodore R. 1973. *The Politics of Medicare*. Chicago, IL: Aldine.

Marmor, Theodore, Jonathan Oberlander, and Joseph White. 2009. "The Obama Administration's Options for Health Care Cost Control: Hope Versus Reality." *Annals of Internal Medicine* 150 (7): 485–9.

Mathews, Anna Wilde, and Tom McGinty. 2010. "Physician Panel Prescribes the Fees Paid by Medicare." *Wall Street Journal*, October 26.

Mayer, Kenneth R. 1999. "The Limits of Delegation: The Rise and Fall of BRAC." *Regulation* 22 (3): 32–8.

Mayes, Rick, and Robert A. Berenson. 2006. *Medicare Prospective Payment and the Shaping of U.S. Health Care*. Baltimore, MD: Johns Hopkins University Press.

Mayhew, David. 1974. *Congress: The Electoral Connection*. New Haven, CT: Yale University Press.

1991. *Divided We Govern*. New Haven, CT: Yale University Press.

Medicare Payment Advisory Commission (MedPAC). 2012. *A Data Book: Health Care Spending and the Medicare Program*. Washington, DC: Government Printing Office.

Merlis, Mark. 2010. "Adding up the Numbers: Understanding Medicare Savings in the Affordable Care Act." Center for American Progress.

Morgan, Kimberly J., and Andrea Louise Campbell. 2011. *The Delegated Welfare State: Medicare, Markets, and the Governance of Social Policy*. New York: Oxford University Press.

Morone, James A. 1990. "American Political Culture and the Search for Lessons from Abroad." *Journal of Health Politics, Policy, and Law* 15 (1): 129–43.

Neuman, Tricia, and Juliette Cubanski. 2014. "The Mystery of the Missing $1,200 Per Person: Can Medicare's Spending Slowdown Continue?" http://kff.org/health-costs/perspective/the-mystery-of-the-missing-1000-per-person-can-medicares-spending-slowdown-continue/.

Neumann, Peter J., Alison B. Rosen, and Milton C. Weinstein. 2005. "Medicare and Cost Effectiveness." *New England Journal of Medicine* 353 (14): 1516–22.

Newman, David, and Christopher M. Davis. 2010. *The Independent Payment Advisory Board*. Washington, DC: Congressional Research Service.

Nixon, Richard. 1972. "Special Message to the Congress on Health Care." March 2. www.presidency.ucsb.edu/ws/?pid=3757 (accessed December 7, 2013).

Obama, Barack. 2009. "Remarks by the President to a Joint Session of Congress on Health Care." September 9. www.whitehouse.gov/the_press_office/Remarks-by-the-President-to-a-Joint-Session-of-Congress-on-Health-Care (accessed December 7, 2013).

Oberlander, Jonathan. 2003. *The Political Life of Medicare*. Chicago, IL: University of Chicago Press.

2006. "Through the Looking Glass: The Politics of the Medicare Prescription Drug, Improvement, and Modernization Act." *Journal of Health Politics, Policy and Law* 32 (2): 187–219.

2010. "Long Time Coming: Why Health Reform Finally Passed." *Health Affairs* 29 (6): 1112–16.

2011. "Throwing Darts: Americans' Elusive Quest for Health Care Cost Control." *Journal of Health Politics, Policy and Law* 36 (3): 477–84.

Oberlander, Jonathan, and Barbara Lyons. 2009. "Beyond Incrementalism: SCHIP and the Politics of Health Reform." *Health Affairs* 28 (3): w399–w410.

Oberlander, Jonathan, and Marisa Morrison. 2013. "Failure to Launch: The Independent Payment Advisory Board's Uncertain Prospects." *New England Journal of Medicine* 369 (2): 105–7.

Orszag, Peter R., and Ezekiel J. Emanuel. 2010. "Health Care Reform and Cost Control." *New England Journal of Medicine* 363 (7): 601–3.

Patashnik, Eric. 2000. *Putting Trust in the U.S. Budget: Federal Trust Funds and the Politics of Commitment.* Cambridge: Cambridge University Press.

Pear, Robert. 2009. "Obama Proposal to Create Medicare Panel Meets with Resistance." *New York Times*, August 13.

Peterson, Mark A. 2005. "The Congressional Graveyard for Health Care Reform." In James A. Morone and Lawrence R. Jacobs, eds., *Healthy, Wealthy and Fair: Health Care and the Good Society.* New York: Oxford University Press, pp. 205–33.

Pierson, Paul. 1994. *Dismantling the Welfare State.* Cambridge: Cambridge University Press.

Pozen, Alexis, and David M. Cutler. 2010. "Medical Care Spending Differences in the United States and Canada: The Role of Prices, Procedures, and Administrative Expenses." *Inquiry* 47 (2): 124–34.

Quirk, Paul F., and Sarah A. Binder. 2005. *The Legislative Branch.* New York: Oxford University Press.

Reinhardt, Uwe. 2010. "The Annual Drama of the 'Doc Fix.'" *New York Times* Economix Blog, December 17. http://economix.blogs.nytimes.com/2010/12/17/the-annual-drama-of-the-doc-fix/?_r=0 (accessed December 7, 2013).

Roehrig, Charles 2011. "Must We Bend the Health Care Employment Curve?" http://altarum.org/health-policy-blog/must-we-bend-the-health-care-employment-curve (accessed December 7, 2013).

Skocpol, Theda. 1996. *Boomerang: Clinton's Health Security Effort and the Turn against Government in U.S. Politics.* New York: W. W. Norton.

Smith, David G. 1992. *Paying for Medicare: The Politics of Reform.* New York: Aldine De Gruyter.

Smith, Mark, Robert Saunders, Leigh Stuckhardt, and J. Michael McGinnis (eds.) 2012. *Best Care at Lower Cost: The Path to Continuously Learning Health Care.* Washington, DC: National Academies Press of the Institute of Medicine.

Starr, Paul. 1982. *The Social Transformation of American Medicine.* New York: Basic Books.

1995. "What Happened to Health Care Reform?" *American Prospect* 20: 20–31.

2011. *Remedy and Reaction: The Peculiar American Struggle over Health Care Reform.* New Haven, CT: Yale University Press.

Steinmo, Sven, and Jon Watts. 1995. "It's the Institutions Stupid! Why Comprehensive National Health Insurance Always Fails in America." *Journal of Health Politics, Policy, and Law* 20 (2): 329–72.

Stigler, George J. 1971. "The Theory of Economic Regulation." *Bell Journal of Economics and Management Science* 2 (1): 3–21.

Truman, Harry S. 1945. "Special Message to the Congress Recommending a Comprehensive Health Program." November 19. www.trumanlibrary.org/publicpapers/index.php?pid=483 (accessed December 7, 2013).

United States Census Bureau. *Voting and Registration: Historical Time Series Tables.* www.census.gov/hhes/www/socdemo/voting/publications/historical/index.html (accessed August 5, 2015).

Vladeck, Bruce C. 1999. "The Political Economy of Medicare." *Health Affairs* 18 (1): 22–36.

Volden, Craig, and Alan Wiseman. 2011. "Breaking Gridlock: The Determinants of Health Policy Change in Congress." *Journal of Health Politics, Policy and Law* 36 (2): 228–64.

Weaver, R. Kent. 1986. "The Politics of Blame Avoidance." *Journal of Public Policy* 6 (4): 371–98.

Weissert, Carol S., and William G. Weissert. 1996. *Governing Health: The Politics of Health Policy.* Baltimore, MD: Johns Hopkins University Press.

Wennberg, John E. 2010. *Tracking Medicine: A Researcher's Quest to Understand Health Care.* New York: Oxford University Press.

White, Chapin. 2008. "Why Did Medicare's Spending Growth Slow Down?" *Health Affairs* 27 (3): 793–802.

White, Chapin, and Paul B. Ginsburg. 2012. "Slower Growth in Medicare Spending: Is This the New Normal?" *New England Journal of Medicine* 366 (12): 1073–5.

White, Chapin, Juliette Cubanski, and Tricia Neuman. 2014. "How Much of the Medicare Spending Slowdown Can Be Explained? Insights and Analysis from 2014." Henry J. Kaiser Family Foundation Issue Brief.

White, Joseph. 1995. "Budgeting and Health Policymaking." In Thomas J. Mann and Norman I. Ornstein, eds., *Intensive Care: How Congress Shapes Health Policy.* Washington, DC: American Enterprise Institute and Brookings Institution Press, pp. 53–78.

2011. "Prices, Volume, and the Perverse Effects of the Variations Crusade." *Journal of Health Politics, Policy and Law* 36 (4): 775–90.

2013. "Cost Control after the ACA." *Public Administration Review* 73 (S1): S24–S33.

White, Joseph, and Aaron Wildavsky. 1989. *The Deficit and the Public Interest: The Search for Responsible Budgeting in the 1980s.* Berkeley: University of California Press.

Wright, Joshua. 2013. "Health Care's Unrivaled Job Gains and Where It Matters Most." www.forbes.com/sites/emsi/2013/10/07/health-cares-unrivaled-job-gains-and-where-it-matters-most/ (accessed December 7, 2013).

Zelman, Walter, and Lawrence D. Brown. 1998. "Looking Back on Health Care Reform: 'No Easy Choices.'" *Health Affairs* 17 (6): 61–8.

10

The Demise of Immigration Reform

Policy-Making Barriers under Unified and Divided Government

Daniel J. Tichenor

INTRODUCTION

Comprehensive immigration reform (CIR) has loomed for some time as one of the most elusive items on the Congressional agenda. Yet twice in recent years – once during unified party control of the branches in 2009–10 and again during divided government in 2013 – the chances for sweeping reform legislation were quite palpable. The failure of CIR in the 111th (2009–10) and 113th (2013–14) Congresses presents different and intriguing puzzles. Why did the Obama administration largely avoid immigration reform in 2009–10 despite its crucial role for the Democratic Party and strong margins of control by Democrats in both the House and Senate? How did Congress come *far closer* to enacting CIR during *divided* party control in 2013, with passage of a bipartisan Senate bill, and why was it ultimately derailed in the House?

As Barbara Sinclair underscores in Chapter 3, high levels of partisan polarization do not make landmark legislative innovation impossible during periods of unified party control of Congress and the White House. In fact, as various chapters in this volume demonstrate, Obama-led Democrats in the 211th Congress passed a major economic stimulus package, historic health care legislation, and other significant reforms targeting regulation of the financial services industry, child nutrition, fair pay, student loans, repeal of a ban on qualified gay and lesbian serving in the armed forces, and other agenda items. This record of marked legislative productivity raises the question of why President Obama and Democratic leaders in Congress did not press their advantage to enact a partisan, pro-immigration law that, among other things, satisfied most Latino and Asian voters by legalizing millions of undocumented immigrants residing in the country.

Strikingly, many pundits and scholars alike thought major immigration reform was a fait accompli following the presidential election returns of

2012. In contrast to many issues examined by Sinclair and others, CIR presented distinctive incentives for many lawmakers to act in spite of divided party control of the branches in the 113th Congress. "We will get immigration reform," David Gergen confidently told CNN viewers soon after the election. "Democrats want it and Republicans now need it."[1] The reason was obvious: more than 70 percent of Latino voters supported Obama, with Asian voters (less numerous overall) voting for Obama in even larger proportions. The fact that pro-immigrant Latinos and Asians represent the largest growing sectors of the U.S. electorate led many to assume that in the realm of American immigration policy making, the philosopher August Comte was right to proclaim that "demographics is destiny." It was a view expressed often by Republican leaders and presidential hopefuls endorsing bipartisan immigration reform during the 113th Congress. "We're getting an ever-dwindling percent of the Hispanic vote," Republican Senator Rand Paul (KY) told reporters. "We have to let people know, Hispanics in particular, we're not putting you on a bus and shipping you home."[2] Republican House Speaker John Boehner (OH) also recently commented that "a comprehensive approach is long overdue.... It's time to get the job done."[3] Amidst increased partisan polarization in both the House and Senate, immigration emerged as an exceptional issue in 2013 where prominent lawmakers in both parties worked together on crafting reform legislation. A "Gang of Eight" formed in the Senate comprised of four Republicans and four Democrats, yielding a compromise bill in the summer of 2013 that garnered sixty-eight votes, which included fourteen Republicans.[4] In the House, a comparable bipartisan group negotiated their own "grand bargain." One year after pledging to place CIR on the front burner of the House agenda, however, Speaker Boehner sounded the death knell for CIR in the 113th Congress by telling reporters that "we have no intention of ever going to conference on the Senate bill."[5] Why did landmark immigration reform legislation almost emerge from a highly polarized Congress, and what explains Speaker Boehner's about-face on CIR?

One could simply chalk up the demise of immigration reform to durable impediments to nonincremental policy change sewn into American government by the Constitutional framers. As Jonathan Oberlander aptly notes in Chapter 9, the U.S. political system is replete with structural veto points that bias the policy-making system against monumental changes such as the Affordable Care Act and CIR. Yet these familiar hurdles do not adequately explain why CIR failed in the 111th and 113th Congresses. Indeed, immigration reform failed in 2009 and 2013 because this issue inspired distinctive inter-and intraparty conflicts and especially challenging policy dynamics that discouraged action under both unified and divided government. That is, immigration reformers of various stripes ultimately faced the nearly impossible task of running two gauntlets: one driven by inter- and intraparty conflicts and another spurred by the bedeviling features of immigration policy making in particular. The purpose of this chapter is to explain how these inter- and intraparty obstacles and challenging policy dynamics derailed CIR in recent Congresses, fuel the current impasse on immigration reform, and shape the future prospects of significant policy innovation.

Most of the political and policy-centered impediments to CIR are nothing new. Major immigration reform presents Congress with institutional and inter- est group hurdles comparable to health care reform, but CIR presents special challenges all its own. Efforts to address porous borders and the presence of millions of unauthorized immigrants in the United States have produced signifi- cant political divides that explode even the most unified party coalitions and that make straightforward problem definition a pipe dream. Campaigns for sweeping reform in this arena typically have followed a tortured path of false starts, prolonged negotiation, and frustrating stalemate. When lightning has struck for passage of major reform, as it did with the Immigration Reform and Control Act of 1986 (IRCA), enactment has hinged on the formation of "strange bedfellow" alliances that are unstable and that demand difficult compromises over rival goals and interests. The result is legislation that is typically unpopular among ordinary citizens, compels key stakeholder groups to swallow bitter pills, draws fire from determined opponents, and places new and often competing policy demands on the national state. These dynamics – intraparty conflicts, elusive problem definition, and the necessity of strange bedfellow alliances and compromises – have presented contemporary propon- ents of CIR with more than their share of daunting barriers. In 2009, the Obama administration was uneasy about expending significant political capital on contentious immigration reform that exposed centrist Democrats in both chambers, presented multiple problems without easy solution, encouraged popular cynicism, and was almost certain to draw fire on all sides.

The growth of mass-based political mobilization on this issue also con- founded the chances for comprehensive reform in the 111th and 113th Con- gresses. One of the most significant developments in American politics in the past two decades has been a marked expansion in the scope of partisan conflict over immigration policy, introducing important grassroots and popular forms of contestation that have altered the policy calculations of lawmakers. According to influential analyses by Gary Freeman and other migration scholars, U.S. immigration reform traditionally has been dominated by "client politics" in which the policy decisions of congressional actors and other offi- cials largely were insulated from popular pressures and fashioned to suit key organized groups. Since the late 1990s, however, U.S. immigration politics has been reshaped by dramatically expanded publicity, popular restiveness, and grassroots mobilization.

The expanded scope of conflict on immigration has cut in two directions. On one side, restrictionist organizations such as the Federation for American Immigration Reform (FAIR) and Numbers USA teamed with Republican polit- icians and conservative media figures to fuel grassroots support for hard-line, enforcement-only policies toward undocumented immigrants. Negative policy feedbacks associated with implementation failures in terms of immigrant enforcement played a key role in this regard. As we shall see, efforts to mobilize the conservative base against legalization proposals and for tougher enforcement proved highly effective. These mass-based and localized campaigns derailed bipartisan reform in 2006 and 2007, advanced restrictive legislation in Arizona, Georgia, Alabama, and other Republican-controlled states, stymied bipartisan reform efforts during Obama's first term, and nurtured a partisan litmus test on immigration reform that few Republican members of Congress or presidential candidates were willing to defy.

On the other side, the ascendance of restrictive immigration positions among grassroots conservatives spurred immigrant and ethnic political agency. That is, immigrants and kindred ethnics, most notably Latino and Asian Americans, responded to these threats by mobilizing in record and growing numbers. Their impact was felt most dramatically at the ballot box where the partisan divide on immigration reform has contributed to a decisive advantage for Democratic candidates among Latino and Asian voters. In the 2012 presidential returns, Obama won 71 percent of the Latino vote with a 44-point advantage that was even more decisive than his 36-point margin (67 percent of the Latino vote) in 2008. When he began his first term, Obama later told Univision reporters, "we could not get ... a single Republican [senator], including the 20 who had previously voted for CIR, to step up and say, we will work with you to make this happen."[6] Fourteen Republicans did cross the aisle to vote with all Democrats to pass an ambitious Senate bill in 2013 and various House Republicans worked quietly on reform in the 113th Congress, yet many House Republicans were far more responsive to conservative grassroots opposition to CIR than to larger demographic pressures that transcended their home districts. Ironically, interparty competition and intraparty heterogeneity on immigration made enactment of the 2013 Senate bill possible, yet inter- and intraparty conflicts also gave Speaker Boehner ample reason to rule out negotiations with the Senate several months later. The complexities of CIR and widespread cynicism over past implementation failures only reinforced House Republican intransigence.

In the pages that follow, our chief aim will be to investigate the inter- and intraparty conflicts and the challenging policy dynamics that shape the politics of immigration reform in Congress and make an overhaul so arduous to achieve. The first half of this chapter examines why the competing ideas and interests associated with immigration reform defy the familiar partisan and ideological divides of American politics, fueling intraparty heterogeneity on the issue. It then considers how these distinctive political fissures make the formation of "strange bedfellow" alliances and difficult compromises necessary for congressional action on major immigration reform. The second half of the chapter concentrates on the emergence of increased popular mobilization in immigration policy battles and the complementary rise of partisan polarization on the issue in Congress and national politics. The flourishing of an immigration restriction movement on the Right and the countermobilization of an immigrant rights movement on the Left over the past decade has yielded electoral incentives for lawmakers that have intensified inter-and intraparty conflicts on the issue. These formidable barriers to immigration reform have spurred dramatic unilateral action by the Obama administration, eliciting a significant constitutional showdown between the branches over executive power.

THE IMMIGRATION POLICY GAUNTLET: DISORIENTING CONFLICTS AND STRANGE BEDFELLOW COALITIONS

Immigration is a potent cross-cutting issue in American national politics, one that defies the standard liberal–conservative divide and often polarizes major party coalitions. Whereas ideational frameworks may help clarify the policy choices and rationales of partisan and ideological camps in other venues (such as the efficiency of markets, deregulation, family values, national sovereignty, and cultural protectionism on the right or cultural pluralism, equal rights, economic security, and work standards on the left), they often clash and frustrate action in immigration policy making. This is hardly new: Americans have been arguing and taking stands on immigration since the earliest days of republic. It was an issue that exercised Franklin, Jefferson, Hamilton, Madison, and Wilson, not to mention the Anti-Federalists. Over time, we can identify four rather durable ideological traditions that have found expression in national debates and political struggles over immigration. Consider two dimensions. The first focuses on immigration numbers, and divides those who support expansive immigration opportunities and robust numbers from those who favor substantial restrictions on alien admissions. The second concentrates on the rights of noncitizens residing in the United States, and distinguishes those who endorse the provision of a broad set of civil, political, and social rights (as defined by T. H. Marshall) to newcomers from those who advocate strict limitations on the rights accorded to noncitizens.[7] These two dimensions of immigration policy reveal tensions between cosmopolitans versus economic protectionists on the left, and between probusiness expansionists versus cultural protectionists and border hawks on the right.

Immigration and American Politics: Four Ideological Traditions

Liberal cosmopolitans embrace the universality of the American experiment, professing deep faith in the social, economic, cultural, and political benefits of diverse mass immigration. Whether Jane Addams in the Progressive Era or Senator Edward Kennedy today, they have supported expansive admissions policies for family reunification, refugee relief, and other legal preference categories, as well as a broad set of legal protections and entitlements for noncitizens. A rich variety of organizations have favored expansionist policy goals over time, including the German American Alliance, the American Jewish Committee, the Japanese American Citizenship League, the National Council of La Raza, the National Immigration Forum, and numerous other ethnic, religious, and humanitarian groups. Organized labor has emerged as critical to this camp in recent years, with the AFL-CIO and Change to Win federations championing immigrants who represent a pivotal target of current unionizing efforts.

By contrast, economic protectionists oppose porous borders and soaring immigration on the grounds that they imperil the material security of the nation's working class and its least advantaged citizens. More than a century ago, Frederick Douglass favored limits on immigration, lamenting that "every hour sees the black man elbowed out of employment by some newly arrived immigrant."[8] He also defended broad rights for Chinese and other workers already in the United States. A later generation of labor leaders such as Samuel Gompers of the American Federation of Labor favored sweeping immigration restrictions because they believed immigrants undercut the wages, working conditions, and job security of American workers.[9] The labor movement traditionally has been the most visible left-wing constituency advancing restrictive policies. Although leading national labor unions and federations today have shifted to the pro-immigration column, building and trades unions as well as many rank-and-file workers have remained protectionist in orientation.[10] Likewise, former Congresswoman Barbara Jordan, who chaired the Commission on Immigration Reform during the Clinton years, made it clear that she supported reduced immigration to provide economic opportunity for disadvantaged citizens but also equal benefits for those already here.[11] Today prominent organizations such as the National Urban League have produced fissures within the civil rights coalition by demanding that citizens "be given the first right" to jobs routinely given to temporary and immigrant workers.[12] A final sign that the Democratic base and its congressional caucus are far from unified on immigration reform can be found in the tendency of many moderate Democrats in Congress from swing states and districts to distance themselves from expansive proposals.

Free market and probusiness conservatives tend to support large-scale immigration to meet the labor needs of business interests and to promote national prosperity. During the Gilded Age, capitalists such as Andrew Carnegie described the flow of tractable immigrant workers into the country as a "golden stream."[13] Contemporary business leaders and conservative politicians from Ronald Reagan to John McCain draw the same conclusion, arguing that the nation's economy benefits from foreign workers willing to do jobs and accept wages that U.S. citizens would not. These pro-immigration conservatives are particularly supportive of newcomers who are economically self-sufficient and do not require government assistance, an orientation captured well by the rallying cry of lawmakers such as Spencer Abraham and Dick Armey in the

1990s: "Immigration yes, welfare no!" Powerful business interests such as the American Farm Bureau Federation, the U.S. Chambers of Commerce, Microsoft, service industries, and numerous other immigrant employers have defended imported labor as essential to U.S. competitiveness in a global economy. The value of immigrant labor to the national economy is a familiar refrain of the editorial pages of the *Wall Street Journal* and conservative think tanks such as the Cato and Manhattan Institutes.

Finally, cultural protectionists and border hawks advocate stringent border control, tough limits on alien rights, and reductions in immigrant admissions. Historically, immigration activists of this ideological tradition have worried about significant shifts in the ethnic, racial, or religious composition of immigration. As Harvard President A. Lawrence Lowell, a supporter of the Immigration Restriction League (IRL), argued during the Progressive Era, "the need for homogeneity in a democracy" justifies policies "resisting the influx of great numbers of a greatly different race."[14] Today many, although not all, border hawks are haunted by cultural anxieties over what Patrick Buchanan dubs as a "Third World invasion" of unprecedented Latino and Asian immigration: "The children born in 2006 will witness in their lifetimes the death of the West."[15] One consistent position of restriction-minded conservatives after the terrorist attacks of September 11, 2001, is that porous borders and mass immigration pose significant security risks. "The consequences of uncontrolled immigration are far more serious than our leaders want us to believe," declared Representative Tom Tancredo (R-CO), leader of the restrictionist Congressional Immigration Reform Caucus. "The safety of Americans and the security of our way of life are on the line." The restrictionist agenda has been advanced at the grassroots by causes such as California's Save our State campaign and the Minutemen movement, while organizations such as FAIR have demanded restrictive legislation for decades.

Problem Definition and Strange Bedfellow Coalitions

These distinctive ideological traditions remind us that American political debate over immigrant admissions and rights reflects a depth and texture that eludes those who try to define a clear "conservative" or "liberal" position on immigration reform. Equally significant, none of these immigration activists has secured nonincremental policy change independently. Over time, major policy innovation almost invariably has required the building of incongruous left–right alliances. These strange bedfellow coalitions sometimes produce large bipartisan majorities in favor of legislation, especially when dealing with legal immigration, in which opportunities for credit-claiming can abound. Such was the case when the Immigration Act of 1990 cheerfully unified pro-immigration Democrats and Republicans behind a 40-percent increase in annual visa allocations, benefiting both family-based and employment-based admissions.[16] Yet nonincremental initiatives addressing illegal immigration yield very different politics in which painful choices, shrill conflicts, and blame-avoidance strategies abound.[17]

The rival commitments of ideology and interest unleashed by illegal immigration make basic problem definition a tall order for policy makers. Indeed, recent immigration reform efforts captured profoundly different assumptions and conceptions of what the problem is, or, for some, whether a problem even exists. Moreover, powerful organized interests and competing constituencies regularly mobilize and clash over immigration reform. The resulting battles not only pit interest groups and constituencies allied with the Republican party against those allied with the Democratic party, but they also divide organized interests within these partisan coalitions and sometimes even among those associated with the same interest or constituency, resulting in internal fights on this issue within the labor movement or among environmental and population control groups.

For cosmopolitans, or pro-immigration liberals, the problem is not *the presence* of millions of undocumented aliens in the United States but rather *their status* as vulnerable, second-class persons. The chief imperative for these activists is to make the estimated 10 to 15 million unauthorized migrants living in the country eligible for legal membership. "What we want ... is a pathway to their legalization," Representative Luis Guiterrez (D-IL) explains, "so that they can come out of the shadows of darkness, of discrimination, of bigotry, of exploitation, and join us fully."[18] Since powerful democracies such as the United States profit from the economic exploitation of unauthorized immigrants, progressives such as Marc Rosenblum of the Migration Policy Institute argue that "all American employers, consumers, and lawmakers – all of us – share the 'blame' for undocumented migration."[19] Legalization or "earned citizenship" initiatives draw strong support today from Latino organizations, the leading federations of organized labor, and various civil rights and ethnic groups.

Economic protectionists have been particularly hostile toward illegal immigration, which they view as enhancing the wealth of corporate and professional America with little concern of the consequences for blue-collar workers or the unemployed. As Cesar Chavez complained bitterly in the late 1960s that undocumented Mexicans were being recruited to undermine his efforts to organize legal farm workers, so Carol Swain recently pointed to the deleterious "impact that high levels of illegal immigration [are] having in the communities when it comes to jobs, when it comes to education, when it comes to health care."[20] CNN's Lou Dobbs regularly sounds similar themes, claiming that illegal immigration has "a calamitous effect on working citizens and their families" and "that the industries in which illegal aliens are employed in the greatest percentages also are suffering the largest wage declines."[21] Economic protectionists endorse employer sanctions against unscrupulous employers who knowingly hire undocumented aliens, and they vehemently oppose guest worker programs that they associate with a captive workforce subject to exploitation, abuse, and permanent marginalization. These views resonate among many rank-and-file members of labor unions and the constituencies of moderate Democrats in Congress.

For pro-immigration conservatives devoted to free markets and business growth, the chief problem is that existing federal policies fail to address "the reality," as President Bush puts it, "that there are many people on the other side of our border who will do anything to come to America to work." In short, the U.S. economy has grown dependent on this supply of cheap, unskilled labor.[22] The solution for this camp lies in regularizing employers' access to this vital foreign labor; if the back door is to be closed, then this labor supply must be secured through temporary worker programs and an expansion of employment-based legal immigration. Powerful business groups in this camp also oppose employer sanctions as an unwelcome and unfair regulatory burden placed on American businesses large and small.

Border hawks today see the illegal immigration problem as nothing short of an unprecedented breakdown of American sovereignty, one that compromises national security, the rule of law, job opportunities for citizens, public education, and social services.[23] Mobilized by conservative talk radio, columnists, and television commentators, many Main Street Republicans are outraged that the nation's fundamental interest in border control and law enforcement has been trumped by the power of immigrant labor, rights, and votes. Amnesty or legalization proposals inspire hostile resistance from this camp as unethical rewards to those who break the rules and as stimulants to new waves of undocumented immigrants anticipating similar treatment. Likewise, temporary worker programs are scorned by these activists because many guest workers historically have remained illegally and because they contest the notion that only foreign workers will do certain menial jobs. Border hawks believe enforcement must come first. They favor a strengthened border patrol and tougher security measures along the nation's borders, as well as crackdowns on unauthorized immigrants and their employers within U.S. territory. They endorse a strategy of attrition in which targeted deportation efforts, workplace enforcement, and denial of social services and other public benefits would persuade many unauthorized migrants to return home.

Grand or Faustian Bargains?

The long-standing linkage between the achievement of immigration reform and so-called "grand bargains" among unlikely political allies should hardly surprise us. The distinctive ideological traditions inspired by American political struggles over immigrant admissions and rights reminds us that none of the four major camps identified above has been able to secure significant policy innovation independently. Over time, major immigration reform almost invariably has required the building of incongruous left–right coalitions. Strange bedfellows abound in U.S. immigration politics, and these uneasy alliances make nonincremental policy change possible. Faustian bargains have been recurring features of national immigration policy making. Let us consider two illustrative examples from the 20th century.

Mexican Braceros and Undocumented Aliens
During the first New Deal, AFL leaders campaigned for legislation that would place national origins quotas on Mexico and other Western Hemisphere countries. In 1924, the AFL's Washington office vigorously pursued legislation that would establish a 1,500 annual quota for Mexican immigrants. But the AFL failed to build a broad coalition of support, and it faced insurmountable opposition from the House and Senate Immigration Committees that were dominated by Southern and Western legislators who favored European and Asian restrictions but welcomed Mexican labor migration.[24] By 1938, the Immigration and Naturalization Service (INS) reported that illegal immigration from Mexico was soaring due to the construction of new highways and "automobile travel."[25] At the start of World War II, southwestern growers and other business interests, joined by their legislative champions, complained to executive branch officials that war-induced labor shortages necessitated a new Mexican temporary worker program. In response, an interagency committee was formed to facilitate the importation of Mexican guestworkers. In 1942, the State Department negotiated a special agreement with Mexico establishing the Bracero Program that Congress swiftly approved. Under the bilateral agreement, the United States pledged that wages, living conditions, workplace safety, and medical services would be comparable to those of native workers. In turn, the Mexican government was to supervise the recruitment and contracting of braceros.[26] One the Bracero Program began, neither employers nor federal administrators saw that the negotiated protections of Mexican laborers were honored. Mexican braceros routinely received much lower wages than native workers and endured substandard living and working conditions. Contrary to the bilateral agreement, the INS permitted growers and other employers to directly recruit braceros at the border. If they resisted direct employer recruitment, one INS official recalled, "a good many members of Congress would be on the Service's neck."[27] Tellingly, the Bracero Program endured for almost two decades after the war ended. Guarded by a "cozy triangle" of agribusinesses, Southern and Western congressional "committee barons," and a lax immigration bureaucracy, roughly 4.2 million Mexican workers were imported under the Bracero Program. Unauthorized flows across the southern border also continued apace.

During the early 1950s, influential restrictionist legislators such as Senators Pat McCarren (R-NV) and James Eastland (D-MS) and Representative Francis Walter (D-PA) fervently guarded stringent limits on Asian, African, and southern and eastern European immigration. The McCarren-Walter bill promised to maintain the national origins quota system. As in the past, the AFL pledged support for the national origins quotas, but it joined other labor organizations in expressing alarm that Mexican braceros and unauthorized migrants had "depressed wages and destroyed working conditions." In 1951, the AFL proclaimed that the presence of hundreds of thousands of braceros coupled with an estimated 1.5 million undocumented aliens compromised the "security" of American workers. Their appeal had no impact on the policy process. McCarren and Eastland shepherded passage of Public Law 78 reauthorizing the Bracero Program in 1951, claiming that termination would be "unfair to the farmer and the Mexican involved."[28]

During floor action on the McCarren-Walter bill one year later, liberal Senator Paul Douglas (D-IL) proposed legal sanctions against those who illegally smuggled aliens into the country and employers who intentionally hired illegal aliens. But McCarran and Eastland successfully defeated the amendment; the final legislation contained language that made it unlawful to transport or harbor illegal aliens, but stipulated that "harboring" did not include employment of unauthorized migrants.[29] This "Texas proviso," as it later became known, highlighted the lengths to which many key congressional defenders of national origins quotas were willing to go to preserve Mexican labor flows, both legal and illegal.

After the 1960 election, the American Federation of Labor-Congress of Industrial Organizations (AFL-CIO) lobbied hard for the Bracero Program's termination. The Kennedy administration and Democratic leadership in Congress lent their support to the effort. Yet growers and other business interests exerted considerable pressure of their own on members of Congress. The American Farm Bureau Federation, the National Cotton Council, the United Fresh Fruit and Vegetable Association, the National Beet Growers, ranchers, and other business interests rallied to save the Bracero Program. In 1961, these pressure groups won a two-year extension of the program but failed to win reauthorization in 1963 despite vigorous lobbying. Sweeping immigration reform in 1965 dismantled national origins quota in favor of a new preference system that emphasized family-based immigration, but it also placed a 120,000 annual ceiling on western hemisphere visas.[30] Reformers did not anticipate that this new ceiling and the end of the Bracero Program would swell unauthorized Mexican inflows.

From Prolonged Gridlock to the Immigration Reform and Control Act of 1986

Unauthorized immigration emerged as the chief migratory issue for congressional reformers during the 1970s. In 1971, Representative Peter Rodino (D-NJ), chair of the House Judiciary Committee's Subcommittee on Immigration, led pro-labor liberals in the pursuit of employer sanctions legislation to resolve the perceived illegal immigration crisis.[31] Rodino's employer sanctions legislation initially passed the House in 1972 but languished in the Senate where Eastland refused to allow the Judiciary Committee he chaired to take action.[32] When Rodino reintroduced his bill a year later, new resistance emerged in the House from fellow Democrats who warned that the measure would lead to job discrimination against Latinos, Asians, and anyone who looked or sounded foreign.[33] By 1977, the Carter administration ignored the warnings of Congressional Democratic leaders when it proposed a comprehensive plan for addressing illegal immigration. The reform package included stiff civil and criminal penalties for anyone who engaged in a "pattern or practice" of hiring undocumented aliens; use of the Social Security card as an identification document for verifying employee eligibility; enhanced Border Patrol forces at the Mexican border; and an amnesty program that would confer legal resident alien status on all aliens living in the country before 1970.[34] The White House proposal galvanized opposition from all sides in Congress: lawmakers with ties to growers and other business interests argued that sanctions were unfair to employers, those aligned with the National Council of La Raza and the Mexican-American Legal Defense and Education Fund (MALDEF) saw the measure as detrimental to civil rights, and law and order conservatives complained that the plan rewarded law-breakers with amnesty.[35] With immigration reform mired in conflict, Congress formed a bipartisan Select Commission on Immigration and Refugee Policy (SCIRP) to study the "illegal immigration problem" and all other facets of U.S. immigration and refugee policy and issuing recommendations for future reform.

The SCIRP completed a sweeping final report in 1981 that portrayed "lawful immigration" as "a positive force in American life," serving the national interest in terms of economic growth and productivity, reuniting families, and advancing key foreign policy imperatives.[36] But it also concluded that illegal immigration was an urgent problem that needed to be controlled before legal immigration could be expanded. The SCIRP noted that unauthorized entries created a vulnerable shadow population that had few incentives to report crimes, health problems, or exploitation by employers.[37] It also asserted that unrestrained illegal immigration encouraged a perilous disregard for the rule of law: "illegality erodes confidence in the law generally, and immigration law specifically."[38] To address the problem, the SCIRP endorsed the familiar scheme of enhanced Border Patrol resources and employer sanctions. But it also underscored the notion that the efficacy of sanctions hinged on faithful enforcement and the development of a tamper-resistant national identification card as the linchpin of a security and universal system of employee eligibility. All sixteen commissioners also agreed on a generous legalization program for undocumented aliens already residing in the country.[39]

Two young lawmakers – Senator Alan Simpson (R-WY), who served on the SCIRP, and Representative Romano Mazzoli, a moderate Kentucky Democrat with ties to the SCIRP chair Father Theodore Hesburgh – took the lead in pressing for immigration reform. Early in 1982, the pair introduced omnibus legislation on illegal and legal immigration. The measure met fierce resistance from a broad coalition of business interests (the U.S. Chamber of Commerce, National Association of Manufacturers, agribusinesses, the Business

Roundtable), ethnic and civil rights groups such as NCLR and MALDEF, the ACLU, religious lobbies, and a new immigrant rights organization, the National Immigration Forum. Left–right opposition to the Simpson-Mazzoli initiative was reflected in the resistance of both the Reagan administration, which saw employer sanctions and national identification cards working at cross-purposes with its regulatory relief agenda, and House Democrats led by the Hispanic and Black Caucuses, which raised familiar concerns about discriminatory impacts of sanctions and other provisions. Gridlock was overcome only after three more years of wrangling, and the resulting Immigration Reform and Control Act of 1986 (IRCA) depended on a compromise package including watered-down employer sanctions provisions, legalization for undocumented aliens living in the country since 1982, and a new seasonal agricultural worker program to appease grower interests.

The measure proved highly successful in granting legal status to nearly three million undocumented aliens, but employer sanctions proved to be a "toothless tiger." This was largely by design: in the absence of a reliable identification system for verifying employee eligibility that the SCIRP described as a linchpin for effective enforcement, the employer sanctions provisions lacked teeth. By the late 1980s, it was clear to national policy makers that the IRCA had done virtually nothing to discourage illegal immigration. But legislators were eager to shift their attention to the politically painless task of expanding legal immigration. The Immigration Act of 1990 unified cosmopolitans and free market expansionists behind a 40 percent increase in annual visa allocations that benefited both family-based and employment-based immigration.[40] The "grand bargains" of the 1980s, like their forebears, left key dilemmas posed by unauthorized immigration for future Congresses to resolve.

The absence of a reliable identification system for verifying employee eligibility made it relatively easy for undocumented aliens to evade detection at the workplace. Soon after passage of the IRCA, an underground industry of fraudulent documents flourished in both Mexico and the United States, enabling unauthorized migrants to obtain work with ease. But if the legislative design of employer sanctions discouraged their efficacy, the Reagan administration was less than zealous in their enforcement. The INS tended to enforce employer sanctions with considerable forbearance toward offenders. Alan Nelson, the INS Commissioner under Reagan, was urged to pursue a policy of "least employer resistance" by stressing business education over penalties.[41] The IRCA authorized a 70 percent increase in the INS budget, with an annual $100 million targeted for employer sanctions enforcement. Tellingly, $34 million was spent on enforcing sanctions fiscal year 1987, $59 million in 1988, and below $30 million annually in ensuing years.[42]

From his perch on the Senate immigration subcommittee, Senator Simpson pressed the Reagan and Bush administrations to take a harder line on employer sanctions. Yet despite his clout as Republican minority whip, Simpson made little headway during either Republican presidency. "Even when we direct the

Administration to do such things as 'study' the employer sanctions verification system and develop a more secure system, if necessary, we get no action," he lamented.[43] Few of Simpson's congressional colleagues shared his alarm over the inefficacy or uneven enforcement of employer sanctions. In fact, the most vigorous oversight of sanctions focused on whether they should be repealed because they unfavorably burdened small businesses (led by Orrin Hatch) or because they engendered increased job discrimination against legal aliens or citizens who look or sound foreign (led by Edward Kennedy). Few conservative politicians of the 1980s, most of whom embraced "regulatory relief" and free markets, or their liberal counterparts, dedicated to universal rights and inclusion, worried about the efficacy of employer sanctions.

IRCA's implementation failures helped fuel the dramatic expansion of illegal immigration in recent decades, yielding an undocumented population in the United States that estimates suggest is three to four times larger than it was in the early 1980s. They also have raised profound doubts among activists, policy makers, and citizens that the federal government either can or would adequately control its borders. The resulting cynicism poses a substantial hurdle to reform.

THE RISE OF A PARTISAN GAUNTLET: HUDDLED ELITES AND POPULAR MOBILIZATION

A little more than a decade ago, Gary Freeman used frameworks developed by James Q. Wilson and Theodore Lowi to argue that immigration policy making produced "concentrated distributive policies and client politics." By this, he meant that political elites advanced immigration policies that rewarded organized groups with concentrated benefits over unorganized bearers of diffused costs. In this fashion, the IRCA was the product of huddled Washington elites who distributed benefits to organized agribusinesses and immigrant advocates, limited sanctions on organized business groups, and did little to please unorganized mass publics. However, antiimmigrant populism, immigrant enfranchisement, and competitive democratic elections have altered this equation. That is, one of the most crucial dynamics of congressional immigration policy making in recent years has been a transition from relatively insulated client politics to more popular engagement via stronger grassroots pressure and greater "electoral connections" for lawmakers. The scope of conflict in American politics over immigration reform is greater now than it has been for generations. [44]

During the 2000 election, Republican national and state organizations drew up plans to attract new Asian and Latino voters. They were emboldened by party strategists who warned that "if we're only getting 25 percent of the Hispanic vote, you wait three, four presidential elections, and we'll be out of business." Then-Texas Governor George W. Bush was hailed by many party leaders as the ideal candidate to court new immigrant voters in 2000, and he reminded Latinos throughout the campaign that early on he had "rejected the spirit of Prop 187," opposed "English-only" proposals, and refused "to bash immigrants" when it was popular. Vice President Al Gore in turn reminded Latino and Asian constituencies that Republicans led the way in stripping welfare benefits and other rights for noncitizens, and assured them that Democrats would continue to defend expansive legal immigration. Yet Bush dramatically outspent Democrats in his appeal to Latino voters in 2000, devoting millions of campaign dollars to Spanish-language advertising and direct-mail appeals. He also gave television interviews in Spanish, and had his bilingual nephew George P. Bush stump for him extensively among Latino constituencies.[45] Bush's "compassionate conservatism" on immigration policy and his direct campaigning had clear electoral ramifications. An estimated 7.8 million Latino voters, or 6 percent of all voters (up from 4 percent in 1996), cast ballots in the 2000 election. Gore maintained the Democrats' traditional edge in Latino voting, but Bush gained an estimated 34 percent among Latinos – 13 points higher than Dole's 1996 total and only 3 points off the previous GOP record of 37 percent attained by Ronald Reagan in the 1984 election.[46] The Bush team clearly was focused on adding more Latinos, the fastest-growing sector of the electorate and a crucial swing constituency in battleground states, to the GOP base.

Bush and Mexican President Vincente Fox took office within a few months of each other, and they soon began bilateral talks about a new temporary worker program and ways to legalize several million undocumented Mexicans living in the United States. Fox and Bush portrayed themselves as "commonsense ranchers" who wanted to make the flow of persons across their shared border "safe, orderly, and legal." During a September 6, 2001, visit to Washington, Fox called for a joint agreement on a guest worker program and legalization "by the end of the year" and Bush replied that he intended to "accommodate my friend" and hailed Mexico as the United States' most important ally.[47] But discussions ended abruptly after the terrorist attacks five days later.

In the wake of the 9/11 attacks and its transformation of the immigration policy environment, the Bush administration felt it had little choice but to set aside comprehensive reform. Border hawks such as Representative Tancredo made headlines in December 2001 by underscoring how porous borders presented an appalling national security problem. Organized interests favoring immigration restriction and strict border control ran ads around the country blaming lax immigration policies for the September 11 terrorist attacks. Plans for a guest worker program and legalization fell off the agenda. Relations with Mexico's Fox also cooled as Bush postponed any relaxation of immigration laws and Fox vigorously opposed the United States-led invasion of Iraq.

During the fall of 2003, the AFL-CIO supported hotel workers when they took the lead in organizing the Immigrant Workers Freedom Ride, a national mobilization intended to evoke the civil rights movement's 1961 freedom rides.

Organized labor became a strong champion of legalizing undocumented workers in the late 1990s when it became clear that foreign-born union membership was growing sharply while native-born membership was dropping.[48] During the Democratic presidential primaries several months later, leading candidates endorsed "earned legalization" programs that would provide green cards for undocumented immigrants. As Democrats described immigration reform as "another broken promise" by Bush in debates, word leaked to reporters that "the White House feels it's got to get its irons in the fire now" or risk losing ground with Latino voters in November.[49] Wasting little time as he kicked off his reelection year, Bush unveiled a major immigration reform plan in the first week of January 2004 that made a new guest worker program its centerpiece. "The President has long talked about the importance of having an immigration policy that matches willing workers with willing employers," White House Press Secretary Scott McClellan explained. "It's important for America to be a welcoming society."[50]

Tellingly, the harshest criticism of Bush's reform blueprints came from conservative members of his own party in Congress. Representative Tom Tancredo (R-CO) made cracking down on unauthorized immigration his signature issue, and he chided Bush for rewarding people who break the law. Ed Gallegly (R-CA) mocked the White House for becoming "the Mexican Department of Social Services."[51] At a Republican retreat in Philadelphia later in the month, senior Bush adviser Karl Rove got an earful from outraged members of Congress who claimed that their constituents were overwhelmingly opposed to the Bush proposal and that "Hispandering" for votes would create a voter backlash within the party's base.[52] Yet the president's closest advisers were convinced that his immigration proposal would help with Latino voters without sacrificing support from his conservative base. "It's more conservative pundits than conservatives," one adviser observed of conservative radio, television, and print commentators versus rank-and-file voters. Grover Norquist, president of the conservative Americans for Tax Reform and a key probusiness advocate of the president's guest worker program, agreed that immigration reform was a safe strategy to win Latino votes without threatening the Republican base. "It's not a vote-moving issue for any bloc of the center-right coalition," he asserted. "People vote on guns. They vote on taxes. They vote on being pro-life."[53] By March of 2004, a truce was called on immigration battles within the Republican party and Bush quietly put his immigration proposal aside for the rest of the campaign.[54]

The Demise of Kennedy-McCain: Fusing Immigration Restriction and the Conservative Right

The 2004 election returns validated Rove's calculation that courting Latino voters with pro-immigrant rhetoric and a relatively expansive reform proposal could be done without losing ground among voters in the Republican base.

Bush's reelection bid produced unprecedented mobilization and support from his partisan base, and it *also* yielded a GOP record 40 percent of the Latino vote.[55] Soon after the election, Bush met privately with pro-immigration House and Senate Republicans on a new guest worker program that would grant legal status to millions of undocumented immigrants. Immigration reform became the key post-election talking point of Secretary of State Colin Powell, DHS Secretary Tom Ridge, and chief strategist Karl Rove, the latter telling reporters that it was striking that Bush did not lose votes among his conservative base in the election.[56] Press Secretary McClellan added that immigration reform was "a high priority" that the president "intends to work with members on to get moving again in the second term." Border hawks were aghast. One lobbyist for the immigration restriction movement doubted that Republican lawmakers would follow the administration "over a cliff" on the issue.[57] He was right. In late November, House Republicans blocked an intelligence overhaul bill to signal Bush that his immigration initiative would split the party and stall action in his second term.[58] Tancredo scorched the White House as abandoning conservative law and order values, proclaiming that "their amnesty plan was dead on arrival ... in January, and if they send the same pig with lipstick back to Congress next January, it will suffer the same fate." [59] His views were echoed by many Republicans leaving a House Republican Conference the same month. One Republican leader anonymously observed that it was "highly unusual for the administration to use their political capital that was given by the base against the base."[60]

Polls indeed found that most conservative Republicans disapproved of plans for granting legal status to undocumented immigrants. In truth, however, the business base of the Republican party was a strong and unwavering supporter of the president's guest worker plans throughout his two terms in office. The most active business lobbyists favoring the Bush initiatives formed the Essential Worker Immigration Coalition (EWIC), an alliance of immigrant-dependent industry associations headed by the U.S. Chamber of Commerce. The coalition would bring together powerful associations such as the American Health Care Association, the American Hotel and Lodging Association, National Council of Chain Restaurants, the National Retail Federation, and the Associated Builders and Contractors. EWIC was initially formed by meatpacking conglomerates to advocate for expansion of guest worker programs, and counts many of the nation's largest employers as members including Wal-Mart, Tyson Foods, and Marriott.[61]

Nevertheless, porous borders and unauthorized immigration were hot-button issues for many grassroots Republicans, and their disquietude was fueled by local and national talk radio, television commentators such as Lou Dobbs and Pat Buchanan, and restrictive politicians such as Tancredo and his House Immigration Reform Caucus. New citizen patrols also propped up along the United States–Mexico border. In 2004, an accountant and decorated former Marine, James Gilchrist, founded the all-volunteer Minuteman Project to patrol the Arizona border armed with binoculars and cell phones. Former California schoolteacher Chris Simcox established the separate Minutemen Civil Defense Corps as an extension of this citizen patrol movement.[62] Described as "vigilantes" by Bush, surveys showed that Republican voters strongly approved of the Minuteman movement.[63]

In the winter of 2005, HB 4437, a punitive bill focused on border enforcement, narrowly passed the Republican-controlled House. It proposed for the first time to make unauthorized presence in the United States a felony, and made it a crime to lend support to undocumented immigrants. From March through May 2006, demonstrations against the bill by primarily Latino immigrants and their supporters, unprecedented in number and size, took place in a wide array of cities and towns across the United States.[64] These nationwide rallies, protests, and boycotts drew negative reactions from most Americans: just 24 percent offered a favorable view of the immigrant rights protests and protestors while 52 percent expressed disapproval.[65] Overall, however, public opinion remained open to varied policy solutions: majorities favored legal status and earned citizenship for undocumented immigrants, stricter employer penalties, and tougher enforcement.[66] Strikingly, 60 percent of Republicans backed Bush's plan, a number that would dwindle steadily in coming months.[67] By the fall of 2006, Bush sought to appease enforcement-minded conservatives by endorsing the Secure Fence Act of 2006 that authorized the construction of a 700-mile fence along the 2,100-mile U.S. border with Mexico. Signed just twelve days before the midterm elections, Bush used the occasion to urge moderation to assembled House and Senate Republicans. "There is a rational middle ground between granting an automatic path to citizenship for every illegal immigrant and a program of mass deportation," he observed, "and I look forward to working with Congress to find that middle ground."[68]

The midterm elections gave Democrats control of the House and Senate, but their ranks now included new moderate Democrats from culturally conservative swing districts that favored enforcement first. In the summer of 2007, a bipartisan Senate coalition led by Edward Kenney (D-MA) and John McCain (R-AZ), old hands at immigration reform, negotiated with the White House on a new compromise bill. The result was the Border Security and Immigration Act of 2007, a "grand bargain" that had the support of President Bush and became the focus of all meaningful subsequent discussion.[69] The bargain included a new Z visa for undocumented immigrants that covered "a principal or employed alien, the spouse or elderly parent of that alien and the minor children of that alien" currently living in the United States provided they pay fees and penalties that could total as much as $8,000 and a "touchback provision" requiring the leader of the household to return home before applying for legal permanent residency status. It also contained a temporary Y worker program of about 200,000 that would allow workers to be admitted for a two-year period that could be renewed twice as long as the worker spent a period of one year outside of the United States between each admission (which eventually had a five-year sunset provision). Incorporating the White House proposal, the bill contained triggers to be met before the Z or Y visas could begin. These triggers included: 18,000 Border Patrol hired, construction of 200 miles of vehicle barriers and 370 miles of fencing, resources to detain up to 27,500 persons per day on an annual basis, and the use of secure and effective identification tools to prevent unauthorized work.

Subject to intense media scrutiny and commentary, the public response to the compromise Senate immigration plan ranged from hostile to tepid. Many members of Congress were deluged with angry phone calls, emails, and letters from constituents and other activists. Surveys indicated that a majority of Republicans, Democrats, and Independents opposed the measure, with only 23 percent in favor. Significantly, most Americans opposed the initiative not because they opposed "amnesty" or other proposals for legalizing millions of undocumented immigrants in the country (roughly two-thirds supported earned citizenship options over deportation), but rather because they had little trust that it would provide genuine border security. More than 80 percent in surveys said they did not believe that the Kennedy-McCain bill would reduce illegal immigration or enhance border control.[70]

This profound cynicism born of past implementation failures was a powerful theme for many lawmakers of both parties who lined up against the "grand bargain." Senator Byron Dorgan (D-ND) recalled believing the promises of the Simpson-Mazzoli Act when he was in Congress in 1986, and later discovered that "none of them were true, and three million people got amnesty. There was no border security to speak of, no employer sanctions to speak of, and there was no enforcement." Robert Byrd (D-WV) vowed "not to make the same mistake twice," while Charles Grassley said, "I was fooled once, and history has taught me a valuable lesson."[71] Dorgan and Grassley would be among dozens of Senators proposing amendments designed to derail the bill.

The Kennedy-McCain compromise had the makings of vintage client politics. As Freeman's theory predicts, organized interests likely to receive concentrated benefits from the reform formed a familiar strange bedfellow alliance. The bill was the result of careful negotiations that ultimately won the support of EWIC and other business lobbies, the NCLR and various ethnic and civil rights groups, the ACLU, and labor unions such as the SEIU, HERE, and the United Farm Workers. Yet the scope of conflict had exploded, and a repeat of the behind-the-scenes congressional deals that produced IRCA in 1986 was not in the offing two decades later. In late June, angry constituents, organized interests from the AFL-CIO to restrictionist lobbies, and both conservative and liberal lawmakers successfully blocked cloture on the Senate bill and thereby dashed hopes of avoiding killer amendments.[72] Fox News polling reaffirmed that conservatives bitterly opposed to the bill and felt disenchanted with Bush, while Democratic poll conducted by Stan Greenburg showed Democratic identifiers to be split 47 percent for and 47 percent against the bill.[73]

With the measure close to death, the White House and a small bipartisan group of Senators worked quietly on a last-ditch effort to save the compromise plan. Their private negotiations drew fire from all sides in the summer of 2007. "The process has been orchestrated by a handful of people behind closed doors," Senator Bob Corker (R-TN) observed, "and they are paying a price for that."[74] In truth, closed-door negotiations represented the primary means by which an unpalatable compromise could be brokered among disparate interests. Yet the forces arrayed against this last-ditch effort were overwhelming, from the grassroots to the halls of Congress. Ultimately, the "grand bargain" developed by Bush, Kennedy, and McCain fell fourteen votes short of the sixty needed to force a final vote. Fifteen Democrats were among those who helped kill the bill, including freshman senators from swing states such as Claire McCaskill (MO), Jon Tester (MT), and Jim Webb (VA).[75]

Bush had pursued CIR out of a strong personal conviction that the best solution to the bedeviling problems associated with unauthorized flows was an expansive guest worker program that matched willing employers and willing laborers. He also believed that stricter enforcement of employer sanctions, improved efforts at the border, and earned citizenship for undocumented immigrants were necessary features of an effective compromise package. Finally, he and his advisers also were convinced that public opinion could be swayed on the issue, that his conservative base would hold and not rebel, and that his compassionate pragmatism on immigration reform would draw large numbers of Latino voters into the Republican fold. Tellingly, whatever inroads were made in 2000 and 2004 with Latinos, Asians, and other new immigrant voters, these gains were forgotten by 2008.

Thunder on the Left: Conservative Threats and Immigrant Political Agency

During the bruising battles that derailed CIR in 2007, FAIR and other restrictionist groups formed alliances with conservative talk show hosts who filled the airways with withering attacks on any policy overhaul that included a "path to citizenship" for unauthorized immigrants. Groups such as Numbers USA rallied grassroots conservatives to demand that their Congressional representatives defeat the Bush plan. They "lit up the switchboard for weeks," Senator Mitch McConnell (R-KY) recounted. If the 2007 demise of immigration reform highlighted how successfully border hawks and other restrictionists had won control of the Republican base, the electoral repercussions were unmistakable in the 2008 presidential contest. Barack Obama ran for president pledging to win a bipartisan compromise package would enhance border control while extending legal status to roughly 12 million undocumented immigrants. In the two previous presidential elections, both major party candidates touted strong pro-immigration credentials as they courted immigrant and coethnic Latino and Asian voters. During the 2008 campaign, however, Obama's position on immigration distinguished him from his Republican opponent, John McCain, who assumed a tough enforcement stance. McCain, once committed to comprehensive reform and guest worker programs, became an eleventh-hour border hawk during the primaries to appease a partisan base adamantly opposed to extending legal status to unauthorized immigrants. When the dust settled, Obama's pro-immigration appeals helped him garner 67 percent of the Latino and 64 percent of the Asian vote in 2008. Equally troubling to Republicans was the fact that Latino turnout increased to 11 million voters (9 percent of the total) in 2008, double the turnout in 2000.[76]

Soon after entering office, the Obama White House announced that an immigration initiative would have to come after more looming priorities such as health care, energy, and financial regulatory reform.[77] Its determination to push the issue off its action agenda was influenced by the reality that the Obama team reflected the interparty divide: it could not find more than one Republican senator and a handful of Republican House members willing to work across the aisle on immigration reform. Yet the White House also worried about maintaining intraparty unity, with centrist Democrats from swing states and congressional districts warning against a partisan, pro-immigration reform. The complexities of CIR and deep cynicism among policy makers and ordinary citizens over past implementation failures also encouraged White House lethargy on the issue. In order to justify future legalization efforts and to attract conservative lawmakers to negotiations, Obama acted unilaterally to station National Guard troops along the nation's southern border and to step up enforcement efforts by deporting a record number of undocumented immigrants.[78] Yet congressional Republicans could not be less interested in compromise on immigration reform.

At the same time as policy stalemate prevailed in Congress, states dominated by overwhelmingly Republican legislatures and Republican governors took the lead in passing restrictive measures that targeted undocumented immigrants for harsh treatment. These state-level policy innovations were anything but spontaneous, with restrictive national organizations shopping for Republican state venues where model legislation could be adopted. Many of these model bills were drafted by Kansas Republican Kris Kobach, a former adviser to Attorney General John Ashcroft whom one Alabama lawmaker described as a "godsend" to conservative state and local officials hoping to crackdown on unauthorized immigrants.[79] Arizona gained notoriety in 2010 when it enacted legislation – SB1070 – requiring state and local law enforcement officers to determine the immigration status of anyone involved in a lawful stop, detention, or arrest where "reasonable suspicion exists" that the person is unlawfully present. Critics charged that the measure would spur racial profiling by targeting people who look or sound foreign, especially anyone of Latino descent. Defenders retorted that strong action was required, and law enforcement would be sensible and respectful in enforcing the law.

Within days of its signing, SB1070 was challenged in federal court as an unconstitutional violation of equal protection, due process, and the supremacy of the national government over immigration matters. President Obama also wasted no time in denouncing the law and its potential for discrimination, declaring that no one "should be subject to suspicion simply because of what they look like." In one of its blockbuster decisions of the summer of 2012, *Arizona v. United States*, the Supreme Court ruled that key provisions of SB 1070 were unconstitutional on the grounds that it violated the Constitution's supremacy clause. In particular, the Court struck provisions making it a crime to be in Arizona without legal papers, making it a crime for undocumented immigrants to apply for or get a job in the state, and allowing for the warrant-less arrest of individuals if there is probable cause that they committed crimes that could lead to their deportation. Finally, the Court provided a narrow window for Arizona state and local law enforcement officers to determine the immigration status of anyone involved in a lawful stop, detention, or arrest where "reasonable suspicion exists" that the person is unlawfully present – if they did so without violating civil rights protections. It is expected that the implementation of this last provision will generate a new round of litigation that ultimately challenges its constitutionality. As MALDEF President Thomas Saenz put it, the Court gave SB1070 "three F's and an incomplete."[80]

Undaunted by the controversy that swirled around SB1070, other states have followed suit with legislation requiring police to check the immigration status of criminal suspects, compelling businesses to check the legal status of workers using a federal system called E-verify, and forcing applicants for public benefits to verify eligibility with new documentation of lawful presence. Republicans in Alabama, for instance, a state where the undocumented immigrant population grew fivefold to roughly 120,000 in ten years, GOP Governor Robert Bentley hailed new legislation in 2011 as the "strongest" and "toughest" in the nation. Along with familiar law enforcement, employment, and public benefits provisions, the Alabama law went further than most in mandating schools to determine the legal status of students and making it a crime to knowingly rent or give a ride to an undocumented immigrant.

Claims that undocumented immigrants would benefit from health care reform also became a prominent talking point for Tea Party activists at vituperative town hall meetings during the summer of 2009. They elicited a strong rebuke from Obama in his health care speech to a joint session of Congress the following fall, serving as the impetus for Representative Joe Wilson's infamous outburst, "You lie!" At the first national Tea Party Convention in Nashville, Tennessee, during the winter of 2010, immigrants and immigration reform were major topics of speeches heard by assembled delegates of the grassroots movement. In one of the most prominent keynote addresses, the failed 2008 GOP presidential candidate and former Representative Tom Tancredo was cheered when he fulminated that Obama was elected by naturalized immigrants and other people "who can't even spell the word 'vote' or speak English."

Warning rapt delegates that "our culture is at stake," he then made headlines by lamenting "we do not have a civics, literacy test before people can vote."[81] The next day, Tancredo joined Roy Beck, Executive Director of the restrictionist Numbers USA, to argue that cracking down on illegal immigration, discouraging "chain migration" from developing countries by cutting family preferences in legal admissions, and denying birthright citizenship (*jus soli*) to the children of undocumented mothers were keys to solving the nation's deep social and economic woes.[82] In the months that followed, the lone Republican senator who had been willing to work with Obama on immigration reform, Lindsay Graham of South Carolina, responded to pressure from his conservative base by announcing that he would seek to amend the Constitution to deny birthright citizenship to the children of undocumented immigrants. "People come here to have babies," Graham told Fox News. "They come here to drop a child. It's called, 'drop and leave.' To have a child in America, they cross the border, they go to the emergency room, have a child, and that child's automatically an American citizen. That shouldn't be the case."[83] A bipartisan congressional deal on immigration reform was impossible. The same year, Congress was unable to pass the DREAM Act, despite broad public support, when no Republican senator dared to cross FAIR or Numbers USA by breaking a filibuster on the bill.

During the heat of the 2010 election, illegal immigration was again center stage. In races across the country, Republican candidates railed against "illegal aliens who take our jobs" and increase taxes by placing strains on "health care, criminal justice, and the educational system."[84] During the hotly contested Nevada Senate campaign, Republican challenger Sharron Angle ran negative ads blaming incumbent Senator Harry Reid for "millions of illegal aliens, warming across our border, joining violent gangs, forcing families to live in fear." By contrast, Obama sought to rally Latino voter support during the waning stages of the election by renewing his pledge to secure CIR. Obama reminded Univision audiences that his efforts were opposed at every turn by "anti-immigration" Republican lawmakers "who are supportive of the Arizona law, who talk only about border security, ... who are out there engaging in rhetoric that is divisive and damaging." Even as Democratic control of the House slipped away, Obama said of comprehensive immigration that he was "committed to making it happen. We're going to get it done."[85]

"Had [my father] been born of Mexican parents, I'd have a better shot at winning this," Mitt Romney quipped in one of his not-ready-for-prime-time remarks at a secretly recorded fundraiser more notorious for his "47 percent" comments. During more scripted moments of an online forum broadcast by the Spanish-language Univision network, Romney assured the mostly Latino audience that he would achieve sweeping immigration reform in office and promised that he would not pursue the mass deportation of 10 to 12 million undocumented immigrants living in the country. The Romney campaign also invested heavily in ads on Spanish-language media in swing states from

Colorado to Virginia, and deployed his son Craig, who speaks Spanish, to help court Latino voters. These efforts represented a last-ditch attempt to minimize Obama's strong advantage among Latino voters, the fastest-growing ethnic group in the United States and a crucial voting bloc in pivotal swing states. Romney's difficulties with Latino (and Asian) voters stemmed from his endorsement during the GOP primaries of punitive state immigration laws that would encourage "self-deportation," but they reflected a deeper estrangement between the Republican party and the nation's growing Latino population.

Obama's checkered immigration record created strains and uncertainties of its own entering the 2012 general campaign. The Obama administration had angered pro-immigrant groups for failing in his 2008 pledge to secure CIR or even to make it a top priority. It also drew the ire of some Latinos and immigration advocacy groups by advancing policies that netted a record number of deportations in his first term. With a decisive edge among Latino voters, the challenge for the Obama campaign was how to energize these supporters enough to turn up at the polls. Demonstrating the advantages of being president, Obama issued an executive order in June granting immunity from deportation for some undocumented immigrants who came to the United States as children (known as the Deferred Action for Childhood Arrivals program, or DACA). He also reminded pro-immigration audiences that the chief hurdle to CIR and some form of legal relief for undocumented immigrants has been the resolute opposition of congressional Republicans. "I am the head of the executive branch," Obama has explained. "I am not the head of the legislature. ... And what we could not get was a single Republican, including 20 who had previously voted for CIR, to step up and say, we will work with you to make this happen." In the end, Obama won 71 percent of the Latino vote with a 44-point advantage that was even more decisive than his 36-point margin (67 percent of the Latino vote) in 2008. Obama also won 76 percent of the Asian vote, an electoral bloc that once provided majority support for Republican presidential candidates.

Troubled by presidential election returns, Republican leaders conceded on election night in 2012 that it was time to come to the negotiating table on CIR. In the months that followed, a "Gang of Eight" formed in the Senate comprised of four Republicans (Jeff Flake, Lindsey Graham, John McCain, and Marco Rubio) and four Democrats (Michael Bennett, Richard Durbin, Robert Menendez, and Charles Schumer) formed a familiar "strange bedfellow" alliance and hammered out a painful compromise package. In June 2013, the Senate approved the 1,200-page by a sixty-eight to thirty-two margin, with fourteen Republicans joining all Democratic senators – a bipartisan exception to the recent norm of partisan polarization in the chamber. The final bill called for a thirteen-year pathway to citizenship for millions of undocumented immigrants, a new visa program for lesser-skilled workers, stronger security measures along the nation's border, and an enhanced system of workplace verification and tougher employer sanctions enforcement. It also would have paved the way for significant changes in the legal immigration preference system, placing greater emphasis on admitting immigrants with desirable work skills and educational backgrounds.[86]

In the House, Republican leaders and rank-and-file members supportive of immigration reform favored a piecemeal approach of enacting a series of smaller bills addressing the issue. Various House committees cleared bills beefing up border security, enhancing interior enforcement, and revamping guest worker programs. A separate bill was being written to extend legalization to young undocumented immigrants who entered the country as minors and passed security tests. Republican leaders also adopted a broad set of principles on immigration reform that was meant to bridge the divide between House Republicans on the issue. Both the Senate bill and the immigration reform principles endorsed by the House Republican leadership elicited a fierce backlash from the base of the party, as conservative opinion leaders and House members lined up in opposition to any form of legalization for undocumented immigrants, including young DREAMers. In the end, inter- and intraparty dynamics of immigration politics played out quite differently in the two branches.[87] In the Senate, a sweeping bipartisan bill was propelled by interparty competition over Latino and Asian votes and by intraparty fissures that allowed the Gang of Eight to build a supermajority for passage. By contrast, both inter- and intraparty conflicts made the stakes too great for House Republican leaders to find common cause with partisan rivals while alienating either conservative voters or border hawks in their own caucus.

CONCLUSION

At the heart of immigration reform's demise in 2009 and 2013 are distinctive inter-and intraparty conflicts and especially daunting and complex policy challenges. During unified party control of the branches during the 111th Congress, the Obama White House chose to postpone a bruising political fight over landmark immigration legislation that they expected to draw Republican fire, divide Democrats, and fail to elicit broad popular support. Amidst divided government in the 113th Congress, diverse business interests and Romney's 44-point deficit with Latino voters convinced fourteen Republican senators to break ranks and join Democratic colleagues in passing a rare bipartisan bill authored by the so-called Gang of Eight. Conservative border hawks in the House Republican Caucus and at the grassroots, however, handcuffed Boehner and other GOP leaders who originally favored a compromise measure that addressed employer demands for immigrant labor, toughened enforcement, and might have improved the party's brand among Latino voters. Despite fissures among House Republicans in 2013, conservative hard liners on immigration succeeded in making the Senate bill's collapse a matter of partisan and ideological fealty.

Legislative stalemate on CIR during both unified and divided government has not meant that policy has stood still. During the summer of 2014, House Republicans refused to appropriate resources the Obama administration requested to cope with thousands of unaccompanied Central American child migrants arriving at the southern border. Instead, Republican House members passed two essentially symbolic bills that pleased party faithfuls who favored tough responses to a full range of immigration issues. The first bill coupled far less emergency funding than the president requested with calls for expedited deportation of unaccompanied minors and funding for gubernatorial deployments of the National Guard to border areas. The measure doomed any chance of brokering a deal with the Senate over the child-migrant crisis. Scolding congressional Republicans for political theater rather than "actually trying to solve the problem," Obama declared that legislative stalemate left him with no options. "I'm going to have to act alone," he told reporters.[88]

More provocatively, the second House bill sought to prevent the administration from continuing to implement a 2012 White House order, DACA, which put off the potential deportation of up to 700,000 undocumented immigrants who arrived in the country as minors before 2007. During its second term, the Obama administration was urged by immigration rights advocates to broaden deferred action to cover more undocumented immigrants, with pressures building from the DREAMer movement of undocumented young people to assorted civil rights, religious, labor, Latino, and Asian groups. Tellingly, the second House bill set about to prohibit the Obama administration from spending any more funds on the Deferred Action program and sought to block it from renewing or expanding work permits to any undocumented immigrants. In essence, the House measure attempted to use the current border issues to roll back earlier Obama administration steps to regularize the status of some undocumented immigrants.[89] This was, of course, a nonstarter in the Democratic-controlled Senate, yet it signaled the buildup of angry political storm clouds.

Undaunted, President Obama elicited a firestorm of protest from Congressional Republicans when he moved decisively a few weeks after the 2014 midterm election to provide administrative relief from deportation for roughly 4.4 million undocumented immigrants. The executive action expands DACA and extends deferred action to the undocumented parents of U.S. citizens and legal permanent residents. As Republican Congressional leaders vow a constitutional showdown over deferred action, typical partisan polarization has drowned out intraparty conflicts over immigration in the 114th Congress. But if and when national lawmakers pursue major immigration reform in the future, landmark legislation can only be achieved in this policy realm when strange congressional bedfellows scrape together narrow majorities in support of an unpalatable, bipartisan compromise. In the meantime, immigration policy has become ground zero in our current state of political dysfunction.

Notes

1. Ted Hesson, "Analysis: Why Immigration Reform Isn't a Guarantee," ABCNews, November 10, 2012.
2. Lauren Fox, "Republicans on Capitol Hill Eye Immigration Reform to Win Back Latino Voters," *U.S. News*, November 21, 2012.
3. "Boehner: Time Right for Immigration Reform," UPI.com, November 9, 2012.
4. Ed O'Keefe, "Senate Approves Comprehensive Immigration Bill," *The Washington Post*, June 27, 2013.
5. Stephen Dinan and David Sherfinski, "Boehner Puts Brakes on Immigration Reform," *The Washington Times*, November 13, 2013.
6. "Remarks by the President at Univision Town Hall," White House Press Release, September 20, 2012.
7. T.H. Marshall, *Citizenship and Social Class and Other Essays* (Cambridge: Cambridge University Press, 1950).
8. Douglass is quoted in Adrian Cook, *The Armies of the Streets* (Lexington: University Press of Kentucky, 1974), p. 205.
9. The views of both of these labor leaders are discussed extensively in Tichenor, *Dividing Lines: The Politics of Immigration Control* (Princeton, NJ: Princeton University Press, 2002), chapter 5.
10. Janice Fine and Daniel Tichenor, "A Movement Wrestling," *Studies in American Political Development* 23 (October 2009), pp. 218–48.
11. U.S. Commission on Immigration Reform, *U.S. Immigration Policy: Restoring Credibility* (Washington, DC: GPO, 1994).
12. Lisa Caruso, "Splits on the Left," *National Journal*, June 30, 2007.
13. Andrew Carnegie, *Triumphant Democracy* (New York, 1887), p. 34.
14. Lowell is quoted in Tichenor, *Dividing Lines*, p. 38.
15. Patrick Buchanan, *State of Emergency: The Third World Invasion and Conquest of America* (New York: St. Martin's Press, 2006).
16. The arduous path to the Simpson-Mazzoli legislation in 1986 is discussed in depth in Tichenor, *Dividing Lines*, chapter 9.
17. On the politics of blame-avoidance, see R. Kent Weaver, "The Politics of Blame Avoidance," *Journal of Public Policy* (October–December 1986), pp. 371–98.
18. Luis Guitierrez interview, Democracy Now Radio and Television, May 2, 2006, transcript.
19. Marc Rosenblum, "A 'Path to Citizenship' or Current Illegal Immigrants?," Online Debate, Council of Foreign Relations website, April 1, 2007.
20. Carol Swain, "Introduction," in Swain, ed., *Debating Immigration* (New York: Cambridge University Press, 2007), pp. 1–16.
21. Lou Dobbs, "Big Media Hide Truth about Immigration," CNN.com, April 25, 2007.
22. George W. Bush, Address to the Nation on Immigration Reform, May 15, 2006.
23. See Tom Tancredo, *In Mortal Danger* (Nashville, TN: WND Books, 2006).
24. American Federation of Labor, *Proceedings of the Annual Convention*, 1934 bound volume, p. 550, George Meany Archives, Silver Spring, MD.
25. U.S. Department of Labor, *26th Annual Report of the Secretary of Labor, 1938* (Washington, DC: Government Printing Office, 1939), pp. 95–6.

26. Arthur Altmeyer, executive director of the War Manpower Commission, to Claude Wickard, Secretary of Agriculture, Memo on Proposed Agreement for the Importation of Mexican Workers, July 29, 1942, Box 35, Folder 26 on Mexican Labor, AFL-CIO Department of Legislation Papers, George Meany Archives.

27. Kitty Calavita, *Inside the State: The Bracero Program, Immigration, and the INS* (New York: Routledge, 1992), pp. 32–5.

28. David Reimers, *Still the Golden Door* (New York: Columbia University Press, 1992), p. 54.

29. Ibid.

30. Author's interview with Rep. Henry B. Gonzalez, March 1996; Calavita, *Inside the State*, pp. 163–9.

31. Andrew Biemiller to Peter Rodino, September 8, 1972; Biemiller to Rodino, March 23, 1973; Rodino to Biemiller, May 15, 1973, Papers of the Legislation Department of the AFL-CIO, Box 71, Folder #28, George Meany Archives.

32. See, e.g., *The New York Times*, December 31, 1974.

33. *Congressional Record*, September 12, 1972, pp. 30164, 30182–3; National Council of La Raza documents made available to the author by the national office of the NCLR.

34. White House Statement, August 4, 1977, Patricia Roberts Harris Papers.

35. "Memorandum to Interested Parties from the Mexican-American Legal Defense and Education Fund: Statement of Position Regarding the Administration's Undocumented Alien Legislation Proposal," November 11, 1977, Papers of the Leadership Conference on Civil Rights, Container #23, "Issues: Alien Civil Rights" Folder.

36. Transcript of SCIRP meeting, May 7, 1980, p. 34, Record Group 240, Box 26, National Archives.

37. Lawrence Fuchs, *American Kaleidoscope* (Hanover, NH: University Press of New England, 1990), p. 252.

38. Transcript of SCIRP meeting, p. 34.

39. *The New York Times*, August 24, 1981.

40. The arduous path to the Simpson-Mazzoli legislation in 1986 is discussed in depth in Tichenor, *Dividing Lines*, chapter 9.

41. Author's anonymous interviews with Reagan administration officials, 1996; see also U.S. Commission on Immigration Reform, *U.S. Immigration Policy: Restoring Credibility* (Washington, DC: GPO, 1994), p. 95.

42. Ibid.

43. Alan Simpson to Lawrence Fuchs, January 24, 1991, Correspondence Files of Lawrence Fuchs, made available to the author by Fuchs.

44. E.E. Schattschneider, *The Semi-Sovereign People* (New York: Holt, Rinehart and Winston, 1960).

45. See *Hispanic Magazine*, January–February 2001; on earlier Republican adjustments, see Dick Kirschten, "Trying a Little Tenderness," *National Journal*, January 10, 1998, p. 54.

46. Robert Suro, Richard Fry, and Jeffrey Passel, "Hispanics and the 2004 Election," Pew Hispanic Center Report, June 27, 2005.

47. Mike Allen, "Immigration Reform on Bush Agenda," *Washington Post*, December 24, 2003, p. 1.

48. Immigrant Union Members Numbers and Trends Migration Policy Institute Immigration Facts, May 2004, No. 7. See also Janice Fine and Daniel Tichenor, "A Movement Wrestling: Labor's Enduring Struggle with Immigration," *Studies in American Political Development*, forthcoming.

49. Allen, *Immigration Reform on Bush Agenda*," p. 1.

50. James Lakely and Joseph Curl, "Bush Will Propose Plan on Illegals," *Washington Times*, January 6, 2004, p. 1.

51. Wayne Washington, "Campaign 2004: Bush Upsets Part of Conservative Base," *The Boston Globe*, January 9, 2004, p. 1.

52. Ralph Hallow and James Lakely, "GOP Slams Bush Policies at Retreat," *Washington Times*, p. 1.

53. Washington, "Campaign 2004," p. 1.

54. Ralph Hallow, "GOP to Finesse the Immigration Issue," *Washington Times*, August 23, 2004, p. 4.

55. Suro et al., "Hispanics and the 2004 Election." See also "The Latino, Asian, and Immigrant Vote: 2004," National Immigration Forum Backgrounder.

56. Bill Sammon, "Bush Revives Bid to Legalize Illegal Aliens," *Washington Times*, November 10, 2004, p. 1; and Daren Briscoe, "Immigration – A Hot Topic," *Newsweek*, November 22, 2004, p. 10.

57. Ibid.

58. Stephen Dinan, "House Shuns Illegals Proposal," *The Washington Times*, November 11, 2004, p. 1.

59. Sammon, "Bush Revives Bid to Legalize Illegal Aliens."12–14.

60. Dinan, "House Shuns Illegals Proposal."

61. David Bacon, "Which Side Are You On?" *Monthly Review*, February 2, 2007, p. 12–14.

62. Jim Gilchrist and Jerome Corsi, *Minutemen: The Battle to Secure America's Borders* (Los Angeles, CA: World Ahead, 2006).

63. "Immigration Issue Remains Divisive," *Rasmussen Reports*, March 30, 2006 (containing earlier survey results).

64. See Victor Narro, Kent Wong, and Janna Sahdduck-Hernandez, "The 2006 Immigrant Uprising: Origins and Future," *New Labor Forum* 16 (1), December 2007, pp. 49–56, and Bill Ong Hing and Kevin R. Johnson, "The Immigrant Rights Marches of 2006 and the Prospects of a New Civil Rights Movement," *Harvard Civil Rights-Civil Liberties Law Review*, 42, 2007.

65. "24% Have Favorable Opinion of Protestors," *Rasmussen Reports*, May 1, 2006.

66. "Immigration Rallies Fail to Move Public Opinion," *Rasmussen Reports*, May 3, 2006.

67. "39% Agree with President on Immigration," *Rasmussen Reports*, May 17, 2006.

68. "Bush OKs 700 Mile Border Fence," CNN.com, October 26, 2006.

69. Robert Pear and Jim Rutenberg, "Senators in Bipartisan Deal on Immigration Bill," *The New York Times*, May 18, 2007, p. A-1.

70. "Support for Senate Immigration Bill Falls," *Rasmussen Reports*, June 6, 2007; and "Why the Senate Immigration Bill Failed," *Rasmussen Reports*, June 8, 2007.

71. Robert Pear, "'86 Law Looms over Immigration Fights," *The New York Times*, June 12, 2007; Stephen Dinan, "Grassley Admits Amnesty Mistake," *Washington Times*, June 22, 2007.

72. On June 8 (34 in favor versus 61 against) in which a majority comprised of conservative Republicans and liberal Democrats opposed the bill.
73. Carolyn Lochhead, "Democratic Poll Finds Tepid Support for Immigration Bill," *San Francisco Chronicle*, June 20, 2007; Angus Reid, "Americans Pick Enforcement in Immigration Debate," *Global Monitor*, June 11, 2007.
74. Gail Russell Chaddock, "Senate Makes a New Try for Immigration Bill," *Christian Science Monitor*, June 21, 2007.
75. The actual vote was on invoking cloture; it was 46 in favor versus 53 against.
76. "Latino Vote Fueling Introspection for Republicans," *America's Voice*, November 11, 2008.
77. Ginger Thompson and David Herszenhorn, "Obama Set for First Step on Immigration Reform," *The New York Times*, June 25, 2009; Michael Farrell, "Obama Delays Immigration Reform – At Great Risk," *Christian Science Monitor*, August 11, 2009.
78. Peter Slevin, "Deportation of Illegal Immigrants Increases under the Obama Administration," *Washington Post*, July 26, 2010.
79. George Talbot, "Kris Kobach, the Kansas Lawyer behind Alabama's Immigration Law," *Press-Register*, October 16, 2011.
80. Author's interview with Saenz, May 2013.
81. Brian Kates, "Tea Party Convention's Racial Brouhaha," *New York Daily News*, February 5, 2010.
82. Ibid.
83. E.J. Dionne, "Is the GOP Shedding a Birthright?" *The Washington Post*, August 5, 2010.
84. See James Coburn, "Candidates Sound Off on Illegal Immigration," *The Edmund Sun*, July 12, 2010; and Josh Kraushaar, "Tennesee Republicans Feud Over Immigration," May 25, 2010, *Politico*.
85. "Univision Transcript: Piolin Interview with President Barack Obama," October 26, 2010.
86. O'Keefe, "Senate Approves Comprehensive Immigration Bill."
87. Dinan and Sherfinski, "Boehner Puts Brakes on Immigration Reform."
88. Katie Zezema, "White House: Obama Has 'No Choice but to Act' on Immigration," *The Washington Post*, August 3, 2014.
89. Lisa Mascaro, "Late Push by House GOP Produces a Border Bill (with Bleak Prospects)," *The Los Angeles Times*, August 1, 2014.

11

It's Hard to Get Mileage Out of Congress

*Struggling Over CAFE Standards, 1973–2013**

Bruce I. Oppenheimer

This chapter is part of a broader effort to analyze U.S. legislative efforts to develop energy policy from the oil embargo of 1973 to 2013. For four decades, there was general agreement on the overall long-term policy goal of making the United States less dependent on foreign sources of energy. Every president from Nixon to Obama and every Congress has articulated some version of an energy independence goal, regardless of which party was in the majority or whether party control at the national government level was unified or divided. What decision makers did not agree upon were the policies needed to reach that goal. It would not be too much of a simplification to say that policy makers, interest groups, and the public were largely split into two camps. One viewed the solution largely in terms of increasing production of fossil fuels to meet the growing energy demand, while the other preferred lowering demand through conservation and less reliance on fossil fuels. Until the last few years, when a sluggish economy slowed energy demand and some major technological break-throughs have significantly increased domestic oil and gas production, U.S. reliance on foreign energy had remained at or above the level at the time of the Organization of the Petroleum Exporting Countries (OPEC) embargo. Even if one believes that dependence would have been much greater if it were not for the policies that were adopted, one could reasonably contend that U.S. energy policy was an example of policy failure.

In the description, analysis, and theorizing that follow, I will examine the legislative struggle over one policy option in the effort to enact and implement an overall energy policy, the use and adjustment of CAFE (corporate average fuel economy) standards on motor vehicles, particularly on automobiles and

* Prepared for delivery at the Conference on Congress and Public Policy Making in the 21st Century at the University of Virginia, June 3–4, 2013.

light trucks.[1] In doing so, I hope to provide some explanations for why energy policy posed such difficulty for Congress and a series of presidential administrations for most of forty years. I will contend that as the hurdles to enacting legislation grew, there has been a decline in congressional policy influence, not just on energy policy, but more broadly as presidents choose to bypass Congress in pursuing their policy goals.[2] In doing so, my findings are generally supportive of and extend the ideas that Terry Moe and William Howell (1999) set forth on presidential exercise of unilateral action. Moe and Howell contend that "it appears the strategy of unilateral action has grown increasingly more central to the modern presidency" (851–52). Their analysis of presidential use of unilateral action rests on the examination of the ambiguities in the president's powers, the growing statutory authority in existing law, and the hurdles that make it so that "neither Congress nor the courts are likely to stop them" (852). Howell (2003) offers refinements and demonstrates that the frequency of presidential use of unilateral action is inversely related to the size of the president's party in Congress. More recent research has placed qualifications and limitations on the breadth of Moe and Howell's initial argument. Rudalevige (2002) theorizes about conditions under which presidents will centralize legislative policy formulation in terms of contingent centralization. And more recently (2014) he evaluated the limits on presidential use of unilateralism in the aftermath of the Obama 2014 State of the Union address. Other work examines the effect of ideological distance between the president and the other two branches on the presidents' use of delegated authority (Rottinghaus 2014) and on the Congress and the Supreme Court as conditioning factors (Chiou and Rothenberg 2014). Rather than focusing on the limits of the Moe and Howell perspective, I will argue that presidents have a greater incentive to act unilaterally when the costs of passing legislation and the likelihood of failure in doing so increase. In addition, other players, such as interest groups and the mass public, not just Congress and the courts, also play key roles because they have incentives to support the presidential use of unilateral action as a means of avoiding gridlock.

In the course of this analysis of the legislative struggle over CAFE standards, I hope to offer insights about a number of aspects of the changing nature of Congress' efforts to affect public policy and its relative influence vis-à-vis the president. These include the following:

1. The effect of the transition from committee government and relatively weak parties and party leadership to conditional party government with more cohesive and polarized parties and with greater authority in the hands of party leaders to hold their members together and address collective action problems;
2. The impact of contextual conditions in terms of the short-term costs of the status quo and the skill of party leaders in disguising the traceability of proposed policy changes;

3. Why close party balance since the 1994 election in the period of conditional party government contributes to the Congress's inability to resolve issue differences and enact legislation; and

4. How the increasing costs of overcoming congressional veto points has led the president to pursue other means to achieve his policy goals, including active engagement in interest aggregation at policy formulation stage and using existing statutory authority to achieve policy goals rather than pursuing new legislation.

To examine these propositions, I have divided this chapter into four sections. The first focuses on the expectations about how the congressional process worked when parties and party leaders were relatively weak and applies them to the struggle to enact the first set of CAFE standards in the 94th Congress as part of the Energy Policy and Conservation Act. The second part examines the efforts to increase CAFE standards beginning in the late 1980s until passage of the passage of the Energy Independence and Security Act of 2007 (EISA) during a period when parties in Congress became more cohesive and more polarized. Despite the existence of what many have labeled as conditional party government,[3] it actually became more difficult to enact energy legislation than when parties and party leaders were considerably weaker. The third section discusses the way that the Obama administration, beginning almost immediately after taking office in 2009, has used its interpretation of existing authority to set CAFE standards far beyond the intent of Congress in EISA, making nonincremental policy change. Finally, in the concluding section, I will argue that what has happened in energy policy, and specifically with CAFE standards, is not an ad hoc tactic on the part of the Obama administration but rather is a strategic change that is at the heart of a more systematic approach to overcome a congressional process that has become more difficult as transaction costs have become prohibitive. In the end, as Congress seemingly has gained policy influence through the increased use of its ability to block legislation, its policy influence is actually declining as both the executive and interest groups have reacted strategically, and the mass public has been willing to tolerate additional extensions of executive authority if it leads to policy responsiveness.

Before analyzing how changes over the past forty years have impacted Congress's ability to resolving energy issues, and specifically to deal with CAFE standards, it is first necessary to discuss one important constant that has inhibited Congress's ability to legislate on energy policy: the nature of the issue itself.

ISSUES THAT SUIT LEGISLATURES

A major problem that Congress has faced in dealing with energy legislation over the past forty years has been that energy issues generally are not the policy type that legislatures and their members are comfortable in addressing.[4] The literature is filled with sound theorizing and empirical analysis supporting the idea that Congress and its members find it easiest to enact two broad types of legislation. One is pork barrel/distributive in nature because it allows members to concentrate benefits and disperse costs (Shepsle and Weingast 1981; Evans 1994; Evans 2011). When effectively logrolling with other members on programs that service their constituencies, pork barrel bills allow members to take credit for obtaining material benefits for their districts and states without seemingly conferring traceable costs on their constituents. Thus, members receive credit from their constituents when elections occur without giving potential opponents a visible basis for criticizing them.[5] The second and related method is one that Douglas Arnold explores in his book, *The Logic of Congressional Action* (1990). Arnold asks how it is that Congress sometimes passes legislation in which costs are not dispersed. He credits congressional leaders with being able to design legislation in such a way that they can persuade members that the costs are not traceable. Often this strategy involves formulating legislation so it produces program benefits in the near term but defers the costs to some later date. Again, the key is that the leaders persuade their members that a potential electoral opponent cannot use public dissatisfaction with policy costs as a campaign issue. As Rich Vallely skillfully demonstrates in Chapter 4, discussing the repeal of "Don't Ask, Don't Tell," other members, not just party leaders, may also employ this strategy.

To these two types, we might also add circumstances where majorities of both parties are willing to support policy changes that confer short-term costs on the public (with deferred benefits), thus providing some insurance against either party using the issue in the upcoming campaign. The 1990 Omnibus Budget Reconciliation Act and the 1990 Budget Enforcement Act provide a good example of an effort to avoid electoral damage. As James Thurber observed: "The bipartisan agreements were intended to ... provide political cover for unpopular election-year decisions" (2013, 324). These three types may not exhaust the ways to enact legislation with short-term costs that might otherwise have negative electoral consequences, but they are the methods that political scientists most frequently mention.[6]

Most energy policy proposals, however, do not seemingly share any of these qualities, at least not in recent decades.[7] Instead, they require the public to incur short-term costs to reap long-term benefits. These costs may come in the form of higher energy prices, increased taxes, increased costs of consumer goods (cars, appliances, heating and cooling systems), increased levels of air and water pollution, unemployment, and safety. Support for policies that inflict front-end costs exposes members to potential electoral vulnerability. Because there are competing sides in the energy policy debate that are highly critical of the policy proposals of the other side, it almost guarantees that opponents will be ready seize upon the issue. Accordingly, as I have argued elsewhere, Congress has only passed significant energy legislation when the short-term political costs from maintaining the status quo exceed the short-term political costs of

adopting policy changes (Oppenheimer 2014). Arnold in his case example
of energy legislation in the mid-1970s properly credits the skill of party
leaders in limiting traceability of policy costs for the success in resolving
some energy issues. Importantly, however, faced with rising energy prices
and uncertainties about the supply of gasoline and heating oil in the aftermath of the embargo, Congress also had to weigh the political consequences
of maintaining the status quo against the short-term costs of policy change.
Even under these circumstances, it took until 1980 for Congress to resolve all
the key energy issues in a series of separate legislative packages. Once energy
prices and supplies stabilized, the incentives for Congress to address energy
policy abated.

ENACTMENT OF CAFE STANDARDS IN 1975

The enactment of the first set of CAFE standards occurred in 1975 in an era
when political parties and party leadership in Congress were still weak.
Although Democrats had sizable majorities, sixty-two senators[8] and a 2:1
advantage in the House, they were hardly a cohesive group. Democrats in both
the House and the Senate had average party unity scores of only 75 percent in
the 94th Congress (1975–76). The recently adopted Subcommittee Bill of
Rights had reduced the power of committee chairs, but it had further decentralized decision making in the House. Some additional powers were seemingly
available to the party leadership. Speaker Carl Albert, however, was reluctant
to use them fully (Dodd and Oppenheimer 1977). In March 1975, the Senate
did change the cloture requirements from two-thirds present and voting to
three-fifths of the membership. The number of cloture votes dropped for the
remainder of that Congress but then increased, and the success of cloture
motions had a modest increase. The rule change did not make Senate party
leadership appreciably stronger in its ability to influence the behavior of its
members. Moreover, the Ford presidency meant that there was divided party
control, with differing preferences for energy policy in Congress and in the
White House. So mobilizing majorities to enact legislation presented a number
of hurdles.

    The existence of high and unstable oil and gas prices and uncertainty about
supplies in the aftermath of the embargo proved critical in reaching an accommodation on CAFE standards and on some other energy issues. Both parties
rejected the use of rationing or higher gasoline taxes. In his 1975 State of the
Union Address, President Ford argued that "neither would achieve the desired
results and both would produce unacceptable inequities" (1975, 5).
Congressional Democrats concluded that "the cross elasticity between gasoline
prices and the fuel economy of new cars is very low, and ... lifetime fuel costs
still have too little effect on consumer automobile purchasing power" (S Rept
94–179, 9). With automobiles accounting for 40 percent of domestic petroleum
consumption, it was impossible to maintain the status quo. The Ford

administration, siding with the domestic automobile companies, opposed imposing fuel economy standards and instead called for voluntary efforts from the auto industry with a goal of a 40 percent improvement in fuel economy by 1980. The United Automobile Workers (UAW), in contrast, was generally accepting of some required mileage standard.

In the Senate, the pieces of a larger energy package were initially considered as four separate bills. The Committee on Commerce dealt with S 1883, the Automobile Fuel Economy Act of 1975. Its hearings in March, 1975 built on nine previous days of hearings beginning in the 93rd Congress that considered a variety of automobile fuel economy proposals. The end product was one largely developed within the committee, albeit one that Democrats dominated. The bill called for instituting of mileage standards for automobiles beginning with the 1977 model year with a fuel economy standard reaching 28 MPG by 1985. The Committee softened the blow on the auto companies, allowing the Secretary of Transportation to modify the 1980 and 1985 standards in adopting an amendment from Senator Philip Hart (D-MI). Hart's fellow Michigander, Robert Griffin (R-MI), provided the major opposition to the CAFE standards in the committee and on the floor. After his floor amendment to delay implementation of the standards for a year was handily defeated, he tried unsuccessfully to recommit the bill to the Finance Committee to be considered with an energy tax bill. At no point did Griffin indicate any intention to filibuster the bill. Hart supported Griffin on the amendment to delay implementation but voted against recommital and for final passage. Even with the Ford administration's opposition to government-imposed mileage standards, the 36 Senate Republicans who voted on the bill split 18–18, and the bill passed 63–21.

The events in the House were very similar to those in the Senate in that it was a committee-dominated process. Unlike the Senate, however, all the nontax aspects of energy legislation were contained in a single piece of legislation, HR 7014, over which the Committee on Interstate and Foreign Commerce had jurisdiction. The major focus of debate was on the sections dealing with the continuation and modifications of oil price controls, not the automobile fuel efficiency provisions contained in Title V of the bill. Nevertheless, the Committee's Energy and Power Subcommittee held an extended hearing on the mileage issue. Clarence "Bud" Brown, Jr., (R-OH), the subcommittee's ranking minority member, tried to delete the 28 MPG standard for 1985 during floor consideration, arguing that "neither Congress nor anyone else knows how to accomplish the 28-mile-per-gallon standard by 1985" (Congressional Record, September 17, 1975, 28934). John Dingell (D-MI), the subcommittee's chair and bill manager and a strong UAW and auto industry ally in the House, surprisingly led the opposition to the Brown amendment, clearly siding with the UAW's position about the manufacture of more fuel efficient vehicles. The amendment was defeated handily, but eight of the other eleven Democrats from Michigan supported Brown's amendment, while Republicans only split 72–62 in favor of it. As in the Senate, the competing coalitions engaged a mix of constituency and party forces. The majority party leadership did not use the rule to restrict the amendment process substantially on the House floor as twenty-four amendments received roll call votes. Although Republicans opposed the bill on final passage by more than 3 to 1 and Democrats supported it by over 5 to 1, this was not a case of the parties moving in lock step.

The conference report scheduled CAFE standards for cars to reach 20 MPG by 1980 in yearly steps and then increase to 27.5 MPG by 1985 and thereafter. The Department of Transportation (DOT) secretary could make downward adjustments, if necessary, and set lower mileage standards for light trucks. Party votes again prevailed in approving the conference report in both chambers. But Majority Leader Tip O'Neill offered a more nuanced and accurate picture of the entire bill when he observed: "This is perhaps the most parochial issue that could ever hit the floor" (*Congressional Quarterly Almanac 1975*, 243). He then went on to discuss all of the geographic cleavages that affected consideration but did not mention party. Despite the congressional Republicans voting against the bill and little evidence that either chamber was capable of overriding a veto, President Ford signed the bill. He expressed reservations but acknowledged the political and electoral realities: "If I were to veto this bill, the debates of the past year would almost surely continue through the election year and beyond" (Ford 1975). Bill proponents in a Democratic-controlled Congress had allowed for changes both in the overall legislation and in CAFE standards to produce a bill that President Ford could accept. It also meant that some issues, most notably a final decision on how to decontrol oil prices, were left unresolved.

The initial set of CAFE standards was enacted in largely a give-and-take context with a mix of constituency, interest group, and partisan forces in play. Opponents to setting standards and to the legislation more generally, however, were not willing to be veto players, even if they preferred the status quo to the proposed policy changes. The potential electoral costs of blocking action in a period of high energy prices and uncertainty about supply meant that it was better to pass legislation and remove the issue from the table before the 1976 campaign began. For much the same reason, those who favored CAFE standards realized that they could support the mileage requirements without suffering electoral consequences. Moreover, with large Democratic majorities in both the House and the Senate, and the expectation that they would persist, there was little incentive for Republicans to engage in a strategy of obstructionism, making the Democrats appear incapable of governing and using that strategy to win control of Congress in the 1976 election. In addition, failure to produce energy legislation would reflect badly on the Ford administration as well and might hurt the reelection prospects of Republicans. Under these circumstances, Republican members had a strong incentive to resolve some of the energy issues.

BLOCKING POLICY CHANGE

The second period is one during which Congress enacted few energy policy changes and most initiatives, including those to increase CAFE standards, were blocked. Without a sustained crisis for more two decades, the short-term political costs for members of making nonincremental changes in policy to achieve the longer-term benefits of reduced energy dependence were too great. Even as energy prices again escalated, especially after 2001, energy issues were more difficult to resolve than had been the case in the 1970s. The presence of stronger, more polarized parties in Congress meant that it was easier to mobilize party majorities, but it also meant that the minority was more cohesive in blocking legislation and more willing to do so. In addition, after Republicans won control of Congress in the 1994 election, increased electoral competition between the two congressional parties made compromise more difficult, lest the majority party be seen as governing competently. Instead of cooperating in producing long-term policy solutions and insulating each other from electoral damage, blocking majority party and presidential initiatives and reaping electoral gains took precedence. In this environment it was not until 2007 that Congress passed and President Bush reluctantly signed a bill increasing CAFE standards.

THE STRUGGLE OVER CAFE STANDARDS, 1985–2006

Gasoline prices peaked in 1981 but remained at levels well above those of 1975 until 1985. As the energy crisis abated, GM and Ford successfully lobbied the DOT through its National Highway Transportation Safety Administration (NHTSA) to roll back the CAFE target from 27.5 to 26 MPG. Congress was unable to block NHTSA from doing so, and the 26-MPG standard for passenger automobiles remained in place until 1989 when it was finally raised to 27.5. By that time, the real dollar cost of gasoline, which had been declining since 1981, was lower than pre-OPEC embargo prices for more than three years (see Figure 11.1). OPEC was seemingly in disarray, unable to enforce cooperation among its members to limit supply in a period of declining demand. The energy crisis had abated, and public and governmental concern focused on the health of the domestic automobile industry, not increasing fuel efficiency.[9]

When the 27.5 MPG standard had been reached, parties in both the House and the Senate were stronger, more ideologically homogeneous, and more cohesive than they had been in 1975 (Rohde 1991). Especially in the House, the majority party leadership had more resources with which to mobilize its membership to pass legislation. Increasingly, the sides on the energy debate organized along party lines, with those favoring production-oriented solutions and reliance on fossil fuels more concentrated within the Republican congressional membership and those advocating conservation and alternative fuels

FIGURE 11.1: Annual mean price of regular gasoline, 1970–2011. 1970–75 Leaded Gasoline. 1976–2011 Unleaded Gasoline. *Source*: U.S. Energy Information Administration, "Total Energy Annual Review," September 27, 2012.

more concentrated within the Democratic party, although there were sizeable minority positions articulated within each party's caucus until the mid-1990s on energy issues. Gradually, however, Republicans won the House and Senate seats that Democrats from oil- and gas-producing constituencies had held, while the number of moderate Republicans from consuming areas in the Northeast declined.[10] In turn, party positions on energy policy hardened. One major crosscutting cleavage party persisted within the Democratic party among members with strong environmental and organized labor constituencies, especially on issues that affected the domestic automobile industry and the UAW.

Until the 2000s when another energy crisis emerged, there was little impetus to enact significant energy legislation, such as increasing CAFE standards, because the short-term costs were too much of a political liability when the benefits were all in the future. With the competing sides on energy policy intense and fairly evenly divided, it was likely that floor consideration would be very time consuming, and in the end no major legislation would be enacted. And opponents to increasing CAFE standards blocked even the potential for such action to occur, just as the opponents of production approaches blocked those as well. Even after energy prices began to increase dramatically, one party or the other continued to prevent major energy policy change until 2007.[11]

This does not mean that there was a total absence of congressional activity on CAFE standards. Most of it, however, was futile. In 1989 as the new Bush administration, Republicans in Congress, and remaining energy-producing-state Democrats began to push for oil and gas drilling in the Arctic National Wildlife Refuge (ANWR), some congressional Democrats countered with proposals to raise CAFE standards. In 1990, shortly after Iraq's invasion of Kuwait set off concerns about a potential energy crisis, Senator Richard Bryan (D-NV) and his Republican co-sponsor, Slade Gorton (WA), undertook an unsuccessful attempt to lessen the opposition of domestic auto producers to an increase in CAFE standards by requiring a percentage increase in company mileage standards over their fleet-wide averages, thus putting a burden on foreign producers of smaller, more fuel-efficient vehicles and not just on domestic producers. Nevertheless, the active opposition of auto companies and the UAW, in addition to that of the Bush administration, defeated a cloture motion as several auto state Democrats, Democrats from energy-producing states, and two-thirds of the Republicans blocked a vote on the bill.

In an effort to pass a major energy bill lasting several years, Senate Energy Committee chair J. Bennett Johnston (D-LA) tried to couple CAFE with ANWR (Davis 1989). He also hoped to take advantage of residual concern over the Iraq War to enact a package that included drilling in ANWR and electric utility deregulation among other things. Johnston recognized the political necessity of a change in CAFE standards if a comprehensive bill were to survive in the Senate and realized that party leaders in Congress were playing a larger role in overseeing legislation that committees reported. Majority Leader George Mitchell (D-ME) had already appointed a sixteen-member party task force on energy that would require energy conservation provisions, including an increase in CAFE standards, before he would schedule a bill for Senate floor consideration (Idelson 1991). President Bush, meanwhile, threatened to veto a bill that mandated CAFE increases, eventually insisting that any decisions to alter CAFE standards be left to the executive branch.

With the Iraq crisis fading, Majority Leader Mitchell delayed bringing the bill to the Senate floor for months, by which time most of the controversial provisions had been stripped from the legislation. Johnston dropped the ANWR provision, and the bill only directed the DOT secretary to study CAFE standards and potential increase. Even if CAFE increases had been included in the Senate bill, it is unlikely that they would have passed the House where UAW and auto industry constituencies were proportionately stronger.[12]

The Gulf War and the resulting energy crisis were relatively brief, even if they again raised concerns about energy dependence. The potential electoral costs of inaction on major energy issues were not as great as the costs of making major policy changes that would yield long-term benefits but impose short-term economic costs on the public. In addition, CAFE standard opponents in 1990 resorted to a filibuster, a tactic that opponents had not employed in 1975. President Ford accepted some modifications, while President Bush threatened a veto. Signs of party and party leadership involvement increased. Johnston and his Energy and Natural Resources Committee did not have autonomy in crafting energy legislation. Majority Leader Mitchell and his energy task force were a significant constraint.

After the enactment of a stripped-down bill, energy policy generally, and CAFE standards in particular, ceased to be front-burner issues for Congress again until the Clinton presidency and even then legislative initiatives were limited as energy prices remained low. The Clinton administration's initial energy proposals dealt with energy taxes as a means of encouraging conservation (and raising revenue) and not efficiency standards. When Republicans took control of Congress in 1995, they ensured that the Clinton administration did not use existing authority to raise CAFE standards. Majority Whip Tom DeLay (R-TX) added a provision to the DOT appropriations bill prohibiting any increases in CAFE standards for cars or trucks, sending a clear message that it was a party position (Hager 1995). For the duration of the Clinton administration, Republicans put this restriction in each DOT appropriations bill.[13] In 1999, Senate Democrats offered an amendment to the bill that would have allowed the DOT to study whether to change CAFE standards. Republicans blocked even that modest step. The conferees again accepted the ban on spending for updating CAFE standards that was in the House bill, and President Clinton signed the appropriations bill. A year later, with gasoline prices quickly rising in real dollars to the highest price in fifteen years, auto state senators did agree to compromise allowing for the DOT and the National Academy of Science to conduct a study of CAFE standards and let the DOT propose increase if the study supported a change. In exchange, however, any change in CAFE standards would require a vote by Congress, and the House rider continued for another year (Plungis 2000).

With the election of President George W. Bush in 2000 and continued Republican majorities through 2006 (in the House for six years and in the Senate for all but part of the 107th Congress), the outlook for anything more than a symbolic increase in CAFE standards was bleak. As gasoline prices increased markedly, especially after the onset of the Iraq War in 2003, other items received the dominant focus of debate during three efforts to enact energy legislation between 2001 and 2006. With Republicans in control, attention focused on increasing domestic energy supplies through tax incentives to encourage fossil fuel production, making ANWR accessible for exploration, and incentives for ethanol production and use. In the 107th Congress (2001–02), neither the House nor the Senate version of the energy bill included mandatory increases in CAFE standards, although the bills provided guidelines that would likely lead to very modest increases.[14] The Senate, however, was unable to invoke cloture on an amendment to allow drilling in ANWR. Without it, no conference agreement was possible. Again, in the 108th Congress (2003–04), even with Republicans back in majority control of the Senate and with House Republicans reluctantly willing to remove the ANWR issue from the energy bill, the bill could not survive a Senate filibuster over liability protection for the MTBE (methyl tertiary butyl ether) additive, a provision on which House Republicans were unwilling to compromise. CAFE standards remained an auxiliary issue.[15]

When Congress finally passed an energy bill in 2005, it did not have a provision on CAFE standards as many controversial elements were purposely kept out of the legislation. Senator Richard Durbin (D-IL) did offer an amendment on the Senate floor to increase CAFE standards to 40 MPG over eleven years, but it was soundly defeated (28–67) with even nearly as many Democrats voting against the amendment as for it. The bill made only modest policy changes, including some pork provisions on ethanol designed to ensure the support of corn state senators of both parties as well as some tax incentives for fossil fuels and some support for renewables. What passed looked more like a public works bill that concentrated benefits and dispersed costs than one that addressed major ongoing energy issues. Most of the controversial energy issues remained on the table.

In 2006, House Republicans did push legislation to allow the Secretary of Transportation to set car fuel economy standards after weighing a number of factors. By then, gasoline prices had risen to an annual average of $2.637 in real dollar terms for unleaded regular (see Figure 11.1), over a dollar per gallon higher than at the time of the OPEC embargo.[16] With the 2006 elections approaching, Republicans felt a need to respond in some way to growing public concern over gasoline prices. They did, however, defeat an amendment that Markey (D-MA) offered to the bill in the Energy and Commerce Committee to increase CAFE standards to 33 MPG by 2015, with auto district Democrats joining with Republicans in opposition. The Bush administration supported the bill. However, when it appeared the bill would face opposition in both chambers, the Republican leadership did not schedule it for floor consideration (Tollefson 2006).

Despite the rise in gasoline prices and projections that they would go higher, Republicans in Congress and the Bush administration were able to block efforts to increase CAFE standards for six years. Democrats with auto constituencies continued to join them in arguing that raising CAFE standards would impose unacceptable costs in terms of the competitiveness of the auto industry, jobs, and vehicle safety and costs. But increasingly CAFE standards, and energy issues more generally, were partisan. Republicans could pass production-oriented legislation in the House, but fairly united Democratic opposition in an increasingly polarized Senate meant the minority party could prevent cloture if it was perceived that legislation was positioned at the Republican median chamber position.[17] And Democrats were unwilling to leave the decision about increasing CAFE standards at the discretion of an administration that they viewed as being against significant increases.[18] Unlike the initial adoption of CAFE standards in the 1970s, compromises were not readily available even as the costs of the status quo increased with rising gasoline prices. Moreover, Republicans preferred the status quo to any position that would be acceptable to a sufficient number of Senate Democrats to invoke cloture. That position, however, became more difficult to defend as gasoline prices and the potential electoral costs increased. In addition, with the parties in tight competition for control of the House and Senate and with the expectations of very competitive presidential elections, the parties were reluctant to enact legislation for which their opponents could claim credit. As in Daniel Tichenor's narrative in Chapter 10 on immigration reform efforts during the same time period, forces blocking nonincremental policy change repeatedly prevailed.

A BREAKTHROUGH IN 2007

With the return of Democratic control of Congress for the first time in twelve years after the 2006 election, increasing CAFE standards had greater agenda priority. President Bush's opposition to a statutory-set increase presented a major obstacle. Rising gasoline prices had been one of the issues on which Republicans proved vulnerable in the 2006 elections and affected the political calculus going forward. Gasoline prices continued to increase in 2007 to new record highs with expectations that they would go even higher (and they did through 2008, exceeding $4.11 a gallon by early July before declining), creating a political context in which the status quo on CAFE standards was no longer an acceptable alternative. Both the Bush administration and key congressional Republicans indicated a willingness to support some changes in CAFE standards as part of an overall energy strategy, although coupled with fossil fuel production provisions. Bush proposed an annual increase in CAFE standards beginning in 2010, but treated it as a goal, not a requirement. And Ted Stevens (R-AK), the ranking Republican on the Senate Commerce Committee, introduced a bill calling for a 40 MPG standard as part of a package that included drilling in ANWR (Raju 2007). Meanwhile, Democratic congressional leaders designed a strategy to avoid splitting their membership on the issue and to limit the political costs of supporting a CAFE increase. They took advantage of bicameralism in an effort to address three energy issues – CAFE standards, transferring tax subsidies for fossils fuels in the 2005 legislation to alternative energy sources, and requiring utilities to use a certain percentage of renewable energy sources in the production of electricity.

Because support for a CAFE standards increase was stronger in the Senate than in the House and the reverse was the case with the other two provisions, Speaker Pelosi used bicameralism to her advantage and did not include CAFE standards in the House bill, instead allowing the Senate to deal with it. CAFE standards remained a difficult issue for some House Democrats who had ties to two core Democratic interest group constituencies, environmentalists and organized labor, especially the UAW, that were initially on opposite sides on CAFE standards' issue. If they were forced to vote on CAFE standards, many House Democrats would anger one of these groups. The House leadership could hold enough member support to pass a meaningful increase in CAFE standards, but the margin would be narrow. Instead of Speaker Pelosi and her members incurring political costs, she persuaded Ed Markey, the CAFE standards' main sponsor, to withdraw his amendment in exchange for Democrats opposed to Markey agreeing to drop their weaker alternative. The bill that passed the House contained provisions on subsidies for alternative fuels and on the use of renewables for electric utility generation but nothing on CAFE standards. By the time that the bill reached the House floor, the Senate had already passed an energy bill that included CAFE standard increases to 35 MPG by 2020 but without the subsidy or electricity generation provisions. Assuming that the CAFE provision survived a conference or other House-Senate negotiated agreement, Democratic House members would be able to support an increase in CAFE standards as part of an overall package without ever having to take a separate vote on a CAFE provision. In this way Speaker Pelosi's strategy insulated her party's members from potential electoral costs of voting for or against a CAFE increase. In the end, Pelosi held auto district Democrats after negotiating an agreement giving the NHTSA greater authority than the Environmental Protection Agency (EPA) in setting standards, as labor opposition to a significant CAFE increase diminished. On the key House vote concurring with the Senate amendment to the bill with an amendment (maintaining all three key provisions), only seven Democrats, all southern conservatives and/or from oil producing states, voted against it.

The Senate's resistance to the electric utility generation provision and the Bush administration's threat to veto the transfer of the tax break provision from fossil fuels to alternative sources meant that those two provisions were eventually dropped from the bill. The final passage vote of 314–100 in the House and the overwhelming support in the Senate on the cloture vote to concur with the House bill stripped to the two provisions understates the levels of controversy and the partisan conflict. Republicans blocked the tax subsidy for renewables and the electricity generation portions of the legislation; blocking the CAFE change was no longer a viable political option, even for many conservative members who preferred the status quo to an increase in CAFE standards. The political dimension trumped the ideological one.

President Bush, who had wanted his administration to retain the authority over mileage standards and had stated in a White House position paper that "Congress should not legislate a particular numeric fuel economy standard" (Baker 2007), signed the bill and tried to share credit with Speaker Pelosi at the ceremony. As I will discuss in the following, although the legislation required new numeric standards, the executive branch still had a role. Between the bill signing and the time Bush left office, however, neither he nor his DOT did much to expedite the implementation of the new CAFE standards.[19]

OBAMA SIDESTEPS CONGRESS

As passed, the EISA was designed to ensure that mileage for passenger and nonpassenger automobiles for sale in the United States would increase to 35 MPG by 2020. It gave authority to the Secretary of Transportation to "prescribe annual fuel economy standard increases that increase the applicable average fuel economy standard ratably beginning with the model year 2011 and ending with the model year 2020" (PL 110–140 2007, 121 Stat 1499). Congress' intent was that the executive branch would write regulations for auto manufacturers to reach that standard in a step-like fashion. The concern was that otherwise the executive would do less. So the law called for vehicles "beginning with model year 2011 to achieve a combined fuel economy average for model year 2020 of *at least* 35 miles per gallon."[20] In addition, for subsequent years 2021 to 2030, the legislation set the standard at "the maximum feasible average fuel economy for that model year" (PL 110–140 2007, 121 Stat 1499). It is fair to say that the parties to the legislation had assumed that as 2020 approached, the DOT would put forth a proposal for additional steps over the following decade or that Congress might then revisit CAFE standards. Instead the Obama administration unveiled a more far-reaching interpretation of its authority under EISA than anyone involved in its passage in 2007 had or could have anticipated and did so without Congress playing a role. Aware of the growing difficulty of enacting legislation because of Congress's increased use of blocking tactics, the Obama administration acted unilaterally, using existing authority to achieve its policy goals.

The strategy the administration employed with CAFE foreshadowed what was to follow on a broad range of domestic policy programs. Because of Congress's more frequent and vigorous use of its blocking powers, the administration chose to avoid it whenever possible, effectively weakening congressional policy influence. In the course of doing so, the executive assumed another policy process function that is frequently associated with legislatures in the policy process, interest aggregation.

When President Obama came to office in January 2009, the price of gasoline was less than $2.00 per gallon, under half of what it had been six months earlier, prior to the economic collapse, and hardly indicative of energy crisis conditions that had been necessary to enact major energy legislation in the past. Even with his party owning larger House and Senate majorities than any president enjoyed since 1994, there was little expectation that Congress would welcome a request for President Obama to revisit CAFE standards, an issue that Congress had seemingly put to bed in 2007. Yet within four months of taking office, Obama made it clear that CAFE standards and the interlocking issue of greenhouse gas emissions from automobiles were very high in terms of policy priority for his administration.[21] Having struggled with Congress over an economic stimulus package immediately upon taking office, anticipating great difficulty in enacting health care legislation, and concerned with the potential of unified Republican opposition to most of its domestic policy initiatives, the Obama administration chose to sidestep Congress and implement the increases in CAFE standards far more rapidly than anyone would have assumed when Congress enacted EISA. In a May 19 Rose Garden ceremony, the President signaled a major change in the decade-long timetable for meeting the goal of

35 MPG that the EISA had set. Surrounded by nine corporate automobile leaders, the head of the UAW, and several administration officials, President Obama addressed an audience that included the governors of California and Michigan, key congressional Democrats, other UAW officials, and the heads of leading environmental and health groups. He announced a new policy agreement among all the parties. That agreement called for meeting a CAFE standard of 35.5 MPG by 2016 and for the DOT and the EPA to set a single national standard on fuel efficiency and greenhouse gas emissions from automobiles and light trucks. In addition, all contending parties would agree to drop a series of pending lawsuits.

The president may have only exaggerated slightly in his remarks when he noted, "Now, in the past, an agreement such as this would have been considered impossible. It's no secret that these are folks who've occasionally been at odds for years, even decades. In fact, some of the groups here have been embroiled in lawsuits against one another."[22] When the EISA passed in 2007, the auto companies and the UAW had argued that they would have trouble meeting the standard by 2020. Less than two years later, they were agreeing to exceed it by 2016.

Of course, with the federal government holding large ownership stakes in General Motors and Chrysler, neither they nor the UAW were in a position to object to the president's actions. Still, there were a large number of other interests involved, including other auto manufacturers, over whom the administration did not have leverage. At a minimum, the administration could sell policy predictability to all players. Certainty about what mileage and emission standards would be and ensuring that different interests would accept the national standards allowed the auto companies to do the long-term planning necessary to produce vehicles, including design, plant construction, and retooling.

It is fair to say that, in the past, one side or the other among the groups at the event would have been at the other end of Pennsylvania Avenue, pleading its case with Congress to rein in the president's abuse of legislative authority and filing briefs in federal court, rather than accepting such an agreement. Beyond the symbolic handful of supportive Democratic House members and senators who were invited to the ceremony as observers, the role Congress was minimal. The EPA and NHTSA would still need to conduct the appropriate rule-making procedures, but it was for all practical purposes a fait accompli.[23] The administration had been able to bring all the competing interests together and reach an accommodation on a major policy change. Interest aggregation started and ended in the executive branch. No player with a significant material stake in either the fuel efficiency or greenhouse gas standards for automobiles and light trucks threatened to take its case for more favorable treatment to Congress. Thus, in this exercise of unilateral authority the president had an insurance policy against either Congress or the courts blocking or resisting him. Beyond all the limitations that Moe and

Howell (1999) discuss about the capacity of Congress or the courts to overturn presidential exercises of unilateral authority to achieve administration policy goals, getting the key interests to accept a change in CAFE standards meant that those groups would not be activating constituency pressure on House members and senators and that those who had been longstanding litigants would not choose to do so.

The effect of the Obama administration's interest aggregation efforts was even more critical when the president announced the second phase of his CAFE changes. In 2010 he requested that the DOT and EPA put together a CAFE proposal for the post-2016 period. Speaking on a stage with the heads of thirteen major automobile companies in July 2011, he announced CAFE standards for cars and light trucks for the 2017–25 model years with a goal of 54.5 MPG by 2025. In his speech the President pointedly observed: "And finally, this agreement ought to serve as a valuable lesson for leaders in Washington. This agreement was arrived at *without legislation.* You are all demonstrating what can happen when people put aside differences – these folks are competitors, you've got labor and business, but they decided, we're going to work together to achieve something important and lasting for the country."[24] That same day the DOT Secretary, Ray LaHood, and the EPA Administrator, Lisa Jackson, signed the appropriate document for publication in the Federal Register, and in early 2012 the agencies held a series of three field hearings.

With Republicans now firmly in control of the House and having taken every opportunity to register their policy differences with the administration on a full range of issues, one might have anticipated a major political conflict and greater resistance to the president exercising unilateral authority than had been the case in 2009. In fact, congressional response was muted and not all that different from what it had been following the 2009 announcement. Darrell Issa (R-CA), chair of the House Oversight and Government Reform Committee and a regular Obama administration critic, charged that the White House had engaged in a secret, and potentially illegal, deal that would increase the cost of automobiles. But in a speech at a battery plant in Michigan, President Obama mocked this criticism, declaring: "I brought together the world's largest auto companies, who agreed, for the first time, to nearly double the distance their cars can go on a gallon of gas. That's what we got done – and by the way, *we didn't go through Congress* to do it. But we did use the tools of government – us working together – to help make it happen" (McCardle 2011).[25]

Few interest groups were available to complain about the policy. Initially, the National Association of Auto Dealers (and others involved in the retailing side of the automobile business) expressed opposition because of concerns about the effect of increases in vehicle prices on sales. The auto companies quickly persuaded them to rethink their opposition. The House Energy and Commerce Committee decided to defer any action until the agencies completed the regulatory process (McCardle 2011).[26] Aside from one hearing at a sub-committee level of the House Oversight Committee at which neither represen-tatives of any of the auto companies or the UAW testified, there was little activity on Capitol Hill. Instead, congressional critics of the administration's energy policy focused their attack on the Obama decision to delay approval of the Keystone XL pipeline, arguably a decision of lesser magnitude than the CAFE standards. As in 2009, there was seemingly nothing in EISA that pre-vented the administration from proceeding as it did. The "maximum feasible" standard allowed under the law certainly left the president a good deal of discretion. But no one would have anticipated a change of this magnitude. The initial standard set in 1975 called for moving the mileage level of autos from 18 MPG in 1978 to 27.5 by the 1985 model year. In fact, that level was not met until the 1989 model year, where it remained until the EISA increase began in 2011 with an assumption of gradual increases, eventually reaching 35 MPG by 2020 and then some undefined amount in the following decade. Instead, the administration was going to exceed the first step in a little more than half the allotted time and nearly double the 1985 CAFE standard between 2011 and 2025.[27]

Despite the Obama administration initiating the biggest change in energy policy in decades, Congress did not even play a supporting role in enacting or opposing the policy change. Rather than downplaying his use of unilateral action, the president was gleeful in pointing to it. Beyond broadly interpreting executive authority in setting CAFE standards, the Obama administration assumed a functional policy process role in which Congress had traditionally excelled: interest aggregation. Although the executive is not a stranger to dealing with interest group demands in the development of public policy, Congress has traditionally thrived at balancing and adjusting provisions in response to the competing claims of affected interests. The literature on Con-gress is replete with research on the symbiotic relationships between Congress and the interest group community (Lowi 1969 and Fiorina 1977). In this instance, the president aggregated interests as a means of undercutting potential congressional opposition. By resolving interest group concerns, the adminis-tration prevented most of the affected groups from appealing to either Congress or the courts.[28]

One might reasonably argue that President Obama's decisions on CAFE standards did not require new legislation. Clearly, however, he stretched EISA beyond congressional intent. Congress might have challenged his actions as an overreach of executive authority. His ability to engage the support of all the interest group players, however, gave the process legitimacy that it would have otherwise lacked. Like the president, those groups preferred working with the executive branch rather than struggling with the delay and uncertainty of the contemporary congressional process. It is not just presidents who find it frus-trating to work with a Congress that is more focused on exercising negative power than resolving policy differences.

A BROADER PATTERN?

It would be one thing if the Obama administration's sidestepping of Congress on CAFE standards was an isolated instance. Then, this chapter would just be a case study of the nearly forty-year struggle over CAFE standards, ending with a president deciding to use existing authority rather than seeking new legislation to achieve the policy change he desired. In fact, CAFE is just one example of the Obama administration avoiding Congress to achieve its policy goals (although at times admitting it would be preferable to pass legislation). True, modern presidents have often found it convenient to use regulatory authority and executive orders to reach their policy goals. What is different is the apparent frequency with which the Obama administration and perhaps other recent administrations have sidestepped Congress and the openness with which they have admitted to doing so.[29]

Although the frequency with which Obama has taken unilateral action seems to have increased after the Republicans won back control of the House in 2010, the administration did not reserve the tactic for periods of divided party control. Instead it appears to have been part of a deliberate strategy in place since early in the Obama's first term. In addition to CAFE standards, there is evidence that during its first two years in office the administration considered achieving immigration reform without congressional action. Four senior officials in Citizenship and Immigration Services of the Department of Homeland Security produced a draft memorandum for the agency director entitled "Administrative Alternatives to Comprehensive Immigration Reform."[30] Although Obama waited until June 2012 to issue the executive order designed to fulfill many of the Development, Relief, and Education for Alien Minors (DREAM) Act's policy goals, the Senate defeated the cloture motion on the legislation in December 2010 when the Democrats still held majorities in both houses of Congress.

The impetus to avoid potential congressional obstruction increased in the 112th Congress. In February 2011, the president ordered the Department of Justice to stop enforcing the Defense of Marriage Act after Congress had not responded to his request to repeal it. Then, beginning in the fall of 2011 under the slogan of "We Can't Wait," the administration publicly announced its decision to use executive action (relying on existing authority) rather than trying to overcome congressional obstructionism. White House chief of staff, William Daley, declared: "We had been attempting to highlight the inability of Congress to do anything. The president expressed frustration, saying we have got to scour everything and push the envelope in finding things we can do on our own" (Savage 2012). The administration then followed with a stream of unilateral actions for legislation on which Congress was not acting, including jobs for veterans, drug shortages, and dealing with domestic violence. In each instance, the president made his bypassing of Congress a theme of his announcement. In cutting fees for federally insured mortgages, Obama noted:

"If Congress refuses to act, I've said that I'll continue to do everything in my power to act without them" (Savage 2012). Although some of these efforts were undertaken to highlight issues for the 2012 election, the trend continued after Obama's reelection. Repeatedly in the his 2013 State of the Union Address, President Obama requested Congress pass legislation but indicated implicitly, and at times explicitly, that he would use existing authority if Congress did not act. In discussing the issue of climate change, he threatened: "But if Congress won't act soon to protect future generations, I will. I will direct my Cabinet to come up with executive actions we can take, now and in the future, to reduce pollution, prepare our communities for the consequences of climate change, and speed the transition to more sustainable sources of energy."[31]

Some presidential threats to proceed, if Congress does not act, are undoubtedly for bargaining purposes or to place blame for policy inaction on Congress. But starting with CAFE standards, it is clear that the administration found that pursuing its policy goals through negotiations with Congress often imposed high costs and few benefits. As Congress has increased the use of blocking power to achieve policy influence, the executive has had a growing incentive to pursue policy change through means other than legislation.

Importantly, the Obama administration has claimed that it would prefer it if Congress negotiated over the passage of legislation rather than requiring the executive to choose between inaction and the use of unilateral authority. Legislation has several advantages over unilateral executive action. First, passage of legislation may provide a greater sense of legitimacy. That may assist with public support for the program and with getting others to cooperate with its implementation. Congressional Republicans have recently sued President Obama over his use of executive authority over delaying employer sanctions as they apply to the Affordable Care Act and the suspension of deportations for some groups of undocumented aliens. Both cases raise questions about the legitimacy of executive action because of the absence of legislation. Second, unilateral executive action may not have the permanence of legislation. In cases of changes that the president makes with executive orders, a president's successor has the ability to reverse the policy with another executive order (although that is not always feasible). Third, using unilateral action through existing authority may limit the available policy formulations and produce suboptimal outcomes because of the legal constraints on existing executive authority. For example, when he was unable to get Congress to pass the DREAM Act, Obama's alternative for dealing with the immigration problems of undocumented young people through unilateral action did not resolve all the issues they faced or produce comprehensive immigration reform, as Chapter 10 documents. The executive order did postpone for at least two years deportation of those it covered and also allowed them to obtain work permits but did not provide for permanent residency or a path to citizenship. Finally, the congressional process might produce better public policy than the president does through unilateral action. The input of Congress in designing legislation can provide useful perspectives that might not be forthcoming when the deliberation is within the narrower confines of the executive branch. It is probably correct that presidents would prefer legislation to unilateral action in many instances, if the former is politically feasible.

CONCLUSION

Getting Congress to enact energy legislation over the past forty years has never been easy. Because proposals to make the United States less dependent on foreign sources normally imposed short-term costs on the public in exchange for long-term benefits, it was difficult to persuade House members and senators to support legislation that might increase their electoral vulnerability. Only when the costs of maintaining the status quo imposed significant political liabilities were the competing sides willing to resolve key issues and produce nonincremental policy change. Often the skill of congressional leaders in packaging the legislation in such a way as to persuade members that they could avoid traceability of costs was also an essential ingredient to the passage of legislation. Those conditions were met in the mid-1970s and again in 2007 with CAFE standards. In the intervening years, efforts to deal with CAFE standards (and after 1980 with other major energy issues) faltered in Congress.

Perhaps surprisingly to many, the movement of parties in Congress to more closely approach the "responsible party government" ideal did not improve the capacity of Congress to enact energy legislation. Barbara Sinclair correctly concludes that during the 111th Congress, with unified party control of government and sizeable party majorities in both chambers, many major pieces of legislation were enacted. And it does stand in stark contrast with the 112th and 113th Congresses. But those results were achieved at substantial political and policy costs. (In Chapter 9, Oberlander demonstrates the political necessity of sacrificing cost controls in the enactment of the Affordable Care Act, for example.) The minority party has increased incentives to block proposals, even as a more unified majority party has given its leadership the power to hold members' support for party positions and as party loyalty has increasingly trumped committee loyalty. As Mann and Ornstein (2012) argue, the congressional parties have taken on the adversarial cast of parliamentary parties but are doing so in a checks and balances constitutional system that limits the abilities of majorities to act. During period of divided party control, the effects of this mismatch have been exacerbated. Even when there is unified party control of government, however, the capacity of and the incentives for the minority to block significant policy change persist. The tight competition between the parties for majority status (the size of the party majority in the 111th Congress is the exception) has meant that the minority party has little reason to compromise. Resolving policy disputes may allow the majority to win governing credit and thus undercut the chances for the minority to gain majority status in the next election. Moreover, if the minority believes that it will be in a stronger position after the next election, it has few incentives to resolve an issue today because it believes that it will hold a stronger bargaining position after the election.

As it has become more difficult and costly for the presidents to achieve their policy goals through the congressional process, they find the exercise of unilateral authority a more attractive alternative. Instead of investing resources to build support for their legislation in Congress, presidents will invest to ensure that affected interest groups are on board with their proposals for unilateral action.

To some it may appear that Congress is exercising substantial policy influence when it blocks policy initiatives or uses its veto powers for bargaining purposes. But in fact, that is not the case. The president and the executive branch instead have decided to bypass Congress more frequently. As a strategic player, the president, faced with a very costly congressional process, has pursued other means to achieve desired outcomes. The analysis of the struggle over CAFE standards that I have presented in this chapter demonstrates how these changes have occurred over time from a period of relatively weak congressional parties to a period during which the parties became more homogeneous and polarized. In the former, policy change was not easy but could be achieved with bargaining at the committee and subcommittee level, compromises, attracting support from members of the other party, and without constant threats of filibusters, vetoes, and electoral revenge. By the 1990s the growing influence of conditional party government and the more adversarial stance of the parties further limited the room for building policy consensus and resolving issues in Congress. Faced with this dilemma, presidents may pursue unilateral action, as Obama did with CAFE standards. Unlike Harry Truman, who used a recalcitrant Congress primarily as a political foil, contemporary presidents possess far greater statutory and administrative authority. As Moe and Howell observed: "it is crucial to recognize that the president is greatly empowered by the sheer proliferation of statutes over time" (1999, 860). Presidents often have other options available to change public policy than getting Congress to pass new legislation or to amend existing law.

Importantly, the interest group community is often a sympathetic player in these efforts. Although Moe and Howell (1999) correctly point to the incentives for presidents to take unilateral action, their primary focus is on the strategic behavior of the president, Congress, and the courts. Interest groups and the mass public may play important roles as well. Unless their preference is to preserve the status quo, interest groups with material, and not just ideological, stakes also find Congress increasingly frustrating. So the opportunity to resolve policy difference through nonlegislative means that the president and the executive branch may offer may prove an attractive option to interest groups. They may gladly cooperate in this transition away from Congress. Where the executive branch once served primarily as an appeals court for interest groups dissatisfied with congressional outcomes, the executive is now their first stop. Part of the president's goal, as in the case of CAFE standards, is to ensure the interest groups' concerns are resolved in such a way that none of them appeals the outcome to Congress. Similarly, the mass public, desiring responsiveness from government, may accept unilateral presidential action rather than gridlock. The end result of these strategic changes is a decline in Congress's policy influence and greater acceptance of new extensions of executive authority.

Of course, these conclusions are tentative. I have not presented data demonstrating that the frequency with which presidents sidestep Congress to achieve their policy goals has increased. Developing a method for measuring that over time is an important next step. What is clear is that the Obama administration is engaging in this behavior very publicly, even to the point of bragging about making major policy changes without Congress. In addition, I have not done enough detailed analysis of other policy areas to be completely comfortable in claiming that the case of CAFE standards is representative. Nevertheless, the analysis of the struggle over CAFE standards over nearly a four-decade period hopefully provides useful insights into the impact that process changes have on the capacity of U.S. governmental institutions to address critical issues of public policy.

Notes

1. One might just as easily examine a policy that those favoring increasing the supply of fossil fuels have advocated, allowing drilling in the Arctic National Wildlife Refuge (ANWR), and reach similar conclusions (Oppenheimer 2014).
2. It is not my intent in this paper to discuss the efficacy of the policy goal of reducing dependence on foreign energy sources.
3. For elaborations of conditional party government theory, see Rohde (1991) and Aldrich (1995).
4. In this sense it is useful to think of policy as the independent variable affecting a process.
5. Of course, this is not always the case. Especially in periods of budget constraints, members with reputations for pork barrel projects sometimes find themselves under attack as "wasteful spenders."
6. It should be noted that it was easier to reach such an agreement in 1990 because the players did not perceive that partisan control of Congress was likely to be in play in the next election. Importantly, however, House Republicans, influenced by the electoral strategy of Newt Gingrich, refused to support the agreement. And President George H. W. Bush did pay an electoral cost because supporting the agreement violated his 1988 campaign promise not to raise taxes.
7. In the 1950s and 1960s, energy legislative issues were treated according to their separate sources (oil, gas, coal, nuclear, etc.) and fit the concentrated benefits/dispersed cost model. Support for ethanol purchase guarantees as part of broader energy packages is a notable exception. It is a more recent example of pork barrel provisions (in these instances efforts to win support of House members and senators representing corn-producing constituencies).

8. The sixty-two includes the Independent who caucuses with the Democrats and the contested Senate seat in New Hampshire that was not decided until September, 1975.

9. The 1988 Republican platform called for deregulation to bring technological change to transportation as "far preferable to outmoded regulation, such as the current design of corporate average fuel economy (CAFE) standards, which create substantial advantages for foreign auto manufacturers and actually promote the export of U.S. jobs."

10. Neither of these groups has totally disappeared. Republicans continued to struggle for support from their House members and senators from the Northeast when pro-energy production policies, such as opening off-shore and environmentally sensitive areas to drilling, were perceived as having negative environmental consequences. In addition, there remained a few Democratic House members and senators from producing constituencies.

11. Modest energy bills passed in 1991 and 2005, but both were stripped of controversial provisions.

12. The omnibus energy bill reported by the Subcommittee on Energy and Power of the House Committee on Energy and Commerce did not contain a provision on CAFE standards. If it had, the full committee chair, John Dingell, would have strongly opposed it.

13. Prior to DeLay's amendment, a Michigan Republican member of the House Appropriations Committee, Joe Knollenberg, placed a provision in the committee report for the Department of Transportation appropriations bill that reduced funding that might be used to implement increased mileage standards on vans and light trucks.

14. In the House bill HR 4, auto producers would have to save about 3.7 percent of gas consumption over six years. The Senate bill, S 517, required NHTSA to increase mileage standards for cars and light trucks but only after considering costs, economic impact, and safety consequences. And only if NHTSA did not act could Congress then decide to raise standards.

15. An amendment Ed Markey (D-MA) offered during subcommittee consideration in the House requiring cuts in petroleum demand for vehicles over a five-year period, thus forcing an increase in CAFE standards in a circuitous manner, was rejected 6–24 (Goldreich 2003b). In the Senate, advocates of CAFE increases complained that the bill's criteria that the DOT had to consider before increasing standards made it more difficult to do so than under existing law (Goldreich 2003a). Thus, had Congress passed an energy bill, it would not have contained any measurable change in CAFE standards.

16. The price data is from "Total Annual Energy Review" U.S. Energy Information Administration, September 27, 2012, www.eia.gov/totaltnergy/data/annual/show text.cfm?t=ptb0524. The price is calculated in chained (2005) dollars.

17. For a more detailed analysis of the effect of "conditional party government" on efforts to pass energy legislation in the 2001–06 period, see Oppenheimer and Hetherington (2008). Ironically, when Republicans attached ANWR exploration to the budget reconciliation process to avoid a Senate filibuster of the issue, a group of environmentally sensitive House Republicans blocked action in that chamber.

18. NHTSA had made incremental increases in the standard for light trucks during the Bush administration. In 2006, it raised the standard to 24 MPG, beginning in 2011. The 1975 law did not set standards for light trucks but left those decisions to the DOT.

19. The administration did propose to increase the target for vans, SUVs, and smaller pick-up trucks to 28.6 MPG by 2015 but discouraged states from adopting stricter mileage standards than provided for in the new law (Bettelheim 2008).
20. Italics added.
21. Work on an agreement as complex and involving as many parties as this one must have begun shortly after the new administration took office, if not earlier, suggesting that it was a high-priority issue.
22. www.whitehouse.gov/the-press-office/Remarks-by-the-President-on-national-fuel-efficiency-standards, May 19, 2009.
23. Jody Freeman provides an excellent analysis of the coordinated rule-making activity between EPA and NHTSA (Freeman 2011).
24. www.whitehouse.gov/the-pres-office/2011/07/29/remarks-president-fuel. Italics added.
25. Italics added.
26. On August 28, 2012, LaHood and Jackson announced that the standards were finalized. The Energy and Commerce Committee took no action.
27. In addition, the new standard covered light trucks.
28. Ironically, those wanting to overturn unilateral presidential action would likely find it more difficult to do in a Congress that was more subject to partisan gridlock. So (undelete) the president might choose to act unilaterally rather than try to pass legislation (delete) it likely became more difficult for Congress to overturn the presidential exercise of unilateral action.
29. Data across administrations on the use of executive orders in place of legislation would certainly be useful but go beyond the scope of this paper. And executive orders are not the only vehicles that presidents have at their disposal.
30. The draft memo is undated. It was later leaked to Senator Charles Grassley (R-IA) and resulted in the resignation of one of its authors.
31. "Full Text: President Obama's 2013 State of the Union Address." www.forbes.com/sites/beltway/2013/02/12/full-text-president-obamas-20.

References

Aldrich, John H. 1995. *Why Parties? The Origin and Transformation of Political Parties in America*. Chicago, IL: University of Chicago Press.

Arnold, R. Douglas. 1990. *The Logic of Congressional Action*. New Haven, CT: Yale University Press.

Baker, Peter. 2007. "Solidarity for Bush, Democrats; Looking Past Disputes, Sides Join Together to Enact Energy Bill." *Washington Post*, December 20: A18.

Bettelheim, Adriel. 2008. "Regulations Provide Fuel for Federalism." *CQ Weekly*, May 5: 1154.

Chiou, Fany-Yi, and Lawrence S. Rothenberg. 2014. "The Elusive Search for Presidential Power." *American Journal of Political Science* 58 (3): 653–8.

Davis, Joseph A. 1989. "Arctic-Drilling Plan Clears Committee." *CQ Weekly*, March 18: 598.

Dodd, Lawrence C., and Bruce I. Oppenheimer. 1977. "The House in Transition." In Lawrence C. Dodd and Bruce I. Oppenheimer, eds., *Congress Reconsidered*. New York: Prager, pp. 21–53.

Evans, Diana. 1994. "Policy and Pork: The Use of Pork Barrel Projects to Build Policy Coalitions in the House of Representatives." *American Journal of Political Science*, 38: 894–917.

2011. "Pork Barrel Politics." In Eric Schickler and Frances E. Lee, eds., *The Oxford Handbook of the American Congress*. New York: Oxford University Press, pp. 315–39.

Fiorina, Morris P. 1977. *Congress: The Keystone to the Washington Establishment*. New Haven, CT: Yale University Press.

Ford, Gerald R. 1975. "Statement on the Energy Policy and Conservation Act." December 22, 1975. Online by Gerhard Peters and John T. Wooley, *The American Presidency Project*. www.presidency.ucsb.edu/ws/?pid=5452.

Freeman, Jody. 2011. "The Obama Administration's National Auto Policy: Lessons from the 'Car Deal.'" *Harvard Environmental Law Review* 35: 343–74.

Goldreich, Samuel. 2003a. "Senate Braces for Floor Battle over Omnibus Energy Bill." *CQ Weekly*, May 3: 1042.

Goldreich, Samuel. 2003b. "Vote against ANWR Drilling Hits Core of Bush Energy Plan." *CQ Weekly*, March 22: 698.

Hager, George. 1995. "As They Cut, Appropriators Add a Stiff Dose of Policy." *CQ Weekly*, July 29: 2245.

Howell, William G. 2003. *Power without Persuasion: The Politics of Direct Presidential Action*. Princeton, NJ: Princeton University Press.

Idelson, Holly. 1991. "Energy: Varying Interests Tie Hopes to Fast-Moving Omnibus." *CQ Weekly*, March 16: 669.

Lowi, Theodore J. 1969. *The End of Liberalism*. New York: Norton.

Mann, Thomas E., and Norman J. Ornstein. 2012. *It's Worse Than It Looks: How the American Constitutional System Collided with the New Politics of Extremism*. New York: Basic Books.

McCardle, John. 2011. "House Oversight Chairman Widens Probe into CAFÉ Standards Deal." *New York Times*, August 12. www.nytimes.com/gwire/2011/08/12/12greenwire-house-oversight-chairm.

Moe, Terry M., and William G. Howell. 1999. "Unilateral Action and Presidential Power: A Theory." *Presidential Studies Quarterly* 29: 850–73.

Oppenheimer, Bruce I. 2014. "ANWR and CAFE: Frustrating Energy Production and Conservation Initiatives over Three Decades." Paper presented at the Congress and History Conference, University of Maryland, June 11–12.

Oppenheimer, Bruce I., and Marc J. Hetherington. 2008. "Catch-22: Cloture, Energy Policy and the Limits of Conditional Party Government." In Nathan W. Monroe, Jason M. Roberts, and David W. Rohde, eds., *Why Not Parties?: Party Effects in the United States Senate*. Chicago, IL: University of Chicago Press.

Plungis, Jeff. 2000. "Congress again Feeling Heat over Surging Gasoline Prices." *CQ Weekly*, June 17: 1461.

Public Law 110–140. 2007. "Energy Independence and Security Act of 2007." 121 Stat. 1499.

Raju, Manu. 2007. "Ted Stevens Gets Ever So Greener." *CQ Weekly*, January 15: 156.

Rohde, David W. 1991. *Parties and Leaders in the Post-Reform House*. Chicago, IL: University of Chicago Press.

Rottinghaus, Brandon. 2014. "Exercising Unilateral Discretion: Presidential Use of Unilateral Powers in a Shared Powers System." Paper presented at the Conference on Executive Politics, Washington University, St. Louis, MO.

Rudalevige, Andrew. 2002. *Managing the President's Program: Presidential Leadership and Legislative Policy Formation*. Princeton, NJ: Princeton University Press.

Rudalevige, Andrew. 2014. "The Letter of the Law: Administrative Discretion and Obama's Domestic Unilateralism." *The Forum* 12 (1): 29–59.

Savage, Charlie. 2012. "Shift on Executive Power Lets Obama Bypass Rivals." www.ny times.com/2012/04/23/us/politics/shift-on-executive-powers-let-obama-bypass-con gress.html?_r=0.

Shepsle, Kenneth A., and Barry R. Weingast. 1981. "Political Preferences for the Pork Barrel." *American Journal of Political Science* 25: 96–111.

Thurber, James A. 2013. "The Dynamics and Dysfunction of the Congressional Budget Process: From Inception to Deadlock." In Lawrence C. Dodd and Bruce I. Oppenheimer, eds. Washington, DC: CQ Press.

Tollefson, Jeff. 2006. "New CAFÉ Standards for Autos Allowed under House Measure." *CQ Weekly*, May 15: 1332.

PART V

REFLECTIONS

12

Explaining Legislative Achievements

R. Douglas Arnold

LEGISLATIVE ACHIEVEMENTS

What makes for a productive Congress? Scholars have struggled with this question for many years. David Mayhew launched the formal quest for an answer with his provocative book, *Divided We Govern* (1991, 2005). For Mayhew, a productive Congress is one that generates many important laws, with importance assessed either contemporaneously by journalists or retrospectively by policy experts.[1] Other scholars have compared the laws that Congress enacted with those that it might have enacted. Scholars mining this vein differ in what denominator they use to compare actual bill passage – presidential proposals, party platforms, issues discussed in newspaper editorials – but all agree that a high ratio of bills passed to bills sought is a good measure of legislative productivity.[2]

It is never quite clear why bill production is supposed to be a good measure of legislative achievement. Why are more laws something to celebrate? We do not assess presidents by the number of executive orders issued, courts by the number of trials held, regulatory agencies by the number of rules established, or firefighters by the number of fires fought. Indeed, scholars do not assess each other by the sheer number of books and articles published; accomplished scholars are those rich in ideas, not those with the most pages in print. So why is bill production, or its variant, bills produced as a fraction of bills sought, something that scholars equate with legislative achievement? Once measured, why do scholars spend so much time working to explain fluctuations over time in bill production?

One possibility is that bill production reflects the common notion that whenever a problem is identified, "there ought to be a law" to resolve it. More laws are a signal that Congress is addressing more problems. Unfortunately, people disagree as to whether some situation is merely a condition to be endured (noisy motorcycles) or a serious problem to be solved (gun-wielding terrorists boarding commercial aircraft).[3] Sometimes doing nothing is the better choice. Even when all agree that something is a problem, people disagree as to whether it should be resolved by private action, local government, or national government.

Equating bill production with legislative achievement incorporates a liberal bias into the assessment. In most domestic policy areas, liberals are more inclined to governmental action than are conservatives. A Congress dominated by liberal legislators might pass 100 bills to create 100 programs to solve 100 problems. Another Congress filled with conservative legislators might pass one bill to eliminate fifty programs and another to reduce funding for fifty others. A third Congress evenly balanced between liberals and conservatives might pass nothing other than a series of continuing resolutions to fund all programs at their current levels. Why is it a good measure of legislative achievement to score the first legislature as highly productive, the second as barely productive, and the third as unproductive? Doing so reflects nothing more than that creating programs requires more and longer bills than killing, slashing, defunding, or maintaining them.[4]

The same liberal bias appears in studies that attempt to adjust bill production for the demand for legislation. Sarah Binder's (1999; 2003; 2014) studies of bill production (and its opposite, gridlock) measure the demand for legislation by counting unsigned editorials in the *New York Times* between 1947 and 2012. It is a reasonable measure. Her results might have been very different, however, if she had counted unsigned editorials in the *Wall Street Journal*. The editorial board at the *Times* believes that new laws are needed to address innumerable problems, whereas the editorial board at the *Journal* recognizes few problems that require governmental solutions, and even fewer that require solutions imposed by the federal government.[5] Measuring demand is not so easy once we recognize that people disagree about whether national government should enact any legislation to address particular problems.

Perhaps a better measure of demand would be rooted in what policies citizens want Congress to enact, and a better measure of legislative achievement would be what proportion of these bills Congress actually enacts. Although normatively appealing, these two measures stumble over the shallowness of public opinion. What do citizens really want? How could we know? Citizens' responses to survey questions are easily affected by small changes in question ordering. Pollsters unveil supportive or opposing publics partly by how they frame questions about policy proposals (Zaller 1992). It is difficult for polls to capture the trade offs inherent in real-world policy choices. Asked separate questions, citizens regularly support increased funding for health, education, transportation, the environment, children, seniors, and many other worthy ends (only welfare and foreign aid are regular candidates for cuts); these same citizens regularly oppose the increased taxes that would support expanding these valued programs (Stimson 2004, 37–50). Pollsters also have trouble measuring the intensity of citizens' opinions. Knowing that a proposal's proponents outnumber its opponents is not the same as knowing that the latter are intensely opposed and would work to punish legislators who approved it, while the former are only moderately favorable and would quickly forget legislators' actions. Legislators are better equipped to gauge intensity than are pollsters. Moreover, it is not a defect of democracy that legislators weigh the intensity of citizens' opinions; they would not survive in office if they did not. In short, public opinion does not provide a firm foundation for political scientists to evaluate legislative accomplishments.

A second possibility is that scholars study bill production because bills are easy to count and sum. Unfortunately, bills are not so easy to categorize. Mayhew (1991, 2005) created sensible decision rules to identify legislative enactments as either important (included) or unimportant (excluded). So, too, did Howell et al. (2000), who divided legislative enactments into landmark, major, ordinary, and minor.[6] The problem is not the dividing line between adjacent categories, but that individual categories still contain vastly dissimilar items. Was the 83rd Congress (1953–54) under Eisenhower, which passed nine important bills, really as productive as the 97th Congress (1981–82) under Reagan, which also passed nine important bills (Mayhew 1991, table 4.1)? The principal news from the 83rd Congress was that Eisenhower, the first Republican president in two decades, did not attempt to roll back the New Deal. The nine legislative enactments were important, but they did nothing to shift the direction of national policy.[7] The principal news from the 97th Congress was that Reagan, the first conservative in the White House since Hoover, pushed two bills through Congress – the Omnibus Budget Reconciliation Act of 1981 and the Economic Recovery Tax Act of 1981 – that dramatically changed the direction of national policy. The first reversed the decades-long growth of domestic spending; the second constricted future revenues so that it would be difficult for future presidents and legislators to restore domestic programs or resume spending growth. These two bills completely overshadowed the other seven bills.[8] Moreover, they were two of the most consequential bills in a generation, as Mayhew notes by coding them "historically important." Despite this notation, the data set that Mayhew and others have analyzed considers the 83rd and 97th Congresses as equally productive. How can that be, when the 83rd Congress merely confirmed the direction of national policy, while the 97th Congress launched a major reversal in national policy, one that is still being felt three decades later?

My argument about legislative achievement is not just about concepts and measurement. It is about how we should view recent congresses. Many commentators call the most recent Congress (the 113th, 2013–14) the least productive in modern history. If one believes a count of legislative enactments is a good measure of legislative achievement, that assessment is close to the truth (the 112th Congress was actually less productive).[9] On the other hand, if one believes that leaving a large imprint on national policy is a sign of legislative achievement, the assessment is questionable. The Republican House in the 112th and 113th Congresses (the important actions span the two) left a huge imprint on national policy by its relentless efforts to reduce federal spending. Beginning with a showdown over raising the debt limit, and then a backup sequestration plan that liberal legislators thought would never be implemented, Republicans cut discretionary spending by a larger fraction than did President Reagan and the 97th Congress in 1981. Senator Patty Murray (D-WA), chair of the Senate Budget Committee, estimates that the budget battles during these two congresses will reduce the federal deficit by $3.3 trillion between 2010 and 2024 (Murray 2014).[10] Why isn't an achievement of this magnitude reflected in political scientists' measures of legislative effectiveness?

The House Speaker certainly rejects the metrics that political scientists have been using. When Bob Schieffer of CBS News asked Speaker John Boehner (R-OH) how he felt about presiding over "what is perhaps the least productive and certainly one of the least popular congresses in history," Boehner replied, "We should not be judged on how many new laws we create. We ought to be judged on how many laws that we repeal" (Jacoby 2013). Of course, the Republican House did not repeal many laws. Repeal would require the cooperation of a Democratic Senate and a Democratic president. Nevertheless, the Republicans achieved many of their goals through budgetary brinksmanship – threatening to default on federal debt, shut down the government, or go over the fiscal cliff – if others did not accept major cuts in spending. If legislative productivity is defined as enacting one's preferences into law, then the recent Republican House was vastly more successful than many congresses that passed longer lists of important bills.

Those who insist that the recent Congress was unproductive argue that citizens did not really want so many programs cut. Of course, that is true when citizens are asked about individual programs. But when they are asked about cutting deficits and balancing budgets, citizens are often enthusiastic about those options too. Which of these contradictory opinions should we believe? House Republicans have long campaigned for smaller government; citizens have given them control of the House for sixteen of the last twenty years. Rather than scoring House Republicans as unproductive, why aren't we concluding that they are finally delivering what they have long promised? If citizens are truly upset by these actions, the Founders created biennial opportunities for them to register their disapproval and dispatch a replacement team.

Enacting important bills is a good measure of legislative achievement, but it is not the only one. As Mayhew admits, it does best when Congress is enacting binding rules (civil rights, safety regulation, taxes) and least well when Congress is adjusting spending programs, especially when those adjustments are made incrementally (or decrementally) in a series of appropriations, authorization, or budget bills (Mayhew 1991, 41). Counting legislative enactments is a great way to judge legislative achievements in the 1960s and 1970s, when a bipartisan surge of enthusiasm for new programs and regulations encouraged

Congress to enact many landmark, important, and major bills. Unfortunately, counting legislative enactments misses much of the action in the early 1980s, when retrenchment was first beginning, and most of the action today, when retrenchment is the dominant story.

Assessing legislative achievements requires that we pay attention to what legislators seek to accomplish. What are their policy goals? What are their priorities? When majorities of legislators seek to create many new programs, a good measure of achievement is how many programs they actually establish. When majorities of legislators seek to reduce or eliminate many programs, a good measure of achievement is how many programs they actually reduce or eliminate. If legislators can fulfill their policy goals in just a few bills – whether called omnibus, reconciliation, sequestration, or something else – it is no less notable than if they achieve their goals with dozens of separate bills.

EXPLAINING LEGISLATIVE ACHIEVEMENTS

Why are some congresses more successful in achieving legislators' policy goals than others? The most important factor is the degree to which legislators share common goals. Common goals facilitate action; conflicting goals sustain inaction. The 9/11 attacks on New York and Washington unified Congress, giving legislators common policy goals that quickly overwhelmed their previously divergent goals on a host of issues. Within weeks, legislators gave the president powers to track, arrest, and prosecute terrorists domestically and to use force against terrorists abroad. Congress nationalized airport security, bailed out the airlines, and appropriated $40 billion for domestic security and rebuilding New York City. Passing any of these bills would have been inconceivable a few months earlier without intense debates about presidential powers, domestic wiretapping, the dangers of bailing out private corporations, or the fiscal constraints impeding massive new spending on anything. After the attack, these concerns largely disappeared as legislators developed common goals of preventing future terrorism and helping the country recover and rebuild.

Such unity of purpose is rare. In most policy arenas, legislators' policy goals are in direct conflict. The rise of spatial thinking among congressional scholars – everything can be explained by noting legislators' ideal points on a single ideological dimension – blinds one to the fact that most coalition leaders operate in a complicated multidimensional world. Health care reform is more than just an ideological battle between leftists who want the national government to do more and rightists who want it to do less. It is a battle between all the private interest groups that are involved in financing and delivering health care, including insurance companies, pharmaceutical companies, device makers, hospitals, nursing homes, home health care agencies, physicians, and radiologists. Not to be forgotten are those who pay the bills (employers, employees, patients, state and local governments), those who care about particular services (mental health, contraceptives, hospice, abortion, cancer trials), those who have vested interests in particular delivery schemes (Medicare, Medicaid, employer-sponsored health care, veterans' hospitals), and those who receive or hope to receive health care and whose current access varies widely depending on their income, age, employment status, geographic location, and health. Given these conflicts and crosscutting cleavages, the surprise is not why it took more than a generation to enact the Affordable Care Act, but why Congress was able to enact any comprehensive reform in 2010. And given the stakes – nearly one-fifth of the American economy – it is no surprise that conflict persisted long after enactment.

There is no easy metric to summarize the degree of agreement or conflict among legislators' policy goals. We cannot say that the congressional unity after 9/11 should be scored 100 and the perennial conflict over health care should be scored 10, 20, or any other number. We are on firmer footing using ordinal categories. Health care and taxes generally belong near the conflictual end of the continuum, since there is so much discord over so many dimensions. Agricultural policy is ordinarily less conflictual, since it is first a contest between organized agricultural producers and unorganized consumers (the organized usually win), and second a competition among various agricultural interests (logrolling allows each group to win something). Providing disaster assistance after earthquakes, hurricanes, tornadoes, and floods usually occupies the less-contested end of the spectrum, as everyone rallies to aid helpless victims. Notice that all three statements include adverbial modifiers, for events can quickly transform the conflictual into the uncontested (think 9/11 and wiretapping), and clever entrepreneurs can reframe issues to increase or decrease conflict. The once-impossible goal of tax reform became possible in 1986 through artful reframing. More recently, disaster assistance and agricultural policy have become more conflictual as conservatives have tried to reduce the role of government in arenas where governmental action had long been accepted.

It helps if we consider separately four types of cleavages that animate most policy debates. First, there is *ideological conflict*, often centered on the proper role of government. Some legislators believe the government should do more to alleviate innumerable problems. Others believe the government – or at least national government – should do less. Second, there is *group conflict* between the various interests that would profit or pay if current policy changes. Coal plant operators see the world differently than nature lovers; so do bankers and borrowers, labor and management, gun owners and those concerned with gun violence. Third, there is *geographic conflict* between the regions, states, and localities that would profit or suffer from policy change. Areas where energy is produced see the world differently than energy-consuming areas. Geographic conflict is actually a variant of group conflict; its importance flows from the fact that legislators represent geographically defined districts.[11] Fourth, there is *partisan conflict* between the majority party, which wants to appear competent, responsible, and productive, and the minority party, which wants the majority to look incompetent, unproductive, and unreasonable.

Most legislators acquire some of their policy goals long before they enter elective politics. Certainly that is true for their basic ideological perspectives on the world, as well as their attitudes toward various groups in society, such as organized labor, corporations, or environmentalists. Many policy goals, however, are shaped by the pursuit of election and reelection. Ambitious career-minded politicians acquire positions on a wide range of policies in order to attract and retain support from contributors, activists, and voters in primary and general elections.

Primary elections tug especially hard at congressional candidates. Although few citizens vote in primary elections, those who do tend to have more extreme and more intense views than do nonvoters (Jacobson 2013). The extremity of primary electorates affects the type of candidates who survive the initial round in congressional contests. Candidates may enter politics with liberal, moderate, or conservative views, but the need to appeal to primary voters pulls Democratic candidates leftward and Republic candidates rightward. The same forces pull candidates with moderate views on abortion toward opposite ends of the abortion spectrum – pro-life for Republican candidates, pro-choice for Democrats. Republicans running for office are asked to sign the Norquist pledge that they will never vote to raise taxes; few Republican candidates risk the fury of campaign contributors or primary voters by suggesting they might have open minds on fiscal matters. Candidates from both parties quickly learn how complicated are the views of various local firms and organization in their districts. It is not *the* banking interest that they must learn to appreciate – for community banks have little in common with large multinational banks – but the views of actual bankers in their districts.

Conflict in Congress today is more intense than it was two or three decades ago. One reason is that more of the underlying ideological, group, geographic, and partisan cleavages align directly. They are reinforcing rather than crosscutting cleavages. A crosscutting cleavage is one where a program's advocates include legislators from both parties, from various ideological persuasions, and from a diverse group of states and localities. Agricultural programs long had this character, especially in the Senate, since most states had significant agricultural interests, and these interests were represented by liberals, moderates, and conservatives from both parties. A reinforcing cleavage is one where all the pressures on legislators shove them in the same direction. Tax policy currently has this character, especially for Republican legislators, as their conservative impulses suggest that lower taxes are always better, their alliances with corporations and the affluent reinforce these impulses, and their taking of the Norquist pledge makes even small deviations from the pledge politically costly.

Political scientists have long noted that the two parties have become more ideologically distinct than they were in the 1960s and 1970s. The Republican party was once populated with liberal, moderate, and conservative legislators;

today's Republican legislators differ only in their degree of conservatism. The Democratic party was once populated with liberal, moderate, and conservative legislators; today's Democratic legislators are mostly liberals, with a smattering of moderates. The most conservative Democratic legislator is now more liberal than the most liberal Republican legislator. This alignment of party and ideology makes it increasingly difficult to build bipartisan coalitions in issue areas where ideology is dominant.

An increasing number of group conflicts also align with the underlying partisan divide. Democratic politicians have long championed the interests of labor, African Americans, and the poor, while Republicans have championed the interests of corporations, small businesses, and the wealthy. Politically it matters that these group interests are geographically dispersed. More recently, other group interests have become aligned with parties, interests that are more geographically concentrated. For example, the production of petroleum, natural gas, wheat, corn, and cotton is now heavily concentrated in Republican districts. Eighty percent of the top thirty oil-producing congressional districts were represented by Republicans in the 112th Congress, as were 80 percent of the top thirty gas-producing districts, 83 percent of the top thirty wheat-producing districts, 77 percent of the top thirty corn-producing districts, and 73 percent of the top thirty cotton-producing districts.[12] This alignment of party with group and geographic interests makes it increasingly difficult to build bipartisan coalitions in these policy arenas.

Many observers misunderstand the role that partisan conflict plays in congressional decision making. To be sure, legislators from the two parties differ in their ideological composition, in the extent to which they champion various group interests, and in the localities where they are strongest. Much partisan disagreement simply reflects these underlying and increasingly aligned ideological, group, and geographic interests. For example, the fact that most Republican legislators support gun rights is better explained in terms of ideology (Republicans prefer fewer governmental regulations) and geography (Republicans represent rural, gun-toting folks) than in terms of partisan conflict. But if one seeks to explain why Republican legislators first supported the Medicare Prescription Drug Act in 2003 and then opposed the Affordable Care Act in 2010, both of which expanded health care by subsidizing private insurance, one needs to know that the former was championed by a Republican president, whom they reluctantly agreed not to embarrass, whereas the latter was proposed by a Democratic president, whom they eagerly sought to portray as an extremist. No other explanation based on ideological, group, or geographic interests does as well as an explanation firmly rooted in partisan competition. Frances Lee (2009) shows how deep an imprint partisan politics leaves on congressional decision making, encouraging legislators to support one policy when they are in the majority or when their party controls the White House, while supporting the opposite policy when they are in the minority or when the other party controls the White House.

It matters a great deal which party controls the House. The House is a majoritarian institution where the dominant party manages the agenda and where not even a unified minority can stop a unified majority from doing exactly what it wants. It matters especially now that the policy goals of Republican House members diverge so sharply from those of Democratic legislators. In an earlier era, when the Democrats controlled the House for forty years (1955–95) and when the distance between Democrats and Republicans was much smaller, competition between the two parties was more sportsmanlike than gladiatorial. Committee and party leaders from one party team did not work persistently to make the other party team look weak and incompetent. By the time Republicans demonstrated in 1994 that they, too, could constitute a majority, collaboration had broken down and relentless combat was the new norm. House parties behaved more like the opposing parties in parliamentary regimes, with each party working to polish its brand while tainting the other party's brand. Partisan conflict was exacerbated by subsequent shifts in partisan control in 2007 and 2011, which together reminded legislators that they were always just one election away from gaining (or losing) something that now really mattered – majority control of the House.

It matters much less which party controls the Senate. First, the ideological distance between the two parties in the Senate is smaller than the ideological distance between the two parties in the House. This reflects the fact that most senators run in larger and more heterogeneous districts than do House members. Second, the filibuster makes the Senate a supermajoritarian institution where minorities can stop even unified majorities from enacting their preferred policies.[13] Since majorities can rarely govern without some help from the minority, switches in party control in the Senate leave a fainter impression on public policy than switches in party control in the House. No matter which party is in the majority, moderate senators – the most conservative Democrats and the most liberal Republicans – have extra influence because they are the legislators most likely to defect from their party's position. Switches in party control simply establish whether the most moderate Democrats or the most moderate Republicans enjoy this extra influence.

It also matters whether the same party controls the House, Senate, and the presidency. Although this is not the conclusion that David Mayhew (1991) reached in his pioneering book on the subject, I have gradually come to believe that important differences exist between unified and divided control.[14] Mayhew's original study combined two measures of legislative productivity: Sweep One, based on the observations of contemporary observers about the expected significance of bills, and Sweep Two, based on retrospective judgments by policy experts on their actual significance. The problem is that his Sweep Two method had a recency bias – policy experts were more likely to recall recent happenings than distant events. Since recent congresses were mostly under divided party control, the method artificially boosted overall productivity during divided regimes (Howell et al. 2000). If one focuses just on Sweep

One enactments, Mayhew's original data from 1947 to 1990 show that nine unified regimes enacted 23 percent more bills that contemporary observers deemed important than did the thirteen divided regimes (10.8 laws per unified regime, compared to 8.8 laws for divided regimes). The same pattern persists in the data that Mayhew collected from 1991 to 2012.[15] Four unified regimes enacted 23 percent more bills that contemporary observers deemed important than did the seven divided regimes (13.0 laws per unified regime, compared to 10.6 laws for divided regimes).

The increased productivity during unified regimes partly reflects the greater agreement on policy goals across the House, Senate, and president. Moreover, unified regimes often enact more ambitious and innovative policy proposals than do divided regimes. Since Democrats and Republicans disagree so fundamentally over the federal government's role in health care, it is no accident that Medicare, Medicaid, and the Affordable Care Act, each of which changed the fundamentals of health care financing, were enacted under unified Democratic regimes. Bipartisan efforts on health care are usually more incremental – health maintenance organizations (1973), health planning (1974), catastrophic coverage for seniors (1988), health insurance portability (1996), and the state children's health insurance program (1997). These five enactments were important – and they certainly boosted the measured legislative productivity of divided regimes – but not even these five bills combined had the sweeping impact of creating Medicare, Medicaid, or Obamacare.

RECENT POLICY MAKING

How has policy making changed over the past decade as the parties became increasingly polarized? Has there been an increase in what I shall call *majoritarian policy making*, instances where the majority party enacts bills over the intense opposition of the minority party? If one defines majoritarian policy making as any enactment under unified party control where more than 80 percent of House members from the minority party oppose the final bill, then 28 of Mayhew's 149 Sweep One enactments (19 percent) fit the bill.[16] There were three from the Kennedy era, seven from Johnson's time, three from Carter's time, three from Clinton's time, five from George W. Bush's time, and seven from Obama's first term. Majoritarian policy making was higher in recent years, but not dramatically so. If one tightens the measure to 90 percent of minority House members opposing the final bill, then only 13 enactments (9 percent) would count, including three from the Johnson era, one from Clinton's time, three from Bush's time, and six from Obama's first two years. Finally, if one tightens it to 100 percent of minority legislators opposing the final bill, there were only three instances (2 percent) – Clinton's 1993 economic stimulus, Obama's 2009 stimulus, and Obama's 2010 Affordable Care Act.

The general sense that majoritarian policy making is increasing reflects more a change of intensity – the majority party is enacting legislation to which the minority is fiercely opposed – rather than a dramatic increase in the number of enactments that the minority opposes. Using the 80 percent standard, both Presidents Johnson and Obama enacted seven bills that most Republicans opposed. For Johnson, it was food stamps, rent supplements, model cities, the war on poverty, Appalachian regional development, the wheat and cotton bill, and creating the Department of Housing and Urban Development. For Obama, it was economic stimulus, health care, equal pay for women, community service programs, financial services regulation, food safety regulation, and allowing gays to serve openly in the military.[17] One difference is that Johnson attracted an average of 12 percent of Republican House members for his seven votes, while Obama attracted only 5 percent of Republican legislators. A second difference is that Johnson's seven bills were only 18 percent of the forty Sweep One bills enacted during his time in office, while Obama's seven bills were 44 percent of the sixteen important enactments in his first two years. In short, policy making under unified control is somewhat more likely to be dominated by the majority party than before, and the minority party is less happy with the enactments, but the differences are not enormous.

The Senate is the principal check on a unified majority controlling policy making. Since the majority party rarely controls the sixty seats required to stop a filibuster, it must routinely appeal to at least some minority-party senators. The only exception to the sixty-vote requirement for action is a reconciliation bill. A reconciliation bill cannot be used routinely, however, because it must be tied to the annual budget resolution. Even with this limitation, creative leaders have used reconciliation to enact many important tax bills, as well as major reforms in welfare, student loans, and health care (including the Affordable Care Act).

This digression into majoritarian policy making underlines how much bipartisan policy making is still the norm. Even under unified party control, most Sweep One enactments enjoy the support of more than 20 percent of minority-party House members. This was true for Clinton's two unified years (75 percent), Bush's four and a half unified years (80 percent), and Obama's two unified years (56 percent). Moreover, bipartisan policy making is the *only* option under divided party control, which continues to be the norm. We have had divided party control for six of the past ten years, eight of the previous ten years, and eight of the ten years before that. Bipartisan coalitions are still the principal vehicle for making policy in Washington, even if they are increasingly difficult to assemble.

The ten papers in this volume take two approaches to explaining recent policy making. Several papers take a macro approach, attempting to explain changes in the overall productivity of Congress or in the nature of laws enacted. The others focus more on policy making within specific policy areas, sometimes across time and sometimes on specific bills. Collectively, they paint a rich portrait of congressional action at the dawn of the 21st century. What is not yet clear is whether we need new tools for appreciating the role of Congress in policy making, or whether the tools of the late 20th century still explain things nicely.

Barbara Sinclair argues persuasively in Chapter 3 that, when the same party controls the House, the Senate, and the White House, increases in partisan polarization actually facilitate the enactment of important bills, both because the majority party is more ideologically homogeneous than it once was and because majority-party legislators have provided their leaders with improved tools to hold the party team together. Under divided party control, however, the same partisan polarization impedes bill passage, both because there are few moderate legislators from the minority party who might defect to support the majority's proposals and because leaders of the minority party have improved tools to keep their opposition team together. Mayhew's recent data support her argument nicely. The unified 111th Congress enacted sixteen important bills, including the Affordable Care Act, while the divided 112th Congress enacted only seven important bills.

Sinclair's argument that Republicans have an inherent advantage over Democrats in negotiating "must pass" legislation, such as the annual budget or extending the federal debt limit, is less persuasive. Her argument rests on the observation that a faction within the Republican party does not believe that shutting down the government or defaulting on the federal debt would have serious consequences, so everyone else must pacify this pertinacious faction to avoid disaster. To be sure, Tea Party Republicans played this hand very well in 2011, insisting on massive cuts in federal spending over the next decade in exchange for raising the federal debt limit. But their success had as much to do with President Obama's overriding goal of doing nothing to threaten the fragile economy while running for reelection as it did with Republicans having an inherent strategic advantage. Once the election was over, Democrats could play chicken, too. In late 2012, Democrats seemed perfectly willing to let the Bush tax cuts expire for all taxpayers rather than approve Republican plans to extend these cuts for all taxpayers. The compromise plan that Congress enacted was much closer to the Democratic plan – extending income tax cuts for most taxpayers, but allowing rates for the richest taxpayers to revert to the Clinton-era tax schedule. Republicans caved again in 2013, after first shutting down the government for sixteen days, once they learned that citizens blamed them for government dysfunction. The compromise plan was to reopen the government on Democrats' terms, with the Affordable Care Act intact and spending largely unchanged.

Republicans would have a strategic advantage over Democrats in negotiating must-pass legislation only if they were united in the belief that default or an endless government shutdown would have no serious consequences. As it happens, they are not. Many Republicans fear the economic consequences of default, have no desire to tie the Republican party brand to disastrous outcomes, and are willing – often at the last minute – to compromise with Democrats. In the congressional game of chicken, there are many hands on the wheel and many different constituencies watching those hands. It takes more than an obstinate faction within the Republican caucus to keep a bipartisan House majority from swerving to avoid disaster.

Alexander Hertel-Fernandez and Theda Skocpol argue in Chapter 6 that, although Democrats and Republicans are miles apart when it comes to their views on federal tax policy, Republicans play the tax-cutting game better than Democrats play the revenue-raising game. Their reasons are four: Republicans are better at timing their efforts to take advantage of favorable economic winds, have superior tactics for controlling legislative and political agendas, are better at keeping their party caucus united, and have a stronger constellation of interest groups to mobilize citizens and legislators for action. The authors make a good case that all four factors contributed to the Republicans' success in cutting taxes in 2001 and the Democrats' failures to reverse those cuts in 2010 and 2012.

My own preference is for a more parsimonious single-factor explanation: It is inherently easier to cut taxes than it is to raise taxes because politicians prefer delivering benefits to imposing costs. Tax cuts deliver concentrated and measurable benefits to citizens, some of whom may choose to reward elected politicians for their bounty, while delivering only diffuse and distant costs in the form of increased deficits or foregone spending, none of which citizens are likely to trace to politicians' tax-cutting actions. Tax increases, however, deliver concentrated and measurable costs to citizens, some of whom may choose to punish elected politicians for their misfortune, while promising only diffuse and distant benefits in the form of decreased deficits or more generous spending, none of which citizens are likely to trace to politicians' tax-raising actions. In short, traceable benefits with untraceable costs are attractive and addictive to elected politicians, while traceable costs and untraceable benefits are politically dangerous (Arnold 1990). It is easy to recollect politicians who suffered electorally for raising taxes, ranging from the one-term Marjorie Margolies-Mezvinsky (D-PA), whom Republicans serenaded with "Goodbye Marjorie" as she cast the deciding vote for President Clinton's 1993 tax increase, to the one-term President Bush, who reversed his 1988 campaign promise ("Read my lips: No new taxes") by agreeing to raise taxes in 1990. But can anyone recall politicians who suffered electorally for cutting taxes? Not since the Kennedy administration has Congress been reluctant to approve a president's request to cut taxes.

The more parsimonious explanation does not deny the roles that Hertel-Fernandez and Skocpol's four factors played in the day-to-day political maneuverings in 2001, 2010, and 2012. It simply provides a foundation for explaining why these four factors were so important. It also explains why Democrats appeared flat-footed when attempting to increase taxes in those freestanding tax bills, while the very same Democrats looked skilled and dexterous in enacting the Affordable Care Act, which contained higher Medicare taxes on earned income for the affluent, as well as a new 3.8 percent Medicare tax on their unearned income. The difference is that these two taxes were connected to huge bundles of benefits that would be delivered to health care providers and to uninsured and poorly insured citizens. Democrats were perfectly willing to tax the wealthy once there were enough traceable benefits to make it politically worthwhile.

Although Democrats and Republicans appear just as polarized on health care as they are on taxes, I do not think that image captures the complicated reality of health policy. To be sure, polarization reached a peak in 2010 when Democrats enacted the Affordable Care Act over the unanimous opposition of House and Senate Republicans, and again in 2013 when House Republicans shut down the government for sixteen days in an unsuccessful attempt to block the act's implementation. When the question is whether the national government should establish a new health care program, Republicans are instinctively opposed. The two parties' irreconcilable differences on the Affordable Care Act, however, do not suggest an inability to tackle persistent problems elsewhere in health care. Jonathan Oberlander argues persuasively in Chapter 9 that Democrats and Republicans have a long history of working together to manage Medicare costs.

What makes Medicare different? First, it is an established program with 50 million active beneficiaries and tens of millions more soon to join those ranks. If Congress were considering establishing a new health program for seniors, Republicans would probably oppose it, just as many Republicans opposed creating Medicare in 1965. An established program, however, is very different, especially a program with beneficiaries that largely reflect the underlying partisan divisions in society. Republican seniors would be just as upset as Democratic seniors to have their Medicare benefits reduced. Second, it is a costly program, accounting for one seventh of all federal expenditures. Unlike Social Security, which has a dedicated payroll tax, Medicare is heavily dependent on general funds (only hospitalizations are covered by a second dedicated payroll tax). Put differently, Medicare is in constant conflict with all other federal programs for general funds. A dollar spent on Medicare is a dollar that could otherwise be spent on defense, education, transportation, or medical research. Oberlander nicely captures how Democrats and Republicans have dealt with these fiscal trade offs by restricting the growth of Medicare expenditures. The trick is not to restrict beneficiaries' access to health care – there would be hell to pay for that – but to limit how much health care providers are paid for their services. Given the fiscal challenges facing the federal government, there is no reason to believe that Democrats and Republicans will not again come together to control Medicare costs. That is where the money is.

Energy policy is another arena where legislators have difficulty finding common ground. Here the problem is not just that Democratic and Republican legislators see energy problems through different ideological lenses but that energy production is increasingly concentrated in districts dominated by a single party.[18] Many oil- and gas-producing areas in Texas, Oklahoma, and Louisiana that were once solidly Democratic are now solidly Republican.

Explaining Legislative Achievements315

This new alignment of partisan, ideological, group, and geographic interests makes it increasingly difficult for leaders to build bipartisan coalitions on energy issues. In Chapter 11, Bruce Oppenheimer shows that after Congress passed the Energy Policy and Conservation Act in 1975, which first set mileage standards for new automobiles, legislators were unable to agree on any plan to tighten those standards for more than three decades. What finally spurred legislators to pass the Energy Independence and Security Act of 2007, which did raise mileage standards, was the doubling of gasoline prices in just a few years. When gasoline prices were stable, it was not that dangerous for legislators to serve oil-producer interests. When gasoline prices were soaring, however, legislators felt compelled to do something – anything – that sounded as if it might help tame prices, even setting mileage standards, which could produce only long-term effects.

Just as the underlying cleavages in energy policy are largely reinforcing, with Republicans generally siding with energy producers for a combination of ideological, geographic, and partisan reasons, so too do the underlying cleavages for inequality-reducing policies reinforce one another. That is the principal finding of Nick Carnes's innovative Chapter 5 about which legislators vote for inequality. His most striking finding is that Republicans in the 112th Congress (2011–12) were unlikely to support *any* policies that explicitly targeted economic inequality, no matter where their constituents stood, no matter what their underlying ideological beliefs, no matter what their sources of campaign contributions, and no matter what their occupational backgrounds. In contrast, Democratic legislators were quite varied. Those Democrats who were relatively liberal, who represented liberal constituencies, who raised substantial campaign contributions from unions, or who came from less elite occupations were more likely to support policies that addressed economic inequality than were Democrats with fewer of these attributes.

The principal limitation of this argument is that Carnes tested it with only a single two-year period. The results would have differed if he tested it with the 111th Congress, rather than the 112th. After all, the earlier congress (a) enacted a colossal redistributive scheme, the Affordable Care Act, which promised health care benefits for tens of millions of beneficiaries, partly through Medicaid and partly through subsidized private insurance; (b) provided vast funds for Medicaid, unemployment benefits, and food stamps in the $787 billion fiscal stimulus bill; and (c) modified a student loan program that is essential for students who could not otherwise afford college. Although Republicans opposed these three efforts, Democrats of all stripes came together to enact programs explicitly designed to reduce inequality.

I also have serious reservations about the inequality index, developed by the Institute for Policy Studies, that Carnes used to measure support for inequality-reducing legislation (Anderson et al. 2012). Why doesn't the index include anything that the 112th Congress enacted that did benefit the working poor? Surely, the most significant inequality-reducing bill during 2011–12 was the one extending the payroll tax holiday for another year, sparing workers from paying one-third of a tax that is highly regressive and that is often the only federal tax that low-income workers pay. That positive action seems far more significant than legislators' inaction in "protecting U.S. call center employees from having their jobs shipped offshore" or "requiring federally funded water infrastructure projects to use American-made products," two protectionist bills that did make the IPS index.

Nowhere are today's policy conflicts deeper than over immigration policy. Unlike taxes, inequality, or health care, disagreements about immigration policy rarely follow standard left–right or partisan cleavages. In Chapter 10, Daniel Tichenor explains well the complexities of these conflicts and shows how they have evolved over time. To be sure, there is an economic dimension to immigration policy. Some people welcome additional workers who they believe will contribute to American prosperity; others worry that new immigrants will deprive citizens of jobs that rightfully belong to them. There is also a cultural dimension. Some people welcome immigrants' contributions to society, celebrate their diversity, and encourage them to become citizens; others worry that new immigrants undermine American society, threaten its security, and should be strictly limited. These two crosscutting dimensions give rise to many small factions advocating or opposing particular policy provisions. Building majority coalitions in such a factious world has always been difficult.

Tichenor's most interesting finding is how immigration politics, which was once relatively quiet and mostly involved conflicts among interest groups, is now very public and involves many grassroots groups working to mobilize citizens during both legislative deliberations and electoral campaigns. The electoral connection pulls legislators every which way. Short-term electoral calculations are especially powerful. Consider the many positions that Senator John McCain has taken on immigration policy over the past decade. In 2005, he cosponsored with Senator Kennedy a bill that would have given illegal immigrants a path to citizenship. Three years later, while running for president, he repudiated his own bill, arguing that border security was the central issue. Two years later, while running for reelection, he praised an Arizona antiimmigration bill that would let local police arrest those with inadequate identification. By 2013, McCain was back where he started, championing a Senate bill that would give illegal immigrants a path to citizenship. If there were nothing but short-term electoral calculations, stalemate on immigration policy would likely continue as legislators worry about how one wrong vote might play out in the next campaign. But layered on top of these short-term calculations are Republican legislators' long-term concerns that their party cannot hope to be a majority party without addressing an issue about which the growing number of Latino and Asian voters care intensely. Of course, it is never easy for legislators to do something for a long-term good that threatens their near-term well-being.

By comparison to immigration policy, the politics of gay rights is much less complicated. First, the basic conflict is single-dimensional. Some people believe that any discrimination against gays – in the workplace, the military, or marriage – is wrong; others believe such discrimination is perfectly acceptable. Second, both public opinion and elite opinion have been moving steadily toward acceptance of gays, with younger people leading the way. Third, the parties have taken opposite positions on gay rights. Democratic party platforms tend to embrace gay rights; Republic platforms do not. One consequence is that gay rights advocates have time on their side. Every year both public opinion and elite opinion become more supportive. A second consequence is that action is far easier when Democrats are firmly in control. A third is that a few moderate Republicans are essential when Democrats are not firmly in control.

Rick Valelly's superb account in Chapter 4 of the repeal of "Don't Ask, Don't Tell," the statutory prohibition on gay men and women serving openly in the military, shows the decisive role that political skill played in overturning this law in the final days of the 111th Congress, just before Republicans regained control of the House. There were many heroes – Secretary of Defense Gates, Admiral Mullen, and Senators Collins, Lieberman, and Reid – who somehow made the impossible possible. But legislative strategy gets top billing in Valelly's account. Legislative leaders deferred to Gates and Mullen, both sympathetic to repeal, so that the Pentagon could prepare for change. They also crafted a bill that would allow military leaders to implement whatever plan they devised without further legislative review. Gay rights advocates supported the plan because it was the best they could achieve in 2010. Legislators who were natural supporters of the military but more skeptical of gay rights supported the plan because it was deferential to military leaders. By introducing this new dimension, it protected conservative Democrats and moderate Republicans from electoral retribution. Strategists transformed what otherwise was a pure vote on gay rights into a vote on supporting two respected military leaders, Secretary Gates and Admiral Mullen. It was a brilliant strategy, beautifully executed.

A century ago, Congress delegated exclusive power over monetary policy to the Federal Reserve Board. Although Congress can limit or withdraw any delegated powers, and legislators are free to criticize or investigate those who exercise these powers, Congress has never seriously interfered with the independence of the nation's central bank. In Chapter 8, Sarah Binder and Mark Spindel explore this puzzle and investigate what drives some legislators to work toward limiting or refashioning the bank's powers. They find that a combination of electoral and partisan incentives encourage some legislators to work toward limiting or changing what the bank can do. Such efforts are especially likely during times of economic stress, ranging from high inflation in the 1970s to the Great Recession. The surprise for me, however, is how small the differences are between Democrats and Republicans. Yes, Democratic legislators

were more active prior to 1978, when Congress enacted the Humphrey–
Hawkins Full Employment Act, forcing the Fed to consider economic growth
and not just inflation. Yes, Republicans were more active after 1978, when their
own favorite concern – inflation – was no longer the Fed's exclusive concern.
But really, why so little partisanship? Even in the increasingly bitter politics of
the past few years, 70 percent of senators confirmed Ben Bernanke for his
second term as Fed chair and 68 percent of senators confirmed Janet Yellen
for her first term as chair. The recent conflict over who would chair the Fed was
largely *inside* the Democratic party, as senators from President Obama's own
party told him that his favorite nominee – Larry Summers – was unacceptable.

In Chapter 7, Nolan McCarty asks two good questions about the decline of
the textbook appropriations process. First, why does Congress sometimes
abandon the regular order of first passing a budget resolution that sets overall
budget targets and then passing a dozen or so appropriations bills that fit
within the resolution? The answer seems to be that departures from regular
order are more common when different parties control the two budget-making
branches, when different parties control the two legislative chambers, and when
legislators are more polarized. As a consequence, delay was common both in
the 1980s (before extreme polarization) and more recently. Second, what
difference does it make when Congress departs from regular order and governs
with a series of continuing resolutions, sometimes for the entire fiscal year?
McCarty finds no evidence that departures from regular order contribute to
(or detract from) deficit spending, and some evidence that these departures may
contribute to policy uncertainty (as measured by how the media covers the
economy).

Although McCarty's paper is a nice start on both questions, what is missing
is any analysis of budgetary *outcomes*. Budget making is how Congress sets
national priorities – choosing between guns and butter, between human capital
and physical capital, between the young and the old. The most compelling
question for me is how a departure from regular order affects these choices.
Is the greater conflict that gives rise to congressional departures from regular
order resolved by making explicit choices to change national priorities and
move money from one function to another? Or does the use of continuing
resolutions simply favor the status quo allocation of spending, cementing into
place the choices of previous congresses? Put differently, we know that over
time Congress has made major changes in the allocation of spending among
functions. What we do not know is whether these changes are facilitated or
hindered by departing from regular order.

Craig Volden and Alan Wiseman remind us in Chapter 2 that the incidence
of costs and benefits affects the politics of policy making. This was James Q.
Wilson's (1980) fundamental insight in his analysis of entrepreneurial,
majoritarian, interest group, and client-centered politics, a distinction based
on whether a proposal's costs and benefits are narrowly concentrated or widely
distributed. The composition of effects also plays a central role in Arnold's

(1990) analysis of congressional policy making, where the incidence of general, group, and geographic costs and benefits influences how legislators calculate the electoral consequences of their actions. The incidence of costs and benefits also plays important roles in many other congressional works, including Richard Hall's (1996) examination of why legislators invest in building coalitions and Eric Patashnik's (2008) analysis of why some policies providing general benefits persist while others disintegrate.

Indeed, the incidence of costs and benefits has featured prominently throughout this essay. My analysis of why cutting taxes is always easier than raising taxes is that the former concentrates the benefits while distributing the costs, whereas the latter concentrates the costs while distributing the benefits. My discussion of energy policy emphasized how rising gasoline prices finally made general costs more salient than the group or geographic costs that usually dominate energy politics. The incidence of costs and benefits continues to be central to congressional politics because legislators care much more about who gains and who loses from policy changes than they do about the abstract totals that are the outcome of traditional cost–benefit analyses.

LEGISLATIVE ACHIEVEMENTS REVISITED

Recent congresses have been enormously productive. By Mayhew's definition, the 111th Congress – the first under Obama – enacted sixteen important laws, four of them historically important (fiscal stimulus, financial services, health care, and the bipartisan tax deal). Since World War II, only two other congresses have enacted as many as sixteen important laws (the 89th under Johnson and the 107th under Bush), and only two congresses have enacted as many as four historically important laws (the 88th under Kennedy/Johnson and the 107th). Although productivity was enhanced by the need to resolve problems related to the Great Recession, the recession accounts for only two of the sixteen enactments (fiscal stimulus and financial services).[19] The real catalyst was that for the first time in fourteen years Democrats controlled the House, Senate, and White House. Most of the sixteen important bills had been waiting for the unity of purpose among legislators that only a decade and a half in the wilderness can provide.

Even if Democrats had not lost control of the House in the 2010 election, the 112th Congress would not have been as productive as its predecessor. Not only was the 111th Congress already an outlier, but the Democratic cupboard was looking much emptier than it was just two years before. It is a mistake, however, to view the recent period of divided government as unproductive. Congress and the president passed budgets, appropriated money, and removed the decade-long uncertainty about the Bush-era changes in the estate and income taxes. By doing so, according to one estimate (Murray 2014), they reduced the cumulative deficit by $3.3 trillion over a fourteen-year period, with a combination of revenue increases and cuts in domestic and defense spending that neither party would have enacted on its own. These fiscal bills are producing enormous changes in what the federal government does in everything from housing, transportation, and weapons acquisition to forestry, justice, and scientific research. The fact that these changes were made in a handful of bills, rather than dozens, does not diminish their importance.

Is it more difficult to enact bills today than it was in previous decades? That depends on who sits in the many Capitol Hill chairs. When Republicans control one house and Democrats control the other, it is enormously difficult to pass anything because the two parties disagree fundamentally on so many things. Enacting must-pass legislation is sometimes all that we can expect. When a single party controls both houses of Congress, however, bill passage is somewhat easier than it used to be because majority-party legislators agree on so many more things. Today the principal limitation on majority-party success is the senatorial filibuster.

Looking forward, it is easy to imagine the filibuster fading away. Democratic senators already took the first step in November 2013, when they prohibited using the filibuster to block votes on executive branch nominees or judicial nominees (other than to the Supreme Court). Their move was largely in response to Republican senators blocking all nominees for some positions, most notably to the influential U.S. Court of Appeals for the District of Columbia Circuit, the court that reviews regulations from most administrative agencies. Having prohibited the filibuster for one class of votes, what is to prevent the majority party from extending the line to embrace votes on Supreme Court nominees or on substantive bills? Once the filibuster is gone, a party controlling the House, Senate, and White House will have fewer impediments to enacting its platform. Majority-party legislators will also lose the ability to hide from the consequences of congressional enactments.

Notes

1. Others have conceived of productivity in similar ways, while using different methods to identify important laws. See Howell et al. (2000) and Clinton and Lapinski (2006).
2. See Edwards et al. (1997) and Binder (1999; 2003; 2014).
3. See Kingdon (1995, 109–113) for a good discussion of problem definition and for a differentiation between conditions and problems.
4. I am not arguing that conservatives do not need to enact laws to achieve some of their policy ends. Lately, conservative legislators in Wisconsin, North Carolina, and other states have passed bills to curb collective bargaining for public employees, abolish tenure for teachers, restrict abortion, and require stricter identification for voting. For all these, legislative enactments were necessary. My point is that many items on the conservative agenda can be implemented with budgetary decisions that reduce or eliminate unwanted programs.

5. Binder might respond that the source for editorial mining should not matter, since the *Times* would be advocating and the *Journal* attacking the same sorts of issues each year. No doubt that is true for the biggest issues of the day (say, health care reform in 2009), but for the lesser issues, the *Times* may be pushing Congress to get serious about bills that are not moving, while the *Journal* may wait until bills advance before calling in the artillery. Until comparable evidence is collected from diverse sources, I am doubtful that what is arguably the most liberal editorial board in the county provides an adequate measure for the overall demand for legislation. (On the extremity of editorial positions, Ho and Quinn (2008) found that *New York Times* editorials on Supreme Court cases were to the left of all nine Supreme Court justices deciding those cases and to the left of all other newspapers in their study; the *Wall Street Journal* editorials were midway between the two most conservative justices and the next two justices and to the left of three of the twenty-five papers.)

6. Clinton and Lapinski (2006) create a more finely grained measure of legislative importance by using an item-response model.

7. The nine were: tidelands oil act, tax schedule revision, Social Security expansion, St. Lawrence Seaway, Communist Control Act of 1954, Atomic Energy Act of 1954, Agricultural Act of 1954, Housing Act of 1954, and Food for Peace program.

8. The seven were: Agriculture and Food Act of 1982, Transportation Assistance Act of 1982, Tax Equity and Fiscal Responsibility Act of 1982, Voting Rights extension, nuclear waste repository act, Garn-St. Germain Depository Institutions Act of 1982, Job Training Partnership Act of 1982.

9. The 113th Congress enacted 296 public laws, compared with 283 for the 112th Congress. There has been a downward trend in the number of public laws enacted for many decades, from an average of 828 for the five congresses in the 1950s, to 739 in the 1960s, 618 in the 1970s, 625 in the 1980s, 472 in the 1990s, and 440 in the 2000s (Ornstein et al. 2014, table 6.4).

10. The total estimated savings include 56 percent from expenditure cuts, 23 percent from revenue increases, and 21 percent in interest savings resulting from lower deficits during this period (Murray 2014). Of course, Republicans opposed the revenue increases, but their own plans included additional expenditure cuts of at least that much.

11. On how the incidence of general, group, and geographic costs and benefits affects congressional decision making, see Arnold (1990).

12. For data on oil and gas production by congressional district, see Independent Petroleum Association of America (2012). For data on agricultural production by congressional district, see United States Department of Agriculture (2007). I have matched these lists with a list of representatives in the 112th Congress as of December 27, 2012 (with vacancies coded by the party of the most recent representative).

13. Although the Senate has eliminated the filibuster for executive nominations and for lower- and middle-tier judicial nominations, it is still in force for legislation. Of course, the majority could also eliminate the filibuster for legislation, but until it does, the Senate remains a supermajoritarian institution for making policy choices.

14. See Binder (2011) for a recent review of the literature.
15. Mayhew (2005) updates the dataset from 1991 to 2002. Five additional updates from 2003 to 2012 appear on Mayhew's website (http://davidmayhew.commons .yale.edu/datasets-divided-we-govern/). There were 211 Sweep One enactments in the original dataset and 126 Sweep One enactments from 1991 to 2012.
16. My calculations, based on 149 Sweep One enactments under unified party control between 1947 and 2012, are from three spreadsheets on Mayhew's website.
17. The other fourteen bills enacted with more than 80 percent of House members from the minority party opposed were the Housing Act of 1961, minimum wage increase in 1961, and Area Redevelopment Act of 1961 (all under Kennedy); Social Security tax increase in 1977, minimum wage hike in 1977, and creation of the Department of Education (under Carter); Omnibus Deficit Reduction Act, Motor Voter Act, and National Service Act (under Clinton); Bush tax cuts in 2001, Medicare reform in 2003, Bush tax cuts in 2003, Central American Free Trade Agreement, and Military Commissions Act (under Bush).
18. See the data cited earlier in this chapter.
19. The Great Recession actually had a greater effect in 2008, when Congress passed an economic stimulus program, a housing relief program, and the $700 billion bailout of the financial sector.

References

Arnold, R. Douglas. 1990. *The Logic of Congressional Action*. New Haven, CT: Yale University Press.

Anderson, Sarah, Chuck Collins, Scott Klinger, and Sam Pizzigati. 2012. *"A Congressional Report Card for the 99%."* Washington, DC: Institute for Policy Studies.

Binder, Sarah A. 1999. "The Dynamics of Legislative Gridlock, 1947–1996." *American Political Science Review* 93: 519–33.

2003. *Stalemate: Causes and Consequences of Legislative Gridlock*. Washington, DC: Brookings Institution Press.

2011. "Legislative Productivity and Gridlock." In Eric Schickler and Frances E. Lee, eds., *The Oxford Handbook of the American Congress*. Oxford: Oxford University Press, pp. 641–58.

2014. "Polarized We Govern?" Center for Effective Public Management, Brookings Institution.

Clinton, Joshua D., and John S. Lapinski. 2006. "Measuring Legislative Accomplishment, 1877–1994." *American Journal of Political Science* 50: 232–49.

Edwards, George C. III, Andrew Barrett, and Jeffrey Peake. 1997. "The Legislative Impact of Divided Government." *American Journal of Political Science* 41: 545–63.

Hall, Richard L. 1996. *Participation in Congress*. New Haven, CT: Yale University Press.

Ho, Daniel E., and Kevin M. Quinn. 2008. "Measuring Explicit Political Positions of Media." *Quarterly Journal of Political Science* 3: 353–77.

Howell, William, Scott Adler, Charles Cameron, and Charles Riemann. 2000. "Divided Government and the Legislative Productivity of Congress, 1945–94." *Legislative Studies Quarterly* 25: 285–312.

Independent Petroleum Association of America. 2012. *The Oil and Gas Producing Industry in Your State 2011–2012.* Washington, DC: IPAA, pp. 22–3. www.ipaa .org/wp-content/uploads/downloads/2013/05/OPIFinal.pdf

Jacobson, Gary C. 2013. *The Politics of Congressional Elections,* 8th ed. New York: Pearson.

Jacoby, Jeff. 2013. "Ought to Be a Law? Don't Be So Sure." *Boston Globe,* July 28, 2013.

Kingdon, John W. 1995. *Agendas, Alternatives, and Public Policies,* 2nd ed. New York: Harper Collins.

Lee, Frances E. 2009. *Beyond Ideology: Politics, Principles, and Partisanship in the U.S. Senate.* Chicago, IL: University of Chicago Press.

Mayhew, David R. 1991. *Divided We Govern: Party Control, Lawmaking, and Investigations, 1946–1990.* New Haven, CT: Yale University Press.

    2005. *Divided We Govern: Party Control, Lawmaking, and Investigations, 1946–2002,* 2nd ed. New Haven, CT: Yale University Press.

Murray, Patty. 2014. *Memo to Senate Democrats: Our Current Fiscal Outlook.* Washington: Senate Budget Committee. February 27.

Ornstein, Norman J., Thomas E. Mann, Michael J. Malbin, and Andrew Rugg. 2014. *Vital Statistics on Congress.* Washington, DC: Brookings. Online. Table 6.4.

Patashnik, Eric M. 2008. *Reforms at Risk: What Happens After Major Policy Changes Are Enacted.* Princeton, NJ: Princeton University Press.

Stimson, James A. 2004. *Tides of Consent: How Public Opinion Shapes American Politics.* Cambridge: Cambridge University Press.

United States Department of Agriculture. 2007. *Census of Agriculture: Rankings of Congressional Districts.* Tables 25, 47, 49. www.agcensus.usda.gov/Publications/ 2007/Online_Highlights/Congressional_District_Rankings/.

Wilson, James Q. 1980. *The Politics of Regulation.* New York: Basic Books.

Zaller, John R. 1992. *The Nature and Origins of Mass Opinion.* Cambridge: Cambridge University Press.

Index